THE EMERGENCE OF CONTEMPORARY JUDAISM

by

Phillip Sigal

Volume Three:
From Medievalism to Proto-Modernity
In the Sixteenth and Seventeenth Centuries

PICKWICK PUBLICATIONS
Allison Park, Pennsylvania

COVER DRAWING—The drawing on the front cover was executed by JoAnne D. Sieger. The basic building blocks of Judaic Theology, as becomes evident in this book, are the concepts of Creation, Revelation, and Redemption, the third often understood in a dual Messianic-Resurrection sense. The front cover drawing seeks to illustrate that. The left panel portrays Creation, highlighted by the Hebrew from Gen 1:3 "let there be light"; the center panel, an adaptation of a portion of the Vision of the Valley of Dry Bones from the Ezekiel Cycle of the Dura-Europos Synagogue (3rd Century) illustrates the dual concept of messianic redemption and individual resurrection which are the themes of Ezekiel 37; and the right panel presents the burning bush as the locus of Moses' original revelation.

PITTSBURGH THEOLOGICAL MONOGRAPHS

New Series

Dikran Y. Hadidian

General Editor

17

THE EMERGENCE OF CONTEMPORARY JUDAISM

Volume Three

From Medievalism to Proto-Modernity
In the Sixteenth and Seventeenth Centuries

THE EMERGENCE OF
CONTEMPORARY JUDAISM

by
Phillip Sigal

Volume Three:
From Medievalism to Proto-Modernity
In the Sixteenth and Seventeenth Centuries

PICKWICK PUBLICATIONS
Allison Park, Pennsylvania

Copyright© 1986 by **Pickwick Publications**
4137 Timberlane Drive, Allison Park, PA 15101

Library of Congress Cataloging-in-Publications Data

Sigal, Phillip
   From medievalism to proto-modernity in the sixteenth and
seventeenth centuries.

   (The Emergence of contemporary Judaism ; v. 3)
(Pittsburgh theological monographs ; new ser. 17)
      Bibliography: p.
      Includes index.
      1. Judaism—History—Medieval and early modern period,
425-1789.   2. Judaism—Relations.
3. Europe—Civilization—16th century.   4. Europe—Civilization—
17th century.   5. Judaism—Italy.   6. Judaism—Netherlands.   7.
Judaism—Great Britain.
I. Title.   II. Series: Sigal, Phillip.   Emergence of contemporary
Judaism ; 3   III. Series: Pittsburgh
ISBN 0-915138-57-3

Printed and Bound by Publishers Choice Books Mfg. Co.
Mars, Pennsylvania 16046

CONTENTS

FOREWORD

Volume III of Phillip Sigal's projected five-volume series, **The Emergence of Contemporary Judaism,** herewith has been published posthumously owing to the author's untimely death on July 6, 1985. During the last year of his life, Phillip completed this book and began to gather material for Volume IV, which was aborted when he was overcome by the malignancy with which he had battled for seven months. Unless his notes for Vol. IV are picked up by another scholar and elaborated upon in the next volume of the series, the modern and contemporary periods of Judaism, whose emergence he sought to trace and interpret, will remain unfinished. Actually, Phillip was dissatisfied with what he regarded as a confining five-volume work on Judaism, for as Professor Jakob Petuchowski noted in his eulogy, Phillip was "'like a spring which wells up with eversustaining vigor,' that is, bubbling over with new ideas" (Aboth 2:10-11). So voluminous was his scholarship that Volume I, overflowing with material, had to be printed in two parts. Thus he dreamed of one day writing a twenty-five volume magnum opus on Judaism which would have allowed for the breadth and depth of research and ideas that would have done the subject adequate justice.

In his Preface to this volume, Phillip thanks many people who helped him prepare this manuscript. I wish to add to those ranks the name of Amy Pattullo for her meticulous work on the index of this book after Phillip's death, which completed the task begun by Marsha Plafkin.

The various stages of Phillip's odyssey uniquely prepared him for writing this multi-volume study of Judaism. His education spanned almost the entire gamut of Jewish denominational expression, beginning with his ultra-orthodox Yeshivah rearing in Toronto and in the United States at Mesifta Torah Vadaat, through his modern orthodox studies at Yeshivah University, climaxing in his more liberal historical and scientific training at the Jewish Theological Seminary of America.

Like the "Renaissance-type rabbi-scholar" of whom he writes in this volume, Phillip was learned in modern secular knowledge, New Testament and Christianity, as well as in rabbinics, and moved comfortably in both Jewish and non-Jewish circles. The period of his Ph.D. studies at the Pittsburgh Theological Seminary was a watershed in his life. It was there, in an atmosphere of openness to new ideas and deep mutual respect, that Phillip began to dialogue with Christian scholars, a dialogue that had its roots in the harmonious relationship that had obtained in the Renaissance between erudite Jews and Christians.

In his introduction to this book, Phillip writes that individualism was "the most significant legacy of Humanism to the modern world." Phillip was clearly heir to that legacy in his originality of thought and in his insistence on total objectivity and intellectual honesty regardless of where they might lead him. Despite his deep love for Judaism, therefore, he did not feel compelled to show its superiority over Christianity, but rather preferred to illuminate the common matrix from which both faiths have sprung and to stress that both provide equally valid paths for the pilgrim in search of God.

Phillip's scholarship reflects the melding of his love for religious and secular knowledge and his love of humanity. He wanted to uncover the underlying truths and values that gave meaning and coherence to the multitude of facts he so carefully documented in his footnotes, in order to enhance human harmony and understanding. In an interview with the religion editor of the GRAND RAPID PRESS at the Passover/Easter season, but a few months prior to his death, Phillip spoke of the redemptive power of love--the guiding principle of his life:

> When this world has love, then we finally will indeed
> have Passover and Easter. There will be redemption!

June 22, 1986   *In tribute to my beloved husband.*

Lillian Sigal
Grand Rapids, Michigan

PREFACE

This volume is intended primarily to explore points of contact between Renaissance Humanism and Judaism, and interrelationships between Judaism and aspects of the Protestant Reformation. The economy of space requires certain limitations. I examine certain features of these themes, and several major personalities in Italy, Holland and England except insofar as the Reformation involves Germany and Geneva. The attention given to England derives from a desire to pick up the truncated English experience described in vol. 2, and to set the stage for the birth of Anglo-Judaism in North America to be explored in vol. 4.

In these pages we will find it presupposed and stressed that twentieth century acculturated western Judaism, especially in its North American forms, owes much to Dutch and Italian Judaism of the fifteenth and sixteenth centuries. These were prototypes. Contemporary Judaism should not be seen as the product of eighteenth and nineteenth century German and Central European modernization which was given powerful impetus in the wake of the French Revolution. On the contrary, the reformed versions of Judaism that emerged in the nineteenth century, becoming the matrix of "the varieties of Judaic religious experience" that manifested themselves in the twentieth century were latter-day expressions of an older acculturated tradition.

I indicated in my Preface to vol. 1 that the premise of this series is that Judaism is a composite religion allowing for a variety of religious affirmations. We will find here again the development of diversity and its legitimations, albeit accompanied by a degree of homogeneity. There were efforts to dogmatize and declare some persons and views out of bounds, "heretical." But this was not long-lasting, and contrasting theology and halakhah (norms of religious practice) continued to thrive side by side.

Although Judaism began to flourish in North America during the seventeenth century, and impressive developments went on apace in eastern Europe during the time-frame of this volume, both these great centers will be taken up in vol. 4. Their seventeenth century developments will be explored there as antecedent to the eighteenth and nineteenth centuries, as will be the rise of the great Judaic reform movements and the vigorous tension in Judaic religious life. That study will set the stage for a survey of Judaism in the twentieth century in vol. 5 which will explore the intense theological problems that inhere in the tragedy called the "holocaust," and the phenomenon of the rise of the State of Israel. In tandem with both the rise of Judaism in North America and the resurgence of an ethnically diversified State of Israel, the differences and points of contact between àshkenaz and sefardic Judaism and interrelations between Judaism and Islam, beyond what was examined in vol. 2, will be explored in vol. 5.

The nature of this volume, unlike the previous ones, was such that I have had to rely a great deal more upon secondary sources since I do not work with Italian, Spanish, Portugese, Dutch or Slavic languages. I am confident that I have everywhere adequately documented my sources. Special note has here to be taken of Professor Robert Paul of Austin, Texas, with whom I worked in Puritanism during my doctoral studies in Pittsburgh. He encouraged my work on Alexander Ross and Menasseh ben Israel, and much of what appears here is based upon research and papers written during 1975-76. Nevertheless, although I arrived at much of this independently I have credited David Katz whose work was not published until 1982, but which I found to be a valuable reinforcement. Wherever practicable, however, I have pursued my preference for primary sources and have checked documents when there were, for example, in Dutch when I could decipher them on the basis of German.

While I do not claim scholarly breakthroughs in this volume I believe that my synthesis of the data and my perceptions are often original, and that especially in exploring the tensions in the relationship of Judaism to Christianity I have reached an ecumenical perspective.

The format of this volume is in keeping with the previous ones, with some variations. The notes to each chapter follow chapter 8. A list of abbreviations, index, and a bibliography have been provided. I have not considered a source index pertinent to this volume, and have not provided a glossary. Hopefully the reader will find me consistent in providing explanations of foreign terms and concepts in the text.

It is self-evident that the themes discussed in this volume deserve more extensive treatment, and that some topics, such as a further exploration of the points of contact between Judaism and Islam, have been omitted. But economic considerations intended to keep this volume within a more limited scope than the previous volumes required a discreet selection of materials.

This volume has been written while I served as spiritual leader of Congregation Ahavas Israel in Grand Rapids, Michigan. To the members of my congregation I offer my appreciation for the opportunity to continue my studies and researches in fulfillment of the tradition that espouses the primacy of scholarship. I also extend my gratitude to Peter DeKlerk, Theological Librarian, to Conrad Bult, to Marion Battles of the Calvin Center and to other members of the staff of the library of Calvin College and Seminary whose assistance and resources have been made available to me with great openness. During summer sessions (1982-1984) while preparing this volume I taught my primary area of research, New Testament, at University of Michigan at Ann Arbor, and wish to express my gratitude for the additional benefit accrued from the Harlan Hatcher Graduate Library.

As in the past I thank Dikran Y. Hadidian, Director of the Clifford E. Barbour Library of the Pittsburgh Theological Seminary and General Editor of the Pittsburgh Theological Monograph Series, who has been graciously supportive of this projected five-volume series. The research for this volume was fertilized by the concurrent invitation to produce a one-volume survey of Judaism, entitled **Judentum.** This is to be published by Kohlhammer of Stuttgart in 1985 or 1986. That German text contains brief adumbrations concerning the period under investigation which are all here amplified, more comprehensively expounded, and documented.

As was the case with vols. 1 and 2, the typing of the first draft of the manuscript of this work from which the publisher prepared the final copy for publication was arranged for by a special grant from Congregation Rodef Shalom of Pittsburgh. For the facilitation of this I once again thank Rabbi Walter Jacob and the Executive Secretary Vigdor Kavaler, and express my appreciation for the generosity and confidence evinced by Rodef Shalom. For the index I am grateful for the diligence and kindness of Marsha Plafkin.

I am indebted for the preliminary typing of this manuscript to Suzanne Dunn of Grand Rapids, and for the final preparation of the manuscript for the printer, to Jean W. Hadidian. It is also my pleasure to reiterate my appreciation to Jo Anne Sieger for her creative contribution to the art on the cover of this book.

Once more I offer my appreciation to my wife, Dr. Lillian Sigal, who is an everpresent support. As I conclude this volume on my birthday, I offer it to her as a reverse birthday gift. This is the first of this series of volumes that has been written without the participation of my daughters, Sharon and Sabrina now residing in Philadelphia. But their continued love and empathy, and that of my son, Sabrina's husband David, is of invaluable significance for the spirit that undergirds my work.

God has granted me the opportunity to dedicate books to the memory of my father, in honor of my mother when she was yet alive, to my wife and my children. I am therefore taking this opportunity to dedicate this volume, to all of them, and to include among them my brothers Manual and Harold Sigal of Toronto, Canada and their wives and children. This is symbolic of what I hope will be a continuing relationship of our family in generations to come, but it is also in recognition that my early life with my brothers has been a source of meaningful reverie for me over the years that we have lived apart. And since this book carries a collective dedication I include therein as well my late father-in-law, Abraham J. Fisher, of blessed memory, and my mother-in-law, Pauline Fisher of Miami Beach, Florida.

It is with gratitude and joy, with deep appreciation for all the blessings that God has granted me in a life worth living that I turn to Him on my birthday and pronounce the traditional praise,

Barukh atah adonay elohenu melekh haolam sheheheyanu, vekeeyemanu, vehigeeanu, lazman hazeh.
Praised be the Lord who has sustained me and enabled me to celebrate this occasion.

Grand Rapids, Michigan
February 24, 1984

INTRODUCTION

This volume carries forward my survey of Judaism during the sixteenth and seventeenth centuries, a chronological overlap with volume 2, but centering on themes that could not be included there. These themes are the Renaissance, the Protestant and Roman Catholic Reformations, the rise of proto-modern Judaism in Italy and Holland, the surfacing of Judaism in England from which it had been banished in 1290, and a discussion of the tensions between Judaism and Christianity as both were becoming seriously transformed to enter the modern world.

At this juncture it will be useful to define the term "proto-modern" and "proto-modernity." I have in mind the acculturated approach of rabbis and scholars, to secular study and to Christian scholars and society, and a more rational, and quasi-scientific and historical approach to Judaic thought and halakhah (religious practice) which at times sharpened the diversity and even the internal dissent within Judaism. Further, I have in mind how some rabbis and scholars transcended medieval categories of Judaic theology and halakhah over a century and a half before the Judaic reformation of the early nineteenth century.

A primary objective of this volume is to adumbrate parallel structures or spiritual phenomena that inform the Judaic and Christian experience. This is encountered in pietistic and messianic movements, as well as in developments that arise out of cultural shock such as the Humanist movement. The purpose is not to pinpoint precise doctrines or practices in Judaism that were specifically affected by the great European forces that swept both Christianity and Judaism from 1450-1650. It is primarily to trace and to comment upon the points of contact between Judaism and these secular and Christian forces, and to briefly highlight how an imperceptible seminal transformation took place in Judaism which was the result of these phenomena. It is also intended here to offer further illustration beyond that of volume 1, of the congenital relationship between Judaism and Christianity that surfaced in an unexpected and yet possibly inevitable manner in the sixteenth century when Christians turned in great numbers to the study of Judaism and had the willing and congenial collaboration of Judaic scholars.

Medievalists have long debated whether Humanism and the Renaissance tended to paganize its adherents, whether they did so only in Italy, or also north of the Alps, or whether there was far more religion in these movements than is commonly attributed to them. H. A. Enno Van Gelder's very perceptive study has pointed to the religious nature of Renaissance thinkers even before the period considered to be one of "Christian Humanism" in northern Europe, and to the religious foundations of Humanistic ethics independent of the Reformation. [1] Within the Judaic sphere the same truth obtained. As will be seen, for example, in chapter four, Judaic Humanist scholars, although in a proto-modern vanguard, continued their pursuit of the holy and their faith in a transcendent and immanent God who made known His will to humans.

It is not possible in this work to examine technical questions about the chronology of the Renaissance, and for the purposes of this volume I am including the period roughly extending from 1450-1650. This is a time-frame generally pertinent to the evolution of Judaism. [2] One of the most significant changes that took place in European society during that period was the emphasis by Humanists upon this worldly social justice rooted in the centrality of the ethico-moral system of the Judaeo-Christian tradition, as over against the sacramental life leading to other-worldly salvation gained through supernatural mediation. [3] This is not to say that the sense of the holy or that all ritual was rejected. It is only to call attention to a sea-change in orientation which ultimately deeply affected both Christianity and Judaism and led in some circles to a secular humanistic and naturalistic philosophy.

This development also took place in Judaism. Since the eighteenth century a growing segment of Jews who consider themselves loyal to Judaism have withheld assent to a doctrine of supernatural salvation and contented themselves with the affirmation that this physical world constitutes the only arena contemplated by the divine plan for the acting out of human destiny. In this respect I use the term Humanism here to encompass a religious viewpoint that includes a theistic idea even when this is transformed into a naturalistic conception of deity. [4]

The long-evolving forces that led to the Humanism of the Renaissance, and the variegated Christian movements usually subsumed under the heading: the Protestant Reformation, ultimately transformed the European religio-cultural environment sufficiently to facilitate the accommodation of Judaism as a participant in the general culture. [5]

These developments led to the transformation of Judaism, the early process of which is explored in this volume. The term

Renaissance in its relationship to Judaism has reference to the new cultural attitudes that arose in Italy during the fifteenth century and spread to northern and western Europe during the sixteenth century. The novel ingredient which infused all aspects of the socio-political structure with an impact upon economics and the religio-intellectual life was individualism. This was the most significant legacy of Humanism to the modern world. It served as an infinitely significant factor in the emergence of contemporary Judaism. Although theological and halakhic diversity was a built-in phenomenon of Judaism since the earliest times, the newly legitimized philosophy of individualism reinforced and expanded it. Individuality underscored flexibility and independence in halakhic and doctrinal options available to the variegated Judaic centers geographically dispersed and culturally diversified. It had a dual impact upon Judaism which became noticeable by the eighteenth century and matured in the nineteenth, but will be more comprehensively explored in the next volume. On the one hand individualism made for recognition and evaluation of the Jew as an individual on his own merit, no longer subject to legislation and attitudes that pertained to the entire Jewish community as a unit separate from the general population. And it served as an important factor in the acculturation of the Jew and in communal decentralization.

It is important at this point to note that even perceptive scholars divide the medieval European religious condition into Christian and pagan, or into respectively those who were "religious," meaning Christians, and those who were irreligious or people of "incredulity." [6] Little attention, if any, is paid to the existence and development of Judaism as an alternative in European civilization. Judaism had its own system of sacraments (ritual relating the person to God and salvation) and doctrine, and was independently affected by the Renaissance and the subsequent developments within Christianity known as the Reformation and Counter-Reformation. And Jewish thinkers during this seminal period varied in their conception of revelation, salvation, the validity of variegated forms of ritual, liturgy and other elements of Judaism. [7] The great waves of theological and intellectual revolution during the fifteenth and sixteenth centuries, however, washed ashore in Judaism as well, and led to significant developments in the ultimate evolution of the faith and the reorientation of Jews. Judaic scholars who were influenced by Renaissance Humanism remained convinced that they were just as faithful Judaists as those who rejected it. And just as it is plausible to argue that Martin Luther was not the primary bearer of authentic revolution in medieval Christendom, it is necessary to emphasize that the revolution in Judaism happened before the rise of the German reform movements of the late eighteenth and early nineteenth centuries. [8] The Judaic scholars to be discussed in this volume were deeply influenced by the new Humanistic values, and it was they who set the train of intellectual progress in motion that led to the multiple reform efforts in Judaism that blossomed in the nineteenth century as the Reform, Conservative and Neo-Orthodox movements.

The sixteenth and seventeenth century proto-modernists consisted of at least two identifiable schools of thought. The first was largely observant of much traditional ritual, maintained a basically traditional liturgy, and within certain parameters subscribed to the traditional set of doctrines. Its adherents were not orthodox, conservative or reform as these adjectives came to be attached to later Judaism. They were individualistic. They diverged much from medieval Judaism insofar as they advocated the desirability of participating in the general culture and the importance of acquiring secular learning including classical languages, Christian sources and history. They were at times prepared to recognize the distinction between authentic halakhah and superstition in Judaism and were irate with Christian scholars who pointed to medieval folk-custom rooted in superstition and scorned that as authentic Judaism. The tension between these scholars and the closed-ended traditionalists was marked, and prefigured the separatist orthodoxy of the nineteenth century.

The second school of thought, however, was more radical. It centered on returned Marranos but ultimately surfaced among others and influenced the Judaic reformation of future centuries. The adherents of this school emphasized humanistic morality as the essence of Judaism, and as in the case of their Humanist counterparts in Christianity, they minimized the role of sacraments in the way God wishes the human to relate to Him and to find one's salvation. Perhaps it might be said that in the person of Spinoza who emerged out of this school and transcended both Judaism and Christianity we find the first flowering of modern naturalistic and humanistic religion. Just as in Christianity the Humanists did not believe they were disloyal to Christianity so, too, in Judaism support could be found in the stirring oracular pronouncements of the biblical preachers we call "prophets." [9] Though once considered "heretics" the basic theology and halakhic approach to these circles has been legitimated in the twentieth century.

This volume explores the rise of the Renaissance and Reformation forces in Christian Europe, and the mutual impact of these movements and Judaism upon one another. As Christian scholars moved into uncharted waters of interchange and collaboration with Judaic scholars in the sixteenth and seventeenth centuries we see the first traces of a new departure in the dialogue between Christianity and Judaism. In place of debates and polemic we encounter gentlemanly discourse. Books were still written with vituperative anti-Judaism passages, but scholars were able to discourse together as equals. The foundations were laid for twentieth century interfaith encounter, a process that still requires much refinement in order to attain a serious form of ecumenical interchange. Christian Hebraism, as it was called, a process I prefer to call Christian study of Judaism, was a potent force at first to discover how to batter the seemingly impregnable wall of Judaic rejection of Christianity. But it soon became a tool for Christian self-understanding, for Christian perception of the matrix out of which emerged Jesus, Paul, the Apostles and the early Church. As more and more scholars of Judaism both in Christianity and Judaism recognize the inestimable value of gaining insight into the essential Judaic nature of early Christianity, and the perspective that neither Jesus nor Paul stood in antithesis to some strands of first century proto-rabbinic Judaism, the floodgates of ecumenical interchange will open and the waters of salvation will wash out upon the adherents of both religions in the revelation of dual covenant theology. [10]

Chapter One

REFLECTIONS

King Henry VIII of England established Regius Professor-ships in Divinity, Civil Law, Medicine, Hebrew and Greek at Cambridge University in 1540, and in 1546 at Oxford. [1] As has been recognized by others, this climax to the Renaissance may be seen as an opening to the modern world. [2] Furthermore, it is reasonable to assume with some that the establishment of the chair in Hebrew was the outgrowth of the interest in kabalah thrust upon the closing era of the Renaissance by Pico Della Mirandola (1463-1494). He had a strong influence upon Johann Reuchlin (1455-1522) especially infusing him and ultimately the world of Christian scholarship with kabalah-fever. Pico also left an even more enduring legacy to the modern world: the syncretism of kabalistic and Platonic mysticism with Aristotelian rationalism. [3] This same Pico, with his emphasis upon the similarities in kabalah, Christian thought and Hellenism may therefore be seen as one of the major foundation stones in the Humanistic link-chain which flowered in modern scientific, histori-cal and religious studies. He translated kabalistic works into Latin to make them accessible to Christian scholars. In these respects Pico represents the Humanistic tradition which recognized that the human spirit expresses truth in variegated shadings in successive eras. [4] Interestingly too the influence of Pico upon Desiderius Erasmus (1467-1536) suggests his widespread and long-term impact upon Northern Europe and the Reformation. [5]

This has no little importance for Judaism. For Italian and Northern European Humanism is the stuff out of which much pre-modern western acculturated Judaism was forged, and from which the eighteenth century German Jewish enlightenment drew much of its fervor. It should be noted that although there was a long continuing tradition of mysticism in Judaism Pico's infusion of kabalah into Renaissance Europe antedated the great classical age of kabalah in Safed in the sixteenth century. [6] It may therefore be asked with some legitimacy whether kabalism did

1

not gain in significance in Judaism because it had won a degree of lustre in Christianity, and whether, in effect the Jewish mystics were not seeking to preserve the pristine Judaic essence of its teachings. For Pico, Reuchlin and others saw in the kabalah virtual Judaic testimony to the Trinity, Incarnation, Original Sin and Atonement through Christ. [7]

The interest in kabalah and the stunning notion that Christian doctrine can be sustained by this vital segment of Judaism led to the sharpening interest in the study of Hebrew as the key to opening the doors to the original sources. Pico had written, "There is no science which can more firmly convince us of the divinity of Christ than Cabala." For Pico kabalah represented a mystical philosophy which applied neo-Platonic principles to the Bible. [8] Pico had close relationships with Jewish scholars, especially Elijah del Medigo who, in 1482, wrote that this man is "very brilliant, and true in his heart [sincere]; truthfully I have not seen in our time anyone to compare to him." [9]

The Jewish Renaissance scholars who were traditionalist in their observance of most aspects of Judaism and were uncritical believers in the basic doctrines of Judaism as they had been transmitted since rabbinic times, were nevertheless different from the traditionalists then emerging in Eastern Europe. The former set the stage for the reforming tendencies that became known as Reform and Positive-Historical Judaism in the nineteenth century, the latter for what came to be called Orthodox and Neo-Orthodox Judaism. [10]

But it is increasingly being recognized that the cleavage between what one might loosely call traditionalist Judaism and modernist Judaism did not really take place as late as the time of Moses Mendelssohn in the late eighteenth century. [11] Furthermore it did not begin only with the antinomian tendencies introduced by the Sabbatarian heresy, as has been suggested. [12] Rather, it was as early as the sixteenth century when the gap began to widen between the Renaissance-type rabbi-scholar and the anti-Renaissance traditionalists. This separation of the ways was not much different from the ancient cleavage between hellenists and anti-hellenists or the continuing contemporary cleavage between the modernists and the anti-modernists. The cleavages generally revolve around the question whether acculturation and current scientific-historical thought will be accepted or rejected. [13]

Many challenges presented themselves in the eighteenth century leading to the inevitable reforms that mark the end of the period surveyed in this volume. But these challenges were already evident during the sixteenth century. They included the dispersion of Marranos from Spain and Portugal to Western Europe,

Poland, and Turkey after 1492 leading to the re-entry of many of them into mainline Judaism, and their participation in the developments of the Renaissance. [14] But whatever the earlier and later challenges were, the great catalyst was the Renaissance, and ultimately, the Reformation. The lives of many scholars were simply reshaped by contact with the culture of their environment and with Christianity. They did not live in intellectual enclaves closed off from the world as orthodoxy sought for its adherents after the eighteenth century.

This phenomenon can be seen especially in the lives of many Italian Jews, although comprehensive studies of more than a few of these men are still lacking. [15] These men were scientifically learned, moved in non-Jewish circles, often had knowledge of Christianity, and were adept at a variety of professions. They influenced and were influenced by the Christian society in which they lived. Thus François Tissard (1460-1508), a French Humanist who lived in Ferrara for three years, provides a rather intimate portrait of Abraham Farissol (1452-1528), a leading Jewish figure in Ferrara. [16] Tissard attests to the fact that Farissol was learned in the New Testament and Christianity along with his knowledge of the Talmud and kabalistic writings, and while he regarded his facility with Latin as inadequate he praised his knowledge of Italian. [17]

The personal relationship between Tissard and Farissol points up another interesting aspect of the involvement of the Jewish scholar in the Renaissance world. Jewish and Christian Humanists were able to dialogue and exchange knowledge. This facilitated the transfer of post-biblical Judaic theological knowledge to the Christian community. But it also increasingly led Christian scholars to the view that by acquiring knowledge of Judaism the Christian would more easily be able to win the Jew to Christianity. This objective was not removed even from the Humanist's agenda, and Tissard, a contemporary of Johann Reuchlin, like him believed and urged publicly that chairs in Hebrew studies should exist at all universities and be a legitimate aspect of classical studies to enable Christians to study Judaism under the strict discipline of academe. [18]

This attitude of Tissard in the early sixteenth century was but a prefiguration of the same attitude to be found in the eighteenth century toward Moses Mendelssohn. Again, here was a Jew who moved comfortably in the fields of knowledge and in the society usually reserved only for Christians. But his admirers and dialogists really yearned to convert Moses Mendelssohn as Tissard would have liked to win the soul of Farissol. Nevertheless this must be seen as considerable progress from the effort to save the Jewish soul by subjugating the person. From this progressive step forward came the next stage in which Jewish-Christian dialogue is conducted without the ulterior motive of proving one or the other wrong, and winning one or the other to an absolute, exclusive truth. The new stage is one in which the two dialogists examine and expound, and allow legitimate theological space for one another. [19]

Therefore, the Italian rabbis set the stage for their younger contemporaries and later colleagues in Holland, and both of these played a role in the life and thought of Moses Mendelssohn and his eighteenth century contemporaries who escalated the movement to modernity. But if Italian rabbis played this significant role for the Judaisms of successive centuries, they also played an important role in the development of Christian Hebraica, the study of the Hebrew and Aramaic primary sources of Judaism by Christian scholars. [20]

Early reformers sought their knowledge of Hebrew grammar from Jewish scholars, and also received from the latter a high degree of assistance in classical Jewish biblical exegesis. It is, therefore, as important to study the Reformation activists with a view to assessing the extent of their involvement in Jewish studies as it is to appraise the Renaissance turn to Judaica. Although Martin Luther, for example, believed that Christian scholars of Judaica were perverting the Reformation, a careful study of his biblical commentaries might reveal the influence of Jewish exegesis upon his own work. As in the case of the early church where judaization was constantly regarded as a nemesis, Reformation leaders saw the study of Judaic primary sources as a nefarious latter-day form of judaization. Ironically Roman Catholics believed that Protestant interest in Hebrew proved that Lutheranism was another version of Judaism. [21] And yet Roman Catholics were also engaged in ever-increasing study of rabbinics. Furthermore, within the reforming Protestant circles there were wide differences as to how Judaica was used. [22]

What stands out in all of this, and what is of importance to the thesis of this volume, is that for a good segment of the fifteenth, sixteenth, and seventeenth centuries there was great ferment in Jewish studies, in what some scholars prefer to term Hebraica, most especially in rabbinics. The drive for acquiring this knowledge arose out of the Humanistic tendencies of the Renaissance, and out of the deeply-felt need to rediscover the sources of Christian theology and practice during the gestation of the Reformation. But one of the results was an interchange between Jewish and Christian scholars such as had not taken place before. Hitherto the exchanges were acrimonious debates and polemics while now they began to assume a more academic nature. Also significant was the actual juxtaposition of Jewish master to Christian disciple. If none of this led to closer social relationships, or to the breakdown of Jewish political and economic isolation which ultimately resulted from Napoleon's wars of liberation rather than from intellectual interchange, this very condition, nevertheless, made it easier for new stages in Jewish-Christian relationship and dialogue to evolve since the eighteenth century.

These Christian students of Judaism must not be underestimated. Their linguistic studies and exegetical analysis influenced many generations of Christian scholars. If the sheer quantity of scholars who knew Hebrew, estimated by one scholar at twelve-hundred, and listed by name, is at least relatively accurate, one can surmise the immense influence they would have had upon succeeding generations. [23] It. is also a matter of some interest that Michael Servetus, the first man to die at the stake under the new dispensation of John Calvin, was also deeply into Judaic studies. [24] It was indeed one of the great ironies that while hundreds of Christian scholars were probing the depths of Judaica, they were each accusing the other of either secretly being Jewish, whether by origin or secret conversion, or in some devilish alliance with Jews. While this reflects the tragedy of medieval Jewish-Christian relations, it should not obfuscate the significant progress that emanated from these studies. The Renaissance and Reformation, as inadequate as they were to redeem the medieval mind from its anti-Judaic prison during the sixteenth and seventeenth centuries, nevertheless helped set the stage for the liberation of the human spirit and the expansion of a philosophy that emphasized intellectual interchange and theological dialogue which have motivated many Jews and Christians since the eighteenth century.

Christian study of Judaism was hardly balanced by Jewish study of Christianity during this crucial era. But as Renaissance and Reformation attitudes, refined by new socio-political ideas taught by the Humanists of the Enlightenment period led to the American and French Revolutions, and to the ultimate establishment of well-rooted western democratic institutions, the emancipation of the Jew ensued. This emancipation, a stunning characteristic of western civilization during the eighteenth and nineteenth centuries, resulted in a deep Jewish interest in Christian studies. Not only were such studies pursued by those who were testing the waters of a new faith, but by those who were genuinely interested in a discovery of the affinities between Judaism and Christianity. The rationalist and naturalist tendencies of the modern age since the rise of the philosophy known as Deism, motivated both Jewish and Christian philosophers to find in their respective religions the spiritual and ethical essence as over against the sacramental and ritualistic forms. Within Judaism this led to a search for the common ethical values in Christianity that would serve to transform our society. Some Judaic scholars, it must be emphasized, preferred to stress the differences as over against the affinities, and continued to claim rational superiority for Judaism over the irrational elements they found in the Christian emphasis upon the Incarnation, the Virgin Birth, the Trinity and the Resurrection. But a new era was at hand, and a new stage of reflective religious criticism had dawned. As some twentieth century Christians groped for their Jewish roots in a revolutionary new approach to New Testament studies, from the standpoint of religious history, Jewish scholars have been able to approach the New Testament and to note the essential Judaic characteristics of Jesus and Paul and their teachings. [25]

From our vantage point of 1984 it appears self-evident that the coming decades will herald a new era in Jewish-Christian studies and dialogue, and a new era in the ongoing formation of Judaism. Both of these phenomena are indirectly, and to an extent, directly related to the Renaissance and the Reformation, and it is to these influences that we now turn.

Chapter Two

THE IMPACT OF MEDIEVAL HUMANISM
AND THE RENAISSANCE

I. Humanism in Italy [1]

Gianozzo Manetti (1396-1459) wrote his **De dignitate
et excellentia hominis** in 1452, in which he argued that what
particularly distinguishes the human from the animal is the intellect
and not the human's ultimate celestial destiny, contrary to the
views of Bartholomeo Fazio. This might be viewed as an early
articulation of what we know as the distinctive turn of culture
referred to as "Humanism." This Humanistic emphasis was the
spirit that informed and animated what we call the "Renaissance."
Manetti stressed that although God created the world, it is the
human that adorns and perfects it with arts, sciences, philosophies,
technologies, cities and commerce. [2] Interestingly enough,
this view was in accord with an old Judaic midrash that stressed
the benefit of the yezer harå (the evil inclination) for the development of civilization. [3] This acceptance of the human capacity
to make life a joyous experience through self-acceptance of
human power led to a weakening of dependence upon supernatural
salvation.

The Humanists followed the ancient Roman writer,
Lucretius, who sought to liberate his readers from fear of the
gods, death, and superstition. He helped them transpose classical
acceptance of the god Fortune into an acceptance of the workings
of nature and the possibility of human effort overcoming its
adverse aspects. [4] What was really being attempted was, as
one scholar has put it, "a synthesis of antiquity and Christianity,"
in the two great centers of Humanism, Florence and Padua. [5]

For the Humanist the concept of God's "grace" signified
the innate human ability to overcome one's evil propensities
that arise from the sensual and material pursuits to which one
is drawn. [6] Renaissance thought ironically brought loyal Christians closer to the rabbinic notions concerning the human capacity

to overcome the evil yezer than had been conventional in medieval Christendom. This contributed to a further recognition of the human capacity to more fully humanize people and in time the world. In the words of Pico della Mirandola the human is "the shaper and moulder of himself, according to his own judgments and honor." [7] Such Humanistic thought appealed to the Italian and Dutch rabbis who came under its influence. In many ways this type of thinking accommodated itself to sundry rabbinic aphorisms on the nature of the human, the confrontation with sin and human free will to deal with it. [8]

This Jewish humanism was well-epitomized by the first century rabbi Ben Azzai, who found the leading principle of Torah to be Gen. 5:1, that the quintessential toldot, the sequence of the development of humanity, is rooted in the human's having been created in the image of God. But it took the humanistic environment of the Renaissance to bring to the fore once more this indigenous Judaic humanism. The Talmud had long ago recorded the teaching that "all is in the hands of heaven except for the reverence of heaven," signifying that although human destiny is beyond human choice, human morality, and therefore a major element of the condition of society, is indeed subject to human choice. [9]

Marsilio Ficino (1433-1498) wrote similarly that although human destiny is not in one's own hands, the human can "separate the soul from the body and reason from the affections of the senses. . . " and can then ". . . reflect thyself as a sempiternal ray of the divine sun." Put another way, Ficino wrote that the human, by act of will, can free oneself from subjection to destiny. [10] This comes close to the proto-rabbinic teaching that "that person is wealthy who is content with one's portion," suggesting that by an act of will the human spirit can refrain from immersing itself in material pursuit in order to liberate itself from temptation and transcend this-worldly destiny. [11]

Ficino and Pico both exemplified this concept by leading ascetic lives, and thereby seeking to point the Renaissance world away from its more hedonistic influences. But at the same time Pico exemplified the turn of humanistic thinkers away from the traditional emphasis upon the importance and efficacy of the sacraments. And in his failure to articulate appreciation of the priesthood he contributed to the weakening of clericalism and strengthening of laicization. [12]

The minimization of sacrament and the sacerdotal role, and the exaltation of the potential of human striving for a this-worldly Kingdom of God, passed from such thinkers as Ficino and Pico through Jewish humanists to Jews like Yehudah Abravanel, better known as Leone Ebreo (1502-1535). [13] These Jewish humanists were a distinctive group of Jews that were spawned by the Renaissance. They served as tutors, translators, professors in universities, copyists, scribes, and secretaries. Some of them practiced many occupations simultaneously. For example, Leone da Modena (1571-1648) was a cantor, preacher, and judge, while he also practiced as a broker and matchmaker. [14]

Ebreo might very well have been a factor in the development of Benedict Spinoza's pantheism, as he was in the thought of Giordano Bruno. Like Ebreo, Spinoza (1632-1677) eschewed such Christian and Jewish notions as the relationship between God and the human that partakes of the nature of judge and accused. Among other theological concepts he also rejected the idea of the existence of two worlds, this real earthly world, and the one termed by religion "heaven." [15] Ebreo influenced general European thought long before his work was translated into Hebrew in 1871, and became part of the nineteenth century repository of Jewish haskalah (enlightenment). The work of Leone Ebreo, written originally in one of Leone's two mother languages, Hebrew and Spanish, first appeared in Italian and was later translated into many languages and diffused abroad. This is a virtual paradigm of the difficulty of tracing authentic cultural influences in an open society such as that of Renaissance Europe. For in 1590 a South American from Peru who had been born into a Spanish Inca family translated Leone's **Dialoghi** once more into Spanish, and it appeared in Madrid. Thus, a writer descended from an ancient Indian culture brought his perspectives to the work of a scion of the venerable Judaic tradition who had in turn imbibed the civilization of ancient Hellas and synthesized it for Christian Europe. Interestingly, this exercise in cultural synthesis took place in the capital city from which Leone and his family were expelled a century earlier, and where now Leone became a significant philosophical influence. [16]

This was the age when disbelief in miracles became more pronounced, and emphasis was placed upon human accountability for deeds, with the doctrine of original sin, predestination and bodily resurrection receding into the background. [17] What is now thought to be a "modern" approach to miracles, based upon rational, naturalistic possibilities, took its cue from Leonardo da Vinci (1452-1519). But disbelief in miracles was only the tip of the iceberg. From it flowed a minimization of the role of ritual, penance, the priesthood, pilgrimages to holy places, the sanctity of relics, indulgences, and the remission of sin. Even the importance of prayer was doubted as its impotence in the face of natural causality was considered. [18] Here is embedded not only the Protestant Reformation, but also the enlightened teachings of Judaic Renaissance figures to be discussed below, and whose writings deeply influenced seventeenth century Judaism long before the emergence of the Judaic Reformation in Germany. [19]

The emergence of "modernity" during the late fifteenth and early sixteenth centuries is vividly attested to by the Lateran Council 1512-1517, called by Pope Julius II, and concluded by his successor Pope Leo X. This led to the vigorous denunciation of irreligion in the **Apostolici regiminis,** and punitive measures were introduced. [20] Nevertheless, the basic impotence of the council in the face of the winds of change was evidenced by the fact that in October of the same year in which the council concluded its work, Martin Luther placed his ninety-five theses upon the door of the church at Wittenberg. It is perhaps even more startling that as late as 1517 the Church was still admonishing against judaizers. [21] It is not clear at this juncture whether the term referred to the New Christian variety (Marranos or Conversos), whether they were Christians emphasizing the Old Testament and Jewish roots which plagued the Church from its earliest years, or whether they were Christians who were now indeed coming under the influence of such Jews as Leone Ebreo, or such Christians as Pico who in turn had imbibed extensive elements of Judaic religion, and most especially the kabalah. [22]

The art of the period also reflected the winds of change. The miraculous became less evident, saints and angels were not so frequently depicted, scholars such as St. Jerome took the place of martyrs, the crucifixion was often omitted, and the representations of the removal of Jesus from the cross, or of the mother and child were designed more to express human emotion than divine mystery. Even the Sistene Chapel built by Pope Sixtus IV only possessed one almost unnoticeable cross in one corner, and even this was added long after it was built. The influence of the Greek and Roman classics upon the portrayal of the Old and New Testament themes attests to the Humanist synthesis which took place in religious art. [23] A poignant example is the painting of Prometheus by Piero di Cosima (1461-1521) in which Prometheus is depicted as crucified. [24] The poems of Michelangelo (1475-1564) point to his also having found the source of his art in this form of Renaissance Humanism. Even when he depicted the creation of the world on the ceiling of the Sistene Chapel, Michelangelo did so according to Pico della Mirandola rather than Genesis, and in his poems one does not encounter a Christian motif. [25]

The Counter-Reformation launched by the Roman Catholic Church during the sixteenth century became the predominant force in Italy in the shadow of the Council of Trent (1545-1563). [26] This vigorous response to the spreading of Lutheranism in Germany and Calvinism in France and elsewhere in western Europe was a massive effort to retrench and preserve what the Roman Catholic Church regarded as the orthodox Christian doctrine. One of the by-products was the decline of the Humanistic Renaissance in Italy, but a rejuvenation of it in northern Europe.

II. Humanism in Northern Europe [27]

A. Prefatory Comments

It has been perceived that the fifteenth century Dutch play, translated into English as "Everyman" is an apt statement of what one might describe as orthodox Roman Catholicism during the sixteenth century. [28] In this scheme of things the newborn infant was baptized for its salvation, the adolescent took part in communion at puberty, the faithful attended mass regularly, took part in confession, and carried out penitential rites. When they were married they received the sacrament of marriage, and at death they not only received the sacrament until recently called extreme unction, but also set aside material means to have masses read and many prayers said for the soul. In addition there were a host of dogmas to believe, and acts of penance and frequent prayers in which to engage. Because there were many reasons to fear the yawning chasm of hell they hoped for the remission of sins by the priests in return for all these appropriate exercises of piety. The use of Latin in the Eucharist was mandatory, for the Eucharistic formula was regarded by the devout almost as a "sacral-magic" act. One receives from "Everyman" the sense of thirteenth-fourteenth century Judaism, and Judaism "circa 1650." [29]

But new ideas began to emerge. Perhaps these were partially influenced by those who went to Italy on pilgrimages, to study, or for commerce. Perhaps they were affected by the Humanist writers whose works became known in the north, or who visited the north and west of Europe. One who was probably influenced by Nicholas of Cusa was Wessel Gansfort who, along with others, showed a tendency to weaken the doctrine of original sin, the potency of a sacramental priesthood, the belief in miracles, the need for fasting, and the sanctity of monastic life. He was also responsible for a newly awakening advocacy of the use of the vernacular in the Eucharistic formula, and for the participation of laypersons in religious matters. [30] This was brought out in the poignancy of the anecdote told of the Parisian who snatched the wafer from the hands of the priest in 1503 and trampled upon it. [31] One cannot help but draw analogies between these proto-reformation tendencies, and similar demands and advocacy by eighteenth century German Jews. [32]

A subtle revolution was afoot when the Englishman John Colet (1467-1519), founder of St. Paul's School, where he emphasized the reading of the classics, lectured at Oxford that Christ did not die to propitiate an unreconciled God. This he termed a "gross heathen conception of religion." He taught that by sacrificing himself Jesus redeemed humans from evil. This he meant in the sense that the sacrament of the mass commemorated that event as a symbol of the fellowship of humans with God and with one another. [33] Colet was taking one small step on the road soon to be more distantly traversed by Desiderius Erasmus.

B. Desiderius Erasmus [34]

Erasmus may be viewed as a bridge between the Renaissance and the Reformation. As a philologist Erasmus issued an edition of the New Testament in which he prefigured biblical criticism of later centuries. More than this, however, his religious views steered a course between what was considered orthodox Roman Catholicism and the emerging reformist tendencies of Lutheranism and Calvinism, the foremost movements in what became celebrated as the Protestant Reformation. Perhaps the irregularity of his birth, sometimes thought to have been to a father who was a priest, had some influence upon his attitude toward the hierarchy. [35] In any event he articulated the anti-clericalism of the sixteenth century which took strong exception to the excesses of the hierarchy expressed in the accumulation of wealth and the exercise of secular power. In a subtle way he struck out at the sacerdotal pretensions of the hierarchy by translating the Greek ekklēsia into the Latin congregatio, a meeting, and presbyteroi into seniores, elders. The translations are correct, but "elders" without any sacerdotal role is undoubtedly what the New Testament and early Church sought to signify with presbyteroi in analogy to the Judaic zekenim (elders), synonym for hakhamim, (sages), used also as a term for nonsacerdotal community elders. The Church, however, had not been using such a neutral term, but rather sacerdotes, a term which implied a mystery-oriented role, more authoritarian, possessing special supernatural force in its theological usage. His vigorous attack on the papacy and its retinue in his **In Praise of Folly,** therefore, took on added significance. [36]

There is no question of Erasmus' impact upon the Tudor religious revolution in England beginning with Henry VIII, and extending well into the second half of the sixteenth century. His emphasis was upon the doing of merciful deeds, the practice of love, restraint from injuring one's fellowhuman, as overt acts of penance. He spoke little of the role of the death of Christ in redemption, and placed at the center of Christian faith the character and teaching of the life of Jesus. It was as if he were arguing that the notion that salvation comes from pisteōs Xristou, usually translated "faith in Christ" should more properly be understood as "the faith of Christ." [37] Erasmus' views found articulation in his **Paraphrases** to the New Testament as well as in his notes to his edition of the New Testament. These views have been characterized as "humanistic exegesis," and the **Paraphrases,** in particular, have been called "The Gospel According to St. Erasmus." [38] These were made part of a mandatory study program for the interpretation of the gospels in every parish in England under the **Injunctions** issued by Archbishop Cranmer during the reign of Edward VI in 1547. [39] In effect, by using his **Book of Homilies** in conjunction with Erasmus' **Paraphrases,** Cranmer returned to James' Judaic emphasis upon faith being expressed in deeds of love, looking toward the fulfillment of the Humanist vision of an ideal this-worldly society. As a matter of interest the Humanist emphasis upon rational moral behavior and the lack of emphasis upon the mystery of salvation was in effect an elevation of the Epistle of James over Pauline Christianity. Whether consciously or not, they were thus returning to a renewed form of Christian Judaism. The judaizing charge that was so frequently hurled at them and their reforming disciples was, therefore, not entirely without reason.

In Erasmus' theological scheme the other-worldly Kingdom of God was transformed into a this-worldly utopian society. This is clearly one strand of the Judaic view of an ideal messianic age. This emphasis by Erasmus, however, was disassociated from Judaism by his reiterated profession of disdain for intensive Judaic ritualism and his near-contradictory elevation of Paul. [40] Although he attributed Jesus' love command to Moses he failed to see the essence of its centrality in Judaism when he wrote that "Christ repeats and perfects" the law of love, in order to teach "not to act like Jews, but to love." And in disdain of the monastic life Erasmus argued that its advocates distort its adherents and "truss him up with various paltry human traditions and clearly drive the poor wretch into a sort of Judaism, and teach him not to love but to fear." [41] Clearly, not even the great Erasmus escaped the tragic failure of so many other Christian scholars to attain a holistic approach to Judaism, and to grasp that in its teaching the fulfillment of sacred acts without acts of love is as futile as Erasmus believed. [42]

But if Erasmus came down hard on Judaic ritual forms, he came down even more vigorously on Christian dogma. He attacked monasticism and its theory that saints could save society by a repetitious round of stereotyped litanies, minimalized the doctrine of original sin as a hypothesis exaggerated by Augustine, and taught that grace is the help to attain their goal which God offers those who earnestly seek to live the moral life. [43] In this set of propositions there is more affinity with Judaism than meets the eye. [44] Furthermore, Erasmus added to the arsenal of modernists an ambiguity about hell: "Nor are the punishments of hell . . . anything else than everlasting vexations of mind . . . ," a passage that was expurgated under the prohibitions of the **Index.** [45] He also reduced the sacraments from rites with innate salvific power to ceremonies which express solemn ideas. [46] In a certain sense, twentieth century humanism which affects the world-view of Christians and Jews who were first oriented to a supernatural form of religion, is a product of the legacy of Erasmus and his contemporaries. As one scholar has summed it up, " . . . he no longer saw Christianity as being, above all, a doctrine of supernatural salvation . . . " Rather, religion came to signify more a philosophy of life than a scheme of salvation. [47]

Sixteenth century Humanists were also active in England, France, and Germany. With these sixteenth century Humanists north of the Alps we can distinguish certain definitive notions that influenced the adherents of every branch of modern Judaism, other than those who style themselves "orthodox," and in some cases even segments of the latter. [48] These notions have been aptly summed up in a Christian context as: 1) the tendency to view religion as a way of life; 2) ritual as symbol rather than sacral and salvific; 3) the individual is in possession of reason which sets him beyond any such supernatural force as demons or satan; 4) there is a recognizable ethical and philosophical similarity in variegated religions; 5) an acceptance of classical Greek and Roman pagan thinkers; 6) the use of reason along with revelation and faith as a significant criterion in the evaluation of doctrine and practice. [49] It is not difficult to see the significance of the prevalence of such ideas in northern Europe during the sixteenth century. These ideas met head-on with the new thrusts of Italian Jewish scholars influenced by the Renaissance which also penetrated beyond the Alps. The combination was found to have a serious impact upon Judaic scholars in Holland, France, and Germany, and ultimately this was indeed the case.

III. Humanist-Renaissance Impact Upon Biblical and Judaic Learning

A. A Ray of Divine Sun

The process of thought-transformation surveyed above had the result of "laicizing" culture. It also opened the path for intellectual interchange between Jews and Christians without the hostility of the polemical debates of earlier medieval centuries. It was as if some individuals were reflecting in themselves the "sempiternal ray" of which Ficino spoke. [50] This process of acculturation was aided by both the penetration of Marranos into the general communal life leading the way for openly professing Jews, and by the rise of an appreciation of the individual for his own sake in the wake of the intellectual and socio-economic changes taking place during the crucial centuries under review. [51] Of further importance was the spread of Hebrew printing. [52] But more important than these factors was the awakening interest of Christian scholars in the study of Hebrew and the Old Testament from the standpoint of rabbinic commentary. Going beyond Nicholas de Lyra they wanted to study more recent rabbinic materials, an aspiration already reflected in the Alba Bible, a project completed in the early fifteenth century in Spain. Simultaneously Jews were increasingly involved in the translation of Arabic works into Hebrew and Hebrew works into Latin. [53]

Christian scholars were oriented to learn from Jews, and among the leading teachers of Christians during the sixteenth century was Elijah ben Asher Levita (1468-1549), also known as Bahur, for whom a Hebrew press was established in Rome with the support of Pope Leo X. Leading scholars imbibed their Hebraic knowledge from Levita in Italy and brought it to Holland, Switzerland, and France. [54] As late as 1690 Richard Simon advocated the study of Levita for those who wished to understand Hebrew. [55] Along with Levita the earlier commentator David Kimḥi was popular among Christian scholars as a result of the work of Santes Pagninus who translated both the Old and the New Testaments into Latin out of the original Hebrew and Greek with much dependence upon Judaic interpretation. [56] This trend ignored such Humanists as Leonardo Bruni Aretino who regarded the study of Hebrew as wasteful, indicating that such stalwart Christians as St. Augustine did not know the language while Jews who know the language are hostile to Christianity. [57] It also overcame the arguments of such people as Franz Joel that those who immerse themselves in Hebrew become Jews! [58] And among these Hebraists were converts from Judaism such as Immanuel Tremellius (1510-1580), a collaborator with Archbishop Cranmer at Cambridge, and an instructor of theology and Hebrew at Heidelberg. [59]

Ficino and Pico found support for Christology in Jewish mysticism. [60] Ficino quoted the Talmud but exhibited sparse Hebraic knowledge despite his efforts to acquire Judaic learning from both translations and oral consultation with people like Elijah del Medigo (Delmedigo) (1460-1497). But Ficino deferred to Pico as one learned in the primary sources. [61] Pico, too, had learned from Delmedigo and other Jews and was a devotee of kabalism. This was a feature among other Christian savants. Cardinal Egidio (1465-1532), a major figure at the Fifth Lateran Council, saw the epoch opened by the ascension of Leo X to the papacy as the tenth and final historical epoch intended by the ten sefirot of kabalism. It was for this reason that Egidio supported the pretensions of David Reubeni in 1524 and his contemporary Solomon Molkho who were preaching that kabalah predicted the inauguration of the new messianic age forthwith. [62]

Christian kabalists of the Renaissance period emerged from the Platonic Academy in Florence. They believed that kabalah represented the pristine divine revelation which was the key to understanding the teachings of Pythagoras, Plato, and the orphic mysteries, as well as the inner essence of Roman Catholic Christianity. Pico had acquired much of his familiarity with kabalah from translations by Samuel ben Nissim Abulfaraj (Raymond Moncada) a learned Jewish convert to Christianity. [63] Many churchmen condemned the kabalah as superstition, as did Erasmus, but others were fascinated by it and by Pico's propositions that it proved the elements of Christology. In time a Christian kabalism was created and the concepts and phrases of Judaic kabalism were adapted to Christian liturgical usage. [64]

Within these currents of thought and change the Talmud became an issue. It had long been a bone of contention between Christians and Jews, and here too the Humanist transformation had its impact. A significant figure in this was the jurist and diplomat Johann Reuchlin. [65] The Holy Roman Emperor Frederick III gave Reuchlin a copy of Targum Onkelos which first acquainted him with rabbinic biblical intepretation. Subsequently, while he served as ambassador to Pope Alexander VI, he studied with the celebrated medieval commentator Obadiah Sforno, then temporarily residing in Rome. While in Italy, Reuchlin acquired a taste for kabalah from Pico. His interests continued to expand; he became fluent in the talmudic literature and developed a superb disciple in Sebastian Münster (1489-1552). Withal, he believed in the need to convert Jews to Christianity and lauded the prayer Pro perfidis Judaeis recited in the churches on Good Friday. [66] Nevertheless, Reuchlin involved himself in what became an international controversy involving thrones and papacy, and had an effect upon the emergence of the Protestant Reformation.

Johann Pfefferkorn (1469-1521), a Jewish convert to Christianity moved to Cologne and became a polemicist against Judaism, as did other Jews drawn at that time to the Christian faith in the wake of the collapsed mission of Asher Lämmlein who announced himself as the forerunner of the Messiah in 1502. [67] When nothing happened despite great faith placed in him by many devout Jews there ensued a wave of conversions. Pfefferkorn was supported by the Dominicans in his approaches to the Emperor Maximilian I in 1509 for the right to seize Judaic anti-Christian writings. The seizure began at Frankfort, center of talmudism. Maximilian directed that the theological faculties of Cologne, Mayence, Erfurt, and Heidelberg pass judgment on Pfefferkorn's accusations, and while Erfurt and Heidelberg were evasive, the other two adopted Cologne's suggestion that all Hebrew writings except scripture be subject to examination, and that any objectionable passages either be rejected or defended by Jews. Rejected books were to be burned, and all others were to become a criterion by which to judge whether Jews are deficient in morals, or are heretics to their own faith. Entirely unrelated to theological matters, the faculty at Cologne recommended that Jewish usury be curtailed, that Jews be compelled to take manual labor, wear badges and listen to Christian sermons. The Mayence faculty even recommended scrutiny of the Hebrew Bibles lest they contain depraved corruptions in passages Christians believed testified to the Christian faith, and that such review of Judaic books take place every ten years. [68]

The lone voice of dissent was that of Johann ·Reuchlin who defended the literature, pointing out, for example, that if all the exegesis of Rashi was excised from the commentary of Nicholas de Lyra little would be left. He went on to urge that Hebrew and rabbinics be taught at German universities (albeit his purpose was to facilitate the ability of learned Christians to convert Jews). And he also urged that Jews be offered full freedom of religion without such efforts at suppression of their sacred writings because they and the Christians "are fellow citizens of the same Roman Empire and live on the basis of the same law of citizenship and internal peace." [69]

What Reuchlin hoped would be understood by his term "citizen" is assuredly not clear. It took some three more centuries for Jews to enjoy this sense of equality in Germanic lands. In any event the anti-Judaic Dominican forces counterattacked by charging Reuchlin with heresy and demanding the burning of his work **Der Augenspiegel** as heretical and insulting to the Church. The proceedings were temporarily halted by the Archbishop, and in this breathing space Reuchlin appealed (via a Hebrew letter through a Jewish papal physician) to Pope Leo X to prevent the Cologne Dominicans from conducting the hearings. The Pope acceded to this request, and ultimately Reuchlin was exonerated. But the Pope also had to give the Dominicans, the guardians of Roman Catholic orthodoxy, their day in court. He was not able to humiliate them at a time when Martin Luther, a defender of Reuchlin, was defying the papacy, and consequently, Pope Leo decided in 1520 that **Der Augenspiegel** was scandalous.

The Dominican battle against the Talmud and Reuchlin's **Augenspiegel** was equally fierce. It was also a battle between pro-Reuchlin Humanism and the dying medieval order. Within the Church the Franciscans defended Reuchlin, and it was a Franciscan, Cardinal Grimani, a student of rabbinics who was appointed judge of the appeal inaugurated by the Dominicans after Reuchlin's earlier exoneration. The University of Paris, scene of the burning of the Talmud in 1248 by command of Pope Gregory IX, joined the anti-Reuchlin and anti-Talmud forces. When Pope Leo X condemned **Augenspiegel** he also condemned Martin Luther. But none of this prevented Reuchlin from being invited to teach Greek and Hebrew at the University of Ingolstadt that same year, thus vindicating his great campaign. [70]

The end of the matter led to Daniel Bomberg's new printed edition of the Babylonian Talmud in Antwerp, for the Pope's condemnation of **Augenspiegel** did not extend to rabbinic literature. [71] Reuchlin's zeal for Judaica subsequently led to professorships of Hebrew in Germany, Italy, France, and Poland. Interchange between Jewish teachers and Christian students increased. The coming of the Reformation, Luther's own study of Hebrew, and a generally renewed interest in scripture accelerated the pace. Even a Dominican was a patron of Judaic study at the University of Paris as early as that same third decade of the sixteenth century. [72]

Intellectual benefits also accrued to Jews. Some studied Latin and even a rabbinic scholar of the stature of Obadiah Sforno was able to translate his own Hebrew philosophical treatises into Latin around 1550. Others became proficient in the vernacular of their ambience and preached and wrote halakhic responsa, for example, in Italian. [73] But this was not radically innovative in Judaic experience. As was noted in volume 2 of this series, Jews long before had adopted the vernacular Arabic, written in Arabic and effected translations from Hebrew into Arabic and reverse.

There is a degree of exaggeration in any appraisal of the medieval Humanist experience as some kind of decisive break with all previous medieval culture, and the rise of "modern" culture. Aside from the new philosophical emphasis upon humanistic values in the scheme of salvation, there was actually only a gradual shading-in of slowly appearing outlines from the thirteenth century renaissance to the sixteenth century, and to subsequent so-called "modernity." This evolution also took place within the Judaic sphere. Cultural development went on in previous centuries. What the Humanist Renaissance did was to serve as catalyst for a new direction in religious thought.

Sir Thomas More, for example, does not mention Jews in his **Utopia,** and has no room for Humanist religious pluralism, but James Harrington had a special role for Jews in his **Commonwealth of Oceana** which was a blueprint for an ideal English society. And while science was on the upswing in the work of Copernicus and Galileo, the masses of both Jews and Christians were influenced by astrology and demonology as well as the practice of magic. [74] So too, with all the advance in Humanistic thought, the sentiment continued that it is proper to compel Jews to baptism. Such paradoxes are illustrated by the work of Sebastian Franck who translated the so-called six hundred and thirteen Jewish commandments into German, but charged that the Jews had nullified them. And although he was critical of Jewish exclusivism it was clear that in his book about the people on all the continents, in which he maintained that "a

Turk, a heathen and others are born in God's image, and are as much the work of God as a German," the hand of toleration could be extended to Jews as well. [75]

B. Shadow Over the Renaissance

Paradoxically it was during this Humanistic phase of European culture that in Italy, the very citadel of the Renaissance, Jews were relegated to ghettos. [76] This sixteenth century urban experience threw a dark shadow on Judaic spiritual development for centuries to come. It became a source of great ambiguity in the Renaissance's foreshadowing of the modern era. Even toward the end of the twentieth century Jews have not entirely liberated themselves from this sixteen-seventeenth century experience. The physical isolation in ghettos resulted in cultural alienation, and inward spiritual orientation. The ultimate product of this inward-turning mentality continues to be evident in the newly fashionable ethnicity current in the last several decades of the twentieth century.

The perpetrator of this historic injustice that scarred Jewish minds for centuries was Cardinal Carafa, a reactionary churchman who ascended the papacy on May 23, 1555 as Pope Paul IV. Among his earliest actions was his July 12 papal bull, Cum Nimis Absurdum, declaring in effect that it is absurd to allow Jews to become acculturated, to enjoy ownership of property in a Christian society, or to employ Christians. Paul IV reiterated all of the bitter legislation of the previous ten centuries, and called for its enforcement. Among the long list of restrictive and oppressive regulations was the one that segregated Jews to a special street, or to a special section of a city, in either case their area to have only one point of entry and exit, and only one synagogue. [77] This was the ultimate consummation of the policy first enunciated at the Third Lateran Council of 1179. By 1625 the ghetto program was firmly established in all urban areas where Jews were allowed to live, and because it was not practical to establish ghettos in rural areas, Jews were soon uprooted from the countryside. The policy was extended well into the eighteenth century to those cities where Jews established themselves anew. [78]

The ghetto experience, however, is one of those historical aberrations that frequently mark a watershed despite themselves. Indeed, many Humanists like Pico still sought to convert Jews. Others, like Erasmus, combined within themselves a liberal attitude in all aspects of their thought except in their attitude toward Jews. But happily none of them was able to reverse the momentum the emphasis their thinking and writing gave to the concept of individuality as over against the corporate approach to society.

Ultimately this emphasis upon judging each human individual according to his own merit rather than by his corporate origin emerged in the later Enlightenment era as a strong motive for Jewish emancipation.

IV. The Significance of the Renaissance for Judaism

Despite the positive aspects of the Renaissance discussed above, some traditionalist-minded Jews would have argued that it endangered the pristine faith. For this reason it is not surprising that there was always a traditionalist opposition to Jewish participation in it, and ultimately a pietistic backlash, as will be seen below. The artistic and intellectual creativity that marked the Renaissance impinged upon all areas of Jewish life. It set the stage for a dramatic shift in the Jewish life-style in Italy and Western Europe, and foreshadowed the twentieth century. For example, Jewish Renaissance families averaged only two or three children. Here we have a socio-demographic fact which illustrates the intellectual and spiritual transformation prefigured by the Renaissance. [79]

Jews subsidized scholars and literary figures, and arranged for an acculturated curriculum in their schools to supplement the study of Bible and Talmud. The teachers taught grammar, the art of writing, rhetoric, and logic in tandem with biblical and rabbinic studies, setting a pattern for eighteenth century Germany. [80]

Art, including ritual objects, was executed for Jews by non-Jewish craftsmen, among whom was Benvenuto Cellini (1500-1571). Occasionally this art indicates the acculturation of western Jews, for example, by depicting them engaged in religious ritual bareheaded. [81] Jews taught their children music and dancing, and for the first time in medieval Europe we hear of Jewish instrumentalists and composers. [82] Jews were active in drama as actors, playwrights, and producers. They took part in metal work. A Jew taught Cellini. [83] Jews participated in science, engineering, mathematics, and astronomy. Their domestic way of life became increasingly refined and gracious.

Nevertheless, certain aspects of their acculturated life might be looked upon with less avidity. For example, they lived in ostentation. They exhibited their wealth by building spacious homes with great gardens, and occupying also summer residences. They participated in competitive sports, kept pets, and maintained male and female slaves. Like those of the ambient culture Jewish masters enjoyed sexual relationship with their female slaves. They avidly engaged in pleasure-reading, a mark of upper class leisure, and followed the custom of the Renaissance era of gathering groups in their homes for story-telling and entertainment, as is described by the celebrated poet Immanuel of Rome, and they hiked and hunted. While most of this would seem familiar to the modern Jew and relatively harmless, these activities generally were not indulged in by previous generations of Jews. Furthermore, they gambled extensively contrary to the great weight of Judaic tradition. The famous Leone da Modena to be discussed below gambled for almost fifty years. Although he wrote a book against gambling he suffered from a serious addiction to it. When Jewish community authorities tried to ban the practice da Modena demonstrated that it was not halakhically prohibited. [84] Actually gambling was "Judaized" and encouraged as an indoor pastime during Ḥanukah and ḥol hamoed (the intermediate days of Pesaḥ and Sukot), on the day of circumcision, and during the seven festive days following a wedding. Gambling became so prevalent and consequently morally acceptable to Jews during the Renaissance that it was transmitted to succeeding generations as ˏa perfectly proper form of indulgence.

In these and many other ways Renaissance Jewish acculturation can be seen as a forerunner of Jewish acculturation in the western world after the Napoleonic revolution. [85] As far as we can determine Renaissance Jews, unlike twentieth century Jews, generally continued to observe kashrut, but they drank non-Jewish wine and were lax in certain Sabbath restrictions such as carrying in a public domain on the Sabbath and attendance at synagogue worship which sometimes lacked a quorum in some cities. Their choice of foods for the home, their clothing styles, interior decor, the Renaissance stress on hygienic fastidiousness were all similar to those of non-Jews. Thus, a Frenchman condemned a rabbi in Ferrara, Italy who used a handkerchief because he thought the rabbi ought to expectorate on the floor like any good Christian! The meal style of Renaissance Jews was like that of their non-Jewish neighbors: long dinners consisting of many courses. And in general they emulated the sumptuous living standards of the Renaissance well-to-do. [86]

Frequently aspects of Jewish acculturation were denounced as a violation of the Torah. " . . . And you shall not walk by their statutes . . . " (Lev. 18:3), was interpreted as prohibiting the cultural modes of non-Jewish society. Many rabbis were opposed to what they considered the damage done to the religious education of the young as a consequence of parental indulgence in their acquisition of music, dance, composition, and a general affluent life-style in which sports, cards, and theatre played a major role. When anti-Jewish legislation did not enforce distinctive Jewish attire, the rabbis frequently filled the breach by opposing Jews dressing in what they considered "gentile-style" clothes. Not until the Renaissance did it become necessary for rabbis to discuss whether Jewish university graduates may adopt "gentile garb" such as academic robes, and if it be permitted, whether there is an obligation to provide ritual fringes (ẓiẓit) at the corners. But despite opposition of a traditionalist segment those with gentile contacts continued to wear the cappa, the scholar's dress, for example, and many were not particular about covering their heads. [87]

In the galaxy of a changing society advantages also accrued to women. Their position rose substantially as they engaged in business and gained economic power, or as with new-found openness they were allowed to seek education. The well-established Judaic study tradition in Renaissance Italy was shared by some women. Renaissance Italy provided a prevalent atmosphere where for the first time and place in history it was possible for women to enjoy a modicum of emancipation with men. Their education was similar to that of men, and women engaged in the same pursuit of individuality as men. This is reflected in portraiture which shows men and women playing musical instruments in mixed company. [88] Such a condition was bound to affect Jewish women. Renaissance scholars were not averse to hearing women and thus we find that the wife of a significant halakhist, Netanel Trabotto (1569-1653) of Modena was, as he referred to her in a responsum, "very erudite" on the lute and viol, and sang the kedushah as she accompanied herself. [89] Some women became physicians, others practiced sheḥitah (Judaic ritual slaughter of animals for food), and others were authors. One, the poet Deborah Ascarelli is known to have translated sections of the prayerbook into Italian. Women excelled in rabbinic scholarship, being educated in biblical and rabbinic studies, and a number of women were widely read in the halakhic digests, Maimonides, and even in the Zohar. Others were adept at the soferic art as manuscript copyists, an occupation hitherto reserved for men. [90]

The impact of the Renaissance extended to all aspects of Jewish life including the sexual. The restrained habits of northern Europe inculcated by the halakhah going back to R. Gershom against polygamy, and to the Talmud against levirite marriages, tended to enforce a more rigid monogamy. But these prohibitions were not practiced in Italy, giving rise to the spread of plural marriage, or to extra-marital sexual adventures. The greater freedom that the Italians allowed themselves is also illustrated by their neglect of the traditional halakhah banning marriages during the sefirah period. Sexual life became so much less restrained that there was even some discussion of establishing a Jewish brothel in Florence. Amorous activities were also engaged in with gentiles, and on occasion even between Jewish men and Roman Catholic nuns. Sometimes these misplaced pursuits of love led to expulsions of local Jewish communities. Jews fervently engaged in activities that traditionally were not considered proper Jewish pastimes, but since the Renaissance have been among the factors that have diminished Judaic spirituality, and constituted the less desirable aspect of acculturation. [91]

Prior to the modern era it was only during the Italian Renaissance that the environment allowed for the establishment of a Jewish academy in Ferrara with privileges never before granted a Judaic school of learning. There was exemption from all forms of taxes for its students, and Judaic and secular studies were combined and accreditation was provided to enable its alumni more readily to enter universities. It is in this atmosphere that a certain fifteenth century scholar, Judah Messer Leon wrote a book in 1478 to demonstrate that Jews were not opposed to secular culture and freely quoted from classical writers like Cicero. It is equally unremarkable that, as in all societies in flux, with liberalism in tension with conservatism, Leon's contemporary, one of the leading rabbis of the period, Joseph (Colombo) Colon (1420-1480) vigorously opposed his views. [92] On the other hand, the ambiguities of the process of acculturation are seen with Leon attempting to ban the reading of both the Torah commentary and the philosophical work, **Milḥamot Adonay** by Levi ben Gershom (Gersonides, 1288-1344) because of the latter's denial of God's knowledge of particulars, and of God's providence in the life of every individual. [93]

Acculturation and traditionalism were in tension. The fifteenth and sixteenth centuries witnessed increasing elements of acculturation and these set up a reaction among traditionalists. Thus, fifteenth century Italy witnessed a proliferation of major centers of talmudic learning at Mantua, Venice, Modena, Padua, Leghorn, and Ferrara. In addition to Joseph Colon at Ferrara, Judah Minz (of Mainz, 1408-1506) presided at Padua where ultimately the celebrated R. Meir Katzenellenbogen, known as Maharam of Padua (1482-1565) prolific responsa author and liberal halakhic authority served for over two decades (1541-1565). His influence upon Moses Isserles extended his authority into Eastern Europe for centuries. Among other famous talmudists of this period was the important commentator on the Mishnah, Obadiah ben Abraham da Bertinoro (1450-1516) who reported how he was venerated as a holy man during a visit to Palermo, Sicily. During the seventeenth and eighteenth centuries such leading lights as Samuel Aboab (1616-1694) and Isaac Lampronti (1679-1756) continued the learned tradition. But despite the spread of talmudism acculturation went on apace aided by the development of the emerging art of printing which played a major role in Italy well into the sixteenth century. [94]

The variety of general Italian style was evident in Judaism, especially in liturgical traditions. Synagogues varied from the dominant German Ashkenazi in the north through the Roman or Italian rite which prevailed in central Italy to the Sefardi rites in Venice and Pisa, and French ritual in Piedmont. At times all the rites coexisted within the same community. This multiplicity of traditions had proliferated from the basic original Italian liturgical rite known as minhag bene Romi or minhag Leoz. This rite had some substantial differences with the standard Ashkenaz and Sephardi rites. [95] In addition to the content of worship there were differences of style and certain rituals. Ashkenazim are reported to have sung more than others, while the Sefardim and Levantine Jews were described as chanting in a Turkish style. [96]

This variegated religious experience was the natural historical product of Judaism. [97] Specifically in Renaissance Italy it was impossible to establish a unified communal system. [98] The most that was achieved was the organization of a multiplicity of regional groupings. There were efforts at an all-Italy communal structure, especially that of 1416 when delegates from most of Italy met at Bologna and attempted to set up a structure to endure for ten years. But neither this, nor other conferences at Forli (1418), Florence (1428) and Ferrara (1554-1555), were able substantially to create a monolithic religious structure. From 1416 to 1586 many conferences were called, but they basically dealt with anti-Jewish legislation, taxes, or particular crises of the moment. They were not rabbinical conclaves and even when they occasionally took up religious matters they in no way affected the continuing variegation of religious practice in general, and liturgy in particular. When rabbis were present and active they were not so in their capacity of rabbinical authorities or for their scholarship, but merely as representatives of their regions or communities. The closest they came to dealing with matters of religion was in discussing and attempting to legislate concerning the extravagances of the Renaissance life-style, enhancing rabbinical authority, regulating gambling, and attempting to terminate sexual licentiousness. [99] But they neither succeeded in these procedural and moral matters, nor even set about the task of attempting to bring centralized authority and homogeneity into the pluralistic ritual and liturgy that prevailed.

Judah Messer Leon attempted to exercise central authority in 1455, and threatened all who disobeyed him with excommunication. There was, however, no indigenous authority for such a "chief rabbinate" in Judaism, and if Messer Leon was unconsciously emulating the papacy, he failed. Any effort to limit individual rabbinic authority was doomed to failure. Historians who attribute failure to organize central religious authority to secular reasons, such as in the case of Renaissance Italy, to "inertia . . . and the objective conditions of a country divided into a large number of states . . . " are missing the main point. [100] Central, mono-lithic religious authority akin to the Roman Catholic episcopacy and papacy, even to synodal bodies of certain Protestant denomina-tions, is not possible in Judaism. It cannot be stressed too often in a work of this nature ranging over the globe and surveying millenia, that in Judaism each rabbi is autonomous and every congregation is independent. [101]

Renaissance artistry affected even the ghetto communi-ties, and synagogues enjoyed a high degree of aesthetic care. This expressed itself in architecture, metalwork, embroidery, illuminated manuscripts, and decorous prayerbook bindings. Most medieval manuscript and later printed book ornamentation and illustration, however, lacked originality. It was largely imitation of the Christian motifs and style. This is evident since the thir-teenth century and continued into the Renaissance period through the sixteenth century. It went so far as even to borrow and use the caricatures of Jews. Curiously, an Italian prayerbook of the sixteenth century even had a figure of Satan adorning it. [102]

In the field of music, among the interesting aesthetic efforts were those of the musician Salamone (Solomon) dei Rossi (ca. 1570-1630) and Rabbi Leone da Modena. Many Italian predeces-sors as early as the fifteenth century such as Abraham Farissol who was a cantor and styled himself menaggen (musician, or possibly even instrumentalist) and contemporaries took an interest in what is termed "art music." These were compositions with scientifically correct scores which were performed in accordance with the notations and were sung by choirs using harmony, antiph-ony and polyphony, and sometimes rendered by instruments. [103] Much music was composed and performed by Jews for gentile audiences for over a century prior to this time, but this secular music is not of interest in this study. Synagogue art music was known in Padua, Ferrara, Mantua, Venice, Pesaro, and Senigallia, mostly related to the kedushah, the "thrice-holy" doxological prayer occurring in the ámidah, the kaddish, a doxology which occurs at several intervals during the worship order, álenu and ádon ólam. When Modena wanted to defend his favoring choral music at Ferrara in 1605 he called upon the rabbi of Venice, Ben Zion Sarfati (d. 1610) who recalled that the great sage R. Meir Katzenellenbogen authorized "the singing of prayers according to the order and rhythm of music," a preferable activity to singing vulgar songs in the streets. Choices often consisted of three or four voices or multiples if larger. This phenomenon originated in Renaissance Italy and became the forerunner and influence of reform in Germany and elsewhere in central Europe. But it had a long history in Italy from 1450 on and was already developed by the time of Farissol at the end of the century. R. Judah Mos-cato of sixteenth century Mantua and R. Abraham Portaleone in the early seventeenth century were advocates of art music.

The sixteenth-seventeenth century scholar R. Judah ben Moses da Fano of Venice wrote in 1605 that after examining the many sayings of the rabbis in the Talmud, midrashim, and Zohar and other works, he can only conclude that all the decisors (the poskim) find hamusikah (music) to be good in the eyes of God. [104]

Modena had pointed out that at Ferrara there were a number of musical experts who sang èn kèlohenu, àlenu, yigdal, àdon òlam and other such liturgical pieces according to specific arrangements. He also informed us that Ferrara had a music school where the art of music was taught and applied to the liturgy so that a performance of yigdal and àdon òlam was rendered on a certain shabbat nahamu, the Sabbath following tishä b'àþ (the 9th of Aþ which commemorated the destruction of the Temple). On that Sabbath the first of six consoling haftarot (lection readings from the prophets supplementing the reading from the Pentateuch) taken from Deutero-Isaiah is read in the synagogue. [105] Modena's contemporary, the aforementioned Solomon dei Rossi led a company of musicians and published synagogal art music in his Hashirim àsher leshelomoh, issued at Venice, 1622-23. [106] In dei Rossi's collection we find, in addition to items already referred to, the barekhu [107] and hashkeebenu [108] prayers, along with many psalms. We also hear of the passage, èleh moàdei àdonay, sung on Festivals. [109]

Nevertheless, as in other facets of Renaissance acculturation, the use of art music in the synagogue was not unopposed in many communities. For Ferrara we have the testimony of Modena. [110] A number of documents have survived to indicate an energetic polemic at Senigallia. One of the main elements of opposition to art music there was the excessive repetition of words in the prayers sung, including God's name or substitutes for it. [111] It is also learned incidentally from a 1645 responsum of Netanel Trabotto of Modena of the wide prevalence of art music. When discussing the repetition of the name of God or of allusions to the names of God, and of other words or verses, he informs us that art music prevailed "in all the regions through which I have passed." [112]

Just as many of these Renaissance rabbis were sympathetic and supportive of the use of art music in the synagogue they were not prone to appeal to the second commandment to prevent the advancement of art. They did not disallow even portraiture. [113] It is true that no Jewish painter of real distinction arose during the Italian Renaissance, but a number of respectable ones are known, for example, the son of a certain German Rabbi Abraham Sachs who was known as Moses da Castelazzo who was an engraver and painter of portraits during the sixteenth century. [114] Acculturation was further evidenced in such lifestyle particulars as Jewish males shaving their beards, and in the easier nature of personal relations between Jewish and Christian people. Regardless of the numerous annoying restrictions that plagued Jewish life in the ghetto era Jews and Christians listened to each other's sermons, mingled, drank, gambled, and even made love together. [115] Above all, however, the Renaissance had a long-lasting effect upon Jewish cultural development in Italy. [116] One historian has aptly remarked that two typical figures out of Renaissance Italy's Judaic community Leone da Modena and Simone (Simḥa) Luzzatto (1580-1663) were "survivors on the one hand, of the inquiring Renaissance spirit, anticipators, on the other, of the nineteenth century learned publicist." [117] I incline, however, to evaluate these and other similar contemporaries, as more than anticipators of the learned publicist. In a very real sense they anticipated modernity in its broadest sense, blending Judaic and secular learning within the framework of an acculturated Judaic life-style. [118]

The post-Renaissance eighteenth century figure, Moses Hayyim Luzzatto (1707-1746) indicates the type of Renaissance residue that influenced Italian Judaic life. But it also points up certain influences that transformed the Renaissance personality into the pietistic adherent of a traditionalism infused with mysticism. Some time prior to Luzzatto's birth Lurianic kabalism migrated from Safed, Palestine, and established itself at Mantua and Modena. [119] Zoharic studies took extensive root. Pietistic emphasis upon minutiae of observance, mystical prayer groups, and special fast-days seemed as in other times and places to serve as a reaction to the more relaxed and tolerant life-style of a community in process of acculturation.

Italian rabbis such as Aaron Berachiah da Modena (d. 1639), Menaḥem Azariah da Fano (1548-1620), Moses Zacuto of Mantua (1620-1697), and Benjamin Cohen Vitale of Reggio (d. 1739) preserved and expanded the Lurianic mysticism long after the fervor of the community at Safed subsided. Ghetto misery and this proliferating kabalistic conviction combined to make Italian Jews ripe for the appearance of Shabbatai Ẓevi, and they experienced sweeping addiction to the latter's messianic movement even long after the messianic pretender was himself disposed of by the Turkish sultan. [120]

It was in the backwater of this tragic period that Luzzatto was caught up. It is thought that at times, after 1727, in the depths of preoccupation with the study of the Zohar, he began to believe himself to be the messiah, a belief that did not gain wide currency beyond his personal fantasy. [121] In his early life, as heir of the Renaissance he served as father to ingredients of modern cultural development within Judaism, including the advancement of modern Hebrew. But later he became enamored with kabalism and devoted himself to its mastery. He was excommunicated and left Italy. He lived in Amsterdam for some time, and there he wrote one of the most significant treatises in the history of Judaic ethical literature, **Mesilat Yesharim**. [122] For Luzzatto this treatise, based upon a well-known early rabbinic saying was designed for spiritual training which would enable the practitioner to attain saintliness and virtual supernatural power, and thus help bring the redemption, the tikun which was at the center of kabalism. [123]

The reaction to Jewish Renaissance acculturation, however, came not only from proliferating kabalism. It stemmed also from the influx of àshkenazi style yeshibot from central and eastern Europe. The drive for education in the Italian Jewish communities was intense. In the absence of organized schools of the style of the Jews of Poland in the earlier days, private tutoring generally characterized the Italian communities. While Humanists were the tutors of the wealthy, heads of yeshibot and other rabbis generally tutored the poor. A shortage of Jewish teachers, however, was endemic, and often led to the use of Christian teachers even in yeshibot. This is attested to by a sixteenth century rabbi of Siena who described the curriculum in his yeshibah. He referred to the segment of the day after lunch which was devoted to secular studies taught by a melamed nozri, a Christian teacher. [124]

The rigor of the schedule at the yeshibah is of interest. In reality it described what was common for several centuries more in eastern Europe, aside from the secular education which was lacking in Poland. In this way it informed us of the interchange of knowledge and style that went on even over vast areas of geography. But what is even of greater interest is that we see here in a sixteenth century yeshibah in Italy more or less the curriculum and style of a twentieth century yeshibah in the United States, a type prevalent in many particulars in my own youth, and still operated among ultra-orthodox circles with variations and modifications. There was a morning session followed by lunch, an afternoon session, and then an evening session that lasted until ten o'clock at night. This was followed by a light supper during which a student expounded a theme and was subjected to questioning until close to midnight. The students then napped until four in the morning. They arose, studied until seven, attended synagogue, engaged in study again, breakfasted, and resumed their religious studies until one o'clock in the afternoon.

The curriculum was advanced and graduated. The students started their studies with Bible, proceeded to its commentaries, and then went on to halakhah. Specifically, they studied the massive digest of Moses Maimonides, **Mishneh Torah**. From this they progressed to a study of the Mishnah, followed by Talmud and the medieval scholastic commentary, the supplementary glosses and annotations to the Babylonian Talmud known as Tosafot. What is clearly evident in the sixteenth century yeshibah is a reaction to some aspects of Renaissance frivolity through the effort to transplant a Polish-type yeshibah to Italy, as in the twentieth century the same was attempted from eastern Europe to the United States. While this did not serve to halt acculturation in either case, it made possible the expansion of the more traditionalist approach to learning and piety, thus allowing for the continuing evolution of that particular Judaic life-style and religious expression. [125]

Generally Italian rabbis were somewhat different from medieval Franco-German and Polish rabbis because Italian Jews were never degraded to the same extent as those of northern Europe. [126] The proto-modern manifestations in Jewish life already referred to earlier included the kind of intellectual openness that allowed for Jews to expound even rabbinism in princely courts before churchmen, and even in the Vatican itself. This had much to do with the emergence of a different style in the Judaic scholar-rabbi. [127]

The Italian rabbis did not yet prefigure modern western rabbis in all of their functions. The pre-modern rabbi engaged in activities the twentieth century rabbi, with the exception of some of the orthodox ones, no longer finds necessary in a radically different type of community. The Italians taught Talmud and its commentaries each morning. They presided as judges in litigations between Jews, preached, kept the records and conducted the correspondence of the community. R. David ibn Yaḥya of Naples is an illustration of how a dedicated rabbi also taught younger children for many hours a week. He taught the cantillation of biblical readings, grammar, moralistic materials and philosophy. The rabbi preached on Sabbaths, and it appears that at least some preached in the vernacular since Christian clergymen sometimes attended. The rabbi also presided over such religious rites as weddings and ḥalizah, the unshoeing of the brother-in-law who declines to perform the levirate marriage with his widowed sister-in-law. [128]

It was not yet universally acceptable for rabbis to receive salaries. This becomes evident from a responsum of the aforementioned Maharam of Padua, R. Meir Katzenellenbogen. [129] This helps explain a rabbinic phenomenon unknown in ancient or modern times, but akin to the Humanist phenomenon that prevailed at the time under discussion. This was the "patron's rabbi." He was a rabbi supported by a specific wealthy person who sustained the scholar primarily to serve as instructor to the patron's family, to copy manuscripts, and to serve as both legal and halakhic counsellor. [130] There was always tension over communal authority between the lay officials and the rabbis, and when they paid them at all, the salaries paid by the communities were lower than those received by the Christian Humanists. [131]

In addition to the rabbi the community frequently had other functionaries. When the rabbi was not a scribe, a scribe was employed. He was usually a person who had special talents, as for example, the poet Immanuel who was engaged as the scribe in Rome. Hebrew was frequently the language used for communal documents, but Italian was also used. During the sixteenth century Italian was often the only language used, although the sefardi Jews continued to use Spanish. The community also employed a cantor, known in Italian as deputato (sheliaḥ ẓibur), messenger of the congregation. He was paid from community funds as were also those who filled the role of sexton, and shoḥet, ritual slaughterer. [132]

As in other places and times, in both microcosm and macrocosm, Italian Judaism testifies to a wide diversity. Synagogues were the primary institutions of Jewish life, and they were many in number, especially in large cities like Rome or Ferrara. [133] These synagogues attest to the diversity of Italian Judaism in that they were frequently organized along ethnic lines in the same manner as western synagogues during the nineteenth and twentieth centuries, and as is even recalled for the ancient world in the early sources. [134] In Italy there were synagogues for those of Italian origin or long-standing Italian domicile, sefardic congregations for those from Spain and Portugal, and perhaps to serve the returned Marranos, àshkenaz congregations for people from northern Europe, and separate Mediterranean liturgies for Jews from Sicily and the Levant. [135] Synagogues were ornamented, including murals and sculptures. Ritual objects were artistic and expensive. [136]

Art and ornamentation, however, did not conceal religious skepticism and laxity in observance. The latter was undoubtedly a product of the former. The former resulted from widespread fatalism and reliance upon the role of astral influences in human destiny, as well as a belief in demons and witchcraft which affected Jews and non-Jews alike. [137] This rejection of the power of free choice to do good and hence the futility of moral living led to unprecedented corruption in Jewish life. Not only were Jews, including rabbis, mired in the same usurious practices that plagued Jews for centuries in persecution and expulsions, but many Jews were murderers and even contracted hit-men. [138] No less a Renaissance figure than Elijah Capsali of Crete (1483-1555), a descendant of the distinguished Capsali and Delmedigo families, a historian of note, informs us that when Austria captured Padua in 1509 Jews joined in the sacking. Capsali writes, "And many of the Jewish populace also donned armor and weapons and joined non-Jews . . . These ruthless Jews did more harm to their fellow-Jews in Padua than did the gentiles. . . " [139]

V. Twilight and Eclipse

The fifteenth and sixteenth centuries had seen a profound development take place among Italian Jews. This development will be explored further in chapter four through an examination of the ideas and careers of several outstanding Renaissance personalities. But by the time we arrive at the end of the sixteenth century we are entering a twilight zone in which reaction begins to set in. The seventeenth century saw the eclipse of that special characteristic of Renaissance Judaism in Italy. But as will be seen, its major elements continued to influence northern Europe, especially Holland, England, and Germany virtually serving as a bridge of continuity leading into what is often termed "modern" Judaism and incorrectly dated to the nineteenth century.

The Renaissance environment was conducive to the growth of Judaic studies among Christians. Many rabbis and lay scholars were in demand as tutors. Some rabbis opposed teaching Judaic classical texts to gentiles but others continued to do so and to defend the practice as perfectly legitimate. Some allowed the teaching of scripture but prohibited the mysterion as talmudic and midrashic literature were referred to in allusion to an ancient midrash. Some allowed only the teaching of Hebrew language. Nevertheless, most Jewish scholars taught rabbinic literature as well. This atmosphere, furthermore, was congenial to Jews and Christians visiting one another's houses of worship. Many dialogues took place between Jews and Christians, especially in enlightened Ferrara. At times these dialogues took on the form of debates, and thousands of people were in attendance. Dominican and Franciscan monks participated with leading Jewish scholars, and frequently these debates or dialogues took place in ducal courts. [140] The **Magen Avraham**, a major work by Abraham Farissol was designed as a source for the purpose of responding to Christian challenges. [141] This work illustrates that the dialogue or debates were conducted in a spirit of mutual respect, and not at all with the venom and negative impact upon Jews that prevailed in Spain and Provence in previous centuries. The spirit of the times suggested more universal human mutual love. A notable biblical exegete, Obadiah b. Jacob Sforno wrote in his commentary to Ex. 19:5 drawing upon Deut. 33:3 that just as God loves all people, Jews must love all people and not only fellow Jews, thus remarkably expanding the apparent plain meaning of the text which has reference only to God's special love for Israel.

Relationships between Christians and Jews were such that at least one rabbi recommended that Jews should use Christian prayerbooks as texts out of which to study Greek; in some cases Christians were godfathers to Jewish children at circumcision ceremonies; and it is known that Azariah dei Rossi (1511-1578) enjoyed personal friendship with Dominican monks. [142] Since the conditions of earlier centuries in France, Spain, and Germany which led to mass compulsory conversions no longer obtained in Renaissance Italy, conversions of Jews to Christianity were scarce. Usually when they occurred they were for purposes of marriage, at least until the seventeenth and eighteenth centuries when political and religious pressure intensified following the introduction of the repressive policies of Pope Paul IV. [143]

The Renaissance environment here described began to enter its twilight in the latter part of the sixteenth century as a result of the negative policies of Pope Paul IV. These new policies increased Jewish conversion to Christianity, but also served to compel some Jews to look inward. In the late sixteenth and early seventeenth century, as noted earlier, Italy became the scene of increased immigration of pietistic and conservative Jews from Palestine many of whom were addicted to kabalism. By 1612, in contrast to the earlier sparsely attended synagogues, the houses of worship at least in Venice were described as well attended on Sabbaths. A leader in this mystical and pious movement known as shomrim laboker (Morning Watchers), was R. Menaḥem Azariah da Fano. [144] Parallel to this movement there arose study-circles which were no longer interested in the academic pursuit of knowledge like the Renaissance Humanist, but only in study as fulfillment of a religious precept. Hence they opposed all secular learning. Members of these study-societies had to eschew the use of God's name in oaths, recourse to gentile courts and gambling. The pietists blamed the burning of the Talmud in 1553 upon the Jewish Humanists and insisted that great penitence is needed, a part of which is to give up interest in secular studies.

The new piety is exemplified by the sixteenth century figure of Yedidiah Solomon Raphael Norzi (Norsa). [145] Norzi authored several works which he believed would have utilitarian value. He offered condensed presentations of belief and conduct, with a great emphasis upon faith, and argued that Hab. 2:4, "the righteous will live by his faith" denoted that he will attain eternal life. [146] Norzi emphasized revelation, the validity of rabbinic interpretive Torah, the election of Israel, belief in providence, and the centrality of love. Like other scholars of the period he granted importance to necessity decreed by the constellations and offered only a small role to free choice. He taught both this-worldly material reward for the fulfillment of miẓvot (religious precepts) in accordance with a literal understanding of the Torah, and other-worldly spiritual reward applied to the soul after its separation from the body. In addition he asserted faith in bodily resurrection for the righteous after the advent of the Messiah. In his thinking this resurrected person will die again, and subsequently will enjoy a spiritual and eternal existence. Against Dante and in accord with Erasmus, Norzi rejected the idea of physical punishment in hell. Rather, he saw the punishment in hell as consisting of the person craving the sensual pleasures through which he sinned on earth and not being able to attain them, while his soul craves union with God but does not know how to achieve it. According to Norzi this frustrating tension is what constitutes the sinner's suffering in hell. [147]

Another expression of the new pietism may be seen in the effort to suppress certain forms of preaching. [148] Provoked by his brother Nissim of Mantua the sixteenth century scholar, Israel Sforno of Modena stirred up a storm in 1598 against David del Bene (Eliezer David Mehatob) a celebrated Mantuan preacher for using quotations from Italian authors, and for using pagan mythological deities in allegorical explanation of rabbinic àgada, to the extent, for example of speaking of santa Diana ("holy Diana"). [149] Sforno brought rabbis of Reggio, Emilia, Padua, Venice, Salonika, and even Constantinople into the fray to issue excommunications. This combination of rabbinic authority compelled del Bene to cease delivering such sermons. Until that time del Bene was a lay preacher, and when he was silenced he went to study under one of his excommunicators, R. Menaḥem Azariah da Fano and he became a rabbi! He served Ferrara for thirty-six years and was esteemed as a leading scholar and responsa writer, and highly praised for his piety. [150] His son wrote a book which he dedicated to del Bene and in which he assailed the study of vernacular language and literature, the very Renaissance pursuits his father had engaged in during his early years. He also attacked the prevailing custom of educating the females in Italian literature as dangerous to morality and responsible for the excitation of romance and loose morals. [151]

This episode is characteristic of a tension in Judaism in all periods, but most especially in one of transition which retrospectively can be understood as a watershed in the history of Judaism. Del Bene was a product of his time. He underwent a degree of acculturation and brought the spirit of the times into the synagogue. In the nineteenth century northern European reform paralleled this with the zeitgeist of that century. The public in Italy, like the public later, responded positively. This type of presentation of new forms and ideas through which to filter the Judaic tradition appeared to meet a need. The reaction of the anti-acculturationist rabbis taking the form of repressive measures was the other pole of the bipolar tension which was known since geonic times. When threats to tradition appeared on the horizon and rabbinic authority feared dissent and pluralism the reaction was to apply pressure and suppression. [152] This reaction of the rabbis in Del Bene's case is instructive for the repression that haunted Yoseph Shlomo Delmedigo in the seventeenth century, and caused him to leave Crete. It also helps explain his negative attitude toward rabbis, his interest in Karaism and his harsh critique of traditionalism. [153]

The study of Torah was another element affected in the twilight era of Renaissance Judaism. There had always been a close relationship between the French and German scholars and Italian Judaism. Italian Jews primarily followed an Italian compilation of halakhah and custom called **Shibbole Haleket,** or its abridgment **Tanya** which went back to the pre-Renaissance period. [154] Much of this material, however, as also was the case with the background to the thirteenth-fourteenth century scholar, R. Menaḥem Recanati's **Pirke Halakhot** was French and German. Aside from the scholars of those countries, especially the Tosafists, the eleventh century Spaniard, Alfasi, was followed, and the twelfth century views of the Egyptian Maimonides were held in high esteem. The German and French influence was furthered by immigration of Jews from those lands to Italy. And thus too the **Sefer Miẓvot Gadol** of R. Moses of Coucy was quite popular in Italy; and the halakhic work of R. Jacob ben Asher, **Arbá Turim** was acceptable to both àshkenaz and sefardi Jews. [155]

It is no surprise, therefore, that àshkenaz-type yeshibot flourished in Italy. Furthermore, àshkenaz yeshibot often migrated to north Italy in toto, the teachers and entire student bodies, reaching a zenith during the sixteenth century. The most famous were the yeshibah of R. Joseph Colon dating to the mid-fifteenth century, and that of Judah Minz his contemporary at Padua. Nevertheless, at that time many Italian yeshibot differed radically from those of the àshkenaz lands in that the students were also given an education in Latin, rhetoric, and other secular subjects. At the height of the Italian Renaissance the yeshibot were also at their zenith and students came, or were actively recruited from France and Germany. Like other medieval students and scholars who migrated from university to university yeshibah students were prone to do the same, always in quest of a better place to study. [156]

Just as many Renaissance figures cherished secular or clerical titles so too yeshibah students pursued ordination to an extent apparently hitherto unknown in Judaism. And as often happens with a commodity in such great demand, those unable to attain it in a regular fashion might seek to buy it irregularly, and there may be readily available those corrupt enough to sell it. This condition obtained in Renaissance Italy, as it did again in early twentieth century America when many a sexton, ritual circumciser, and shoḥet, styled as "reverend," and many a "graduate" of doubtful rabbinical schools, many illiterate in Judaic rabbinic classics assumed the role of rabbis ostensibly certifying their ordination. [157]

Adherence to minhag (custom) was very strong in Italy precisely in order to preserve historical Italian traditions against the overwhelming power of àshkenaz halakhah and custom. Italy was a land of great diversity and was therefore a center of prolific responsa literature. Constant problems arose, many of them utterly new in the halakhic literature as a product of the unprecedented life-style and socio-economic conditions of the Renaissance.

The policies of Paul IV referred to earlier were inimical to the continuation of Renaissance-style Judaic study. The attacks on the Talmud became widespread and after a reasonable interval of this many yeshibot began to lack copies of the Talmud. They used instead the writing of Maimonides, R. Asher ben Yehiel, and his son's digest **Arba Turim**, and above all the talmudic abridgment by Alfasi. Yeshibah learning declined increasingly throughout the sixteenth century, and Italian scholarship lost its previous high rank, the laurels now left solely to Poland and Russia. [158]

VI. Summary

Despite the emphasis upon excellence, rationalism and individuality that pervaded the Humanistic Renaissance there were paradoxical contradictory tendencies inherited from medievalism that were not entirely shed. There was a curious addiction on the part of many to superstition and to a belief in the potency of magic. [159] Even Jewish scholars were caught up in these irrational trends, and sometimes also in a belief in astral power, ghosts, demons, and the efficacy of witchcraft. [160] The irrational belief in witchcraft and the fear of it were so intense that Italian Jews conducted a double marriage ceremony, the first in a closed room attended only by witnesses, and the second in public, although it is not quite clear how this could ward off the destructive power of a designing witch. [161] Jews no less than gentiles were often fatalistic, sometimes finding the locus of irreversible decree in God, sometimes in the stars. This type of conviction led to a reduction in religious faith, for it told the individual that righteousness and repentance cannot determine his destiny.

Superstition led to a variety of forms of spiritual distortion. Crises in the various stages of life were confronted with dramatic efforts to employ magical solutions instead of seeking God with prayer and faith. For example, a woman suffering excruciating labor pains would have a Torah scroll placed on her lap. [162] Along with the common people scholars were addicted to superstition, sorcery, and the belief in the power of witchcraft. So serious was the problem and so intensely did gentiles believe that Jews were adept at sorcery to an extent far exceeding gentile command of the art, that Pope Paul V ordered their expulsion from papal lands in 1569. [163] Jews also engaged in alchemy, a pseudo-science seeking a method to extract gold from other less precious metals. Leona da Modena's uncle was murdered by a confederate in alchemy and his son died of arsenic and other toxic chemical fumes resulting from experiments, but Leon continued the researches. No less a scholar than Johanan Alemanno (ca. 1435-1504) pursued research into an elixir which would enable him to experience physical immortality. Similarly, Alemanno and other Jewish scholars did serious research into the subject of demons, and claimed to have proven their existence. [164]

A consequence of the vigorous emphasis upon individuality and the unlimited human capability to shape events that was at the diametrically opposite pole of Renaissance thought led to an increase in many forms of violence and corruption. This along with the allurements of both a refined life-style and gambling resulted in the widespread practice of moneylending with all the attendant moral debasement that arose from usury and the insistence upon collecting it. Scholars generally did not inveigh against this evil in their preaching or writing. [165] It was only at the twilight of the Renaissance that R. Samuel Archivolti (1515-1611) denounced this avaricious practice as leading "to the pursuit of robbery, alienation of family, hatred of friends, animosity of the masses, and an overwhelming anxiety . . . " [166]

Certain aspects of the Renaissance Jew prefigured the modern Jew. First, there is testimony of lax ritual observance. [167] Second, in the pursuit of the well-rounded life values and role-models were often not those traditionally associated with Judaic spiritual figures. Under the inspiration of Johanan Alemanno, for instance, they viewed Lorenzo the Magnificent as the perfect example of the type of human being one might aspire to become, in their estimation a virtual parallel to Solomon, who enjoyed the mystique of being the wisest human, and paradigm for all to emulate. [168] Third, there was a proneness to ostentation such as gold-covered walls in a synagogue and the coveting of titles, honors, and coats of arms, lavish funerals and lavish cemeteries with elaborate and expensive tombstones, and flattering portraiture on medallions. [169]

In a more positive vein just as in modern times, people expected to hear sermons on Sabbaths and at happy religious events such as weddings. They prized gifted orators, especially those, for example, who added pleasant comments in Italian after reciting the Hebrew liturgy at a wedding. [170] As noted earlier there was an interesting development of quality art music to elevate public worship. Congregations became more prone to expect it, and to seek opportunities to sing at worship. R. Netanel Trabotto had testified that "in all the regions through which I have passed," there can be found the practice of art music. [171]

Here we have a significant aspect of acculturation that transformed traditional worship and led into the modern practices of instrumental and choral music. Thus, musical elaboration in the Reform and Conservative movements in the nineteenth and twentieth centuries was not an innovation of the modern period but merely a continuation and adaptation of a Renaissance phenomenon.

Why this development occurred precisely when it did in the sixteenth century is also of importance in our evaluation of the processes of religious change and development. Contrary to the view of one student of the subject this should not be attributed to the establishment of the ghetto and the subsequent inner-orientation of the Jew. This view argues that when the Jew and his music was shut out from the general public by the Counter-Reformation's tendency to negative relations with Jews, the Jewish musician turned to art music in the synagogue. [172] This should be taken with caution. Thus, even the proponent of that view recognizes that art music was practiced in Padua in the early 1550's, and the ghetto in that city was not established until 1601. [173] Even if our documentation of the practice of art music in some communities indicates it began after the ghetto was established, this will not militate against consideration of a different theory. It appears, rather, that in an open society of the type of Renaissance Italy Jewish acculturation first takes place in emulation of the general society in what may be termed a secular sense. The acculturated Jew eats, dresses, reads, laughs, sings, and houses the family in the manner of the non-Jewish neighbor of the same social or economic class. In time some of this secular acculturation, especially as it relates to intellectual matters, fine arts, and belles lettres, becomes, for want of a better term, "sacrilized." That is, it is turned to sacred matters that relate to religious study and worship in general, and to the synagogue in particular. This happened, for example with rhetoric, and with aspects of educational methodology and curriculum. The secular was sacrilized or "religionized," and the art music practiced by Jews in the general society was in such favor that hardy souls began to pursue its use in the synagogue. Advances in Judaic spirituality should not be related to persecution. This leads to a fallacious view of the history of Judaism. It results from a lachrymose theory of Jewish history. But worse, it encourages opposition to acculturation and the favoring of separatism and segregation as a necessary condition for the flourishing of a richer spiritual process. Certainly persecution, repression, and segregation often lead to an inner-orientation on the part of the more desperate who then become pietistic and very restrictively conservative. But this should not confuse the matter at hand, for such conservative backlash takes place whenever there is innovation and change even in the absence of persecution, and perhaps even more so in an open society. This is experienced in twentieth century North America.

The Renaissance, like the twentieth century bears witness to the fact that in an ambience of freedom Judaism will flourish despite the tensions of conservatism. When art music proliferated in the synagogue despite traditionalist opposition to it, it was not because of segregation of the Jew but was a remarkable dividend that the Jew had acquired from the open Renaissance society that benefited religious life long afterward.

In these and many other ways, both negative and positive, the Renaissance Jew prefigured the contemporary western European and North American Jews. This was also true, despite occasional breakdowns in amiable relations, of the basic congeniality that obtained between Jews and Christians. These relations often persisted in the face of both Christian and Jewish ecclesiastical opposition based upon mutual fear of the influence each will have upon the religion of the other. The Counter-Reformation weakened this tendency and Jews were prohibited by Rome from teaching Christians. Elsewhere clerics discouraged Christians from social intercourse with Jews. But prior to the Counter-Reformation Jews also expressed the pursuit of the well-rounded life in political awareness, patriotism, support of the various factions in the recurring Renaissance wars, and in a literature that dealt with political science and diplomacy. [174] Such sentiments also persisted into the modern era whenever the Jew was permitted to exercise them.

The Renaissance Jew was a type that went into temporary eclipse more or less from 1650-1750, although this type makes its appearance here and there in certain individuals. On a more general level it surfaced once more with the winds of change blown in by the Napoleonic Revolution and Emancipation. But this eighteenth and nineteenth century version is not to be considered as de novo, but rather as a continuity type that never fully ceased to exist. This Renaissance Jew and the rabbis who exemplified the era, to be explored in chapter four, were proto-moderns and stand as testimony to the thesis that so-called "modern Judaism" was gestated in fifteenth and sixteenth century Italy, and not in nineteenth century Germany.

Chapter Three

REFORMATION AND COUNTER-REFORMATION [1]

I. Introductory Comments

Although the Protestant Reformation had a major impact upon both the history of Jews and the development of Judaism, no adequate study of the relationship between Protestantism and Judaism has yet been made. [2] The main consequence of the rise of Protestantism for Judaism was the Reformation's influence upon the diversification of medieval Christian religion, the subsequent decentralization and weakening of absolute religious authority, and the role played by these forces in the thrust to democratic nationalism and the secularization of modern civilization. That is not to say that such movements were not already in the making. Incipient capitalism and consequent individualism were in formation, and these forces along with a rising tide of nationalism were cracking at the solid wall of corporate medievalism, whether of the Holy Roman Empire, the guilds or the Roman Catholic Church. [3] The Humanists had remained Roman Catholic. Even Johann Reuchlin disowned his grandnephew Philip Melanchthon (1497-1560), a disciple of Martin Luther, and did not bequeath his promised library to him. But eventually the work of the Humanists contributed to undermining the Roman Catholic Church, most especially through their critical philological approach to the Bible. This led to new translations of the Bible from the Hebrew and the Greek into Latin and other languages. Skepticism about the validity of textual translation and the discrediting of the Vulgate led to doubt concerning the authenticity of doctrinal interpretation. As historians of the Reformation have seen, this resulted in an appeal for the return to scripture as the only valid source of religious truth and salvation, and to placing greater trust in individual conscience. [4]

The Reformation embodied one more aspect of the individualism vigorously emerging in all phases of European civilization. Late medieval capitalism led to an emphasis upon individual economic enterprise, Humanism stressed cultural individualism, and Protestantism brought forward the claim to individualism in religion. [5] Corporate religious authority was eschewed by the individual confronting the text of scripture with the aid of the holy spirit. Such ideas of individualism inevitably pierced the medieval corporate structure, and opened the sluices for Jews as well. It enabled them to gain identity as individuals and surmount the confinement engendered by medieval group-status patterns which judged and offered mobility to persons not as persons but as members of a group. When this sea-change occurred, as will be seen later, modern Judaism became a reality.

II. The Matrix of Reformation

The Protestant Reformation did not spring live out of the minds of several figures like Martin Luther, John Calvin and John Knox who are so popularly identified with it. The process was a long and complex one. The parameters of this volume do not permit a comprehensive discussion of the social, political, cultural, and economic causes and influences that led to the schism in the Christian Church. I will limit myself to a brief survey of religious developments and the points of interaction of these with Judaism.

Historical convenience might be served if we accept the notion that dim origins of the Reformation may be glimpsed in the life and work of the Englishman, John Wyclif (ca. 1320-1384), and not only since the importation of Humanism by John Colet (1467-1519) of Oxford in the late fifteenth century. John Colet was brought into contact with Ficino and Pico in Florence, and after his Italian encounter he began to preach the supremacy of the moral life and to play down the role of ritual and sacrament. [6] Colet, indeed, began to preach the concept of Christ not as having offered his life to reconcile humans with God, but rather as redeeming them from the power of evil. Therefore, he interpreted the eucharist not as a sacrifice but as a commemoration. [7] With this we come to a closer approximation of the Jewish idea that the Passover is a commemoration of a one-time sacrifice. Seen as the paschal lamb, Jesus was himself the sacrifice, from this point of view, but all who take the eucharist are only commemorating it and not participating in a sacrifice. Here as in so many other matters the Reformation comes closer to Judaism, although reformers charged the Roman church with being too Jewish.

It must be recalled that Wyclif was master of Balliol College at Oxford during the middle of the fourteenth century, and that placed him in contact with a great Judaic library, a legacy of the expulsion . of the Jews from England in 1290. [8]

Although Henry III had forbidden Jews to take books as pledges for their loans, this was not strictly enforced and their libraries continued to grow. Furthermore sometimes intellectually curious Jews borrowed books from people and did not return them, or purchased books from people who preferred to sell them rather than borrow on them. The large number of books found in the possession of the Jews of Oxford arrested in the mass round-up on charges of coin clippage in 1278 astounded the authorities. The books of the condemned were sold in 1280, but it is believed that this sale did not affect the Hebraic-Judaica collections. After the expulsion of the Jews from England Jewish real estate in Oxford, exchanged for other adjacent properties, went to Balliol College, and along with this a great number of the volumes of Jewish libraries which could not be transported. [9]

Whatever might have been the influence in Wyclif's experience, he initiated the first English translation of the Bible, thus providing Christians in England with the tool for interpreting scripture without reliance upon priest and church. Just as Calvin later used the Mosaic Commonwealth as his model, Wyclif used ancient Israel as an example for his arguments against the right of priests to hold property. Furthermore, he denied the miracle of transubstantiation by which the bread and the wine of the eucharist was believed to become transformed into the body and blood of Jesus, thus rejecting a dogma proclaimed by Innocent III. [10]

Wyclif influenced restless innovators on the continent, and especially John Hus (1369-1415). Later on, when condemnatory scurrilous rumors passed around about Martin Luther, one of them was that he was born in Bohemia where he imbibed the doctrines of Wyclif in his youth. This surely points to a consciousness of a link-chain from Wyclif through Bohemia to the Lutheran Reformation. The Hussite movement in Bohemia emphasized the Old Testament, and John Hus argued that no doctrine is to be affirmed as a requisite for salvation unless it can be theologically demonstrated from scripture. His major theological work, **Tractatus de ecclesia** followed the earlier work of Wyclif. But what influence Judaism had on Hus, beyond his deferment to the Old Testament and possible contacts with Jewish scholars when he studied Hebrew cannot be determined. Better known is the fact that in the mass of variegated sects at the time, all loosely termed "Hussites," there were judaizers who demanded the observance of Judaic dietary practices among other Old Testament practices. When Hus was burned at the stake at Constance in 1415 he was accused of counselling with the Jews, and an impression was circulated that Jews, Hussites, and Waldenses were allied in the reforming movement. [11]

Hus not only repeated many of the traditional violent arguments against Jews for denying the trinity and their refusal to validate Christian truth in general, he also excoriated the church's toleration of Jews while it was persecuting reforming Christians. But he never identified Jews with the Anti-christ, and argued instead, along with his forerunner Matthew (Matej) of Janov that Jews will be converted and will serve as exemplary models for Christians. But Hus' disciple Jakoubek was scurrilously anti-Jewish and especially attacked the judaizing tendencies referred to above. [12] This was not a good omen for any greater chance of ultimate Protestant reconciliation with Jews than had existed in the Roman Catholic Church.

The Hussite reforming movement was the opening of the dykes that led to the larger and more significant German reformation. German scholars had imbibed Renaissance ideas directly from Italians, and brought these Humanist views to the universities. For example, Mutianus Rufus (1470-1526) had been influenced by Ficino and Pico, as had John Colet of England. In addition to the Italian factor, Desiderius Erasmus was having widespread influence all across Europe after 1511. Under these Humanist influences a strong believer like Mutianus began to doubt whether a wise and educated person really has need of formal religion. The Humanists did not reject the dogma of original sin, but they insisted that there is a divine aspect of human nature which can surmount the bodily passions. They argued that these passions, rather than be suppressed, ought to be nurtured toward the good by reason, with attention to the example of Jesus. This was a reversion to the Jewish idea that the mastery of the yeẓer hará (the evil inclination) is fully possible. And hence instead of an emphasis upon supernatural salvation, resurrection, and heaven as an abode of the dead, the Humanists tended to elevate moral conduct as the essence of religion and prerequisite of salvation. [13]

Such Renaissance artists as Albrecht Dürer and Lucas van Leyden, disciples of Humanism reflected these ideas in their art, ignoring such traditional themes as the death of Jesus on the cross, portrayal of divine miracles, and the veneration of Mary. [14] But when Dürer came under the influence of Martin Luther later in life and adhered to Luther's continued teaching of the need for sacraments, Dürer went back to the former style of painting. This underscores the fact that Luther was not a Humanist and that some of his basic thought remained entwined with traditional Christianity. [15]

III. Martin Luther (1483-1546)

Humanism made two important contributions to Christian religion. These two trends also became manifest in Judaism.

First, Humanism influenced a shift from preoccupation with the idea that religion is a doctrine of salvation to a significant recognition of religion as a pattern of conduct. Second, Humanism ultimately generated a minimization of ritualism. Martin Luther, in this latter respect was partly addicted to a Humanist trend, but as regards the former he was not on a Humanist wave-length. He saw the rituals of penance, indulgences, monastic abstentions and even prayer, in terms of "works of the law" which were rejected by Paul as having lost salvific potency. But Luther argued that faith in the Passion alone provides salvation and that good conduct without faith did not suffice. He even thought that Erasmus took the "works of the law" too Jewishly. The great difference between Erasmus and Luther was that Erasmus saw salvation as the fruit of moral living while for Luther it was the product of faith. [16]

In point of fact it is probably correct to assess Luther's reforming movement as a last glow of medieval faith rather than the beginning of modernity. Luther related to medieval movements and sought a return to St. Augustine, who was not only a representative of the classical age prior to what Luther regarded as the era of the church's corruption, but also the prototype medievalist. Nevertheless, Luther was also a harbinger of change. [17]

Martin Luther studied at the University of Erfurt from 1501, and became a priest in 1507. [18] But prior to that he imbibed traditional medieval ideas prevailing in the rural German area where he was raised. He believed in witches and evil spirits, and took seriously clergy processions into the fields in bad harvest years to read the gospel and purify the air from the poisons of these demons. He believed that disease, insanity, and fevers are all caused by demons. When he grew older and matured intellectually he rejected all that, and along with it most aspects of astrology, except for the ill omen of special celestial phenomena such as the appearance of comets. [19]

After his entrance at Erfurt University in 1501 he spent a decade there and in the convent. At the university he began to partake of the Greek and Latin classics, but it is difficult to ascertain to what extent he was influenced by Humanist thought since he railed against the ancient writers in his dispute with Erasmus. He began to use Erasmus' works before 1515, but came to object to many of his ideas, especially what Luther perceived to be too little emphasis upon faith in Christ and the gift of grace, and Erasmus' elevation of the scholar Jerome over the theologian Augustine. Yet he was inevitably influenced by Erasmus' notes on the New Testament and by his friendship with Johann Lang and Georg Spalatin as well as familiarity with the work of Mutianus. [20] It was this Humanist failure to accentuate faith that made for the chasm between Luther and Humanism and prevented the Humanist cultural revolution from channelling the forces of reformation. Yet, when Luther issued his ninety-five theses on October 31, 1517, constituting his historic attack on the entire ecclesiastical system Erasmus saw him as an ally in the struggle against medievalism. Nevertheless, after 1524, Erasmus detected the inevitable schism in Christianity, and eschewing the growing violence among mutual opponents, he withdrew his support from the Reformation. [21]

These events do not negate the reality, however, that in some ways the Humanist reformation in religious thought had the more significant influence on the rise of modernism. Humanism promoted the idea of God as one that is predominantly expressed by canons of reason, almost an abstract idea, while for Luther God always remained the grim and mysterious deity before whom the human stands in awe, full of despair, having to believe that His justice is merciful. In traditional medieval fashion, still somewhat influenced by childhood faith in witches and demons when he looked to the saints of the church for protection, Luther remained a medieval believer: opposite the transcendent God the human is unworthy and incapable of good, tainted by inherited sin and inclined to evil. [22] The Humanist believed in the dignity of the individual person. In a real sense Humanism shared with Judaism the ideas that a person is rational, free, and accountable, and must battle the evil within himself. Humanists saw victory over the evil as salvation. For Luther the human can be directed either by God or by Satan, and that whether it is God or Satan directing him he has no choice in the matter. Like John Calvin, to be discussed below, Martin Luther rejected any iota of free will, and here is the key distinction between the Protestant Reformation on the one hand and Renaissance Humanism and Judaic thought on the other. Erasmus, like other Humanists, taught a very Judaic idea of an inner struggle in which the human engages, the struggle within of yeẓer hatob and yeẓer harả (the good and the evil inclinations). Luther and Calvin denied the independence of the human will. Luther continued to believe in the efficacy of sacraments, albeit only in the two: Lord's Supper and Baptism, as the means to restore the breach between the human and God which was brought about by Adam's fall. Erasmus, like other Humanists saw the value of sacraments only as vehicles to edify morality. [23]

This dichotomy between Humanism and the Reformation appears in the case of Faber Stapulensis (Jacques Lefevre d'Etaples, 1450-1536) who translated the New Testament into French. He was an admirer of Ficino and Pico and believed that the only true service of God which he termed reverentia is to live by the ethics willed by God. He regarded the eucharist as a commemoration as did other Humanist thinkers, and looked upon sacraments as no more than "ceremonies" designed as symbols or spiritual exercises to elevate the doer but not as prerequisite vehicles of salvation. He was condemned in 1519 by the theology faculty of the University of Paris for reducing the veneration of saints, the worship directed to Mary and for undermining the devotion of the people. In his philosophy the world was entrusted to the providence of God, but he did not agree with Luther and Calvin that humans are incapable of choosing the good, and that salvation is not related to the accountability people have for freedom they possess to act in accordance with God's will. [24]

Lefèvre was a strong influence in France, and his disciple Guillaume Briconnet, Bishop of Meaux taught that the sermon should begin with the Lord's Prayer, and not as their custom with a veneration of Mary, that the proper veneration of saints is not in adoring them but in emulating them, and that since God's grace is granted gratis all sacrifices and ceremonies are superfluous. But he was compelled to withdraw instructions of this nature to priests when Luther's teachings were seen to parallel his. Similarly this influence of Lefèvre and another French Humanist, Guillaume Budé (Budaeus, 1467-1540), were influential in the development of John Calvin. [25] Withal, the gap between Humanism and Reformation, especially on questions of freedom of will and the requisites for salvation were never fully bridged. Humanism stood closer to Judaism in these matters.

In the early days of his dissent Luther had a moderate approach to Jews. He appreciated the Judaic origin of Jesus, and empathized with the refusal of Jews to convert considering the perverted role-models he thought the "papists, bishops, sophists and monks" presented. He, therefore, argued that Christians should cease slandering Jews and terminate all their base charges against them such as the Jewish use of Christian blood, offer them greater economic freedom to engage in labor and business in order to give up usury, and to engage them in social fellowship. He urged they exercise Christian love toward them in the hope of thereby winning them to Christianity. At that time Luther wrote, "We must receive them cordially and permit them to trade and work with us that they may have occasion and opportunity to associate with us, hear our Christian teaching, and witness our Christian life." [26]

In time, however, as Luther became enmeshed on the princely side in the wars against the peasants during 1524-26 he emerged a vigorous supporter of nationalism and absolutism. Nevertheless it must not be thought that the peasants' uprising was what first drew Luther to support of constituted authority against insurrection. He was already opposed to the use of violence by reformation groups who were chafing at the bit against the Catholic Church, urging instead that the constituted regional authorities unshackle the Christians from "the pope and his anti-Christian regime." He urged the people to pressure the authorities, but to make no insurrection of their own. In 1521 or 1522 he wrote, "I am and always will be on the side of those against whom insurrection is directed, no matter how unjust their cause; I am opposed to those who rise in insurrection, no matter how just their cause, because there can be no insurrection without hurting the innocent and shedding their blood." [27] Luther even sought scriptural evidence for his opposition to violent overthrow of injustice, and concluded that insurrection "is nothing else than being one's own judge and avenger, and that is something God cannot tolerate . . . God is not on the side of insurrection." [28] It is this trend in Luther's thinking which makes it possible for an autocratic atheistic communist state in East Germany to celebrate the five-hundredth birthday of Martin Luther, and hail him as a great national hero.

One cannot adjudge Luther as a pacifist or even as anti-violence, however, on the basis of this pamphlet. One can only see him as favoring entrenched secular authority. For in his search for allies in his ever-growing struggle with, and estrangement from the papacy, he became more and more reliant upon the ultimate schism he hoped would be declared by the regional princes. He was led by this logic to oppose the peasants in their uprising and he saw the princes as God's ministers and the peasants possessed by every devil of hell. With his violent outbursts against them, typical of Luther's mercurial temperament he inspired and even specifically articulated the need for savage vengeance against the rebellious peasants. [29]

This tendency in Luther's thinking to emphasize the absolute authority of the civil regime indirectly affected his attitude toward Jews, for the Jews retained their loyalty to the Emperor and he to the papacy. Further, his growing frustration with the failure of a massive Jewish conversion to materialize exacerbated his antagonism despite his interest in Hebrew. This interest was intense, and he preoccupied himself with the Old Testament. He believed the Hebrew language to be the source of all wisdom, a theory then gaining currency in the search for the original human language. [30] Luther is known to have had conversations about the Hebrew text of the Bible and rabbinic exegesis with Jewish scholars and he also received aid from Jews who had converted to Christianity. In one of his sermons in 1526 he said, "Ich hab selbo mit den Jüden davon geredt, auch mit den allergelertisten . . ." ("I have myself spoken of this with Jews, even with the most learned . . .") He thus became familiar with rabbinic exegesis from them as well as from the **Postilla** of Nicholas de Lyra (1270-1349). This, however, did not ameliorate his anti-Judaic views which were additionally fueled by his growing anger with bankers, and therefore Jewish moneylenders who backed the Catholic imperial forces. Finally, as his German Bible became a classic it increased German nationalist fervor and had a further negative impact upon Jews. He saw Jewish interpretation of scripture as the influence of Satan and distinguished between the ancient Israelites whom he admired and the Jews since the rise of Christianity for whom he had distain. During the 1530's some of his Table Talk comments excoriated Jewish usury. [31]

Luther was also concerned over the traditional identification of sectarians with judaizers, a charge now being levelled at reformers. There was a degree of reality in this since Hussite successor groups were practicing Old Testament usages such as circumcision and the seventh day Sabbath. The judaizing charge was made at the Diet of Augsburg, 1530, at which time there also took place a debate between the celebrated Josel of Rosheim (ca. 1478-1554) and a convert Antonius Margarita (Margolis) before the Emperor Charles V. Luther was impressed by Margarita and this relationship undoubtedly had additional negative influences upon Luther's approach to Jews and Judaism. It is after this event and certain other encounters with Jews that his Table Talks evince increasing hostility. [32] This hostility is also evident in several of his pamphlets which were directed to obviate judaizing charges against him. One was published during 1538 and another 1543. [33] One was against "Sabbatarians," as those who reverted to the seventh-day Sabbath were called in various periods of church history. They proliferated especially in Bohemia and Moravia during the early sixteenth century. Since they were condemned by all major reformation groups such as Lutherans, Zwinglians, Calvinists, and Anabaptists, as well as Roman Catholics, they must have been numerous enough to appear dangerous. Furthermore, the charge of judaizing which each party made against the other could be reduced if specific Judaic trends within reformation circles were vigorously denounced. Luther, for one, blamed the Sabbatarian trend on Jews. And in order to put off any suggestion that his Jewish contacts were of direct influence upon him as they were on Sabbatarians, Luther more than once decried their stubborn addiction to rabbinic exegesis. [34]

It is of some interest in this connection that Luther wrote his pamphlet against Sabbatarians only a few months after he wrote a letter to Josel of Rosheim refusing to intercede for him for safe passage in Saxony because Jews "misuse" his service and "undertake things that we Christians simply shall not bear from you." This must be an allusion to the continuing practice of usury, not to speak of their continuing refusal to allow him to "win some from your venerable tribe . . . and bring them to your promised Messiah." [35]

The worst of Luther's outbursts, however, are found in "On the Jews and their Lies." This pamphlet was even decried by Luther's reforming colleagues, Philip Melanchthon and Andreas Osiander (Heiligmann; 1498-1552). [36] This was a long diatribe full of venomous contempt and violence, wholly unbecoming a great theologian, and explainable only as the aberration of a near-demented frustrated evangelist who failed to win the Jews to Christianity, and even more had failed to win Germany to his cause. He originally misunderstood Jews who hailed him as forerunner of the messianic age because of the sharp reformation return to Hebrew scripture. He thought they alluded to the notion that he heralded the Christian Second Coming. What they actually had in mind was that the schism in Christianity and the return to the Old Testament heralds the coming of the Jewish Messiah. Later Luther began to sense that Jews were actually engaging in converting Christians and was deeply upset by a treatise he read in which a Jew engaged in a dialogue with a Christian and "dares to pervert the scriptural passages which we cite in testimony to our faith." While he disclaimed the desire to dispute them, he used a great part of the pamphlet to attempt to show how Jews pervert scripture and live in utter blindness to the true meaning of their own scripture. [37]

In his commentary on Genesis Luther charged the rabbis with obscuring the word of God, being too preoccupied with grammar as over spirituality, the corruption of the text (a charge that goes back to Ebionite indictment of rabbinism in the second century), and being inspired by the Devil rather than the Holy Spirit. [38] Clearly, delivering these lectures from 1535-1545, Luther evinced some years before his scurrilous pamphlets against Jews an already-developed pejorative attitude toward the rabbis. In his very first lecture on Genesis 1 Luther referred to the rabbis as "prattling most childishly." In comments to different verses he noted that the great Nicholas de Lyra was "confused" by the rabbis, the rabbis themselves "blundered miserably," and that the important Christian scholar of Judaica, Sebastian Münster, was influenced by rabbinic fabrications. But then again one must remember how Luther even lashed out against the Epistle of James in his intemperate way, even suggesting that "Jimmy" ought to be consigned to the flames, and argues that at Wittenberg they would prefer to throw the Epistle out of the Bible. [39] An exhaustive study of Luther's commentary, and the extent of his borrowings from rabbinics, and the relative merits of his interpretations as over against that of rabbinic exegesis and midrashic excursuses where he is in vigorous disagreement, is a desirable project for future execution. One thing is clear: from many predecessors he was able to imbibe much rabbinic learning, and a great number of rabbinic interpretations show up in his commentary. Frequently he disagrees with them or dismisses them, but he obviously goes to great pain to do so evincing a below-surface awareness of their threat to his veracity.

This apologetic exercise of these massive lectures on Genesis over a decade point to a very important aspect of Luther's theological battle with the rabbis that descended into the carnal level of crude attacks upon contemporary Jews. What was at the heart of Luther's battle was keen disappointment over Jewish failure to respond to him. This withholding of their souls from Luther's blandishments caused him psychological distress. This was not so much the product of having lost a challenge as it was a direct confrontation with his assertive posture that his version of Christianity as over against the Roman Catholic church which they rightly rejected was true and pure and, therefore, deserving of Jewish conversion. Luther's Christian love was drowned in a sea of frustration.

Martin Luther did not create the atmosphere of sixteenth century Germany. This had been the long-term product of developments since the rise of Christianity to triumphalism in the fourth century. But in a certain way, despite the positive features of the Italian Renaissance, and the emergence of some Jews into proto-modernity, the Jews were soon subject to cumulative woes in Germany half-a-century subsequent to the expulsion from Spain at the end of the previous century. [40] A German reformer contemporary to Luther, Martin Bucer (1491-1551), engaged in serious anti-Jewish suggestions as well in a treatise **On The Jews** published in 1539, in which he recommended that no new synagogues be allowed, Jews be compelled to attend Christian sermons and to reject the Talmud, and be assigned to menial labor. Luther's opponent John Eck published a similar treatise in 1541 which escalated the venom and deplored the security and freedom Jews enjoyed. And thus Luther's treatise of 1543 appears almost as part of a game of one-upmanship. [41] Yet one must remember that during all this time Luther was working himself into a frenzy with his lectures on Genesis.

Even before these reformers, however, Jewish converts had written works that offered support to the charges against Jewish exegesis and rabbinic interpretations later duplicated by Luther. Yet Luther depended chiefly on medieval predecessors such as Nicholas de Lyra who imbibed rabbinism from Rashi, and Paul of Burgos (Burgensis; 1350-1435), a converted Spanish Jew who wrote **Scrutiny of Scripture (Scrutinium Scripturarum)**, and a gloss to de Lyra's commentary. Behind all of these was the influential **Pugio Fidei (Dagger of Faith)** by the thirteenth century Raymund Martini. [42] Further, also underlying Luther's vile pejoratives is his enslavement to the medieval superstitions involving sorcery, evil spirits, the devil and all the vivid images related to this culture, and which bound it all up with Jews. Withal Martin Luther's anti-Jewishness cannot be explained without also considering that he was an utterly hostile man who functioned with what one scholar has called "an immense capacity for hatred" and he expressed this in a way that "in each case quite obscured the human countenance of the opponent." He used similar pejoratives and foul expletives against papists and Muslims, and anyone who disagreed with him. Furthermore, toward the end Luther was functioning in a defensive manner. His failure to witness the conversion of the Jews while he placed so tremendous an import upon their scriptures began to mean for him that Christian exegesis is on the block. After suggesting that Roman Catholicism and discriminatory political treatment alienated the Jews he was disoriented by the failure of his congeniality and his "true" Christianity to win them over. In his pamphlet "On The Jews" written while he was expatiating on Genesis and acting the role of Don Quixote against the windmill of massive rabbinic commentary he rose to tempestuous heights unprecedented for a noted theologian and recommended against Jews: burning their synagogues, reducing them to abject serfdom, and finally expulsion. [43]

That the theological sub-stratum always played a major role in Luther's thinking rather than any socio-political considerations can be seen from the fact that as early as 1514 he gave up the Jews as unregenerate, and in his lectures on the Psalms between 1513-1516 he also attacked the "lies" of rabbinic literature. [44] It was only after his struggle with the papacy began that he contemplated the possible conversion of Jews to his pure Christianity, a victory which would have given him virtual evidence that he was teaching truth and Rome falsehood. He therefore withheld further references to their refusal to convert and began speaking in conciliatory tones. It was this that led to his publication of "That Jesus Christ Was Born a Jew." [45] The reaction that set in during the 1530's was the product of his great disappointment, and his serious concern that Moravian Jews were influencing reformers in an untoward manner. [46] Luther made this progression clear in his "On The Jews" when he revealed that he had hoped for their improvement but saw that his hope was futile, and that indeed, the Jews were luring Christians to Judaism. [47]

In conclusion it must be pointed out that Luther's most anti-Judaic works did not sell as well as "That Jesus Christ Was Born A Jew," and his last work on Jews in 1543, a more moderate, "The Last Words of David" which was recommended by Melanchthon. And while one agonizes over Luther's vile language toward Jews one must recall that he termed the Pope a "Roman Anti-Christ," "apostle of Satan" and "a son of depravity." At times he railed that Christians "cared naught for Christ . . . were worse than the pagans and the Jews." [48] This was Luther's style and must be seen in that context. Even of James, the brother of Jesus, as noted earlier, Luther had brashly declared that he ought to make rubble of the epistle and throw "Jimmy into the stove" because of his teaching the centrality of works. [49] And finally, Luther's troublesome psychological state and mercurial personality should not be underestimated in assessing his contribution to modern "anti-semitism."

IV. Reformation Diversified

A. Parameters

In a pre-modern "domino theory" there was a reiterated prediction that one breach in the "seamless garment" of the Holy Catholic Church would result in a continuous process of differentiation of one sect out of another. As a foremost historian of the Reformation has made clear, however, there was not "a continuous process of separation." [50] Certainly the Reformation was not monolithic, but the new varieties of movements arose independently, and were not inevitably offshoots of a previous plant. The Reformation occurred in various stages and in various degrees across a good part of Europe from England to Russia and from the North Sea to the Mediterranean and Black Seas and was inspired by men of different interests and temperaments. The impact upon Jews consequently differed from place to place, and with the variegated reformation trends. The foregoing cursorily reviewed certain aspects of the Lutheran trend in its encounter with Jews and Judaism. In this section I will briefly discuss certain aspects of non-Lutheran trends before going on to John Calvin and the Roman Catholic Reformation. No effort will be made to trace political questions or the complex transformations that occurred in Jewish legal status, for better or for worse, depending upon the place and decade of the sixteenth or seventeenth century. In general, Jewish social, political, and economic vicissitudes have been amply discussed elsewhere. [51] We are here only concerned for certain aspects of the religious encounter which point to a new age, and ultimately a new orientation in the relationship between Judaism and Christianity.

B. Reformers in the Footsteps of Luther

1. Melanchthon and Zwingli

Some successors to Luther, for example, Philip Melanchthon and Andreas Osiander were milder than Luther in their attitudes towards Jews. Osiander was more independent of Luther and was more competent in Hebrew than both Luther and Melanchthon. Osiander had studied with a Jewish tutor and corresponded with Elijah Levita. Melanchthon lacked an appreciation for post-biblical Judaism, and although he insisted upon the use of the

Hebrew language in the church he deprecated talmudic and medieval Judaism. Like Luther, he charged the talmudic and medieval biblical commentators with hallucinations and fantasies. Yet in 1539 Melanchthon was instrumental in setting right an old injustice in Brandenburg in which thirty-four Jews were martyred and the rest were banished. Melanchthon facilitated Jewish readmission. [52] Levita's pupil, Sebastian Münster was generally free of the anti-Jewish animus exhibited by Luther, but at one time he did refer to the Jews as "perfidious" and suggested that it was only because "the Redeemer himself wished that the infidel race survive into the end of the era as an example to His faithful . . . " that they should be allowed to live in Christian lands. [53]

Ulrich Zwingli (1484-1531), a German reformer with major influence in German Switzerland from 1519 was the least expressive on the Jewish question. He was a strong advocate of the study of Hebrew because he urged the sole authority of scripture, and lauded Hebrew over Greek. He wrote, "No other language expresses so much with so few words . . . none so greatly delights and quickens the human heart . . . " It was largely due to his persuasion that a Christian Hebraist, Conrad Pellican (1478-1556), was brought to Zurich in 1526, where there soon developed a considerable circle of scholars who studied the Old Testament in Hebrew. Pellican was versed in rabbinics and thus the Christian scholars resorted to rabbinic exegesis. [54] Zwingli argued that ignorance of Hebrew leads to erroneous exegesis. Although he used the term "judaizing" in a negative way when he sought to accuse the Catholic Church of perverting pure Christianity, this did not express anything more than a popular term already at hand to describe a theological process which was Judaic in character, as for instance, placing emphasis upon ritualism. But it was not intended as what would be termed "anti-semitism." For he risked the same charge when he compared baptism to circumcision and removed it from its root in faith, arguing that baptism is potent even if the individual makes no personal commitment. Furthermore, he linked the Lord's Supper to the Passover and saw it as a "memorial" rather than a sacrifical act. [55] Zwingli consulted Jews, and when criticized for this, he appealed to St. Jerome who had been an advocate of it. He had little interest in post-biblical Judaism, but unlike John Calvin (1509-1564) he conceded that righteous non-Christians were eligible for salvation.

2. Martin Bucer

Martin Bucer (Butzer), referred to earlier voiced a typical Christian view that Jews must be physically preserved until their ultimate salvation, and advocated to Christians to win them over by exemplary conduct. Nevertheless, because he was himself accused of being descended from Jews, Bucer was moved at times to disprove the charge by showing antagonism toward them. Thus, when Philip of Hesse asked him in 1538 to react to an anonymous document that contained seven proposals of toleration, Bucer maintained that both Jews and Catholics were to be mildly tolerated. But this was to be within tight parameters. There was to be recognition of only one true religion by the civil authority and this was to be the Protestant faith. In connection with Jews his so-called "Cassel Advice" of 1539 recommended that Jews not be allowed to blaspheme Jesus or Christianity, build new synagogues or dispute with Christians, that they be required as families to attend churches to hear Christian sermons, and to be quiet in their synagogues. The Hessian materials were all gathered together in a little volume entitled **Von den Juden,** which Bucer published in 1539. Here he also argued for the imposition of longstanding pre-Reformation disabilities upon Jews: a Christian is not to be a servant to a Jew; that since their financial activities impoverish Christians, Jews be barred from trade and commerce, and restricted to manual labor. But also in typical pre-Reformation Roman Catholic style Bucer insisted that Christians are not to harm Jews, but to treat them with love. He pronounced Jews and Catholics to be similar in status and that both are not God's children. It was at a conference at Frankfurt-am-Main in 1539 called for the purpose of attempting a settlement between Catholics and Protestants in Germany, that the opportunity arose for Josel of Rosheim to reply to Bucer's **Ratschlag,** the Cassel Advice, in discussions with Bucer and other leading figures of the day. [56] Actually prior to his Cassel Advice Bucer had already written **The Dialogi** in which he used the ancient Justinian Code as a basis for laws to be applied to Jews. Such laws were to include that Jews were not to proselytize, mock Christianity, or hold positions of authority. At that time he also ambivalently expressed the notion that Jews ought to be required to hear Christian sermons and possibly be converted by friendly treatment. Bucer, like others, evinced this degree of ambivalence and it is difficult to ascertain when the person was seriously anti-Jewish in the modern sense of "anti-semitic," when he was only theologically anti-Judaism, and when we was simply recording facts and explaining the condition of Jews. For example, when Bucer argued against usury he pointed out that the princes sponged up Jewish wealth and left them dry, causing them to charge more usury and amass more wealth, and he prayed that the princes would treat them better, allowing them economic opportunity so that they would give up usury. [57] Bucer labored with a divided self, arguing from Rom. 11:28 that the Jews are God's people and therefore he supported toleration until the time of their conversion. He offered arguments for and against toleration as if he was either an objective outside observer, or was struggling with inner tensions. The latter is most plausible.

One of Bucer's arguments to defend legislating disabilities against Jews was from Deut. 28:43f., which he interpreted to mean that Jews must be subservient to Christians, and never rise above them in wealth or power. And he pointed to Christians improperly "serving" Jews at menial tasks "when they make fire, cook, wash, and do other work for them on the Sabbath." [58] It is in one of these moods of wrath that Bucer penned his argument that Jews ought to be relegated to menial and manual labor such as mining, breaking stones, making charcoal and the like, but that in return should be protected, treated mercifully and not tormented. [59] Bucer, however, did not originate this idea of confining Jews to unpleasant labors. This was actually originally recommended by the Jewish converts Johann Pfefferkorn and Antonius Margarita. [60]

In any event, Josel had written a Hebrew response to Bucer's tract, entitled, "Letter of Consolation from Joseph to His Brethren Against the Booklet by Butzer" which was to be read on Sabbaths in Hebrew in the synagogues. This pamphlet was translated into German. It was designed to give the Jews faith in the future should the worst of Bucer's more antagonistic suggestions be introduced. But of great interest was Josel's statement that as far as listening to Christian sermons is concerned the individual must act on his own conscience. For himself he asserted he believed a person of faith would not be swayed, and disclosed that he had often listened to Capito. [61] One last word might be in order on Bucer. It was the darker side of Bucer and Martin Luther, and the negative vibrations Josel sensed from some Protestant princes that led him on the one hand to declare Jewish neutrality in the brutal civil war between Christians in Germany, and on the other to have Jews pray for the Roman Catholic Emperor's victory. And in his memoirs Josel exults at Emperor Charles V's victory over the Protestant princes in 1547. [62]

3. Wolfgang Capito

Bucer's close associate, Wolfgang Capito (Kopfel; 1478-1541), frequently had Josel of Rosheim in his audiences listening to his sermons or lectures. But this did not bring him any closer than the others to magnanimity toward Jews that might have led to universal toleration and thus elevate Judaism from its centuries-long subordination. Early Protestantism made no direct progress in this direction, and it remained for secularism and Humanism to effect this emancipation. Capito was a good Hebraist, however, having studied with the convert Matthew Adrianus at Heidelberg, and emerged as a leading Christian Hebraist. He also consulted Josel of Rosheim often. It was he who gave

Josel a letter to Luther in which he asked Luther's help for Jews in Saxony which Luther refused. In his message to Luther, however, Capito was unable to raise himself out of the historic animosity, and while urging Luther to follow God's model of supreme mercy and plead the Jewish cause, he added, "so that they may realize that we are prepared to do good not only to pious Christians but also to our enemies." [63]

Capito reveals a good knowledge of the entire range of Judaica from the Torah to the literature of his own time, including the targums, rabbinic halakhic and àgadic literature; medieval exegetes and the Zohar. Like other reformers, however, his dual purpose in writing the material was " . . . either that I might refute their errors, or confirm our religion by means of their testimonies . . . " Here again we receive a picture of ambivalence. Judaism is either in error, or it is true. When it conflicts with Christianity it is in error. When it can be shown to uphold Christian doctrine it is God's own truth spoken in God's language. Capito regularly moves along this two-track road, praising and blaming, reflecting, as one scholar has aptly put it, the two poles of Christianity in its attitude to Judaism: an empathy that came from the realization that the two religions have affinity, and hostility engendered by Judaic rejection of christology. Unlike some others, however, Capito never recommended maltreatment of Jews. [64] And it is evident that his more benign attitude was transmitted to his disciple Caspar Hedio, the first Protestant Church historian. He read Jewish history as a saga of Jewish rebellion and God's forgiveness, but averred that since their rejection of Jesus they will not cease to suffer until all the gentiles and then the Jews came into the church. Nevertheless, although convinced that the Jews are doomed, he cited Jesus weeping over Jerusalem (Lk. 19:41-44). For him this implied that Christian pity and love is called for rather than hatred, for while God's justice is done, one must nevertheless succor the victim. [65]

It must be emphasized that many of the reformers wrote many tracts, treatises, letters, and pamphlets, and delivered hundreds of sermons. Some of this work has been published, much of it remains unpublished. This sheer quantity of written material over many decades, is reason enough for the reformers to evince inconsistency in many areas of thought, and also toward Jews and Judaism. An example of this can be seen in Heinrich Bullinger (1504-1575), successor to Zwingli in Zurich, and one of the Pellican circle. On the one hand he sounds almost like Martin Luther excoriating Jews for not having learned the truth after fifteen hundred years bereft of their country, temple, sovereignty and prophets, and yet not turning to Christ. And on the other hand in his commentary on Rom. 11:25ff. he correctly understood Paul, as few did, that Jews continue to possess the covenant promises. [66] This again underscores the great desideratum in Judaeo-Christian studies for a careful and exhaustive analysis of these writings from the perspective of their Judaic or Judaic-oriented content.

C. Sectarian Encounters

Judaizing among a variety of newly arising sects was vigorously resented. This usually signified a sharp return to the Old Testament and Judaic ideas. Sometimes it took the form even of denying the divinity of Jesus, claiming that Jesus was not sufficient answer for one's spiritual search, or that he pursued a this-worldly messianic goal. This judaizing element was a factor that turned major reformers away from empathy for Jews. They blamed Judaism and Jews for sectarian deviations among Christians. Anabaptists, for example, were charged with heterodoxy, heresy, and judaizing by fellow-reformers such as Zwingli and Luther. But, in fact, the Anabaptists often practiced severe anti-Jewish measures. [67]

Nevertheless, the idea of toleration unknown to Luther and Calvin arose among the Anabaptists. While Luther, and as will be seen later, Calvin inspired harsh repressive measures against those whom they deemed heretical, the Anabaptist leader Balthasar Hubmaier (1485-1528) argued that whoever slays a heretic is guilty of heresy. From this type of thinking came the impetus to social and religious reform, as well as a new trend to advocate non-violence. This in turn led to a wave of passive martyrdom on the part of Anabaptists. Out of these ranks arose also the movement for total abstinence from alcoholic beverages as a means of character improvement to help the believer to attain a true ethical life. Total abstinence had never been advocated by Catholics, Lutherans or Calvinists. From these Anabaptists also emerged the Mennonites under the inspiration of Menno Simons (1496-1561). Analysis of a large variety of other movements might yield much interesting data on the extent that these sectarian groups borrowed from Judaism. Although they would not have borrowed abstinence, it is likely that Jewish medieval martyrdom served as an example for the non-violent response of beleaguered Anabaptists. This might be said of the Bohemian and Moravian Brethren successor movements to the Hussites, as well as Sabbatarian groups in Transylvania. The pacifist position of many Anabaptists was stated by Felix Mantz of Zurich who said, "A Christian will not wield the sword nor will he resist evil." It was the proliferation of these sects, each demanding religious liberty, the urgings of Humanists in France and England, and the vast socio-economic and political changes, rather than the mainstream reformation, that ultimately led to universal toleration that included Jews in the late seventeenth and eighteenth centuries. As will be seen, however, a decisive factor in this universal toleration was indirectly injected by Calvinism's ultimate influence upon the separation of church and state, a decided reversal of Calvin's own Geneva theocracy. [68]

The Italian rabbi, Joseph of Arli, was not alone when he saw the proliferation of heterodoxy in Christianity and the attack on Rome in 1527 by a mixed imperial Army of Spaniards, Italians, Germans, and French as signs of the messianic advent. Messianism was rife among Anabaptists. The latter were often chiliasts, those who emphasized the doctrine that Jesus will return to earth to rule for one thousand years. Other Protestant sects also regarded papal Rome's imminent fall as being the fulfillment of the Danielic apocalyptic vision of the destruction of the fourth beast (Dan. 7:23-27). Protestant thinkers generally looked upon the pope as the anti-Christ and the Roman Church as a latter-day Babylon doomed to destruction. Millenarianism (the idea of the thousand-year reign, chiliasm), although not a matter of doctrine among major Protestant groups, was a fervent belief among the sectarians. Chiliasm motivated the peasant revolt in Germany and this might have been part of the reason Luther was so opposed to the revolt. For it is clear from the Lutheran Augsburg Confession of 1530 that along with the condemnation of Anabaptists, chiliasts who taught there would be a rule of saints on earth were condemned for teaching a "Jewish doctrine." Philip Melanchthon drew up the confession based upon earlier creedal articles only one week after being agitated by the apocalyptic excitement stirred by Solomon Molkho, of whom more below. At least one Anabaptist leader, Melchior Rinck, had been predicting the beginning of the millenium for Easter, 1530, and the Augsburg Confession was presented on June 25, 1530. [69]

Similar messianic fervor was proceeding apace among Jews. The current period of this agitation began with Asher Lämmlein who was influenced by Abarbanel's calculation of 1503 as the year of the messianic advent. Lämmlein appeared near Venice in 1502 and proclaimed the imminence of the Messiah. A year of great penance ensued among Jews, and when the Messiah failed to come and Lämmlein died many Jews went over to Christianity. [70] Soon thereafter David Reubeni (ca. 1490-1535) and Solomon Molkho (1500-1532) made their tragic appearances.

Reubeni appeared in Egypt in 1522 with fantastic claims of being descended from Muḥammad as well as being a brother to a fictional Jewish king, Joseph of Khaibar in Arabia. He claimed that this land consisted of northern Israelite tribes. He told Jews in Muslim countries that Joseph was preparing to attack Rome, and to Christians he offered Joseph's armies to attack the Turks and expel them from the Holy Land. He entered Rome on a white horse and met with Pope Clement VII in 1524. The idea that the Messiah will present himself to the Pope as Moses to Pharoah, and say "send my people forth that they may worship me . . . " was traced to a statement made by Naḥmanides in his famous debate with Pablo Christiani. Reubeni was received by kings and princes, was deeply influential among Marranos, and sent Solomon Molkho (Diago Pires), a functionary in Portugal's High Court, into ecstasy, and to his death. Actually Reubeni never claimed to be the Messiah, only modestly asserting that he was a Davidic soldier working for the restoration of Jews to Palestine. But his appearance excited Jews everywhere, and incited Molkho to return to Judaism. Molkho became involved with mystical circles in Palestine and became convinced that the Messiah will come in 1540. The sack of Rome in 1527 encouraged his faith, and his pretensions to being the herald of the Messiah. Together he and Reubeni went to Emperor Charles V of the Germanic lands in 1532, a year certain kabalists believed was designated by the Zohar to be the year of the resurrection of the dead in Palestine. Molkho, as a Portugese Marrano, however, was subject to the Inquisition. The latter tried and burned him in Mantua. In this way ended his messianic career which began with ecstasy, kabalism, a liason with the celebrated Joseph Karo of Salonika, and a stay in Palestine. That land was then in messianic fervor as a result of kabalists who since 1522 undertook to bring the Messiah through prayer, fasting, and the manipulation of the Tetragrammaton. Molkho originally predicted the messianic advent for 1540, but it is thought by some that after his visit to the Pope popular excitement brought him to accept the role of Messiah for himself. [71]

Messianic millenial speculation was only one aspect of the relationship between the reformation sectarians and Jews. Because of their radical positions on many questions affecting theology, church polity, and state organizations, the sectarians, often subsumed by reformation historians under the rubric "The Radical Reformation," came to understand the medieval condition of Jews. [72] Messianic fervor for Anabaptists, as for Jews, was the instrument by which they looked forward to overthrowing the power that made of them persecuted heretics, and reduced their socio-political and economic conditions to dreariness. [73] Owing to their outlook, antitrinitarian sectarians were classed with Jews, Turks, Tatars, and Arians because they argued for a purer monotheism and the prophetic status for Jesus as over a divine status. They were consequently declared to be outside of the Christian order and incompetent to interpret the New Testament. Many sectarians, like Jews, were uprooted from their lands of origin. German Anabaptists and Hutterites migrated to Moravia, and these and others undergoing persecution and suffering saw themselves as an elect covenantal people in exile. [74]

The testimonies of the famous Rabbi Judah Löw of Prague (1520-1609) and of his associate, the historian David Ganz. (1541-1613), indicate that although there were a number of expulsions of Jews from various communities during the upheavals brought on by internecine Christian strife and the many years of international war during that century, Jews lived in greater tranquility than during the fourteenth and fifteenth centuries. Part of the reason for this might well have been the preoccupation of Christians killing each other over theology and ritual and the substitution of Anabaptists for Jews. According to Ganz' perspective, during the fifty years from about 1540-1590 one million Christians were slaughtered while the Jews went unharmed. [75]

The interchange as well as tension between Jews and reformation sectarians are seen in antitrinitarian arguments against other Christians which were also used by Jews to justify themselves in turn before antitrinitarians. Both groups also used similar prayers for the welfare of the secular ruler in gratitude for even a modicum of toleration. Both groups were able to look out at the world and find people who were politically and economically successful despite not living in accord with the true faith. For sectarians the wealth and power of the Roman or Lutheran churches in contrast to their misery and exile, had to be explained, just as the success of Christendom as a whole in contrast to Jewish subordination had to be justified by Jews. Both grappled with the important (anti-Calvinist) doctrine that worldly success cannot be interpreted as the product of divine favor. On the other hand the sectarian argument for their own election as over against Jewish election was based on the notion that voluntary, formal alienation from the majority constitutes their divine election rather than the perpetual chosenness of a natural people which is the basis of the Jewish claim. In essence this was an argument that divine election was evident in self-willed separatism under conditions of humiliation and not under the externally imposed suffering under which Jews labor. [76] Even a Jewish scholar who continued to regard sectarians with the same contempt as he regarded all Christians, and perhaps largely out of fear that the sectarian virus might infect Judaism, nevertheless conceded that they were daily groping for the truth while Jews seemed to be drawing away from it. As enigmatic as this might appear, although undoubtedly aimed at sixteenth century Judaic Humanism, even more enigmatic was his statement that Christians were, after all, of the holy seed. [77] At the heart of the fear of some Jewish scholars that the sectarians might attain divine election was the ongoing process of sectarian judaization, a process Jews were unable to evaluate or to prognosticate as to how far it might go. On the other hand R. Judah Löw countered his own brother by denying the possibility of divine election bestowed upon any group outside of those within Israel by birth or by proselytization. [78]

V. John Calvin (1509-1564) [79]

While the Lutheran tendency of the Reformation found its most fertile ground in Germanic provinces and in Scandinavia, John Calvin's influence was greatest in Holland, England and Scotland. Emanating from France where he was converted to the Reformation between 1530-1534, he fled to Basel when peril to Reformers was imminent in 1535, and there studied Hebrew with Sebastian Münster. His origins resulted in some influence on the French Huguenots but after much repression they were driven out of France in 1685. And even in the British Isles, Calvinism early became only a dissenting faith. The strongest unmitigated influence, therefore, was upon Dutch Christianity. Nevertheless, Calvinist influence on British Christianity went far afield to the New World, and it was there that its most significant political import took place, as well as its long-range impact upon Judaism. [80]

Several major differences emerged between John Calvin's views and those of Humanists. First was the fact that for Calvin a person's responsibility to God requires that he act virtuously, while for Humanists virtuous action is derived from human dignity and responsibility to fellowhumans. Second, religion, Calvin insisted, is concerned with salvation through the mystery of Christ, in contrast to Humanists who understood religion to be a way of life. Third, for Calvin salvation was deliverance from sin and death, while for Humanists it meant attaining happiness on earth. [81] During Calvin's formative years Humanists were active in France, the Netherlands and England. [82] This Humanist position of the sixteenth century is basically well-articulated by the Netherlander, Dirck Volckertz Coornhert (1522-1590) who believed that true religion is inward, expressed by venerating and loving God as the supreme good and manifesting this love in the deeds of love performed for fellowhumans. This was a relatively Judaic position, with its emphasis upon imitatio dei the call to imitate God: as He is compassionate so is the human to be compassionate, as He is gracious so is the human to be gracious. In this Judaic mode it was also a late medieval throwback to the early Christian Jewish position of the Epistle of James, offering the essence of religion without reference to christology or to supernatural christologically-oriented salvation. Coornhert regarded ritualism, which included sacraments, as valid only for the personal benefit of some people but not for the service of God. He rejected both predestination and original sin as taught by the Dutch Reformed Church after the impact of Calvinism. [83]

As in this so too the Humanists were closer to other strands of Judaism than to the Protestant Reformation of the sixteenth century. For Coornhert, and others who associated with his views, grace is the power of God poured into the human to enable him to do good, but the human receives this grace by preparing for it with knowledge, and using one's free will to attain it. For him, as for Philonic and certain strands of rabbinic Judaism, a person surrenders one's will in order to let God's will live, but this does not negate the freedom not to do so. Again, we have here the Judaic notion of "allign God's will with your own will . . . and annul your will before His . . . " within the parameters of freedom of choice not to do so. Coornhert added to this that Christ is divine love extended to humans, but is a love present also to those who stand outside of the baptized community. [84]

Calvin had received an intensive Humanist education, but it was a strong emphasis upon law that he garnered from his teachers rather than these views concerning human-divine relationships. Furthermore, he did not have the same degree of contact with Jews as Luther had. There had been no Jews in France since 1394. In Geneva there had been none since 1491. He, therefore, was not prompted to an interest in the immediate questions concerning their legal status, nor had he direct contact with their scholars. One scholar has suggested that the only real contact Calvin had with Jews was between 1539-1541 when he lived in Strasbourg, and when he travelled to assemblies in various German cities, or to Basel. It is also possible that when he visited Ferrara in 1535 or 1536 that he might have had some contact with Abraham Farissol. [85]

It is thought, furthermore, that Calvin never read Luther's worst anti-Jewish tracts, and that if he did, he never commented on them. In 1545 Calvin sent some writings to Luther, but Melanchthon did not show his letter to Luther, and there were no further contacts between the two men. Nevertheless, it is clear from another letter of Calvin's, this time to Melanchthon, that Calvin knew Luther to be a person whose "impetuosity is ungovernable . . . " and that his vehemence breaks forth "with all the greater violence when all show themselves alike indulgent to him. . . " [86]

In general it appears that very few writers on Calvin, despite the massive literature that exists, chose to inquire into Calvin's relationship with or outlook on Jews and Judaism. [87] It is also significant that Calvin's more open attitude to usury would obviate the vigorous resentment that anti-usurians had toward Jews. In seeking to align Calvin with other moderately anti-Jewish reformers, albeit more benign than Luther, some scholars may stretch a point here and there beyond accuracy. For example, one scholar indicates that in his commentary on Is. 60:6-7 Calvin "indulged in gibes at contemporary Jewish greed." But it must be noted that in this commentary on Isaiah's words on the transportation of the wealth of nations (v. 5) by the multitude of camels that will cover the land, Calvin was relatively evenhanded. He argued that it should not induce Jews to interpret as they have "foolishly" that "under the pretense of prophecy" they have the right to "devour with their insatiable avarice all the riches of the earth;" but also adds "and not less absurdly do the Papists torture these words to support their luxuries, wealth and magnificence." [88] It is within his meticulous biblical commentary that one can find any number of negative comments by Calvin about Jews. These are, however, more the product of traditional theological pique over the refusal of Jews to accept Christ than to what is in modern times called "anti-semitism." Thus, in his commentary to Is. 29:11-13 he referred to the superstitions, hypocrisies, and impieties of the Jews resulting from their blindness to Jesus which leaves them in continuing darkness. But at the same time he again included the Roman Catholics in his indictment when he added, "We may easily conclude from this what value ought to be set on that worship which Papists think that they render to God . . . useless ringing of bells, mumbling, wax candles, incense . . . for God holds them in abhorence." [89]

That Calvin had access to Judaic commentaries at a minimum through the agency of Christian commentators, like de Lyra, or consulted Jewish scholars is evident when he wrote "for I do not approve of the childish attempt of the Jewish writers" in reference to explaining "the waters of Judah" at Is. 48:1. [90] It is highly questionable whether Calvin was "impressed by the anti-Jewish teachings of most German reformers" as one scholar put it. [91] If indeed Calvin learned most about contemporary Jews in Strasbourg he might have gained a positive perspective from the toleration practiced in that city despite Martin Bucer's anti-Jewish views and his general theological influence upon Calvin. [92]

What would be perhaps more important than the effort to ferret out every possible anti-Jewish nuance from Calvin's commentaries would be an analysis of both his commentaries and his **Institution** for the manifestation of Judaic influence upon his thought, or for his adaptation and assimilation of Judaic thought to his work. For example much is yet to be done to uncover the extent of rabbinic rhetoric used by Calvin. It is also interesting to contemplate the astute observation of a leading contemporary scholar of Calvin that John Calvin's theology "defies ultimate systematization: it is a salvation-history faith; it must be told as the story of Israel, narrowly begun in the Old Testament, but in Christ embracing all nations." [93] In this sense, as distant as Calvin might have been from Old Testament theology on the question of free will, he closely approximated the Judaic phenomenon: a virtual inability to construct of Judaism a systematic theology, the essence of it being a faith rooted in salvation history.

Calvin, like other Christian polemicists before him, was hasty in hurling the epithet "judaizer" at anyone with whom he was in opposition. Thus he considered Lutheran liturgy as too Jewish. But his most vigorous antipathy he reserved for Michael Servetus (1509 or 1511-1553) a leading antitrinitarian and Hebraically learned biblical scholar who credited much of his work to medieval Judaic exegesis. Servetus was ultimately burned at the stake by Calvin's Geneva as a result of Calvin's campaign against him. [94] As early as 1545, in the heat of correspondence with Servetus in which the latter was offensive in some of his strictures against Calvin's theology, Calvin wrote that if Servetus ever came to Geneva " . . . I will never let him depart alive." [95]

Michael Servetus was a Reformation Spinoza and irritated all branches of Christendom. His major arguments were against the trinity and infant baptism. Using Jesus as his example he argued that as Jesus was baptized at age thirty so all baptism should be at that mature age. [96] His antitrinitarianism was argued sharply and consistently. Along with all reforming movements of the sixteenth century Servetus believed the church had fallen into corruption, but Servetus saw that corruption as originating as early as the Council of Nicea, 325, with the doctrine of the trinity. He therefore used ante-Nicene patristic literature prolifically in order to reconstruct pristine Christianity. But he also used Judaic sources, the targums, rabbinic literature, medieval commentaries, and kabalistic writings extensively. Thus, along with charges of judaizing there also circulated rumors that he was a Marrano. [97]

How Servetus became knowledgable in Judaic sources is not known. But his arguments against the trinity were rooted in two main points: there is no mention of it in the New Testament or in other apostolic writings, and no role for it in Judaic thought even where it discusses multiple manifestations of God. [98] He used such Jewish philosophers as Philo, Maimonides, and Isaac Arama, a fellow-Spaniard. Isaac ben Moses Arama was born around 1420 and became a leading Jewish philosopher in his day. He was conversant with all branches of Judaic literature and non-Judaic philosophical works. [99] Arama must have been especially appreciated by Servetus because while he was a penetrating critic of Christian doctrine on a theological level he was benign toward the attendance of Jews at Christian worship and discourse, neither concerned over their exposure nor critical of the Christian requirement that they attend, if indeed it was obligatory. [100] In fact, Arama's own experience of these discourses influenced him to his conviction that more profound and interesting preaching is required in the Jewish pulpit. Further, he used Christian emphasis upon faith as primary, and like Christian theologians he argued that where philosophy is in collision with faith one must opt for the principles of faith. [101] For Arama the primary doctrines of Judaism were creation and revelation, and the concomitant doctrine that God governs the universe and history. The human's obligation, he held, is to bend his will to that of God by living by the precepts of the Torah. He rejected the Christian notion of original sin and asserted that the human is not tainted at birth. He took pleasure from the tendency of Christian theologians to support their views from the Hebrew Bible thus indicating that they agreed with Jews that Judaic Scripture bears supreme authority. [102] It might not have been any consolation to Arama to know that a man like Servetus, drawing so extensively from Judaic writings and from those of Arama especially, met his death at the stake for judaization. For Arama had argued that it is special providence that led Jews to live amidst Christians and Muslims who basically subscribe to the principles of Judaism. [103] Thus, for Arama, the theory of galut was in a special sense, a Jewish mission to the world. By the same token Servetus could take no consolation from Arama's clear critique of Christian doctrine.

Servetus drew upon Arama's writings in his penetrating critique of traditional Christianity, arguing especially that to understand the God-idea it is necessary that Christians refer to Judaic sources. Interestingly the Roman Catholic Church labelled antitrinitarians as trinitarii in a sense of opprobrium for their agitation concerning whether God is three "persons" or manifests Himself in multiple modes, and excommunicated them in annual papal bulls from 1583 to 1770. On the other hand, Christian scholars such as Reuchlin and Protestants such as Paul Fagius (1504-1549) labored vigorously to prove the trinity out of Judaic sources. It is, therefore, no surprise that Servetus drew severe censure from all sides. [104]

The nature of syncretism and eclecticism is such that the practitioner of these patterns must naturally take ideas and data out of context and create a new synthesis. Servetus did this with both church fathers and Judaic scholars, and often he extrapolated and reinterpreted his sources in a manner not meant by the original. But contrary to some, it is not accurate to designate such activity as "distortion," for all systems that build upon other systems of antiquity rely only on those aspects of the older knowledge which support contemporary revision and aspiration. [105]

It seemed destined, however, that whatever wrath Servetus incurred elsewhere, it was by John Calvin and Geneva that he was undone. He roundly reciprocated Calvin's charge of "judaizing" by counter-charges of Calvin's having adopted "Jewish legalism." Calvin had indeed left himself open to such charges with his great labors at building a new Christian republic in Geneva largely imitative of the Mosaic Pentateuchal system. But Calvin had the last word when at Servetus' trial in 1553 Calvin's condemnatory articles of accusation led to Servetus' burning. Among his strong anti-Servetus statements ran the charge, that Servetus " . . . excuses the Jews' blasphemies . . . approves and extols Mohammed's execrable words that the three persons in the Trinity . . . are the sons of Beelzebub . . . " Finally when Servetus was burned at the stake other Protestants such as Melanchthon and Bucer congratulated Calvin. [106]

Servetus' death was assured because despite all his Hebraic learning and his Judaic monotheism or "unitarianism" Servetus was not empathetic to the adoption of Judaic legal provisions. His attacks against the Torah as "irrational" and "tyrranical" sounded like veiled attacks on Calvinist Geneva, and in fact he epitomized Calvin's labors as "Jewish zeal." [107]

Even more significant was Servetus' use of Jewish commentaries negating Christian interpretations of Old Testament passages to support the concept of the trinity or as referring to Jesus. This inspired almost a Luther-like venom in Calvin for he often engaged in polemics against commentaries on these matters. Thus when he learned of Don Isaac Abravanel's commentary to Daniel in which Abravanel offered six arguments to counter the interpretation of the fifth monarchy in Daniel in reference to Jesus, Calvin not only engaged in an effort to refute Abravanel but also indulged himself in such epithets for the Jewish scholar as "imposter" and "dog," and accused him of suffering hallucinations. [108] It is nevertheless somewhat suggestive that Calvin refers to the "greatest" Jewish crime as, not the crucifixion or deicide, but incredulitas, disbelief. What he would not tolerate in a Jew Calvin would surely not excuse in a Christian like Servetus. [109]

Calvin wrote an undated treatise called **Ad quaestiones et obiecta Judaei cuiusdam Responsio,** "An Answer to Some Jew's Questions and Objections," reviewing the basic disagreements between Judaism and Christianity. It has been supposed that this might have been written after his trip to Frankfurt in 1539 and was the outcome of an encounter he had there with Josel of Rosheim. [110] In his memoirs, Josel referred to theological discussion with Christians in Frankfurt aimed at refuting Luther and Bucer, but did not name the participants. [111] It is of much interest that this treatise does not contain the kind of venom emitted by Luther. There are twenty-three questions dealing with the messiahship and divinity of Jesus as well as the Jewish role in the crucifixion. Considering the penetrating nature of the Jew's alleged refutations of many Christian claims Calvin's rather objective mood says something for assessing Calvin as a far different critic of Judaism than Luther. Furthermore,

Calvin was never as harsh against Jews as against Christian heretics who, he believed, ought to be coerced by the sword, and
in no way did he seek to harm contemporary Jews in Germany
or in the then-flourishing Jewish community of Poland with some
of whose Protestants Calvin had much influence. [112]

In the end, if Calvin's relative neutrality neither harmed
Jews nor extended any particular help to them, Calvinism as
seen from a long-range perspective generated much influence
in bringing toleration and emancipation to the Jews of Europe.
Despite his tyrannical regime in Geneva, or because of it, a drive
against heresy-hunting and theocratic despotism was launched,
and a call went forth for liberty of conscience. This call was
not only, as mentioned earlier, the cry of sectarians in their
struggle for survival, but of Calvinists in their ensuing battle
for the right to religious liberty in Great Britain. [113] This
was a movement that benefited Jews.

Calvinist emphasis upon Mosaic law, as seen in the comments on his relations with Servetus, was another factor of great
importance to a trend to search out Old Testament verities and
rabbinic interpretations. Calvin's approach to the decalogue and
to other aspects of the "law" was very close to the rabbinic.
He placed Paul in better perspective, abandoning the standard
interpretation of Paul as antinomian and adopting the so-called
"legalistic" approach for which Jews had long been excoriated.
The battle for toleration and the emphasis upon Hebraic learning
and what one might term a "halakhic" approach to religion generated greater empathy between one major trend of the Reformation
and Judaism. [114]

Another element of Calvinism that facilitated integration
of Judaism in western society was the role of Protestantism
in the development of capitalism and individualism which had
a far-reaching effect upon Jews. This was also true of the unwit-
ting impact Calvinism had upon democracy by generating the
concept of the separation of church and state, a step deemed
necessary by proliferating sectarianism within Christianity and
for the avoidance of any future Genevas. Because Calvinists
were persecuted in France and reduced to dissenter status in
England they were alienated from a nationalist point of view,
placing their religious freedom above nationalist unity, thus facili-
tating pluralist democracy. Thus, in contrast to Lutheran states
that banished Jews, and Lutheranism's general tendency to espouse
a mystical German nationalism, states that were early inspired
by Calvinists such as Holland, England, and the United States,
became the first to include Jews in the benefits of democracy.
[115] Furthermore, Calvin's enduring influence upon the English-
speaking democracies should not be underestimated. A major
channel for this influence was John Knox who fled from Mary's

Catholic reign in England and came to Geneva. There he studied Hebrew, and from there he returned to Scotland in 1559, leading the establishment of Protestantism in Scotland. [116]

A final word should be said about Calvin's theology and attitude toward Torah as reflected in **Institution,** and the relationship of this to Judaic religious thought. It is evident from the very structure of the work that Calvin had a very special approach to the Torah's precepts that hewed closer to the demands of the Torah than Luther's attitude. Calvin began his discourse on the decalogue by affirming that God is a just judge, and that by the very nature of being such He will take harsh vengeance upon the sinner. But immediately he mitigated that view by also affirming that God is merciful and gentle and prepared at all times "to receive the miserable and poor that flee to his mercy. . . " [117] Along with this view of God as wielding both justice and mercy, derived largely from the Old Testament and basically Judaic, Calvin also asserted that when Adam sinned the image of God in him was "effaced" and "he lost all the benefits of divine grace." No outward show of good is real, Calvin argued. It is only an illusion, and "the mind stays in its inner state of filth and perversity . . . however much of a dazzling appearance of holiness man may have . . . it is nothing but hypocisy . . . the thoughts of the mind, ever depraved and corrupted, lurk beneath." It was in this "anthropology," or his doctrine of man, that Calvin and the Reformation were not in tune with the Old Testament whether they were aware of that or not. For the potent words of God to Cain (Gen. 4:7) "but you can master it" [sin] are powerfully reinforced in Deut. 30:15, 19, with God's assurance that the human is capable of choosing life by "loving the Lord . . . obeying . . . cleaving unto Him" (v. 20). Regardless of the confusion that arises in rabbinic literature over the paradoxical conflict between providence and free will, the underlying premise of the Torah and prophetic exhortation as well as the wisdom texts of the third division of the Bible, is that the human is capable of choosing the righteous way. [118] The ancient sages who erected the structure called "rabbinic Judaism" did not confuse the human tendency to sin with an inherent guilt that cannot be expiated. And they appear to have decided to live at peace with the paradox that human free will and divine providence can co-exist. [119] Similarly the ancients decided to live in peace with the paradox that God has knowledge and the human can act out of freedom. [120]

Calvin compounded the human tragedy by averring that despite the absence of freedom to choose, the human is like an "impoverished debtor" who nevertheless continues to owe his debts. That is, although the human can in no way satisfy the call of God Calvin taught that he remains subject to God's commandments. And in the absence of paying his debt to God the human deserves eternal death. This, Calvin asserted, is all the more poignant because "Indeed there is no one of us with either the will or the ability to do his duty." [121]

This basic view: that the human is subject to God's law but is depraved and has not the will or the capacity to fulfill it, and therefore deserves eternal death, recurs again and again in Calvin's writings. It is the keystone of his theology. Calvin averred that the Torah promises eternal life at Lev. 18:5, incidentally applying a rabbinic-style midrash interpreting the word "life" to mean eternal life without evidence for that in the text. But he immediately mitigated that view by indicating that nobody is able to fulfill God's expectation. [122] For Calvin the solution to this great theological conundrum and tragedy was "to partake of Christ" through whose death the person is granted the grace that Adam lost, and through which power the individual overcomes the tragedy of depravity and sin from which, because of the absence of freedom of choice, he is unable to liberate himself by choosing to be righteous. "On the other hand," he wrote, "those who have no part in Christ . . . whatever they may do . . . depart . . . into the judgment of eternal death." For this Calvin had no Old Testament source and had to rely upon the New Testament.

An interesting approach taken by Calvin which gave the western world its heritage of what was popularly called the "blue laws" of Sunday, was his transfer of the restrictive Judaic seventh-day Sabbath to the Lord's Day. On Sunday, Calvin taught, "we are to stop all mechanical and manual labor, and all pursuits which have to do with the conduct of this life." [124] But Calvin was conscious of the intense judaization that this implied, a process which was anathema to every branch of Christendom, precisely because every branch of Christendom suffered from the "affliction." Calvin proceeded to explain that it is not because religion requires the observance of a Judaic-type Sabbath on Sunday, but only because it is for the good of the common polity, and necessary to enable Christians to meet for worship, and logical to have the same day for all. He went on to denounce "sophists who have infected the world with the Jewish notion that the ceremonial part of this commandment has been abrogated . . . but that the moral part remains . . . Yet this is nothing but changing the day to spite the Jews . . . " [125] Thus far one would think Calvin was saying that Christians ought not to fall into the heresy of sabbatarians and observe a restrictive Jewish-type Sabbath on Sunday. But he did not cancel what he said previously, and merely boxed himself into a corner with dialectic. In effect he said all days are equal in God's sight (Rom. 14:5), the Jewish Sabbath has been abrogated, and true religion no longer requires the Jewish-type Sabbath. But, he asserted, since it is for the good of society to have one day on which all can join for worship, it ought to be on the Lord's Day, Sunday, and since in order to make this into a proper day of worship, to hear the Word and talk of sacraments, it is important to have total cessation of labor. The Old Testament restrictions were, therefore, to be transferred to Sunday. Calvin was innocent of seeing the inherent contradiction between the product of his argument and his denunciation of sabbatarians who did the same thing. To cap his argument Calvin added that the Jews had an important consideration in sabbatarianism, "the preservation of equity among men" by remitting the labor of servants and animals. [126] And Calvin unabashedly advocated this judaization of Sunday. It should have been no surprise to him when Servetus accused him of judaization.

Thus, if Calvin eschewed the doctrine of free will, distancing himself from Judaic theology, he took a giant step forward in Judaic halakhah by adopting a restrictive Sabbath. The pleasant thing, however, in Calvin's exposition of the decalogue, is the absence of pejorative denunciatory remarks about Jewish or rabbinic interpretations. Here and there he has a stray mild lapse such as "The Pharisees had infected the people with the perverse opinion . . . " or the charge that the true law had been "obscured by the Pharisees' lies and fouled with their leaven." [127] Nevertheless, Calvin proceeded to insist upon observance of the law. He disagreed that the law had been abrogated, and argued that all that has been changed is that because of the grace that comes with faith in Christ, the law can no longer condemn the believer to inevitable eternal death. There can be no question that on this ground of the continued validity of Torah, Calvin stood close to Jesus and Paul. [128] Nevertheless one should not take this to imply that Calvin de-emphasized the doctrine of "justification by faith." He understood the gap that exists between God's expectation and human capability, and just as the rabbis affirmed that God's grace fills the gap to provide salvation, Calvin emphasized that faith in Christ is the ultimate resort of the believer for attaining salvation. [129]

Calvin sought to establish his ideal new covenant community in Geneva. Here the "true Israelites" would live the righteous life under the law, and here the purity of worship against Baal, Catholicism, would be nurtured. But the punishments inflicted by the government of Geneva for the most trivial of violations went far beyond anything we know of biblical society. Nuns were ordered to marry or leave Geneva, anyone who denied predestination was banished, and Servetus was burned. [130] Predestination was another keystone of Calvin's teaching, and was bound up with his view on providence and free will. If humans do not have freedom of choice and must rely upon grace, it can never be known whether the grace has in truth been bestowed, whether the believer's faith is sufficiently firm. Neither outward confession, nor success and prosperity in life, attest to one's having been saved. That is a mystery known only to God. Rooting himself in Rom. 8:30 and 11:1-36, Calvin taught that before one is born God has already predestined His chosen elect, and then calls, justifies and glorifies him. [131]

Predestination in that sense cannot be accommodated to Judaism. Jeremiah was called to be a prophet before he was formed in the womb (Jer. 1:5) but this is a calling for prophetic destiny rather than the status of "people of God," or salvific destiny. Salvation in Judaism is the product of deeds succored by grace and can only be attained after birth. Membership in the elect is a gift of birth or conversion, and membership in the elect guarantees salvation to almost everyone in the body of the elect but only almost everyone. [132] Without incurring the guilt of overgeneralizing a massive and highly variegated literature one can point here and there in rabbinic literature to sayings concerning the prerequisites of salvation. These generally include questions of both doctrine and ethical and moral behavior. One such saying, for example, is "When a person is brought to judgment he will be asked, 'Have you transacted business in an honest manner? . . . Have you hoped for salvation?' " Furthermore, contrary to certain thinkers who believe that Judaism was mono-lithic and required that everyone observe all of the so-called six-hundred and thirteen commandments, a virtually fictional proposition, there is evidence that some rabbis understood the multiplication of miẓvot only as offering greater selectivity. They saw this as offering more "opportunities" to acquire salvation and held that salvation was possible on the basis of concentrating on even one solitary miẓvah. Thus, even if there were sages who believed a Jew must fulfill every conceivable miẓvah pertinent to him, there were others who denied this. The Jew who sided with either group would be legitimately adopting a valid option. Thus, we find recorded the idea that one miẓvah alone can play a salvific role in parallel passages derived from Psalm 15 and Ezekiel 18. [133]

The so-called "curse of the law" which played an important role in Calvin's thinking, derived in turn from Paul's thought, was not so perceived by Paul's proto-rabbinic contemporaries and successors. Furthermore, Paul believed that the ethical segment of Torah continued to have validity and required its practice. [134] Calvin also required the fulfillment of concrete deeds even if he phrased his position differently from both Paul and the ancient proto-rabbis. Calvin, in effect, was saying that if one did not live the virtuous life it might be evidence that he was not predes-tined for salvation. And thus, in summary, while it is fair to say even in the face of great diversity generally, that Judaic thought emphatically endorsed the notion of freedom and equally emphatically rejected the concept of predestination, Calvin and

Judaism both endorsed the requirement for righteous living. [135] Calvin's vigorous denunciation of the notion that works can over-come the great gap between the human and God was matched in fervor on the part of some rabbis for such ideas that far from works acquiring salvation they were really only the believer's outward form of giving witness to God. [136]

The student must bear two things in mind regarding rabbinic literature. The first is its massive proportions with almost every saying being matched by its opposite. For any thinker, Christian or Jewish to delineate "rabbinic" theology is to become guilty inevitably of inaccuracies born of overgeneralization and oversimplification. It is this inadequacy that is present in the writings of both Christian critics of rabbinism and Jewish apologists for rabbinism. The second vital consideration is to understand that because the literature is so diverse, and there was never a central body or hierarchy to enforce a monolithic creed, Jews can comfortably adopt an eclectic posture on rabbinic literature and more or less form a personal theology by careful selection from variegated options.

VI. The Catholic Reformation [137]

A. Stirrings of Catholic Renaissance

Calls for church reform, understood as renewal of the institution aside from reform or spiritual rebirth of an individual can be traced to Pope Gregory VII during the eleventh century. Often these calls for internal church reform were defused by the establishment of monastic orders. At other times councils were called to deal with abuses. Thus reforming and renewal activities went on within the Catholic Church. But when the protesting reform movements began to form churches no longer obedient to Rome the Roman hierarchy began to respond in a way that has given us the rubric, Roman Catholic Counter-Refor-mation. This movement, undertaken to resist the decentralization of the church, set into motion a series of brutal religious wars. These were wars of rebellion on the one hand, and of suppression on the other. Some scholars date the Counter-Reformation to the period of 1540-1650. This covers the span from Jesuit moves against reforming tendencies, and the opening of the Council of Trent (1545-1563) to the Thirty Years' War which ended in 1648. But one must take lightly the standard portrayal of the internal Catholic Reformation as only being a reaction to the Protestant challenge. Many scholars correctly see a Roman Catholic renaissance in progress long antedating the excitement of Witten-berg. [138]

Scholars who argue for the Catholic renaissance within

pointing to a pre-Protestant Catholic reformation point out that Humanism was not essentially an anti-religious movement, but rather had strong regenerative influence within Christianity. It transferred to Christianity a legacy of philology, the search for authentic texts, and the use of the original languages for both scriptural and classical literature. It motivated critical and historical scholarship which, in turn, promoted theological reorientation among both Protestants and Catholics. [139] This is amply demonstrated in the work of the major reforming figure, the Spanish Cardinal, Francis Ximenes de Cisneros (1436-1517), founder of the University of Alcala in 1508. This university became a center of Humanism where the classical languages, Hebrew, Greek and Latin were prominently studied, and patristic studies were emphasized. There it was that the famous and highly influential Complutensian polyglot Bible was developed before Erasmus' work was done. [140]

A symptom of the ferment within the Catholic Church was the tragic figure of the Dominican Girolamo Savonarola who was born in Ferrara in 1452, excommunicated in 1497 and executed in 1498. He spent his most active charismatic years in Florence where he preached for eight years against papal wickedness and corruption in the church. Savonarola believed in his prophetic powers and claimed unabashedly that through him spoke God and not himself. Although Savonarola ended on the scaffold his call for the renewal of the church was not in vain. [141] Just at the time that Savonarola was excommunicated there was founded a new Order, the Fraternity of Divine Love, which emphasized the practice of charity, care of the sick, and the doing of benevolent deeds. [142] These examples of internal reform can be multiplied, and attest to the fact that while fifteenth century reforming tendencies went on among such people as Wyclif and the Hussites, there was deep ferment within the Roman Catholic Church which was engaged in its own reformative process. The serious divergence of the two processes which led to the rise of multiple Christian denominations only came after the Fifth Lateran Council of 1512-1517 and the posting of his theses by Martin Luther in 1517. The church was predominantly following the view of Egidio da Viterbo, General of the Augustine Order, to which Luther belonged, who said at the opening of the Council, "Men must be changed by religion, not religion by men." In effect Luther and later, Calvin, and the other branches of the schismatic reforming movements were saying the reverse of Egidio. [143]

One must, however, wonder about the effort to "reform" the church by strengthening ecclesiastical power and rooting out every form of deviational thought. Thus, the reform bull of 1514 called for driving out "all false and fictitious Christians of whatever race or nation, especially those tainted with heresy, and Judaizers," with "careful investigation to be made everywhere." It was apparent that "reformation" within the church was not conceived then, nor since, of allowing for diversity of thought and expression. [144] For this reason such important Roman Catholic Humanists as John Colet, Desiderius Erasmus and Jacques Lefèvre d'Etaples, all of whom have been referred to previously, were unable to carry forward their designs for church reform. Even Pope Adrian VI, the first papal reformer, who confessed that it was Rome itself that serves as fountainhead of evil and corruption in the church, deflected his energies in concern for Roman Catholic power and orthodoxy rather than internal reform. [145]

In 1518, Johann Maier von Eck, later to be a leading Catholic contender against Protestantism in Germany denounced Luther's theses. Von Eck grouped Jews and Protestants together as enemies of the church. This led to Leo X's order for the suppression of Luther's works in 1520. But the church was still not fully aware of the serious challenge of Lutheranism nor were the leading prelates, including the papacy, seriously confronting true internal reform. They were, as even Adrian VI demonstrated, more interested in crushing diversity in order to maintain political supremacy in Europe as well as absolute religious authority and conformity. To this extent something must be said for the standard popular view that minimizes the Catholic internal reformation and maximizes what is called the Counter-Reformation. One is compelled to wonder whether, had there not been a serious schismatic contention by Lutherans, Calvinists, and Anabaptists, there would indeed have come about internal reform within the Roman church. The church was preoccupied with the notion that Jewish New Christian heretics and mischievous Jews were disseminating Luther's writings because they were impressed by his empathetic pamphlet of 1523, "That Jesus Christ Was Born A Jew." [146]

The turning point came in 1536, when Pope Paul III assembled a commission of churchmen who later played a leading role in the Catholic reformation. The report they presented to Paul III in 1537 was in itself a scathing indictment of church corruption, but became a guidepost for future reform. [147] The report candidly declared that "so many abuses and such grave diseases have rushed in upon the Church of God that we now see her afflicted almost to the despair of salvation . . . " [148] The report excoriated the ordination even of adolescents as priests, and men who are vile and immoral; it denounced the habit of handing out ecclesiastical benefices which enriched the holder and impoverished the people, the manipulation by which clever legalists found ways to leave to their heirs the church properties entrusted to them, and that some bishops held more than one diocese; it attacked the absenteeism of priests and bishops from their flocks, and a host of other abuses. But again, even this report concerned itself with prohibiting freedom of intellectual interchange in the universities and the churches, for careful scrutiny of all books to be published, and certain books were not to be allowed in grammar schools. [149] The most significant force, however, for Catholic Reformation was none of these, but the Society of Jesus. [150]

B. The Society of Jesus [151]

The Spanish nobleman, Ignatius of Loyola (1491-1556) was a Humanist who was almost destroyed by the Inquisition. He became a born-again Catholic, was attracted to mysticism, and emerged as a zealous missionary. He organized the Society of Jesus in 1540. In its zealous devotion to the church this society considered one of its major objectives to be to convert Jews, Muslims, heretics, and pagans. While the Society called for inward spiritual renewal of each individual, it also professed absolute obedience to the church, which meant to the papacy and hierarchy. This would make it a natural enemy of Protestantism and every form of pluralistic religion. Thus in his rules for thinking with the church, Loyola set forth as the first proposition, "We must put aside all judgment of our own . . . to obey in all things . . . the hierarchical Church." And further on he stated quite candidly, "What seems to me white, I will believe black if the hierarchical Church so defines." [152]

In 1552 a grandson of Elijah Levita became a Jesuit. He was known as Salomone Romano and became a Catholic missionary among Copts and Maronites. [153] As a matter of interest, certain Jesuit founder-associates of Loyola were former Jews, and one of these, Diego (Jaime or Jacobus) Laynez, who played an important role at the Council of Trent, was the second leader of the Jesuit Order (1558-1564), and might have been considered for the papal seat when Paul IV died in 1559. [154] But in 1573 King Sebastian of Portugal persuaded Pope Gregory XIII to prevent the election of a New Christian (converted Jew) or candidates supported by them to head the Jesuit Order. At the time the Roman Catholic Church, under the instigation of the Spanish and Portugese Inquisition, was in the throes of a wholly un-Christian effort to define Jews by blood, and keep Christianity "pure" by not allowing descendants of Jews, Marranos or New Christians, who should have been recognized as totally Christian, to hold high office in the church. This effort went by the name of limpi-eza, blood purity, and highlights the ambiguity that prevailed in the effort to convert Jews. It was not until 1886 that Pope Leo XIII formally abolished such discriminatory practices as they related to people who had female Jewish ancestry, and only as late as 1923 was this extended to male ancestry. As can be expected, these discriminatory practices led Jesuits to spy upon one another in the search for blemished ancestry of anyone they opposed for membership or advancement in office. It contributed to a conspiratorial atmosphere and was in part reponsible for some of the unsavory reputation with which the Order was sometimes stigmatized. Nevertheless, the Jesuits had a leading hand in promoting Jewish conversion, and urging authorities to admit them to citizenship along with born Christians. They insisted, however, that new converts must marry born Christians, and eschew all Jewish ritual, including burial rites. [155]

C. The Council of Trent [156]

This council was the nineteenth ecumenical council of the church. It opened at Trent, Italy, convoked by a bull of Pope Paul III on December 13, 1545, and after a brief period at Bologna it continued sessions at Trent. After further meetings under the auspices of Popes Julius III, Marcellus II, and Paul IV, it closed at Trent during the pontificate of Pius IV on December 4, 1563.

The Council was the ultimate consequence of the sobering of the papacy that followed the seven-day pillage of Rome in 1527. The Hapsburg Emperor Charles V had summed up the feeling of both Catholic and Protestant reformers with his explanation of how it came about that his army so savagely attacked the holiest city of Christendom. He said, "It all happened by the judgment of God rather than by my order." [158] It was no surprise that some Jewish messianists believed this event to be the portent of the advent of the Messiah, for in the sheer cruelty of plunder, looting, the raping of nuns and massacre, Jews were able to see retribution for what previous Christian devotees had done to Jewish communities. And in the pathos of fathers killing their daughters so that the lustful soldiery could not violate their purity Jews were able to remember how many a Jew first killed his wife and children and then himself during earlier massacres in the Rhineland. As synagogues were pillaged, so now were churches, and even St. Peter's itself. [159]

Calls for reform had been reverberating throughout the church for decades. New orders set up during recent years were concrete manifestations of this. The crisis with Henry VIII of England compelled Pope Paul III to take a firm stand and to seek a united church in the struggle against heresy in the face of further schism. His first important steps were to name as aides and high officials men who were convinced reformers and even Humanists, and to select from these a commission whose task was to recommend reform of the curia and standards of learning and living that would apply to every priest from parish to papacy. But Paul III also revived the now-defunct Inquisition to combat anyone "who had departed from or who attacked the Catholic faith and to unmask such persons as were suspected of heresy." Concomitant with this he established lists of books which were adjudged harmful to orthodox thought and whose publication and dissemination were to be severely penalized. [160]

The Council of Trent had made little concrete progress between 1545 and 1555 when Cardinal Carafa was elevated to become Paul IV. His major interest was the Inquisition which he directed under Paul III, and his concept of reform was repression. He formalized Paul III's book-lists into the dread Index, another suppressive weapon in Paul IV's armory of reform. It was left to Pius IV, however, to promulgate the Index in 1564, and while this included a ban on the Talmud and all its commentaries, it added that if it can be published without the title Talmud and without any calumnies against Christianity it would be permitted. [161] Soon after his election on May 23, 1555, the pope issued his bull cum nimis absurdum requiring that all traditional legislation restricting Jewish life be renewed, requiring all Jews living in papal states to be confined to ghettos, and that all real estate held by Jews be sold to Christians. [162]

The tightening of policy toward Jews, however, should not be seen in terms of arbitrary anti-semitism as is often charged against the church, but rather as an integral aspect of Paul IV's anachronistic view of the world with which he had to cope. He could not see reform and rejuvenation of the church as a process admitting rethinking old errors, but as a process of reinstituting old repressive measures. As he hoped to stamp out Protestant heresy by force, he sought to keep all alien religious influences away from the faithful by segregating Jews and restricting their socio-economic opportunities in order that they might see the wisdom of conversion. The attitude toward conversion of the Jews was growing more assertive in the Roman Catholic church, and had already been playing a stronger role under previous sixteenth century popes. Thus Julius III had issued a bull in 1554 which required that each synagogue in the papal states pay an annual tax to maintain the House of Catechumens for Jewish converts in Rome. And it was during Julius III's pontificate that the future Paul IV, then Cardinal Carafa, the Grand-Inquisitor, hoping to forestall the spread of Jewish learning among Jews or the contamination by it of Christians supervised the burning of all Palestinian and Babylonian Talmuds. This took place in Rome itself as well as in Bologna, Ravenna, Ferrara, Mantua, and Venice, in 1553. A decree accompanying this ordained excommunication and other penalties for any Christian, clergy or layperson, who aided Jews in retaining such works, and for anyone reading them. [163]

This attitude was also self-evident in the bull cum nimis in which Paul IV attested to his goal of bringing Jews to "recognize their errors, and make all haste to arrive at the true light of the Catholic faith . . . [and] as long as they persist in their errors they should recognize through experience that they have been made slaves while Christians have been made free through Jesus Christ . . .." [164]

The theological justification for Paul's actions is found at Galatians 4:21-31 in which the Apostle Paul midrashized the story of Ishmael and Isaac. There Paul represented Ishmael, the son of the slave Hagar, as the son of flesh, and Isaac, son of the free woman Sarah as the son of promise. These two sons stood as symbols for the two covenants. Isaac, born of a free woman, reflected the freedom of heavenly Jerusalem; thus Paul likened him to the church. By contrast, Ishmael, born of a slave, reflected the enslavement of earthly Jerusalem, oppressed by Sinai's decrees; accordingly Paul likened him to the Jews. Paul concluded that just as the child of flesh, Ishmael, persecuted the child of promise, Isaac, so in his day, the children of real Jerusalem persecuted those of heavenly Jerusalem, and that just as scripture relates that the child of flesh, Ishmael, was to be cast out (Gen. 21:10) and the child of promise, Isaac, remain as the elect, so the church, as child of the free woman will remain the elect of the line of Isaac. This midrash by Paul was obviously reversing the roles of Isaac and Ishmael. It rendered Jews as Ishmael, just as he also had them represent Esau in another midrash. Both these midrashim prevailed throughout medieval history as the premise for subordinating Judaism and Jews, and now served their purpose for Paul IV. [165]

In 1559 Pius IV was elected to the papacy, and finally in 1562 he reassembled the Council of Trent where final study was made of great issues of doctrine and church regulation, and a vast array of dogmatic decrees were drawn up and signed. It has been adjudged that no other council in church history, (I would qualify by saying prior to Vatican II), has had such consequences. The Council of Trent re-established the canon, ordained that the Vulgate be the authorized scripture and that reading the Bible is inadequate for the knowledge of Christianity, which is to be understood rather only in accordance with the interpretation of scripture as transmitted in the traditions of the church. The Council rejected the Lutheran emphasis upon faith alone as the source of salvation and the Calvinist doctrine of predestination. It declared in a canon that anyone who declares himself a sinner is justified by faith alone and need not be aided to grace by his own will; he is anathema. In general the Council opposed the contempt Luther and Calvin had for human nature, and far from seeing humans as irredeemably depraved, it upheld the Humanist and Judaic views that despite the tension between good and evil within the human, a person possesses free will and the capacity to cooperate with God's grace in seeking salvation. Contrary to the reformed view, the Roman Catholic dogma argued that when a human is guilt of mortal sin he or she will be deprived of grace despite possessing faith. In popular idiom I have often expressed the Judaic view to be that God requires that the human achieve "A" for effort which is within the human capacity. This in turn leads to God's blessing of salvation-enabling grace. [166]

In these respects, the emphasis upon the authority of evolving tradition alongside scripture, the importance of conduct alongside faith, and the teaching of free will, among other particulars, Roman Catholic doctrine reaffirmed at Trent was closer to Judaism than Reformation theology, despite the latter's reorientation to the Old Testament.

In consequence of the massive body of doctrine and discipline formulated at Trent, Pope Pius V, elected in 1566, set about to rearrange the church and regain Catholic supremacy on all fronts. He threatened to excommunicate Maximilian II of the Holy Roman Empire for seeking compromise between Catholics and Protestants and prevented equality being granted to the former. He excommunicated Queen Elizabeth for formalizing the Anglican Church, encouraged Catholic sovereigns in heresy-hunting and war against schismatics, and kindled many an auto da fe for people and books alike. [167] It was Pius V who extended the authority of the bull cum nimis, referred to earlier, from governing Jews who resided in papal states to Jews residing anywhere and required all secular princes to cooperate in enforcing it. Conversion was as much Pius V's objective as it was that of Paul IV. In 1566 he wrote of his great pangs that the Hebrew people suffer damnation and that he will leave nothing undone to lead them "from the path of error to the way of sure redemption . . . " He took much pride in the fact that since he became pope " . . . many indeed of both sexes have accepted the Christian religion . . . " and that converts have become "such a multitude." Nevertheless, Pius V's success with Jews seems to have been rather limited, and in 1569 he demonstrated his frustration by expelling Jews from most papal territories. [168]

Although the Council of Trent did not deal with Jews or Judaism, papal policy toward Jews in the wake of Trent was one strand of a general condition set in motion by Trent. In one sense, it might be said the Council of Trent was neither a "reformation" nor a "counter-reformation." Rather it inspired or compelled retrenchment in orthodoxy, and a reinvigoration of repression. On the other hand, it is considered a "reformation" because it improved both the decorum and sanctity of the churches, advanced the morals of the clergy, and promoted centralization in the hands of a regenerated papacy. Yet, again, it also strengthened the monarchical and absolutist style, established the trend which resulted in the dogma of papal infallibility and put an end to a burgeoning tendency toward independence which might have led to national churches in the style of England. [169]

VII. Summary

The Protestant and Catholic Reformations of the sixteenth century set in motion strong forces that affected Jews and Judaism. More will be said of this interrelationship in Chapter Seven. Like Humanism, which opened breaches in Jewish traditionalism, as seen in Chapter Two, and as will be further discussed in its Dutch setting below, these great religious movements equally affected how Jews lived and how they perceived themselves.

As noted earlier, it was not always, however, the mainstream movements that had interconnections with Judaism. Frequently it was the sectarian groups that came close to adapting aspects of Judaism that aroused the ire of both Protestants and Catholics. There can be no doubt that the tragic burning of the Talmuds in 1553 and on a subsequent occasion in Cremona in 1559, was directly related to the threat seen by the Inquisition to be manifest in Judaic literature as it influenced various branches of Christianity. [170] Among the most startling threats perceived by both Protestants and Catholics was the spread of the seventh-day Sabbath in many areas, but especially in Russia and Hungary. [171] Not since the earliest decades of the church had there been such proliferation of sabbatarians among Christians. But the church understood well the threat. For these sabbatarians, known as Sobotniki in Russia also practiced circumcision, denied the divinity of Jesus, rejected the trinity, and were iconoclasts, barring images. [172]

The Russian Sobotniki even called their places of worship a "schule" or schkola, as did Jews. [173] But the Russians were only one visible judaizing sect. Even more intensive was the development of the Hungarian sabbatarians known as Szombatosok. Many of these ultimately joined Judaism. [174] This group originated in Transylvania where the sixteenth century reformation ultimately produced a unitarian movement which moved from Catholicism to Lutheranism, Calvinism, and finally in 1566 to Unitarianism under the influence and inspiration of a certain Francis David. It was out of this Unitarian Church that a small sect arose around 1588 which became known as Sabbatarians. [175]

This Sabbatarian sect developed a hymnal which reveals that the group also observed the New Moon, Passover, Shabuot, Sukot, Rosh Hashanah and Yom Kippur. Curiously its members observed modified dietary practices, but unlike the Sobotniki did not observe circumcision. Interestingly they based their Sabbath observance upon the example of Jesus, and perhaps unwittingly they paraphrased the Gospel of Thomas, when they said, "He who keeps not the Sabbath will have no portion in the inheritance of Christ." And they related the Passover to the Second Coming of Jesus. [176]

These Sabbatarians evince definitive parallels to early Christian Judaism, but the scope of this present chapter does not allow for more exhaustive investigation of this question. [177] The emergence of such sectarian groups that skirted the edges of Judaism in Hungary, and as will be seen below, in England, is an interesting historical phenomenon. It points to a certain logic that emanates from devotion to the Old Testament, and highlights the threat seen in the study of Judaica and an intensive interest in Judaic practice that agitated Luther, Calvin and many popes. It also underscores the inevitable relationship that obtains between Judaism and Christianity, and the irrevocable historical bond between them which both persist in severing. [178] It is this lingering tension between mutual recognition and mutual rejection that inspired both the turn to Judaic studies during the sixteenth and seventeenth centuries and the contradictory persistence of both Protestant and Roman Catholic prejudices against, and efforts at the subordination of Judaism, matters to be more fully discussed in Chapter Seven.

Chapter Four

PROTO-MODERNITY IN ITALY

In this chapter we will explore examples of personalities who differed radically from the traditional Jew locked into his Judaic study, ritual observance, and social life. Some individuals, whether ordained rabbis like Leon da Modena or lay scholars like Abraham Farissol, were paradigmatic. They might be viewed as prefigurations of a certain class of modern scholars and rabbis that emerged in central and western Europe during the eighteenth and nineteenth centuries.

There were others, such as R. Judah Minz, referred to earlier, who reacted to all these vast changes in the social sphere and lifestyle with a program of traditionalist retrenchment. They saw the Renaissance as a threat, while a Farissol or a Delmedigo saw broad opportunities for enrichment, and for a new and radical synthesis unknown since Hellenistic times. Minz saw the Renaissance as bringing dissonance into Judaic life, and what a Modena would view as an opportunity for intellectual advancement a Minz would perceive as cause for despair.

The Renaissance was a window into the last half of the eighteenth century to the present time. It had its own constructs which served as threats to traditionalist Judaism. Astrology and magic played havoc with Judaic ideas of the role of God and of human free will. New philosophical currents and a complexity of new religious movements and tendencies to syncretism affected Judaic insularity despite the rise of the ghetto. The great new geographic discoveries opened new vistas for the curious and adventurous, and in their frequent and wide-ranging travels it became more and more difficult or unimportant to observe the minutiae of the traditional ritualistic regimen.

As in the present era, since approximately 1750, acculturated Jews then too grappled with the challenges, seeking a creative synthesis, while the traditionalist much like the so-called "ultra-orthodox" of this era, rejected the challenges and turned inward to conventional piety and rigorous observance. The many criticisms of laxity, and even opposition to observance of Judaic ritual that one reads in sixteenth and seventeenth century literature indicates that many more Jews existed who were of the acculturated type evident in the writings of such men as Farissol, Delmedigo and Modena but who wrote no books. Thus, we should not attempt to judge the numbers of Jews striving for a proto-modernity by the scarcity of sources. The Renaissance experience transformed southern Europe from which, for a variety of reasons that cannot be expanded upon here, vibrations resounded to Amsterdam and Hamburg. This led to a proto-modern acculturated class of Jews in nothern Europe long before the rise of the Judaic reformation at the beginning of the nineteenth century.

The personalities to be discussed here, and the Dutch experience to be discussed in the next chapter, compel a paradigm shift in historical analysis. Modern Judaism is usually dated to the rise of the Reform Movement and then usually either to the educational reforms of the 1790's or to around 1810 when Israel Jacobson installed a reformed liturgy, choir, and organ into his synagogue next to his school at Seesen. [1] But careful examination of certain elements of the lifestyles and the intellectual and theological viewpoints of a segment of sixteenth and seventeenth century Jews indicated that these prefigured the reforming movements. Thus to see the "origins of the modern Jew" as dating to the period between 1749 and 1824 as some scholars surmise, has some merit, but omits the exceptionally significant factor of gradual evolution in thought and social atmosphere that prepared the way for radical revolution. [2] There can be no question that a radical break with the past resulted from the mid-nineteenth century rabbinical synods in Germany that spawned Reform and Conservative Judaism. But the origins of these movements must be seen in the evolving processes of acculturation that began with the Renaissance in Italy and filtered into Amsterdam and Hamburg. They were also fertilized in part by the widespread return of Marranos to Judaic life during the sixteenth and seventeenth centuries.

The focus of this chapter does not allow for an exhaustive biographical and intellectual exploration of any one of the personalities to be discussed. I am concerned to present here only several highlights of their lives and work that are germane to the thesis adopted in this volume that sixteenth century Jewish Italian Renaissance personalities and their society constituted as important a part of the matrix out of which emerged the Judaic reformation in eighteenth and nineteenth century Germany as did east European traditionalism and its ritualistic minutiae. The latter evoked a reaction leading to reformation, but that reformation must also be seen as the product of the positive intellectual and spiritual forces unleashed by the growing body of Renaissance scholars and their post-Renaissance successors and emulators.

II. Abraham ben Mordecai Farissol. [3]

Farissol was born in 1452 in Avignon, an international and cosmopolitan center of Humanist scholarship going back to Petrarch in the fourteenth century. The "Babylonian Captivity" of the papacy from 1309 when Clement V ensconced himself at Avignon until Gregory XI returned to Rome in 1377 propelled Avignon into intellectual pursuits. But the papacy was gone from Avignon only a decade when it split in a serious schism, with one pope, Urban VI claiming legitimacy in Rome, and another, Clement VII, removing himself to Avignon and their claiming papal authority. This schism continued until 1417 when it was ended after the election of Martin V. [4] Meanwhile Avignon had benefited for over a century and had become a great center of manuscripts, and housed a significant scriptorium where much writing and publication took place. This in turn made the city into a book center and an attractive oasis for Humanist scholars, poets, and their patrons, and a significant cultural influence in the lives of Jews born and raised in its orbit. [5]

Farissol moved to Italy and ultimately settled in Ferrara where he served as cantor of his synagogue, mohel (ritual circumciser), scribe and calligrapher, and as teacher of both secular and religious subjects. It is apparent that he had acquired in Avignon the acculturated capability to teach grammar, composition, logic, letter-writing and sermonics. Although he was teaching these subjects for Judaic purposes, and generally in Hebrew, this type of education was in emulation of general society, and not common in the traditional centers of northern Europe. Thus Farissol followed the ancient rabbinic curriculum, but integrated the biblical and rabbinic materials with grammar lessons by using these materials as the texts for compositions and exercises. [6] In an age when biblical study was generally neglected among traditionalists in favor of Talmud and its commentaries, Farissol insisted on biblical study. This in itself was an aspect of acculturation, and often a symptom of reforming tendencies among Jews no less than it became so among Christians.

But Farissol had not had the authority or the interest to bring decorum into his synagogue as we learn from a gentile visitor, François Tissard, who wrote, ". . . one might hear one man howling, another braying, and another bellowing; such a cacophany of discordant sounds do they make . . . I was almost brought to nausea." This, written of a synagogue at the beginning of the sixteenth century in Italy, was not unlike what Samuel Pepys later wrote in his diary of his visit to an English synagogue a century and a half later. [7] Indeed, it was not until the Jacobson reformation at Seesen in 1810 that the synagogue began its long and arduous transformation into a house of worship with decorum and order, and with prayers read in unison.

Farissol had already become familiar with Christian scholars before François Tissard came to Ferrara, and participated in discussions with two Christian theologians in 1487. He dialogued with Franciscan and Dominican scholars and ultimately wrote his dialogical or polemical work, **Magen Avraham** as a consequence of such discussions. [8] Farissol was a proper participant for such dialogues because he was widely learned in both Christian and Judaic sources as well as in secular wisdom. His Judaic erudition was extensive. This is seen from his citation of biblical, rabbinic, and medieval writings covering all phases of the literature, midrashic, àgadic, halakhic, and philosophical. Perhaps his weakest area was kabalah. But his non-Judaic Christian and Humanist learning was also extensive. He was at home in the New Testament, the apocryphal literature, patristic materials, and in Greek and Latin classics, except for the philosophers. He also shows familiarity with Christian writers and the Christian kabalists. [9]

That he followed various trends of Christian thought is seen in Farissol's familiarity with the views of a celebrated charismatic heretic at the end of the fifteenth century, Giovanni Mercurio da Correggio, who dressed in sackcloth and girded himself with ropes, and for decades preached in France and Italy. He argued that prophecy is not divinely granted but is attainable by anyone who properly develops his innate abilities, adopts a spiritual guru, and masters the science of the occult. Such a one, he preached, can even reach the level of Jesus Christ. This denigration of the special divine attributes of Jesus, denial that scriptural miracles were divine events, and that the church is the only repository of the truth of what constitutes miracle, prophecy, and the divinity of Jesus, set the church against Mercurio. Important to us is that Farissol shows his familiarity with these teachings and with the internal controversies of Christendom. [10] Such debates and currents of thought were not remote to Judaism, and the intellectual forces that brought them on were active within Judaism as well. This will be seen below in connection with returned Marranos. Arguments for individual attainment of prophecy and denial that the church was the repository of absolute truth had parallel implications for Judaism, and these currents of thought flowing through Renaissance Italy among Jews who were not insulated from their contemporary society later produced far-reaching ripples in the north.

More significant, however, is how this knowledge of the Mercurio incident in Christianity also reveals Farissol's penetration into the esoteric knowledge of the Hermetic tradition by which Mercurio was captivated. The first fourteen documents of the great corpus of Greek and Latin literature of the third century attributed to Hermes Trismegistus was translated by Marsilio Ficino in 1471 and became widespread during the sixteenth century. This was a body of theological, philosophical, astrological, occult, and mystical literature. It included material on the ascent of the soul through the spheres of the planets to celestial realms beyond, and on the liberation of the soul from its material prison which allows the human to be suffused with divine power. Such notions deeply influenced Mercurio. In his introduction Ficino argued that Hermes Trismegistus lived at the time of Moses and that both Pythagoras and Plato derived their wisdom from the Egyptian priests who studied and taught the sacred writings of the god Thoth. Greeks had in turn identified Thoth, the god of wisdom and the scribe of the gods, with Hermes, and because Thoth was often described as thrice, or even five times great, Hermes in his capacity of revealer of knowledge was given the epithet trismegistus, the Greek for "thrice-great." [11]

In any event Renaissance scholars accepted a judgment going back to early church fathers, such as Lactantius of the third century and Augustine of the fourth, that Hermes Trismegistus was a historical person of great antiquity. Lactantius used Hermes in his disputes with gentiles showing that Hermes also referred to God as Father and to a "second god" as "son of God." So too in **Poimandres** the Hermetic writer spoke of creation having been effected through a luminous word which was in line with Christian thought from both the Old and New Testaments (Gen. 1; Jn. 1). This early Christian scholar saw Hermes Trismegistus as a significant gentile prophet who foreshadowed Christianity, and although Augustine was less sanguinary about him the Renaissance philosophers looked back to him as a vital fount of wisdom through whose magical writings great things can be achieved. [12]

Disciples of the Hermetic writings formed astral cults and espoused the idea that the true practitioner with the proper knowledge of this wisdom had the power to channel into his person the life-force of heaven which pours down in invisible vertical rays from the stars. This could be done with the proper technique, incantations, and names of celestial persons. [13] In this connection, it is also important to note that Hermetica ascribed no importance to ritualism or sacraments, the all-important theurgia of the Judaeo-Christian tradition. [14] The revival of Hermetica in the fifteenth century and the fascination it held for many scholars had an impact upon this aspect of Judaism and Christianity that was very important to traditionalists. This, indeed, did become a major issue between Protestants and Catholics, and between proto-reforming Jews and traditionalists.

It is interesting, furthermore, that there is present a certain amount of Judaic influence in the hermetic writings. For example **Poimandres** shows much knowledge of Genesis, and resemblances to material in Philo, but no evidence of Christian teaching. Even the discussion of a "second god" in Christian-sounding phrases such as "son of God" and "image of God" could be influenced by Philo's logos rather than Christianity's Jesus. There was no savior in the Hermetica. Each individual could save himself by the proper technique of channelling astral rays and thus bringing the heavenly life-force into one's own person. For the Hermetists each human originated in heaven and returned to heaven, having been incarnated only temporarily. [15] This is fullsome gnostic thought and makes of each person a Christ-like figure. Consequently it can easily be understood why the church opposed any sign of Hermetic thought. Furthermore there are fragments in the Hermetic writings that refer to Christians only as a menace to society and as an enemy seeking to overwhelm the Graeco-Roman world.

There is another aspect of Hermetica of considerable interest. This is the connection between Moses and Hermes. This connection antedated the church fathers in both Judaic and pagan hellenistic sources. In one tradition Moses was credited with being the teacher of Orpheus, a great inventor, originator of philosophy, and creator of the Egyptian religion. This tradition added that in recognition of his interpretation (hermeneia) of the sacred writings the Egyptian priests named him Hermes. [16] This is an interesting sidelight to the fact that the Greeks had named the Egyptian god Thoth, Hermes. Thus, Moses, Thoth, and Hermes were all brought together, and it is Moses who was seen as the original teacher. There might be some interest in the appearance of this cosmic educator in the transfiguration scene in the New Testament, after which the heavenly voice commands that henceforth they are to listen to Jesus whose transfiguration is in a special way connected with the cosmic knowledge of Moses (Mt. 17:5 and parallels).

The **Corpus Hermeticum** which played a great role in the fifteenth and sixteenth centuries first appeared as a collection of works in the fourteenth century. It has been variously divided into from thirteen to twenty separate documents. Ficino's claim that Hermes was a contemporary of Moses, that the priests of Thoth had transmitted their knowledge to Pythagoras and Plato and they in turn to succeeding generations, implied that whatever came from Hermes had been the divine knowledge possessed by Moses. The pavement of the Cathedral of Siena illustrates this, and is of considerable interest. The pavement contains an artistic design dated to 1488, and like the transfiguration scene it depicts three figures. The first is a long-bearded man wearing a mitre who represents Moses. This figure hands a book to a turbaned man who represents Hermes Trismegistus. This second figure hands the book on to a beardless person wearing a hood who represents the pagan philosophers. Again we have here the cosmic educator Moses as fount of all wisdom. [17]

By this time medieval writers loyal to the church professed to find the doctrine of the trinity explicitly stated in the writings of Hermes, as the same school of thought found it articulated in Jewish kabalah. The legitimacy of having these pagan figures represented on the pavement of a cathedral is therefore obvious. The notion was expressed that not only had pagans unconsciously taught the truth of Christianity, but had indeed received it from Moses. This was the thrust of Christian Hebraists and kabalists all during the next century. It was often the same coterie of scholars who immersed themselves in both Hermetica and kabalism. For example, a disciple of Mercurio, Ludovicus Lazzarelli was intensively involved in Ficino's work and claimed the Judaic kabalistic work **Sefer Yezirah** as his source for the view that a terrestrial human can become a god and actually vivify a new man by the proper disposition of letters which is the method of God's own generation of life. Others who attached themselves to both corpuses of literature were Pico and Ficino. That the **Sefer Yezirah** was important in these occult circles is not surprising when one recalls that **Sefer Yezirah**'s main theme is the function of the twenty-two letters of the Hebrew alphabet in the creation of the world. It was believed that the infinite number of combinations of letters into words and compounds can become the creative generating power for any devout practitioner. [18]

It is important to note in concluding this digression on the Hermetica that Farissol's knowledge of the Mercurio controversy and involvement with Hermetica is one more significant symptom of another Judaic scholar-model from that of the conventional medieval Judaic scholar immersed in talmudic and halakhic study that most people are accustomed to think about. His knowledge of Christian sources and interest in current Christian matters set him apart from the traditional Judaic scholar. And in order to keep abreast of this material he also read and used previous Jewish polemical works, as is evident in his **Magen Avraham.** [19]

It appears, however, from a study of the many manuscripts of this work that some chapters were added later, and that some were actually copied out of Isaac Troki's **Hizzuk Emunah** which was not written until 1593. [20] But the literary problems related to this work need not detain us for our focus is rather the reality that the interreligious interchange between this Renaissance Jewish scholar and Christian contemporaries took place as it did in an atmosphere of friendship and academic interest. This was in contrast to earlier medieval forced debates in which it was hoped to convert the captive Jewish audience.

Like other Renaissance figures Farissol evinced strong faith in astrology. He saw it as influential even in the case of Jews. [21] Like Christians Jews had to contend with the inherent contradiction between faith in God's response to prayer and in

God's omnipotent direction of destiny, and the conviction that conjunctions of constellations and planets determine human affairs. Farissol overcame this problem by referring to astral forces as divine messengers, thus preserving the traditional idea that the divine will determines cosmic, historical, and personal fortunes. He even defied logic by arguing that God interrupts the astral order to intervene for Jews. He did not labor at reconciling the other inherent contradiction, that dependence upon astrology was profoundly at odds with the Jewish theory of free will. He merely saw the stars and free will as two basic paradoxes in a tension which remains a constituent reality of the natural and human orders. [22]

Aspects of Farissol's thinking marking him as a proto-modern can be seen throughout his work. He was a Renaissance historian who articulated an evolutionary approach to Judaism. [23] Thus he indicated that the Old Testament speaks of material rewards for righteous obedience to God's will only to meet the needs of a historical phase within the context of Egyptian and other pagan cultures. Their religions were based upon the fertility cult which promised and symbolized blessing in all material concerns: the produce, flocks and herds, and the safety of humans, in effect in all matters pertaining to health and prosperity. [24] He argued that the pagan neighbors of Israel had no concept of the immortality of the soul. Therefore they could not conceive of spiritual salvation. Israel, he added, had not yet risen beyond the pagan level. But later Israel arrived at a stage of development when she was able to grasp this concept, and the rabbis showed that spiritual salvation is implicit in the Torah. [25] One might question Farissol's oversimplification on this complex issue, but it is at least superficially true that certain rabbinic views sought the correction of imbalance between suffering and righteousness in this world in an expanded doctrine of a spiritual afterlife. Certain rabbis believed in the spirituality of the soul and articulated the belief that it departs from the body after death to live on either, if the person was wicked, in a place of punishment, or in the case of a righteous person, in a place of bliss to await the resurrection. [26] Farissol was able to demonstrate, therefore, that spiritual salvation was henceforth the doctrine of Judaism and not a carnal interest in materialistic rewards. Thus he not only defended the higher moral grasp of Judaism, but also evinced a proto-modern historicism concerning the development of Judaic doctrine despite his belief in revelation.

But Farissol was not able to rise above the apologetic that Judaism represented rationalism in its doctrines and was superior to Christianity which abounds in irrationality as well as grave distortion of Old Testament texts. He pointed to such doctrines as original sin, the trinity, transubstantiation and the potency of baptism. [27] But like Judaic thinkers since and even at the present time he was not willing to concede the equal irrationality of Judaic doctrines such as revelation, election, miracles, and resurrection.

Farissol showed an interesting originality in the heretofore unexpressed idea that there was a distinction between the Messiah for Jews and the Messiah for Christians. He not only went so far as to grant that the Messiah of the gentiles might have come, but that indeed it might have been Jesus of Nazareth. Nobody prior to Farissol, at least nobody known to me, had made even this limited concession in interreligious interchange. But he argued the conventional points that Jesus could not have been the Jewish Messiah because he did not fulfill all the conditions spoken of by the canonical preachers of ancient Israel and Judah whom we call the prophets. In other words, Farissol, like others before him and since, had questioned whether this can be the redeemed world promised in scripture when so much poverty, misery, war, and hatred continue to prevail. [28]

Another aspect of Farissol's proto-modern style is seen in his approach to the Bible, which emphasized the use of primary languages. That this was characterisic of other Renaissance scholars does not diminish the significance of this in our estimation of Farissol. For it was in this very fact that Farissol and the other personalities we discuss in this chapter were of the Renaissance model that they were proto-moderns. They prefigured and influenced the reformation of Judaic scholarship of the eighteenth and nineteenth centuries. Farissol was in the company of many Humanists when he argued with Christian dialogists that the inadequacies of the Jerome Bible render it deficient as a source for biblical quotation, and that only the knowledge of the original Hebrew text is a legitimate vehicle. Not only were there an enormous number of versions of the Vulgate, but there were also new Latin versions prepared by a wide variety of Humanist, Catholic, and emerging Protestant scholars. Farissol examined many texts and discussed their variations with Christian scholars on his journeys to Rome, Mantua, and Florence. [29]

At times the new intellectual currents to which we have had reference, both the mystical and the halakhic agitated traditionalists and "modernists" alike. Thus, it appears from Farissol's **Magen Avraham** that there were groups of Jewish apostates in Pico's circle who argued that the Torah was only intended for living in the holy land, and that outside the land the Torah intended for Jews to live a spiritualized faith. These people argued that Christianity was the true expression of the Torah's intent. Farissol registered his opposition to these, and erroneously accused some of them of forging midrashim in order to prove the incarnation of God and other aspects of the birth and passion of Christ. Farissol also argued against christological conclusions derived from Jewish kabalistic writings in Pico's circle, of which a leading exponenet was a Jewish convert Mithridates. It seems, however, from modern research that Martini's **Bereshit Rabbah of R. Moshe Hadarshan** from which this material is taken was genuine. [30] These experiences involving the Christian use of kabalism led Farissol many years later to urge students not to discuss kabalah publicly. The fear of Christian use of kabalism led some Jews to oppose the publication of the Zohar in 1558 because they regarded it as a weapon of Christian evangelism. [31]

Reference was made earlier to François Tissard, a French Humanist who studied with Farissol in Ferrara from 1502-1505. [32] His basic motives were both the acquisition of the proper competence to pursue theological learning, and evangelism. He was convinced that only if Christians will be able to read the Old Testament in the Hebrew they will be capable of adequately disputing with Jews and consequently more efficaceous in their conversionist efforts. As noted previously he was deeply disappointed by the physical reality of the synagogue which was equalled by a total absence of spirituality. He described the Jews he saw as "lazy, vulgar, and obstinate," and discussed dietary practices, holy days, the Sabbath restrictions and circumcision. He referred to the prevalent custom of Jews using gentiles to perform forbidden tasks for them on the Sabbath, and accused them of hypocrisy. Some of Tissard's strictures against Judaism were undoubtedly among the sources of later writers like Bucer who picked up on similar themes. But Tissard had a high respect for Farissol and for the internal civic life of Jews which kept the crime rate low and support for the poor high. [33]

While Tissard referred unquestioningly to some absurd fictions about Jews, such as that men menstruate, other of his references that appear strange were not fiction, such as that bigamy was still practiced in Ferrara during the sixteenth century and that Farissol defended it on the basis of scripture before a Christian court. [34] Here we have an example of how even the more advanced scholars of that time, just as is true of many modern enlightened scholars, often slip into defense of obsolete ideas when confronted with the need for apologetics, and to protect the honor of the Torah. Similarly Farissol defended all the traditional concepts of miracles, demons, angels, divine intervention in human affairs and reward and punishment.

In effect on a Jewish level he defended the dogmas proclaimed by the Fifth Lateran Council for Catholics, which were at that time being subjected to heavy criticism by Pietro Pomponazzi (1462-1524) of Mantua who argued for reliance only upon reason and natural causes. The Fifth Lateran Council had ruled a dogma on the immortality of the soul and its subjection to hell, purgatory, and paradise. Farissol defended the notions of God's particular providence, divine retribution, and immortality of the soul in his biblical commentaries to Job and Ecclesiastes, and in his commentary on Mishnah Abot. Many Jews were following the arguments of Pomponazzi and others, bringing into serious question the balance between faith and reason postulated by medieval Jewish and Christian philosophy. Deeply involved in much of this philosophical speculation and in what were being considered heretical views were the Marranos who were then migrating to various places, many of whom settled in Italy. [35] In defending traditional theology Farissol also clung to the traditional inferences from scriptural verses that the universe was earth-centered, and for some scholars he seems not to have been aware of the heliocentric theories of Copernicus. [36] Considering Farissol's broad scientific and medical knowledge it might be questioned whether he was not aware, or that he prudently refrained from teaching what was heresy for the church in order not to ruffle any feathers. It need only be recalled, as will be discussed in the next chapter, that this was precisely the tragic issue that confronted Spinoza. It is one thing to teach new ideas within Judaism that have no impact upon Christians, and to become acculturated to the Christian ambience, as Farissol and others did, and quite another to teach ideas that strike at the heart of certain basic dogmas and whose dissemination would upset the church.

One final word might be said of Farissol's geographic interest. He wrote a book on geography, **Iggeret Orḥot Olam** in order to discuss the importance of the new global discoveries of the fifteenth and sixteenth centuries. This book ultimately played a role in the English discussions of the mythical "lost ten tribes" who were supposedly found. This was a topic of great fascination during the sixteenth century because of the importance it was imagined to have for the nearness of redemption. To discover the "lost tribes" was to be a harbinger of the discovery of the famous Sambatyon River, and subsequently the Garden of Eden. Farissol, however, rejected all messianic episodes of his time and all calculations of the coming of the Messiah. Nevertheless, he was also fascinated by the accounts of Christian explorers, and his **Iggeret** is oriented to a discussion of the "lost tribes." But he also wrote of the entire known world, including the sub-equatorial realms, and provided travel routes for the adventurous. The book was repeatedly republished and was a major educational tool in geography, especially for Jews who engaged in secular learning. [37]

The foregoing cursory adumbration of certain aspects of Farissol's interests and views depict a Judaic figure wholly unlike the pietistic type of the east European Jew later denominated as "orthodox." The latter was a spiritual descendant of the composite one often reads about in medieval Europe from northern France to the Ural Mountains. Farissol was also unlike the acculturated savant of the Spanish "Golden Age" whose interests were more cosmopolitan than merely talmudic and halakhic in the style of northern Europe. Farissol evinced the broad range of intellectual concerns and pursuits, the cosmopolitan cultural life-style and the easy-going mingling and theological exchange with Christian scholars that is more typical of nineteenth and twentieth century western Europe and North America. In this respect he was a forerunner and a part of the matrix of the Judaic reformation that took place three centuries after he died.

III. Elijah Capsali [38]

Farissol exemplified one type of proto-modern. We will have examples of other types. It is also of interest to explore the many-faceted spectrum of Judaic religious life by examining an anti-type of Farissol. The coexistence of such diversity in the Italian Renaissance ambience is not unique. It reinforces the consistent evidence of such diversity in Judaism since its inception.

Elijah Capsali (1483-1555) was not as urbane and cultured as Farissol, and far more immersed in traditionalism. Nevertheless Capsali was not like his yeshibah teachers at Padua. A member of a leading family of Crete or Candia, which was ruled by Venice from 1204-1669, Capsali was also a descendant of two distinguished families, Capsali and Delmedigo. [39] He pointed to proto-modernity in another way. He wrote a history of Venice in 1517, and a history of the Ottoman Empire in 1523. [40] Capsali was an avid chronicler and pioneer historian, among the first major figures since Josephus to attempt the writing of both general and Jewish history, and the forerunner of a great array of historians who appeared in the eighteenth and nineteenth centuries. [41] He was careful about chronicling his material in proper order, conveying the data with accuracy and using his sources properly. [42] When he dealt with matters that impinge on legend or faith, miraculous or revelatory material, he left it to his reader to decide on the plausibility of such matters. This was possibly a conscious imitation of Josephus whose advice to readers regarding matters that could not be verified was to form their own judgments. For example, when Josephus discussed the longevity of the personalities in Genesis he said, "But on these matters let everyone decide according to his fancy." [43]

While Capsali was concerned for accuracy his history was not written as only objective fact. He interpreted events in a messianic light and was strongly influenced by the traumatic episode of the expulsion from Spain in 1492 as so many interpreters of late twentieth century Judaic history are governed by the holocaust of 1942-45. Capsali saw the Ottoman conquerors in Europe in a messianic light. He justified the cruelty of sultans, and rationalized the deeds of Muhammad II (1451-1481) who, to Christians, was virtually the anti-Christ. [44] He interpreted the fall of Constantinople to the Turks in 1453 as a Christian debacle that presaged the messianic advent. Ottoman sultans who welcomed Jews to Turkey were compared to Cyrus of Persia who allowed the return of the Jews from the Babylonian captivity, and with Solomon who was considered a type of the ultimate messianic ruler. Sultan Selim I (1512-1520) was compared to Solomon for his possession and exercise of supreme wisdom. In his great concern for objectively reporting facts he did not conceal how in some circumstances of unrest and siege the Jews were among the worst perpetrators of violence and looting as, for example, at Padua in 1509, after its conquest by Austrians. [45]

Capsali was in touch with many leading scholars of the time in Venice, Constantinople, Egypt, and Safed, and is referred to in many responsa. [46] He was a leader of traditionalist religious life in Crete. A believer in kabalist ideas he also accepted the ideas of the àgadah. In his synagogue he established the custom that on Simḥat Torah, the aliyah (honor of ascending to the Torah) known as ḥatan torah (the person called to the completion of the reading of Deuteronomy) would be offered only to a scholar, a custom which prevailed among most communities until modern times. His traditionalism and interest in establishing tight ritual control was the product both of his upbringing as well as his yeshiḇah studies. His father was R. Moses Capsali who wielded much authority over his contemporaries because of their "fear of the royal power." And Elijah studied at Padua under two of the major talmudic scholars of the fifteenth-sixteenth centuries, R. Judah Minz and R. Meir Katzenellenbogen. [47] R. Moses was punctillious in his ritualistic stringencies, rejected the Karaites as non-Jewish, and barred all non-Jews from Judaic studies. [48]

In his traditionalism, his messianic interest, his kabalist beliefs, Elijah reveals one side of his personality. As a historian he exhibits another side. It must be clarified here that as we speak of proto-moderns in the Renaissance ambience we speak not only of those who by circumstance of history would have become reformers in the nineteenth century. We speak also of people who were forerunners of the neo-orthodoxy which arose in nineteenth century Germany in reaction to the Judaic reformation. Men like Capsali were the presagers of the Samson Raphael Hirsch school of thought, while the non-acculturated traditionalists like his father, Minz or Katzenellenbogen were the spiritual ancestors of the east European anti-haskalah ultra-orthodoxy.

IV. Azariah Dei Rossi (1511-1578) [49]

     In Azariah dei Rossi we have another interesting personal-
ity whose differences from Farissol and Capsali are instructive
for forming the variegated portrait of Renaissance Jewish scholars,
and for comprehending their proto-modernity. Azariah wrote
a treatise called **Mèor Éynaim** which explores Judaic religion
and history with an underlying purpose of firmly establishing
its essence as revealed religion. The work consists of three parts,
the second of which is a paraphrase of the Letter of Aristeas.
It is, however, the third and longest part, Ímre Binah ("words
of understanding"), which is the heart of the treatise on Judaism.
[50]

     By the judgment of the leading Jewish historian of the
twentieth century dei Rossi's **Mèor Éynaim** marks him as the
greatest Jewish historian between Josephus (first century) and
I. M. Jost (nineteenth century), although he fell short of the
other major non-Jewish medieval historians such as Machiavelli.
Dei Rossi lived in various Italian communities, spent much time
in Ferrara where like Farissol he had close relationships with
Christian scholars from whom he imbibed much. As a Renaissance
man dei Rossi differed from more traditionalist figures of the
time. He stressed a return to the original sources, and used antiquity for his themes, seeking to explore such difficult matters
as the Essenes, or the life and work of Philo. [51]

     It was inevitable that he would encounter matters of
opinion where traditional rabbinic or other Jewish sources were
in conflict with non-Jewish scholars, especially in matters of
science and history. While it was still unthinkable for dei Rossi
to question the absolute veracity of a biblical text, he was more
prone to qualify his acceptance of rabbinic and medieval Jewish
sources. Thus, he laid down as a prerequisite that before accepting
a rabbinic view which conflicts with later knowledge one must
be certain that the rabbis received it from scripture or prophecy,
or derived it through the hermeneutical rules. Otherwise he suggested that the rabbis might have received error from scholars
of their own time, and that it is not encumbent upon us to persist
in this error, for to adhere to their views when we do not believe
in these views would be to act as hypocrites. [52] In effect
this was a new approach to source criticism, unprecedented in
traditional Jewish scholarship in which halakhic decisions might
have been questioned and decided differently in accord with
alternative sources, but ideas and historical events were not
questioned. Thus, his researches led him to argue that the traditional chronology since creation used in the Jewish calendar
was erroneous. In consequence a group of Italian rabbis proclaimed
a ban on the book, while Joseph Karo in Safed actually thought
of excommunicating dei Rossi, but fell ill and soon died. Other

important proto-modern figures, however, who will be discussed below, such as Leon da Modena, and Joseph del Medigo of Italy, and Menasseh ben Israel of Holland, among others, approved of the work. [53]

The book, **Mèor Èynaim** was highly praised by Christian scholars such as Johannes Buxtorf, both father and son. They quoted it and translated chapters. Similarly Jewish scholars who played a large role in the development of modern scientific Judaic scholarship such as Nachman Krochmal and Leopold Zunz attributed to dei Rossi a major role as forerunner of their efforts. [54]

When a scholar's work is banned by contemporary traditionalists as being dangerous to faith, and is more highly esteemed by other enlightened scholars of his time, by Christians, and by later Judaic reformation scholars, it is clear that he represented what is here being termed proto-modernity. The very fact that Delmedigo who, as we will see, sowed seeds of enlightenment everywhere, including Amsterdam; and Menasseh ben Israel, an enlightened Amsterdam scholar, both appreciated dei Rossi's work indicates the tenability of the thesis that the Italian and Dutch Renaissance and post-Renaissance scholars formed the mold from which modern Judaism was cast. The basic premise upon which the modern structure was erected was source and historical criticism. Although independent judgment on matters of halakhah and the right of autonomy in the interpretation of certain areas of theology had always been acceptable in Judaism, as long as actual doctrines were not brought into question, certain basic premises were to be challenged only at the risk of being considered near, or in a state of heresy. [55] What dei Rossi was bringing into question was the very nature of religious truth, what constitutes revelation, and the sharpest challenge of all for its many ramifications: the accuracy of the calendar.

Nevertheless, it cannot be said that dei Rossi was not relatively conventional in his faith. He believed in so thorough a doctrine of creation ex nihilo that he even rejected the notion that "time" existed before God's creative word brought the universe and time into being. He even argued against using the term "before" creation, for "before" is a temporal term, and when there is no time there can be no "before" or "after." This, among other things led him to criticism of Philo for having accepted the Aristotelian notion that there was primordial matter. He believed in the immediacy of God's guidance of the world since creation, and had no room for Philo's logos. Further, in his discussion of Philo's writings at one point he took up the question whether one may make use of them in the light of their differences on many points from Palestinian tradition. But he did not settle the issue. It appears here that he recognized the need to study Philo but wanted to cover his tracks for antagonists. [56]

Dei Rossi was neither a Platonist nor an Aristotelian, but eclectic and independent. Yet he had to face the internal contradictions that scientific findings offered to religion. Did God bring an earthquake, cause it to rain, or subject people to pestilence, premature death and famine? Are the catastrophies of nature God-sent phenomena? Once dei Rossi posited an immediacy of relationship between God and His world he had to account for the terrors of nature as well as their beauties. For dei Rossi God had created nature, that is, a principle with its own laws, to perorm all the necessary operations in the universe. Only when God decides to use the activities entrusted to nature for moral ends, by punishing or rewarding humans, does God intrude Himself into the operations and directly guide them. [57] Try as he might, however, dei Rossi was unable to solve the challenge to God's omnipotence inherent in a ravaging natural phenomenon which strikes at innocent humans and brings disaster to large numbers.

As a typical Renaissance man dei Rossi believed that the tides, the moon, and other celestial bodies all exert influence on humans. For example, he believed that eclipses are warnings of trouble ahead. But he exempted Jews from these influences, and was not clear as to whether individuals are able to study the cosmic movements and thereby foretell, and perhaps forestall events. [58]

Like so many enlightened scholars although dei Rossi placed a great emphasis upon sense perception and rationalism, he was not wholly addicted to science and reason. He maintained a healthy skepticism. But in his case, as in the case of other Renaissance figures, especially those of both the Protestant and Catholic Reformations in order to stress revelation over reason, his skepticism of reason combined with faith in revelation led him to a belief in demonology. Arguing that preternatural and supernatural phenomena can be as real as natural ones he agreed with halakhists of his time who saw no reason to doubt demonic interference in human life. In dei Rossi's own days Joseph Karo, who thought of excommunicating him, had included in his halakhah the view that one may recite verses for a person to protect him from mazikin (demons), and while he prohibited one from burning incense to a demon in order to compel the demon to act in the person's interest, as a form of idolatry, the very nature of the formulation of the halakhah indicates an unquestioning belief in demons. [59] In accord also with traditionalist Judaic theology dei Rossi stressed the reality of miracles and affirmed his faith in such metaphysical and metahistorical doctrines as immortality of the soul and resurrection of the body. [60]

Yet dei Rossi was different from other traditionalists.

Where science contradicted rabbinic literature, as noted earlier, he was willing to recognize rabbinic error. But there were also some contradictions of scripture where he was willing to accept science over the biblical text. Thus, in an age of great interest in geography the new discoveries must have been noticed by dei Rossi. Perhaps he read Farissol's geography. In any event he rejected Ezekiel 38:12, that Jerusalem sits on the "navel" of the earth, as evidence that Jerusalem is really at the center of the earth, relying rather upon his knowledge of geography. And withal, the inner tension between his modernity and his traditionalism seen again in his belief in the legendary exploits of Prester John and all the legends about the ten lost tribes. In this connection it might be recalled that Farissol's geography was greatly oriented to the question of the so-called ten lost tribes. Despite this show of naivete dei Rossi remained firm in refusing to rationalize and harmonize all conflicts with rabbinic literature as his contemporary Moses Isserles did in an apologetic work called **Torat Haolah.** Concerning this work, dei Rossi said, "it is better to be silent than to justify the righteous with arguments that cannot be substantiated." [61]

Dei Rossi exhibited elements of intellectual confinement, however, in his expressed belief in the superiority of the Jewish people, the direct creation of the Hebrew language by God, and in the idea that no other language existed before the human debacle at the Tower of Babel (Gen. 11:1-9). He saw Hebrew as the most beautiful and perfect of all languages. Galen said something similar about Greek, and referred to all other languages as the "bleating of cattle and the twittering of birds." For this dei Rossi accused Galen of "self-praise and racial complacency" without stopping to consider, as one historian has pointed out, that he was similarly guilty. [62]

Dei Rossi argued the conventional idea discussed earlier in reference to Hermetica which had been disseminated since hellenistic time, that all wisdom came from Judaic sources. [63] While he had to concede that in certain respects the gentiles had surpassed the Jews in science he saw the compensation for this to come when the Jews once more attain a superior position in the messianic era. That is not to say that he saw the messianic era as a culmination of history. In fact he followed Maimonides in holding that the messianic era is only to be a period in which Jews are free of oppression and once more settled in the Holy Land and able to observe the mizvot of the Torah that apply only to Palestine. The real goal of history, however, he saw as the advent of the supernatural world to come. [64]

Despite his views on the messianic era dei Rossi, harking back to Jeremiah's famous letter, believed that as long as Jews lived among gentiles they must pray for the welfare of their land. He was conscious that many gentile scholars will read his work and this element of it was undoubtedly designed to win their approval and empathy for Jews. He pointed out that international wars frustrate Jewish prayers, and that it is therefore important for Jews to pray for global peace. And in citing Isaiah in this matter, Azariah dei Rossi emerged as one of the earliest advocates of international peace. [65] There can be no doubt that Menasseh b. Israel's later writings that dwelt upon Jewish loyalty to the state and their interest in peace in order to facilitate their readmission to England were influenced by dei Rossi. [66]

The interesting tension that pervaded a person of the wide secular classical and rabbinic learning is evinced on the one hand in dei Rossi's comments on Christian scholars, and on the other hand in his firm halakhic conservatism. Unlike the usual traditionalist dei Rossi has the highest esteem for men like St. Augustine whom he called "the leading Christian sage," and for other men such as Eusebius, Jerome, Aquinas, and other theologians. Jerome he described at one point as "their learned translator." He admitted that in matters of science the ancient Jews took their knowledge of astronomy from men like Hipparchos and Ptolemy and used this in their work on the calendar. In conceding this he was saying that sacred time, when the holy days occur, is not a matter of perpetual revelation, but rather that Judaism was deeply influenced by secular gentile scientists. This intellectual "softness" on Christians and even pagans incurred the antagonism of some of his contemporaries as did Delmedigo, and he was even accused of heresy. It must be understood that the rabbis who barred **Mèor Èynaim** did so for more reasons than his remarks on calendar and chronology. They wanted to discredit dei Rossi for encouraging the study of other languages and reading non-Jewish books. [67]

Dei Rossi's writings show wide acquaintance with classical and hellenistic studies, Christian literature, early church fathers, later theologians, and Hermetic writings, not to speak of the scientists and philosophers of his own time. He cited at least fifty Graeco-Roman authors, including the great poets such as Homer, Virgil, and Ovid; leading philosophers such as Plato and Seneca; scientists such as Euclid, Ptolemy, and Galen; historians such as Herodotus, Livy, and Dio Cassius, to name only a few. But what is even more striking is Dei Rossi's extensive use of the entire range of New Testament books and early Christian authors such as Justin Martyr, Irenaeus, Origen, and others, along with the later church fathers such as Eusebius, Jerome, and Augustine, and medieval Christian writers such as Isidore of Seville as well as Muslim authors. His knowledge extends to works ranging from antiquity through the medieval era: Christian, Humanist, and Muslim, Italian, French, Spanish and German. What is most striking about Azariah dei Rossi is that unlike most medieval and Renaissance writers who omitted acknowledging their sources, dei Rossi always named his source. [68]

In his time other Jews indulged in these studies but Azariah dei Rossi, like Farissol, did not simply imbibe them as private enrichment. He drew upon them in writing about Judaism. Dei Rossi devoted considerable space in **Mèor Èynaim** to defend himself and others against obscurantist views that favored maintaining a distance between Judaism and non-Jewish learning, between gentiles and Judaism, and Jews and gentiles. To soften his approach he also argued that no gentile sources are acceptable when they are in direct conflict with halakhah, or if they run counter to a tradition arising with Moses at Sinai or with the prophets. Unlike Abraham Zacuto, an earlier contemporary, however, he also used many non-Jewish sources in his **Yuḥasin** but added yemaḥ shemo (may his name be obliterated) after citing select Christian writers such as church fathers, dei Rossi was invariably polite even when he disagreed. [69] It was, however, not so much his mingling with and respect for Christian scholars, but that the traditionalists realized that dei Rossi's methodology and some of his conclusions were dangerous to conventional ideas, that led them to suppress the book in Poland, Germany, Turkey, and Italy. It was generally obscured until the nineteenth century. But some people read it earlier, and along with the work and influence of other Renaissance figures dei Rossi contributed to the enlightenment of Menasseh ben Israel in the seventeenth century and both of them played a role in the modernizing intellectual process of Moses Mendelssohn in the eighteenth. [70]

Another interesting aspect of dei Rossi's inner tension, or divided self, as a Jungian analyst would refer to it, was his traditionalist halakhic stance, unlike that of Delmedigo and Leone da Modena. He rejected halakhic change, and his vigorous defense of the status quo might possibly have been the influence behind Mendelssohn's reluctance to seriously consider halakhic modification. While such halakhic prudence was diplomatic in its way as these scholars perceived their relationship to the vast majority segment of Judaism, it was also historically a brake upon an earlier reformation. [71] Dei Rossi believed that all halakhot are equally important, and that all sins are equally evil. He recognized no hierarchy of values in religious deeds or prohibitions, and applied this severe standard not only to torahitic or serious rabbinic halakhah but also to the great proliferation cf minhag (custom) accumulated through the middle ages. This also led him to an inability to recognize religious pluralism, and he battled vigorously against Karaites. Thus, at one point after quoting a Karaite scholar he added, "May the soul of the father and that of the son descend to hell." [72] In this vein too he accepted kabalism as containing the truth, even over Maimonides, and referred to it invariably as hokhmat haèmet, "the true wisdom." [73]

Azariah dei Rossi must thus be seen as a typical product of the Renaissance, struggling albeit not always successfully, to arrive at a viable synthesis which would allow him to retain credibility among the less educated masses, as well as with savants, dilettantes, scholars, and traditionalist rabbinic authorities. Only a far more detached analysis of his works will enable us to grasp whether there are times when his defensiveness and traditionalism are merely camouflage to divert the rabbinic powers or to avoid traumatizing the masses. In any event his work marked him as a man upon whose shoulders others would be able to sit and see farther. This was certainly the case in eighteenth and nineteenth century Germany.

The highwater mark of dei Rossi's work was historiography and yet even here we detect the inner tension between the medieval pietist and the proto-modern Renaissance man. There was a sudden spurt of historical interest among Jews in the sixteenth century among whom dei Rossi took leading rank. [74] Unlike contemporary historians such as Joseph Hakohen the title of whose work, **Emek Habakå**, describes his lachrymose view of history, and Ibn Verga who wrote in a depressing way and in the hope of bringing Jews to repentance, dei Rossi's view was that the major purpose for studying history is to understand the sources of tradition. [75] It was this attention to sources which he investigated with care, as primitive as his critical method might have been compared to the twentieth century, which marks him as a significant proto-modern. He used older editions, pursued many variant manuscripts of the same texts, and even used the newly emerging science of numismatics as did other Italian historians. [76] But his lingering piety would not allow him to suspect biblical or talmudic texts, and unlike the critical approach he took to the septuagint or the works of Josephus he believed the extant masoretic text and talmudic texts to be perfect, except in the case of several minor tractates, as for example Soferim, which he recognized to be "inexact . . . and . . . does not offer the same degree of correctness as do the other books of our ancient sages." As one historian has put it, "Azariah did not hesitate to give preference to dogma when it conflicted with science." Nevertheless, he did have certain reservations about the historicity of àgadah as he exhibited in the case of the famous story of the gnat which entered Titus' nostril and made its way to his brain when that celebrated Roman conqueror of Jerusalem entered the holy of holies in the Temple. [77]

It was again with Philo that dei Rossi exhibited his divided self. He studied him assiduously, dissected his views, argued against them, and tried to explain them. But in the final analysis, perhaps to avoid the wrath of traditionalists dei Rossi shrank from bringing Philo back into the pantheon of Jewish scholars. He wrote, "I do not wish to decide whether this Yedidiah or Philo . . . is pure or impure; I shall call him neither master nor sage, nor a heretic and Epicurean [unbeliever] . . . I do not propose to enter him into the intimate circle of my people . . . " [78]

Azariah's detached scholarly interest in Philo led to one of the earliest studies of Pseudo-Philo's **Biblical Antiquities,** and to his pinpointing the many parallels between that work and rabbinic literature. It impelled him to argue that the very antiquity of these sources indicates that certain midrashim that seem so bizarre apparently were authentic ancient tradition. Among other reasons dei Rossi suggested that since **Biblical Antiquities** and Philo's other works invert the commandments not to murder and not to commit adultery by placing adultery first, it appears that the same person wrote them all. But this scholarly interest in Philo did not sway dei Rossi on an emotional level. It took still another two centuries or more for Philo to be reclaimed and understood as a pious Alexandrian Jew, even somewhat conservative in his halakhah. Moreover, far from being "deviant" from Palestinian halakhah Philo actually preceded the later halakhah to which his writings were compared and by whose supposed "orthodoxy" he was measured. [79]

Had dei Rossi entertained a more decisively favorable attitude toward Philo the history of Philo's reclamation might have been swifter. As it was, Christian students of Judaica of the seventeenth and eighteenth centuries read **Mèor Eynaim,** but did not pick up on the critique of Philo, nor did Jewish readers until recent times. [80] Perhaps the greatest flaw in Azariah's views on Philo was his conclusion that Philo was an Essene! [81] But Azariah approved of many Philonic ideas such as immortality of the soul, the eternal validity and superiority of the Torah, and the importance of the literal meaning of scripture despite the usefulness of an allegorical reading. [82] He attributed four errors to Philo, however, that brought into question for him Philo's reliability as a Jewish scholar, and devoted all of Chapter Five of the Imrei Binah segment of his work to these problems. The first was that Philo did not use the "true text" of scripture but the Septuagint. He further expressed the conventional assumption that is by no means established in modern scholarship, that Philo did not know Hebrew and could not have read the scripture in the original. [83] The second major flaw in Philo, as dei Rossi saw it, was Philo's belief in the pre-existence of matter, referred to above. [84] Dei Rossi's third major criticism of Philo was that he used the allegorical method to deny the historicity of certain events, such as the creation of the world in six days, and that the Garden of Eden was a real place. Philo saw the six days as merely depicting the order of creation through the use of a mystical number, and the Garden as a concept. [85] The fourth breach in correct thought that dei Rossi saw in Philo was his failure to accept traditional masorah or "rabbinic" reading of scripture. [86] That is, dei Rossi, without realizing the anachronism of what he was saying was condemning Philo who lived before rabbinic Judaism arose for not conforming his halakhah to the rabbis. This speaks more of a flaw in dei Rossi than in Philo, for it exhibits the anachronistic error that flows from the traditionalist assumption that what is found in the later corpus of rabbinic literature had already always been, in toto, the masorah, the transmitted tradition of Moses. In this discussion of a number of examples of Philo's halakhah Azariah dei Rossi became the first scholar to explore Philonic halakhah. He concluded on the basis of his anachronistic premise that Philo's views were "vain imaginings not in accord with the masoreh . . . " and that Philo's "traditions of the ancients" were the views of pseudo-scholars. [87]

To dei Rossi's credit, however, he used a chapter to try to vindicate Philo's views and find ways to exonerate him. In the process he even used rabbinic parallels, explained Philo's use of the Septuagint as logical for his Jewish Greek-speaking and gentile audiences, excused Philo's belief in primordial matter as not intended to preclude creation ex nihilo but rather as misunderstanding the term tohu, chaos, as signifying matter, and praised him for denying that allegorical interpretation justified abrogation of any literal observance. Yet in his final appraisal of Philo part of which was quoted above, dei Rossi added ". . . in every place where he is mentioned in these chapters of mine he will be treated like one of the gentile scholars . . ." [88] This led to Philo's continued ostracism until the late eighteenth century, and underscores the inability of dei Rossi to fully liberate himself from medieval convention.

As he was reluctant to break the anti-Philonic tradition he was totally unwilling to open himself to harsh criticism in his views of the rabbinic literature, and advocated the rigorous approach to halakhah. But once dei Rossi passed the talmudic era he exercised far more independent judgment. Thus, he did not accept unquestioningly the geonic material. He dealt quite independently with post-geonic authorities even of such stature as Ibn Ezra and Maimonides, and polemicized with such major scholars as the tosafists, Jacob b. Asher, Karo, and Isserles. [89] Furthermore, he did not accept the seriousness of àgadah, seeing this genre more as something to induce a state of mind in the reader, parables, and metaphors, and compared many of the àgadic passages to ancient pagan allegories that were used to illustrate philosophical discussions. He considered the rabbis as indulging in symbolism. [90]

These considerations added to his critique of traditional chronology, his respectful use of extensive Christian sources and his denial of the divine origin of the calendar, along with innumerable details of theological and halakhic judgment that surfaced despite his traditionalism, incited contemporary traditionalists to force his **Mèor Èynaim** into oblivion. But dei Rossi was read and despite his basic conservatism in halakhah became a role-model in the process of acculturation in the northern European enlightenment. Perhaps the historian Heinrich Graetz said it well when he wrote of dei Rossi that he "would have been able to purify Judaism from the dross of centuries of hardship if the tendency of the age had not run counter to this endeavor, or if he had had greater courage in opposing it." [91]

IV. <u>Leone Da Modena</u> (1571-1648)

The Renaissance era was a bridge between medieval piety oriented inwardly in the Jewish community, and the modern era with its outward orientation. [92] Contrary to some historians who see the Renaissance as not relevant to the history of the Jews the personalities we cursorily review in this chapter exhibit how vital a role the Renaissance played as a period of transition and prefiguration. A dei Rossi was not yet a Leopold Zunz, but Moses Mendelssohn was not far beyond a dei Rossi, and da Modena, or Delmedigo, to be discussed next, were undoubtedly well on their way to reformation had political and sociological conditions allowed for Jewish community schism.

The Renaissance produced such universalistic philosophers as the physician Judah Abravanel, also known as Leone Ebreo, already referred to in Chapter Two. Ebreo believed that all created things, both the animate and the inanimate are related by the universal principle of mutual love. Love was seen as the dynamism that motivates all of life, and to express his philosophy he wrote **Dialogues on Love.** [93] The Renaissance also produced such interesting people as Leone De Sommi Portaleone (1527-1592), member of a distinguished family in Mantua who was deeply involved in Italian theater which had many Jewish players and musicians. The paths of Portaleone and dei Rossi crossed in 1574 when the latter visited Mantua to publish **Mèor Èynaim.** The Mantuan actors observed the Sabbath, and Portaleone built a synagogue. [94] These examples can be multiplied endlessly. Some had no major impact upon the future of Jewish religious development. Others played a vital role in reforming Judaism. But all together they constituted a milieu and created a mode. They left a legacy, which was carried over to Holland, and Hamburg, from where it was spread to the rest of Germany and set in motion reformation Judaism. The Renaissance synthesis might not have produced the Judaic Reformation, but it was seen as a paradigm, and stood out as an unfinished portrait of what might be.

Leone da Modena was a major figure of transition. The very controversy that swirled about him later in life as to his so-called "orthodoxy" testifies to the synthesis at which he labored, and which he transmitted for the modern generation. [95] What has been anticipated by a historian with a high degree of tentativeness when he wrote that Modena "may perhaps be considered the first of modern rabbis" (emphasis mine), I would say decisively. [96]

Modena had been given an acculturated education as well as the traditional rabbinic learning, and was ordained a rabbi at Venice. Although a scholar and master of the sermonic art he was compelled to earn a living through a potpourri of activities such as teaching children, proof-reading, publishing and lecturing. This frustrated his yearning to engage in scholarship and creative literary activity. This and various personal family tragedies led him to seek respite in gambling to which he became addicted. He wrote a book in which he denigrated gambling but was unable to liberate himself from it, and wrote a responsum upholding its halakhic permissibility. [97]

Modena had an extensive relationship with Christian scholars. He was mentioned from their pulpits and they came to hear him preach. Like the author of the Letter of Aristeas, and to a lesser extent Josephus, he wrote a survey of Judaism designed to be read by non-Jews. He numbered gentile scholars among his pupils, including an eminent person, Jean Plantavit de la Pause, Bishop of Lodève from 1610, and others as far away as England, such as the eminent jurist, John Selden. [98] Modena was undoubtedly the first Judaic scholar to vindicate Jesus as a Jew and to accept both Josephus and the New Testament as historical sources. This might have been under the influence of Azariah dei Rossi, for again in conformity with dei Rossi he looked askance at Philo and branded him an Essene. Taking into consideration the full range of Modena's writings, one historian has concluded that the "atmosphere is that of the nineteenth century, and of the full tide of Jüdische Wissenschaft ("the scientific study of Judaism"). Like Menasseh ben Israel he denied the role of the Jews in the crucifixion. He was among the first Judaic scholars to identify Jesus as a Pharisee, a judgment I consider erroneous but which has prevailed in recent decades in many scholarly circles. For its time, however, it was a giant step forward to include Jesus in the circle of Jews then incorrectly understood to be the forerunners of rabbinism. [100] In an unusual style for his time when rabbis generally corresponded with each other in Hebrew, Modena corresponded with a rabbi in Rome in Italian, and in what was probably an unprecedented gesture for a Judaic scholar, he wrote his comprehensive survey of Judaism, **Historia de' Riti Hebraici**, for James I of England as much as to overcome some of the pejorative negativism found in Johannes Buxtorf the Elder's **Synagoga Judaica (Hebraica).** [101]

The **Historia de' Riti Hebraici** was originally written in Italian in 1616, but problems that arose out of the ecclesiastical censorship imposed by the Catholic Reformation delayed its publication in Italy until 1638. [102] While Buxtorf included pejorative aspects on what might just as well be considered an objective basis as well as to demean Jews, Modena was not yet capable of fully rising above defensive apologetics. Consequently he omitted discussion in the **Riti** of those elements of Judaic practice that he surmised were repugnant to Christians, and hence failed to alleviate the damage done by Buxtorf in his ridicule of some of the practices and notions that came down through the medieval era and bordered on superstition. For this reason, but also because he exaggerated the objective elements in the **Riti** Graetz was critical of Modena for publishing a work which in itself would bring ridicule upon Judaism. [103]

It was for this apologetic reason that Modena sought to prove the superior rationality and morality of Judaism, and included such gratuitous information as that Jews no longer owned slaves, were forbidden to practice the black arts, and were enjoined to have special compassion upon parents, teachers, and the elderly. He also defended their business ethics. [104] But he did not discuss certain folk practices that bordered on superstition, or others that were legal fictions, and were taken seriously by pious Jews because they were included in the **Shulḥan Arukh,** at that time growing in authority. The fact that he chose not to refer to them rather than refer to them and reject them, would lead people who read about them in a book like Buxtorf's to have no reason to think that not all Jews practiced them or cherished them. I have in mind such practices as the order of donning and tying one's shoes when arising in the morning; the deliberate placing of pieces of bread around the house for the ceremony of supposedly "searching" for any remnant of leaven (bedikat ḥamez) on the eve of Passover; the unsavory details of the ḥalizah ceremony (the unshoeing of a brother-in-law) which replaced the equally reprehensible levirate marriage, but continued with the ancient custom of the widow spitting in the face of the levir and proclaiming an imprecation upon him; details concerning the halakhah of proselytes (gerim) which, when enforced, denied the proselyte full equality and acceptance; and a host of other matters. This selection could be multiplied many times over, and was by Buxtorf. All of the Judaic ritual practices enumerated by Buxtorf as superstition were either minimized or suppressed by Modena. Where Modena conceded their existence and minimized their importance he was correct in doing so and exhibiting objectivity. Where he suppressed them he was only intimating that Jews did practice them and that he had no valid way to refute the practices, thus allowing Buxtorf's negative view to stand, although he had himself explained in a letter to a Christian theologian that he left out "those items which have been considered by our own people (by the intelligent men among them) as superstitions." [105]

The occasion for writing the **Riti** seems to have been a request made by Sir Henry Wotton, the English ambassador to Venice in 1616, for a work on Judaism for King James I. Wotton sent the manuscript to a certain William Bedell in England who in turn gave it to one Sir William Boswell who gave it to the jurist John Selden. This Bedell had translated the Bible into Gaelic and later became a bishop, and apparently was in correspondence with Modena. Bedell worked under Wotton in Venice and studied with Modena there. Modena also corresponded with many other Christian savants. [106] Boswell was a pupil of Philip Ferdinand (Polonus) the former Jew Paul Jacob, who taught Boswell at Cambridge in 1606. Wotton was quite interested in all things related to Judaism and indicated he had pondered Judaic religious practice as early as 1592 in Rome, and that when he went to Venice he lived in the ghetto. In Venice he also studied with Leone da Modena. Thus, the **Riti** circulated in England long before its publication because of the copies Leone gave to Wotton, although it was not actually published in England until Edward Chilmead translated it in 1650. An interesting sidelight to this is that a French text was published in 1733 in London with illustrations of Judaic rites. One of these, of a Passover seder has a black person seated at the table. The supposition is that Jews admitted their black slaves to Judaism, and this qualified them to participate in the seder. This is further reinforced by the fact that contemporary prayerbooks contained a circumcision ritual designed for slaves. [107] This naturally retrospectively had to raise questions of Modena's credibility in his apologetics denying Jewish connection with slavery, and underscores the fact that there is little advantage in a Judaic scholar losing his objectivity for a mess of apologetic pottage.

Reminiscent of Tissard's description of his visit to the synagogue at Ferrara and Pepys' in London was another account of a visit to a synagogue in Venice in 1608 by Thomas Coryat when he also observed the ghetto and met Modena. He wrote that the ghetto stood on an island and had five-thousand Jews. He described the Europeans as wearing red hats, the sefardim as wearing yellow turbans, and that there were seven synagogues in Venice to which men, women, and children came on the Sabbath. He described what he called a "levite," the Torah reader who recited the weekly portion not in a distinct, sober manner but "by an exceeding loud yaling, indecent roaring, and as it were a beastly" manner. [108] There can be no doubt that even in these times of twentieth century interfaith exchanges on a broad and regular level many a Christian takes away from many a synagogue a rather curious impression of sparse attendance, late-coming, gossipy conversation, general irreverence, and inattention on the part of Jewish worshippers, but is restrained by modern politeness from commenting or writing about it. And yet, as in the sixteenth and seventeenth centuries this must still reinforce the Christian's idea that Jews have a defective faith which lacks in-depth spirituality.

Modena was opposed to kabalism although he shared the Renaissance tendency to believe in select esoteric ideas, in the potency of amulets and in dreams. He believed that Elijah appears at circumcisions. [109] Against kabalism Modena wrote his two works, **Ari Nohem** and **Ben David**. He also wrote a work called **Magen Veḥereḅ**, designed as a critique of Christianity, but in which he evinced a high degree of toleration. For example, he rejected the popular and widely-circulated anti-Christian tract, the Toledot Yeshu as a fabrication, and declared that any Jew who believed such slanders against Jesus should be ashamed. [110]

As a rabbinic scholar Modena was lenient in halakhic decision-making, and while he had a strong and vigorous position on the authoritative and revealed nature of the interpretive Torah ("oral law") he injected new constructs into halakhic discourse with which we are more familiar today but which were novel in seventeenth century Italy and unprecedented elsewhere. In what is perhaps a historically underestimated responsum he argued for the importance of time and place in halakhic consideration, and thus established the case for historicism in halakhah. In accord with that he urged necessary innovation and modification, albeit by twentieth century standards they appear rather mild. Perhaps his outstanding positions were taken in favor of art music in the synagogue, and on the question of bareheadedness. In the case of the latter he argued that the custom of covering the head was an appropriate act of piety in the ancient east but no longer in a society where "we Italians," as he put it, cannot see that as "good manners." [111] The basic arguments offered by Modena were later upheld by the great Polish Halakhist R. Solomon Luria, and became the standard position of all reforming tendencies in later centuries. Modena correctly interpreted the Mishnaic terms that one must pray in koḅed ròsh and not in kalut ròsh ("heavy of head" and "light of head") to refer to attitude, signifying that one must be mentally attuned and respectful in prayer and not frivolous. Others used this source as a basis for requiring the covering of the head and idiomatically referred to the uncovered head as kalut ròsh. Once Modena correctly interpreted the Mishnah, eliminating it as an ancient authoritative source for covering the head, no ancient support existed to mandate covering the head. [112]

In this same responsum Modena anticipated many a modern halakhist by offering arguments that are used at this time, and which I have used myself in arguing for and demonstrating the need for various modifications, abrogations and innovations in Judaic religious practice. For example, he argued that when people think something is prohibited which is really not prohibited one may inform them of the power of heter, that is, the priority of the permissive approach. And even more, Modena stressed that when he saw that his congregation, and most Italians, do not conduct themselves in a matter as if it is prohibited he cherished the power to permit these practices outright and deflect the claim of Levantine and German rabbis that Italians are sinners and the stringent ones are pious. [113] In Modena's few lines in this responsum we have encased a basic proto-modern halakhah. He virtually upheld the legitimacy of diversity aside from the well-known variegation of liturgies, and denied that religiosity can be measured by a prohibition index and pietistic ritualism.

Modena's halakhic leniency and creative philosophy, however, should not be misunderstood. He was still a cultural product of his time, and toleration had narrow parameters. Thus he was a vigorous opponent of Karaism and of any approach deemed heresy in the middle ages. Any assault upon the fundamentals of rabbinism was unacceptable. And during the seventeenth century there surfaced a new and distinct non-Karaitic tendency to reject rabbinic halakhah, and fundamentally to denigrate the idea that there was a revealed interpretive Torah that supplemented the Torah of Moses. This Renaissance tendency was often initiated or reinforced by Marranos who were finding their way back to Judaism in Christian countries where they faced no further danger from the Inquisition. While this was sometimes true in Italy, it was not as secure a place for such lapsed Christians as Holland or other Protestant areas. And it was to Amsterdam in 1617 that Modena addressed his **Magen Vezinnah**, a vigorous refutation of the eleven theses of Uriel da Costa who exemplified the surfacing returned Marrano heretical movement. In this treatise Modena appeared as a firm traditionalist and gave no quarter to those whom he considered dangerous heretics. [114]

In this tract Modena curiously even defended such particulars as the custom of mezizah (sucking the blood during circumcision from the cut membrane of the penis), but his major thrust was to argue the case for the rabbinic halakhah as revelation. Nevertheless, even here Modena's basic proto-modernity came through and he qualified his stance in what might perhaps have been a hope thereby to win the sympathy of the critics of rabbinic Judaism. He argued for what might be termed "progressive revelation" when he said that the oral Torah was designed to be the unfolded interpretation of contemporary scholars in each age. He saw no final halakhah, no absolute. And thus he was cognizant of the danger then arising in many parts of central eastern Europe where the **Shulḥan Arukh** of Joseph Karo was rapidly becoming the absolute authority in matters of Jewish practice. He referred to a person as "ignorant" who had said, "With the **Shulḥan Arukh** under my arms I have no need of you rabbis." [115]

In another anti-heretical tract called Shaågat Åryeh (The Roar of the Lion) Modena published an anonymous work called **Kol Sakhal** (The Voice of the Fool) and responded to it. The scholarly debate over the authorship of this book and the relationship of Modena to it is not germane to our chapter, but it deserves special attention here because of its close approximation to the arguments of Judaic reformers in the eighteenth and nineteenth centuries. [116] In both the argument and the counter-argument we have depicted for us the internal tension in seventeenth century Judaism which, I submit, never departed, and ultimately broke forth in the reformation of one-hundred and fifty to two hundred years later. [117]

The first part of **Kol Sakhal** is a survey of traditional Judaic theology. The author professed faith in God as creator ex nihilo, revealer of Torah, in both providence and free will, in God's knowledge of human affairs, and reward and punishment. He accepted the doctrine of immortality, and an afterlife in which the injustices of this world will be brought back into balance. [118]

The author continued with an attack upon the Pharisees as those who distorted the Torah transmitted by Ezra because they were pietistic and sought separatism from gentiles. Only later, he argued, did their ritualism spread among the people. In this section the author correctly understood several things although his error, still made in our time, was to identify Pharisees with rabbis. He understood that Jesus was not a Pharisee although he errs, first, in his conclusion that therefore Jesus was compelled to set up a new sect, which Jesus did not do. And second, he failed to see the distinction between rabbis and Pharisees on the one hand, and the elements of conformity between Jesus and the proto-rabbis on the other. The author cannot be faulted for failing to arrive at a sounder position concerning Pharisees, Jesus, proto-rabbis, and rabbinic Judaism over three centuries ago, when these matters are still in vigorous debate and conventional wisdom is still maintaining a basically inexact viewpoint. And thus, he expounded a partial truth when he said that the post-70 rabbis proliferated the halakhah with no biblical basis, and further distorted religious practice by bringing to bear ågadah and kabalah. More to the point would have been the argument that they adopted elements of Pharisaism in order to win the allegiance of the masses who followed them and felt comfortable with the emotion-laden ritualism that was rooted more in the esoteric than in the rational. [119]

In the third part of the book the author particularized his rejection of rabbinism. In many ways this can be read as a proto-reform treatise, and there can be no doubt that its content was influential in late eighteenth and early nineteenth century reform. The writer oriented his critique of specific practices to the sequence of halakhah in Jacob b. Asher's **Árbah Turim** (Four Rows). [120]

The author of **Kol Sakhal** was theologically opposed to granting authority to post-scriptural scholars, in this case specifically the rabbis since the first century, and took it for granted that the entire content of rabbinic literature is their product, none of it attributable to any greater antiquity coextensive with scripture. Thus he opposed the use of tefilin (phylacteries), the mezuzah (capsule on the doorpost containing the shema, the confession of monotheistic faith, Deut. 6:4 and Deut. 6:5-9). He advocated curtailing prayers to Sabbaths and Holy Days, limiting them to one hour only and the eschewal of the berakhah formula in which the rabbis attributed to God their own inventions. The scriptural premise for liturgical change would obviously be difficult to ascertain, but that only gives evidence that so-called "heretics" or proto-reformers of the seventeenth century could no more rely strictly upon scripture than the seventh century so-called heretics or Karaites were able to allow scripture to suffice. The writer favored restructuring the conception of melakhah, work prohibited or permitted on the Sabbath in order to eliminate the massive corpus of rabbinic prohibitions. He advocated a seven-day observance of the prohibition of leaven during Passover in accord with scripture (Ex. 13:6f.) as over the rabbinic eight days. With this he also urged the abolition of the ceremony of bedikat hamez, the search for leaven, in which the householder places pieces of bread about the residence and then supposedly searches for them in order to eliminate leaven. He also called for a more Torah-oriented simplified practice of the Passover hamez (leaven) prohibitions, abolition of the massive rabbinic accretions and the use of the Hagadah for the seder. He called for the total abolition of the second day of each holy day observed in the diaspora which had been added to each of the Torah's holy days. He opposed the roster of fast days, arguing that Yom Kippur alone was legitimate, and that for historical consideration the only other fast that ought to be retained was the tenth of Tebet since that was the day upon which the siege of Jerusalem began and signalled the fall of both Temple and city. He favored sounding the shofar when Rosh Hashanah occurred on the Sabbath as was done in ancient times and discontinued by the rabbis, and with that he argued the removal of the minutiae of halakhah connected with the making and the sounding of the shofar, as well as the abolition of such folk-customs as eating apple dipped in honey on the eve of Rosh Hashanah and the practice of kaparot (swinging a chicken around one's head and the recital of a formula which declared the chicken, soon to be ritually slaughtered to be a vicarious atonement) on the eve of Yom Kippur. He argued that even the taking of lulab (palm branch) and etrog (citron) on Sukot were only meant for the priestly cult in the Temple and should no longer be used. He argued that the calendar had been manipulated by the rabbis and that, therefore, no holy days actually occur on the day designed by God. He went on to attack and urge abolition of all the detailed halakhah connected with circumcision, shehitah (the slaughter of animals for kasher use), the whole complex of dietary practices, the writing and reading of the megilah (the scroll of Esther), the prohibition on the use of gentile bread, food and wine, and any other practice that contributes to the social barrier between Jew and Christian, and is therewith directly responsible for hatred of the Jew. He urged the abolition of the baptismal practices for menstruants and other purposes, the institution of hatarat nedarim (the annulment of vows), the institution of mamzerut (bastardy), except in cases of incest and adultery, and all the privileges of priests and levites. He opposed the minutiae of divorce halakhah, and in fact, in a rather conservative manner, expressed himself against divorce in general, advocating it be permitted only in cases where one partner was guilty of immorality or adultery. And in this same vein he opposed halizah, (unshoeing of a levir) to allow a widow to remarry, and conservatively urged a return of the priority of the biblical practice of yibum (levirate marriage). For the whole complex of Jewish civil and criminal law gathered within Jacob ben Asher's division of halakhah in Turim called Hoshen Mishpat (Breastplate of Judgment) the author of Kol Sakhal urged the use of reason and general law, and an end to the practice of earlier Jewish law and separate Jewish courts.

In all the foregoing, the author of Kol Sakhal, whether he wrote in 1500 as Modena attested or around 1620 just before Modena received the book in 1622 (or indeed, if Modena wrote it himself), evinced a number of characteristics that must not be overlooked. First, he showed an extensive and intensive knowledge of Judaic tradition and the traditionalist regimen as then practiced by pietistically observant Jews. Second, he evinced a strong proto-modernity in what he advocated be shed, although he might have taken many ideas from Karaism. Third, in the very fact that he could have joined Karaism and did not he exhibited the proto-modern characteristic of changing Judaism within the rabbinic parameters in defiance of the communal-rabbinic power axis. Fourth, although not all the ideas of Kol Sakhal were incorporated into the early reforming movements in Judaism during the nineteenth century, very little was added by the latter aside from the equality of women.

Some comments about Leone da Modena's preaching are in order before concluding our discussion of this unusual person. He was reputed to be a great preacher. Thus, his sermons should tell us something about him although scholars have so far only been able to identify twenty-one of his sermons, while he referred to "hundreds." [121] These sermons indicate that Modena had a theological conception of Jewish history. Quite possibly these surviving sermons constituted an independent collection on the theme of suffering and redemption. In them Modena exhibited an other-worldly orientation both for the elect community and the individual. He stressed that while this world is of utmost importance for it is the arena in which the person gains his salvation, salvation will be experienced through other-worldly eternal bliss. On the collective historical level he provided no new concept with which to deal with the perennial question of why God's chosen people suffer so consistently throughout history. Modena interpreted Jewish suffering as the retribution for sin. He saw the exceptional divine miracles that saved Jews at crucial times, such as from Pharoah or Haman, as being special divine signs, paradigms of redemption. These were to teach Jews that God can and will redeem them ultimately. Thus, suffering was to be the normal condition of Jews with redemption to be experienced at the end of this-worldly history and to be enjoyed metahistorically. [122]

Modena also took up halakhic questions in his sermons, apparently especially when he could use that avenue to shed some light on the historical destiny of the Judaic elect community and his theme of redemption. A celebrated controversy of the schools of Hillel and Shammai is the one over how to kindle Hanukah lights. Bet Shammai advocated eight the first night with one less each succeeding night down to one on the last night. Bet Hillel urged one the first night with one more each succeeding night up to eight on the last night. [123] The Talmud records two fourth century explanations. The first indicates that Bet Shammai believed it important to signify the number of days yet to be observed, while Bet Hillel thought it important to signify the number of days that are in process of departing. There is no explanation offered for these positions. An alternative view was that Bet Shammai drew an analogy to the offerings at the Sukot festival when less offerings were presented with each passing day, while Bet Hillel thought it more important to observe the principle that in holy matters one adds and does not diminish. [124]

Modena preached that the two schools taught the same basic lesson in two different ways. Bet Shammai taught that with each passing year the years of suffering, or galut of the Jew are diminished for they come closer to redemption. Bet Hillel taught that with each passing year represented by the additional lights each night the years of suffering have increased until they will reach their end and redemption will come. [125]

Modena thus used this enigmatic halakhic controversy to emphasize the theme of redemption and to reconcile the difference as being only methodological or pedagogical, with both views looking to the ultimate salvation of Israel. In this way the spiritual aspect of Ḥanukah as paradigm of redemption was heightened in his preaching.

Unlike his general interests which included secular and Christian learning Modena's sermons were oriented to pious exhortation and based only upon Judaic sources. In this way he differed from the earlier Renaissance preacher Judah Moscato who illustrated his sermons from non-Jewish literature, although it is reasonable to suppose as some have argued that in his philosophy and themes chosen for sermons Modena might have been influenced by Judah Moscato (1530-1593). Moscato was a contemporary of dei Rossi. He was an accomplished theoretician of rhetoric as can be seen from his collection of sermons; and as Messer Leon had tried to uncover classical rhetoric in the Bible, Moscato sought to rediscover it in rabbinic literature. What motivated such efforts on the part of Renaissance scholars was the psychological tension involved in conceding that certain elements of knowledge and wisdom originated among gentiles and that not all learning was implicit in God's Sinaitic revelation. They labored to demonstrate that scripture and rabbinic literature were antecedent in possessing the humanist spirit of classical and Renaissance style. [126]

Modena was a contemporary of another great preacher in Venice, Azariah Figo (1579-1647) a leading talmudist who had also been steeped in Renaissance Humanistic studies. [127] But in later life Figo regarded his pursuit of secular learning as vain, and wrote that by the grace of God " . . . I saw myself covered with shame for having placed the accidental above the essential . . ." and for neglecting "divine laws that must rule our lives." He subsequently gave himself over entirely to talmudic study. His sermons were serious exhortations to the lax in observance to attain greater piety and a higher level of social morality. Like Moscato he followed classical rhetoric, and like Arama, to be discussed below, and like his contemporary Modena, he based his sermons on biblical and supporting rabbinic texts. But unlike Moscato, he rarely used non-Jewish sources for illustration and quotation. [128]

Modena also differed from Isaac Arama (1420-1495), the earlier Spanish preacher who gained great popularity as a stylist and left his imprint upon synagogue preaching. Arama, a traditionalist, and by no means a Renaissance figure, nevertheless peppered his sermons with citations and illustrations from apocryphal literature and classical philosophers. Arama's sermons dealt with the fundamental doctrines of Judaism: God, sin and repentance, the soul, immortality, freedom of choice, creation, revelation, providence, the truth and mystery of miracles and prophecy, the importance of living by the ritualism of Judaism, the efficacy of prayer, and the function of Israel. His collection of sermons **Akedat Yiẓḥak** displays a technique which was also used by Modena: providing two primary texts from which to proceed with the body of the sermon, one from the Bible and the other from rabbinic literature. Arama was a forerunner of the early modern mussar movement, and unlike Modena, his sermons did not emphasize collective redemption so much as individual salvation. He saw the purpose of the daily regimen of ritual derived from the Torah and rabbinic extensions to be the cultivation of the individual soul, discipline, the curbing of passion, spiritual enrichment and the sanctification of life. He individualized the essence of Passover as being the contemplation of the mystery of birth and Sukot as inspiring sensitivity to the mystery of death. [129]

This unusual approach taken by Arama was theologically correct: Judaism was designed for individual salvation, and redemption was not to be seen as primarily a group function. This is the essence of Gamaliel's passover seder formula: each person is to see oneself as if he (or she) had gone forth from Egypt. The redemption, in Arama's terms was rebirth, and like spring represented new life. But this approach by Arama might also have been the product of strong Christian influence upon the sermonic art for Arama himself informed us that many Jews attended churches in late fifteenth century Spain, whether voluntarily or involuntarily is not always clear, and were impressed by the style and content of the preaching. Individual salvation is of the core of the Christian message and Arama was wise in centering his preaching on this aspect of Judaism. [130] Modern preaching has again departed from stressing the individual mussar style and the salvation of the individual to embracing an emphasis upon collective redemption by which is frequently meant less the metahistorical eschatological redemption than the temporal political-national success of the current State of Israel.

This digression on Arama highlights the fact that Modena was not a pioneer in the medieval sermonic art. But while he built upon previous preachers like Arama and Moscato his emphasis was oriented to his time. Thus, it has been suggested that in eschewing illustrations from non-Jewish literature Modena was responding to the waning interest in non-Jewish culture that characterized seventeenth century Italy. But it is also quite likely that the presence and competitive preaching of Figo in Venice inhibited Modena from using non-Jewish sources. [131] Whatever influence it had on Modena's sermons this waning interest, and the increasing inward orientation that resulted from the intensification of ghetto life, which was further exacerbated by the debacle of Sabbatian messianism, contributed to the hiatus between the Renaissance and the eighteenth century enlightenment and temporarily procrastinated the Judaic reformation.

V. Joseph Solomon Delmedigo (1591-1655)

Delmedigo, also known as Yashar of Candia, was born in Crete when it was governed by Venice. He spent seven years as a student at Padua after the Italian Renaissance had waned, and lived at Frankfurt-am-Main in Germany during the era of the Thirty Years' War (1618-1648). During this time eastern European Jews suffered the traumatic event of the Chmielnicki massacres of 1648-1649. The influence of kabalah was increasing, and the anti-rational, esoteric, and mystical mood was expanding. This was happening at a time when western European intellectuals were moving forward with the new science and concomitant naturalistic philosophy. [132]

Yashar embraced the new scientific rationalism and became a vigorous critic of many aspects of Jewish life which he witnessed both in Crete and Italy, and in Germany and Poland. More than Farissol, dei Rossi or Modena, Delmedigo was a forerunner or prototype of the enlightened Jewish scholar-rabbi of the eighteenth century. Others comparable to him were written off as heretics and not included as Judaic thinkers, such as Uriel da Costa and Barukh Spinoza in Amsterdam. But like other seminal rationalists produced by the Renaissance who had preceded him Yashar was a spiritualist and mystic, and engaged in the occult, as can be seen from his written works. Among non-Jews the same phenomenon was experienced in the case of the Frenchman Jean Bodin (1530-1596), and the Englishman Francis Bacon (1561-1626), both of whom were believers in magic, astrology, and alchemy. Delmedigo believed in the potency of the right conjunction of constellations and accepted the popular beliefs in angels, and in reincarnation and metempsychosis. He gathered large numbers of pagan, Jewish, and Christian sources to illustrate the absurdity of some of the popular superstitions, but at the same time drew attention to their presence in the Talmud. [133]

The records of the Jewish community of Candia as reflected especially in the takanot (decrees, statutes) of the community indicate that despite the high intellectual level of Jewish scholarship and literary activity there, widespread laxity in ritual observance, and especially in public prayer was also a reality. In 1549 it was apparently felt that synagogue attendance was so sparse that a takanah was passed suspending shibah worship at home and requiring mourners to come to the synagogue. Sexual permissiveness and questionable patterns of behavior in business and social life were also rampant. [134]

Yashar's grandfather Eliezer studied under Jacob Berab and Joseph Karo in Egypt and taught at the Candia yeshibah for forty-five years. His father Elijah Delmedigo was also rabbi at Candia and was internationally considered a major halakhist and talmudist. Yashar studied talmudics and halakhah with both his grandfather and father, and while he never published a specific halakhic work it appears from his writings that he had considerable knowledge of the Talmud and its commentaries. Like other figures of the era he studied languages other than Hebrew and Aramaic, was adept at Greek and Latin, corresponded with Christian scholars, and translated sections of Philo. Since Padua had long been a great center of both secular and Judaic studies and especially of medicine, Yashar found his way there. He studied with Galileo and made reference to his new telescope. At Padua he studied philosophy, natural sciences including botany, zoology, and chemistry, mathematics, astronomy, and medicine. [135]

From Padua he returned to Candia, but when he ran into ideological difficulties with his fellow-Jews, and especially because he desired to pursue more secular knowledge he left Crete. Candian co-religionists were not amenable to Delmedigo's acculturated ways. He was not of the hoi polloi unobservant, but as son and grandson of Elijah and Eliezer Delmedigo, and as burgeoning major scholar in his own right, his relaxed attitude toward halakhah and the vision he had of a future acculturated Judaism went counter to the emphasis his colleagues placed on the status quo. He believed in freedom of thought, and the Jewish community of Candia, locked into its takanot was not going to allow it to him any more than Amsterdam to Spinoza several decades later. Thus, in 1617 Delmedigo set out upon widespread travels that took him to many countries over a period of some years. He travelled to Egypt, Constantinople, and on to Poland. By this time the Polish Jewish community was the largest in the world, but it was intellectually ghettoized and culturally narrow. It provided no secular education for its young, and its talmudic-halakhic studies were mired in pilpul, hair-splitting dialectics, which was robustly denounced by Delmedigo. [136]

It was perhaps his discovery of so much status quo traditionalism wherever he travelled that impelled Delmedigo to seek out Karaites, and he developed close relations with far-flung Karaite colleagues, including Zerah of Troki, son of Isaac of Troki, author of the well-known anti-Christian polemical work, Hizzuk Emunah (The Strengthening of Faith). If his disappointment with or alienation from rabbinic Jews influenced his relationship with Karaites, this latter relationship could only serve to further alienate him from the rabbinite Jews. After an extended stay

in Poland Yashar went on through the German provinces and
the Low Countries, and one of his sad impressions everywhere
he came throughout the diaspora of Poland, central and western
Europe, was that Jews were living in meḫuot hametunafot, "dung-
filled alleys."

Yashah functioned for awhile as a rabbi in Hamburg
and then went on to Amsterdam where he was befriended by
Menasseh B. Israel, and where he taught at the yeshiḫah and
preached in the synagogue on Saturday. By 1630 he was living
in Frankfurt-am-Main, one of the largest Jewish communities
in Germany, and there he made his living as a doctor. He was
apparently destined to travel and we find that he died in Prague
in 1655. [137]

It was not always clear from Delmedigo's writings when
he was serious and when he was sarcastic. He was capable, for
example of using Shalshelet Hakabalah (Chain of Tradition) as
a source to support a position, and then turn around and pun
on the name of a work by Gedalyah ibn Yaḥya, as a "chain of
lies." A view in modern scholarship has it that Yashar was frequently camouflaging what was then considered deep-rooted heresy.
Another way to look at Yashar's method of using irony and even
hyperbole was his desire to be either objective or candid, or
both, in his critique of rabbinic Judaism as he witnessed it especially in Candia and Poland. It must be remembered that Delmedigo
lived at a time when seventeenth century so-called heresy was
reaching its peak, and if his arguments gave those circles support
he would suffer guilt by association. Furthermore, he was caught
in the tension between rationalism and the occult, in a belief
in the basic virtues of scripture and Talmud, and the recognition
that both these great works of Judaism contained much unsavory
material. He was a proto-modern scholar, and like Spinoza, more
so than Farissol or Modena, he underscored copyists' errors in
the biblical texts, insertions by masoretes, and the influence
of foreign languages upon Hebrew. In a very real sense he antedated Spinoza as a modern Bible critic. It is possible to argue
that he opposed allegorizing biblical stories of angels, demons
and the revival of the dead in order to expose the primitive
elements of scripture. But it is also possible to take the view
that he preferred to expose the difference between faith and
reason, and to indicate that one cannot truly rationalize all irrational and esoteric elements of Judaism, but must either take them
on faith or relinquish them. [138]

On the other hand Delmedigo evinced a hint of an argument used by other so-called heretics of that era. He argued
that Moses knew the reasons for the obscure commandments
of the Torah but thought it better for the people to remain in
the dark and to act out of total obedience. The similar notion

that the rabbinic proliferation of ritual was designed to keep the masses subordinate to the rabbis who had to teach and explain all the massive obscure details, also undergirded the arguments of Uriel da Costa and the **Kol Sakhal** mentioned earlier. These were arguments that originated with Averroism and became popular in Italy during the previous century and earlier. [139] Furthermore, there are instances in which Delmedigo and da Costa argued against the same passages of scripture, but no specific link between them has been proven. Nevertheless there is little reason to doubt that they had opportunities to meet one another in Amsterdam (both were there some time between 1618-1630), or at least read or hear one another's views. [140]

Barukh Spinoza (1634-1677) again used the same passages, and is in agreement with Delmedigo on many other questions. It is not germane to our chapter to systematically analyze their respective writings. It must suffice here to say that there is reason to surmise direct influence of Delmedigo upon Spinoza. When one considers that Moses Mendelssohn was in turn deeply influenced by Spinoza the links between enlightened thinkers of the sixteenth and seventeenth centuries, the proto-moderns, and the reformers of the eighteenth and nineteenth centuries becomes clearer. [141]

Delmedigo engaged in a vigorous critique of traditionalist rabbis for their intellectual narrowness, pursuit of material gain, interest in power as heads of academies and judges of communal courts, and for their casuistry. [142] Again he can be seen as an objective critic or as an angry heretic. Certainly he lived at a time, as has been seen earlier in this chapter, and in Chapter Two, and will be explored further in the following chapter, when the anti-tradition posture was increasing. What is called heresy and what is deemed as alternative and legitimate option and criticism will always be open to dispute. Farissol, dei Rossi, and Modena were more circumspect and not alienated. Therefore they have not been as suspect of hidden heresy as Delmedigo, albeit Modena suffered a degree of suspicion of having authored **Kol Sakhal.**

Yashar shows that the irrational elements of Judaic practice that border on superstition in matters related to birth, marriage and death, food taboos and the like are often traceable to àgadot in the Talmud, and that many of the esoteric ideas of kabalah can also be found there. By thus substantiating the irrational in talmudic literature Delmedigo was either condemning the latter of being a candid critic. Those who wish to condemn Delmedigo, and perhaps through him all so-called heresy, will take the former position. Those who uphold the idea that legitimate diversity of thought and practice was the historical pattern of Judaism and the charge of "heresy" was political rather than theological will see Delmedigo as a candid critic preserving a degree of intellectual integrity in an environment in which he suffered great tension between the quest for collegiality and alienation.

This was an age when rabbinite scholars took no interest in Karaism, Delmedigo being a rare exception. [143] He gained many disciples among them and admired them for their interest in secular learning. He wrote his work **Elim** in response to a series of questions put to him by a Karaite. In this work he pointed out that becoming a rôsh yeshibah (a talmudic teacher in a higher academy of learning) among rabbinite Jews offers one the best profession for wealth and authority, even over that of medicine and business, while being occupied in the handicrafts is the lowliest. This was a description of the social and economic realities of eastern Europe during the seventeenth century. Certainly the yeshibah field was a large one and such schools proliferated all over Lithuania, Poland and Russia. [144]

Yashar's kinship for Karaites was based upon their interest in secular learning and his disdain for the traditionalist rabbinite indifference to it; their basic rejection of àgadah and kabalah, albeit some did show an interest in kabalah; and their role as paradigms for revisionism. Finally, his interest in Karaites allowed him to demonstrate that he was capable of transcending the narrow divisions among Jews and that he had a broader approach that encompassed a nascent pluralism in religion.

There are those who will argue that both his relationship with Karaites whom he considered as true Jews, and his critique of the limited parameters of the rabbinites contributed to the denigration of the prestige of talmudic learning in Europe. When he derogated elements of halakhic content of Talmud as trivial, and used midrashim and àgadot as witnesses to superstition, as mentioned earlier, he was in effect spreading disdain for the study of rabbinics. But his interest in Karaites went beyond this. For he was also inclined to have a positive attitude toward Christians, and argued that gentiles also enjoy immortality of the soul. He opposed the kabalist position that gentiles were impure kelipot (impure shells) without souls that share in the celestial destiny of Jews, a view still held by those who are of the ultra-orthodox persuasion. He praised the gentile pursuit of secular education over the Jewish immersion in religious texts alone. [145] In this he became a forerunner of the school of Herzl Wessely and Moses Mendelssohn who promoted the idea of secular education as part of the upbringing for all Jewish children in the eighteenth century.

It is not fair to Delmedigo to see these attitudes as evidence for "an inferiority complex with regard to some aspects of Jewish culture and institutions" as one modern scholar has anachronistically phrased it. [146] Delmedigo did not think in twentieth century terms of such an entity as Jewish "culture." He neither thought of "institutions" in the modern sense, nor was his admiration of the broader horizons of general culture evidence of an inferiority complex. This is a modern anachronistic evaluation in sociological and psychological terms of a phenomenon which was intellectual and spiritual. Rather it was Delmedigo's maturation out of parochialism that led him to Karaites, Christians, the sciences and humanism. In this way Delmedigo joined the other paradigms of proto-modernity and although in his own day he was alienated and stood alone he became a harbinger of the eighteenth century enlightenment and acculturation. Unlike a Spinoza who withdrew to solitude, having given up on Judaism, Delmedigo, far from being accused of showing symptoms of an inferiority complex, should be recognized as a vibrant mind who pioneered modern Judaic pluralism. He studied Judaic sources objectively, measured them by the standards of scientific methodology as known in his time, and favored open-ended ecumenical relationships with other branches of the great Judaeo-Christian religious tree. Finally, it is of some interest that in pursuing the winding threads that lead from medievalism to modernity, we find that **Sefer Elim,** Delmedigo's collection of responses to the Karaite Zeraḥ ben Nathan was printed by R. Menasseh b. Israel in Amsterdam in 1629. [147]

Chapter Five

THE DUTCH EXPERIENCE

I. Introduction

The seventeenth century was one of great change in Europe. On one level it was the century of traditionalist Judaic retrenchment as can be seen in the widespread authority of the combined sefardic-àshkenazic halakhic digest, the **Shulḥan Arukh** of Joseph Karo and **Mapah** of Moses Isserles. [1] On another level, however, Jews participated in the encroaching modern world. In contrast to the ever-growing circle of talmudists and halakhists who eschewed modernity, secular education and acculturation there was a David Ganz in Prague who was a universal historian and a competent astronomer who contributed to the work of the Danish astronomer Tycho Brahe (1546-1601) who worked with Johannes Kepler (1571-1630) in Prague. Italian, Dutch and German universities were open to Jews before 1700 although the process had been uneven, and in some places was not consistent. A Jew, for example, did not matriculate as a doctoral student in Germany until 1721. [2]

What was said of changing religious and social lifestyle in Renaissance Italy in chapter 2, can also be said of seventeenth century Germany. There was a laxity of observance, a greater social mingling of the sexes, and permissiveness in sexual behavior patterns, along with the adoption of leisure pastimes such as card-playing and smoking tobacco in place of religious study. There was frequenting of public taverns and drinking with gentiles to the point of public drunkenness. These tendencies are clear from the statutes of such Jewish communities as Altona and Wandsbek for 1686 and 1687, where going to non-Jewish taverns was banned, attending theatre and fencing schools on the Sabbath and holy days was prohibited, and women were denied the right to attend opera even on weekdays. [3] While there were sound reasons already alluded to above for disorientation of Judaic religious life in such destructive events as the Thirty Years' War, the Chmielnicki trauma and the Sabbatian messianic disaster, there were other factors of equal and greater significance that must be considered. There was the residue of Renaissance acculturation that infiltrated Germany and Holland and imperceptibly transformed the western European Jew. To the causes of this turn to modernity must be added the great influx and dissemination of a new view of Judaism borne by returning Marranos who were neither Karaite nor rabbinite Jews, but sought to transform rabbinism. This element had a decisive influence upon how things evolved in Holland and Hamburg, and both areas were, like Italy, the matrix of the Judaic reformation a century later. [4]

II. The Marrano Factor

The phenomenon we identify as "marranism" is basically related to Spain and Portugal. It actually originated, however, at the end of the thirteenth century in Naples, when that area was ruled by the Angevine kings and the Jewish residents were forcibly converted. At that time these forced converts to Christianity were termed neofiti (neophytes), and it was to ferret them out that the Inquisition became active in Naples during the sixteenth century. [5] But "marranism" became an extensive problem only at the end of the fourteenth century, and not in Naples, but in Spain, when there took place a severe onslaught upon the Jewish community and a massive compulsory conversion of Jews to Christianity in 1391 and again in 1444. Perhaps hundreds of thousands of conversos (converts) emerged. These converts were also called New Christians; and among Jews were called ànusim ("the compelled ones"). Their ranks were augmented in 1492 when the order for the expulsion of Jews from Spain was issued, and again after 1497 by tens of thousands of Jews who took refuge in Portugal. [6]

Inquisition records are helpful in determining the religious views and practices of the Marranos, for they were questioned and rigorously investigated in order that the Church might determine their fidelity to Christianity. They invariably believed that salvation will come through the Torah and not the gospels, and they had an earnest belief in messianism. [7] They often did not practice circumcision and allowed themselves that indulgence on the basis that Israelites did not do so in the wilderness. Nevertheless there were times when outsiders came for brief visits and performed circumcisions as is told of R. Menasseh ben Israel, and others. [8] Hebrew had largely disappeared as did their familiarity with any religious writings beyond the Latin version of scripture. They prayed in the vernacular those prayers that had been handed down, Latin psalms and curiously, the Lord's Prayer. They washed their hands before worship, faced Jerusalem, covered their heads with a white cloth as a substitute talit (prayershawl), and kneeled at worship, Roman Catholic style. [9] They observed few dietary practices and only scarcely observed the Sabbath by changing linen on Friday night and kindling Sabbath lights concealed in a jar so as not to risk their being detected by the Inquisition or an informer. All festivals except Passover and Yom Kippur were eschewed to avoid the heavy risk of detection. [10] They had a few variations of traditional observances of mourning, such as the taharah (washing the deceased for burial), and a seven-day shibah period which, unlike the general custom, was concluded by a fast. Secret Jewish weddings invariably followed the church ceremony. [11]

These people often had sons who became priests. These and the Marranos' own study of the New Testament in their open Christian lives, were instrumental in criticizing the accretions of rabbinic Judaism. They conventionally identified these accretions with Pharisaism concerning which they received negative impressions from both the New Testament and post-biblical church tradition. It was out of circles such as these that new voices were heard that were condemned by their contemporaries as heretical. [12] These groups saw rabbinic Judaism as restrictive, unspiritual, and addicted to irrationalism, and they used a literal approach to scripture to undermine rabbinism. Some of them went beyond restricting revelation to scripture, only rejecting rabbinism; they adopted the growing common denominator of scientists and philosophers, the religion of nature and reason that matured from Descarte to Locke. Rabbinic halakhah appeared utterly unnecessary and its minutiae irrational. We know from the Italian rabbi Immanuel Aboab that Marrano intellectuals in Italy were questioning the validity of the interpretive torah. Such groups were also found in south France, Holland and Hamburg. [13]

The theological and halakhic problem related to readmitting either those who were themselves baptized under compulsion or those who had lived as crypto-Jews beyond a generation went back many centuries. A liberal policy had prevailed toward readmitting apostates since the time of R. Gershom in the tenth century. After the serious event of 1391 R. Isaac ben Sheshet Perfet drew a distinction between those who became truly devout and even zealous Christians who tried to suppress other Jews living in their midst, and those who would seek to extricate themselves from their predicament but were economically unable to move themselves and their families and to seek subsistence elsewhere. [14] This problem naturally grew astronomically after 1492, and became a matter of grave urgency especially in the early seventeenth century with the constantly increasing influx of Marranos into Judaism. While many Jews followed the liberal tendency there were those who were rabidly opposed to the New Christians and accused many of them of having been cowards or of having been too materialistic to give up their wealth and flee to safer areas, and regarded them as ineligible for Jewish status. The irony of this position is seen in the tension that beset the celebrated rabbi Saul Morteira (1596-1660) who was a Portugese New Christian whose so-called "semitic" ancestry during the limpieza period prevented him from becoming a Jesuit. In frustration he returned to Judaism and became a Jew and then a rabbi. He then argued that the New Christians were not really Jews and that only people such as he who were first truly devout Christians and were nevertheless unfairly suspected and punished, and exiled by virtue of fear of the Inquisition should be readmitted. The crypto-Jews who pretended to be Christians in order to retain their wealth and position and declined to flee those worldly advantages, he declared, should be regarded as Christians, told to give up their Judaism and when presenting themselves for readmission should be treated as Christians. Morteira and his followers did not appear fully logical and their position never prevailed halakhically. [15]

The fact was that during one period after 1507 the conversos previously barred from leaving Portugal in order that they not transfer their wealth, were allowed to leave and those remaining were granted commercial advantages and freedom from further Inquisition harassment. At that time many left, and many resumed Judaism in Italy and in the Ottoman lands. The majority, however, remained in Portugal to enjoy their new freedom from the Inquisition and quasi-citizenship on a par with so-called Old Christians. This new freedom ended in 1536 and a harrowing period of searching for and punishing crypto-Jews ensued. As some sought to leave, legislation was enacted to prevent them. The tragedy of these people occurred on a variety of levels and those, like Morteira, who refused to forgive them argued they could have left after 1507, or could have given up their wealth and fled even after 1536, and that if they did not do so they were not worthy of readmission to Judaism as Jews but should be treated as any Christian would be. [16] The argument was, in effect, that these seventeenth century returnees were often reentering Judaism for financial reasons, to ally themselves with the expanding and increasingly successful sefardic community in Holland. [17] This, however, left unanswered why they would not instead seek to join the Reformed Christian faith. This leads to my judgment that they still retained memories of their remote Judaic origins and were living in a tension between the past and the present. It varied with different generations and families and with external socio-economic and political events, as to when some chose to return to Judaism while others did not, and why others chose to do so at another time, or yet again others remained ensconced in their Christianity continuing to live in a no-man's land on the border of the two faiths.

The intense inner spiritual struggle that many of these conversos underwent is exhibited in the literature of the period, especially in poetry written by returnees and in personal journals written in Spanish and Portugese. They loved the pleasant life in Iberia and concealed their Judaic beliefs. But they feared there was no forgiveness before God for this dissimulation and worried profoundly that they would not enjoy salvation. One rabbi, Moses Rafael D'Aguilar was theologically reassuring when he wrote a responsum to the question whether conversos will inherit the world to come. D'Aguilar's position was that a person who believes in what we might today define as the values of Judaism but does not practice the observances is not excluded from God's redemptive love. D'Aguilar, in fact, saw the conversos as martyrs and enunciated the view that if a converso was burned by the Inquisition he had indeed died for kiddush hashem, the sanctification of the Name. That is, D'Aguilar was saying that even if one lives a Christian life but is put to death for being a Jew then indeed he died as a Jew and as a martyr, fully eligible for salvation. But there were others who came closer to Morteira's more limited reflections upon the status of Marranos, and like Mortiera they pronounced the more severe view that they were subject to God's judgment for sin and falsehood, and were not to be considered Jews. Isaac Aboab was one who assumed a centrist position, declaring that the theological maxim, "even if one sinned he remains a Jew" applied only to the period after divine punishment has purged him of his alienation from Judaism. Morteira, however, did not accept that view and argued that conversos who had not repented would suffer eternal punishment. [18]

It is also of some interest that returned Marranos not only sought to evangelize among others, but also expressed a theological view of history that saw the prolongation of Jewish exile and suffering to be the consequence of the existence of innumerable descendants of Jews outside of Judaism. Thus, it was argued by one, Ishac Orobio, that it was not the continued rejection of Jesus that causes God to neglect the welfare of Israel, but rather the ongoing absence of so many descendants of Jews from their true religious haven. He pointed to the convents in Spain and declared that there is not one without a Jew, and that priests, and even members of the Inquisition, were former Jews, and because so many Jews "have adopted the abominations and sacrileges of Christian idolatry and practice their profane rites," Jews will continue to suffer the hardships of God's judgment. [19]

This view of a zealous repentant does not correctly mirror the medieval view of Judaism which regarded Christianity as monotheistic and not constituting idolatry, as has been mentioned previously in these volumes. But it is possible to see this argument as the product of the zeal of one who wishes to save other souls from the fate from which he had himself only recently narrowly escaped: the fate of eternal damnation. It might in fact be this theology of history that explains Judaic suffering as a consequence of massive and repeated Judaic apostasy, rather than as a consequence of sinfulness within Judaism that soon impressed itself upon traditionalists. This explains the early modern rigor with which apostasy and mixed marriages were regarded. In effect those called "orthodox" in the nineteenth century would see in exogamy the spectre of increased apostasy, and in the continued proliferation of descendants of Jews living as Christians they would see the source of continued suffering. The suffering of Jews, from this point of view, would continue until every Jewish soul is brought back into the fold. This is an earlier theological version of the inherent danger of exogamy to the future of Israel, which has been replaced in current times by the sociological argument that the physical survival of the Jewish community is at peril. It might also be suggested that the great influx of Marranos into Judaism during the seventeenth century helped set the stage for the Sabbatian debacle, for this massive repentance was seen as a sign of messianic advent.

The Marrano influx gave rise to a polarity in Judaism at that time. On the one hand a certain degree of penitence and religious piety swept the returnees. But on the other hand there arose among them a proto-modern approach to Judaism which has been stigmatized as "heresy." One of the major havens of Marrano migration was Amsterdam after 1579 when the Treaty of Utrecht prohibited religious persecution, and especially after 1581 when Holland declared its independence from Spain. [20] It was therefore at Amsterdam that we find this interplay of pietism and heresy most vivid. One of the most vigorous critics of traditions was Uriel da Costa who was among a group of university educated conversos who found rabbinic Judaism as then practiced unacceptable. This school of thought confronted as unacceptable also the defenses of a person such as the aforementioned Orobio who had studied Catholic theology at Alcala and later, in response to the dissent of a da Costa, applied his strict faith in revelation to Judaism. Orobio argued, "Of what importance is it that this or that limitation appears to be inappropriate to our understanding? Of what significance is it that the prohibition to eat dairy products and poultry together is incomprehensible to us? . . . Whoever loves the Torah . . . does not seek reasons . . . " He saw rabbinism as God's "means for hundreds of years to interpret His Torah." [21] But the school of thought represented by Uriel da Costa rejected this rabbinic authority all through the seventeenth century and without doubt became the prototypes who presented a strong argument for the reforming tendencies of the next century. Orobio, on the other hand represents the reaction to reformation in his denial of the right or merit to dissent and the advocacy of uniform observance of ritual and all its minutiae.

The odyssey of Uriel da Costa is of interest for what it mirrors of a later generation. Although the reforming generation of the late eighteenth century was not coming out of a Christian past, its immersion in a Christian society was a parallel condition, and their arguments paralleled da Costa's even when they were not directly dependent upon him. Da Costa lost faith in salvation by the rites and dogmas of the Catholic church, and turned back to what he knew to be his primary heritage, the Old Testament. Returning to Judaism in Hamburg he was soon disillusioned with extant rabbinic Judaism and in a Martin Luther-like fashion he published eleven theses against rabbinism. In these theses he denied scriptural validity for tefilin (phylacteries), mezuzah (capsule containing Deut. 6:4-9 attached to doorpost), the particulars of circumcision, the second diaspora day of the festivals, and many other ritual practices. Ultimately da Costa rejected any form of revealed religion in favor of rationalism. In 1618 Venetian rabbis issued a ban against heretics. The motive was to silence them in their evangelism and alienate them from the rest of the Jewish community. They had stated in the proclamation of the ban that if the heretics had spread their views " . . . only in their dwellings and only among themselves, we should have held our peace . . . " [22] Eventually the rabbinic opposition escalated from a verbal ban to physical or economic punishment when possible, and ultimately to the venom expressed by one rabbi who wrote that whoever mocks the words of the sages is culpable for the death penalty and "who is quickest to kill him is meritorious . . . " That this proliferation of so-called "heresy" was not deemed a light matter is to be deduced from all of the major figures such as Aboab, Modena, Simone Luzzatto, Menasseh b. Israel, da Silva, Saul Morteira, and others, who participated in energetic efforts to refute it. [23]

Withal, it would be an exaggeration to blame or to credit the Marrano infiltration with the interesting transformation that began to take place in Holland as it had in Italy, and also at Hamburg, and then England. Other factors were involved, most especially the new European enlightenment, the revolution in the natural sciences and philosophy, and the development of a trend toward the establishment of nation states in western Europe in which the base of political participation was increasingly broadened.

III. Amsterdam

By 1564 it was hyperbolically reckoned that "countless" Jews lived in Antwerp, the leading city of the southern Spanish Catholic Netherlands. They were said to be frequenting synagogues and observing circumcision and other rituals openly. This implied that either the Inquisition was no longer active there, possibly weakened by the spread of Calvinism in Antwerp from the northern areas, or that at least some of these many people practicing Judaism openly were Jews and not Marranos. Although the north, Holland, declared its independence from Spain in 1581, it was not until 1648 that Spain recognized its independence, and effected the separation between the Protestant north and Catholic south, which later became the nation of Belgium. After Antwerp was subdued by the Spanish in 1585 many crypto-Jews fled to Amsterdam. Those who remained in the Catholic south continued as Marranos until as late as 1792 when the Napoleonic armies occupied Belgium.

Holland, the independent Protestant north became the leading mercantile nation in the world, and Amsterdam the leading financial center. Jews flocked here, and were received as a valuable financial and trading resource. Marranos were able here to come out of the closet and practice their Judaism openly. This was not immediate, nor welcome to everyone. At times it took the competition offered by provincial cities like Haarlem and Rotterdam, and even the gracious invitation to the Portugese Jews from Christian IV of Denmark to settle in Glückstadt and elsewhere in Danish domains, to inspire the goodwill of Amsterdam's municipal authorities. Even in progressive Calvinist and enlightened Holland there were still many who were under the influence of such a pejorative remark as even an Erasmus was capable of uttering in his encomium to France, that "France alone is not infected by heretics, Bohemian schismatics, Jews or half-Jewish Marranos." Arminians or Remonstrants, and their opponents, the Counter-Remonstrants were all negative toward Jewish immigration. [25] It must also be realized that Protestant Holland might justly suspect that some of the semi-Catholic Spanish and Portugese Jews still harbored loyalty to Holland's major enemy. Thus, it was largely the secular leaders motivated by economic and political interests who welcomed the Jews, beginning with William of Orange, known as "the Silent," the first leader of the Dutch revolt from Spain (1574-1584). It was during his rule that the Treaty of Utrecht was signed in 1579 uniting the northern provinces against Spain, and guaranteeing that there would be no religious persecution in the new nation. [26]

The first Jewish settlers in Amsterdam were probably Portugese Jewish merchants who were active on the trade routes running from Holland to Portugal. Such settlements by Portugese merchants took place at other important cities prominent along vital trade routes between 1585 and 1610, such as Hamburg, London and Rouen. The first synagogue established in Amsterdam was apparently founded in 1597, and the first rabbi to serve there was Joseph Pardo of Venice. This resulted in the traditions of Venice becoming the pattern of Amsterdam Judaism, and explains why it was to the rabbis of Venice that the Amsterdam rabbis turned for help against da Costa and other heretics. Most of the Jewish residents of Amsterdam for a long time were Portugese Jews, or Marranos, or people born in Antwerp and descended from them, probably a few from Spain, France and Venice. This again helps explain why Amsterdam was so great a center of so-called "heresy" and spawned a figure as notable for his dissent as Barukh Spinoza. But it also explains why it was there that pietistic opposition to heresy was at its strongest. [27]

One of the people highly instrumental in 1615 in regularizing Judaic rights in Amsterdam was the person who became a leading scholar of international law, a Christian scholar of Judaism, Hugo Grotius (1583-1645). Grotius presented a memorandum with forty-nine articles. He expressed the conviction that non-Jews would benefit in their knowledge of Hebrew and Judaica if Jews resided in their midst. He thought Jews should not see Christians as adversaries, and advocated that the Dutch Reformed Church should show hospitality to all aliens; arguing that expulsion of any group should take place only on the basis of what they did in violation of law, but not for who they were. He saw the Jews as being a special case, unlike other unbelievers, for they were of the stock of Abraham, Isaac and Jacob, the elect people, as Paul taught, " . . . of whom is the adoption and the glory and the covenants, and the Torah and the worship and the promises" (Rom. 9:4-5). It was from them, Grotius emphasized with Paul, that Jesus came, and the apostles and the earliest Christian teachers. Thus, theology played a major role in Grotius' arguments, perhaps more than either politics or economics. He argued that although Jewish hatred for Christians is deplorable it will be dissipated once Christians no longer subject them to harsh treatment as they have during the Middle Ages. Grotius believed Jews ought to have the right to live in Amsterdam. He pointed out that once that premise is accepted, there remain three options: a) they must adopt Christianity; b) be allowed to practice no religion; c) be permitted to freely practice Judaism. Grotius rejected the first two as immoral and, therefore, urged the toleration of Judaism in Amsterdam. [28]

But Grotius was still encumbered by certain notions that influenced other medieval scholars as we saw earlier, even those who were positive in their attitudes to Judaism. Among other provisions he suggested Jews be requested to listen to Christian sermons, forbidden to circumcise Christians, persuaded to baptism, and be barred from marriage or sexual relations with Christians. But he opposed any form of segregation of Jews, and in harmony with what was already practiced in Haarlem he eschewed the wearing of the yellow badge or any special garb for identity. [29] If Grotius had not brought Amsterdam quite as far as the general legislation of Haarlem, he was probably influenced by it and by the liberal provisions offered by Rotterdam and Alkmaar, which all acted before Amsterdam. Haarlem, for instance, allowed Jews to hire live-in Christian servants as long as they did not seek to teach them Judaism or have sexual relations. Jews were not to blaspheme Jesus or in any way evince disdain for Christianity, were to keep their places of business closed on Sundays and other Christian fast and prayer days, but were not to be disturbed on their Sabbath. The Christian Hebraist Joseph Scaliger hailed these arrangements as conducive to Jewish immigration, and looked forward to finding among such immigrants a tutor in rabbinic literature. And the fact that the Haarlem proposals were found among Grotius' early manuscript of his memorandum for Amsterdam indicates that he was aware of them and used them. [30]

There was inevitable graduation toward true equal citizenship. Ultimately the Dutch government declared in 1657 that Dutch Jews were citizens, and that foreign countries had to treat them no differently from Christian citizens. This unprecedented development can in some measure be attributed to Grotius. In general, however, while Grotius helped pave the way for a great Jewish community to evolve in Amsterdam, sometimes referred to by historians hyperbolically as the "Dutch Jerusalem," he by no means had attained the level of John Locke in England half-a-century later in what he contemplated as toleration of Judaism. Nevertheless, it appears to some historians that while Grotius was privately inclined to the full equality of Jews as citizens of Amsterdam he was prudent in attempting not to go too far and thereby endanger their status by a reaction on the part of their opponents. For example, in 1619, one such opponent urged that interfaith sexual relations should be specifically forbidden by law, and that Jewish representatives were to take an oath guaranteeing observance of the law. An important contribution made by Grotius was that his approach was no longer based upon deciding Jewish rights on the basis of corporate group status, but rather to deal with individuals, and on the whole the Amsterdam city council imposed and enforced few restrictions upon Jews. That Jews could claim individuality is evident from the fact that they were even able to appeal over the heads of the leaders of the Jewish community to the civic authorities in cases where they regarded their religious rights were infringed upon unduly. This was especially the case when rabbis used the ban too freely, denying some Jews the right to worship in the synagogue. [31]

As Holland liberated itself from the Inquisition and Marranos could become Jews again openly without fearing arrest and death for heresy, an irony developed. The now-returned Marranos still used Spanish and Portugese as their official languages. But in other ways too they maintained their previous Catholic heritage. They had learned their lessons well on how to control the religion of a community. Now as they took command of synagogues and developed a formal Judaic community the parnasim or officers of the congregation wielded near-autocratic power. They even attempted an inquisitorial system, and a precensorship of books. There was, nevertheless, great intellectual ferment and the proliferation of Judaic studies. Very early on Jewish education in Amsterdam included secular subjects, and it was first in the Talmud Torah that rabbis such as Saul Morteira, Issac Aboab, Menasseh ben Israel and David Pardo prepared the earliest candidates for the rabbinate. These studies were conducted in the Etz Hayim academy of higher Judaic learning which produced men who were adept at halakhah, just as was later done in the yeshibah established there. These institutions soon produced native rabbis of whom Menasseh ben Israel had been among the first. Menasseh later established the first Hebrew printing press in Amsterdam in 1627 and thenceforth Amsterdam displaced Venice as the leading center of Judaic publishing. [32]

The effort to censor thinkers, purify thought and erase heresy, rife in both the recent Catholic establishment of the Index, and in various branches of Protestantism, as seen earlier, was carried over into Jewish Amsterdam by the erstwhile Marranos. In cases where rabbis could argue that communal members bordered upon heresy the civic authorities did not interfere with their use of the ban. It was this "orthodox" mentality that led them to try to dissuade Spinoza from publishing his ideas, and to impose upon him a thirty-day excommunication. When this did not move Spinoza the community declared a permanent excommunication upon him as a person, and banned all his writings from being read by a Jew. [33]

Upon the development of the Spanish-Portugese community of Amsterdam there also came an influx of German Jews, and after the Chmielnicki massacres of 1648-49 there came a flood of Polish Jews. Soon these àshkenazi Jews outnumbered the sefardim. Both the sefardim, only recently liberated from their strange Marrano existence, and the àshkenazim, refugees from the Thirty Years' War and Chmielnicki, were ready for the miracle of redemption, were mystically attuned to its proximity, and were swept up in the Sabbatian movement in the next decade or two. Amsterdam's major rabbis, Isaac Aboab da Fonseca and Raphael Moses D'Aguilar were carried away with Sabbatian enthusiasm in 1666, and the leaders of the Amsterdam Jewish community wrote a letter to Shabtai Zvi assuring him of their discipleship. Books were published that included on their title pages the good news of "the year of the Messiah." [34]

The intellectual, social-economic and even political opportunities offered by the ascendancy of Amsterdam in the world community attracted intellectuals. Among these came R. Jacob b. Aaron Sasportas (1610-1698), of Algeria, who later spent a decade in London, a number of years in Hamburg and Leghorn, and finally ended his life with almost two more decades in Amsterdam. Here too came Joseph Solomon Delmedigo, referred to in the previous chapter, who was suspected of heterodoxy because of his **Sefer Elim** written to the Karaite. But Amsterdam's variegated Judaic ambience also influenced non-Jews, among them a number of Christian scholars of Judaica such as Joseph Scaliger, referred to earlier, a subject still inadequately researched. This ambience also attracted artists. Rembrandt van Rijn is only the best known and most widely studied for his portraits of rabbis, "The Jewish Bride" and other themes. But while art historians have given much time to Rembrandt there were others who had a strong interest in Jewish themes. The significance of this artistic concern with Jews is in its highlighting the extraordinary integration of Amsterdam's Jews into the general social ambience of the seventeenth century, and their extensive relations with Christians on a basis hitherto unprecedented in northern Europe. [35]

Christian scholars were compelled in this society to take a new look at the type of work done by Menasseh ben Israel. For example, his book, **Conciliador**, expounding upon and reconciling contradictions in the Old Testament was criticized at the University of Leiden because of Menasseh's interpretation of certain passages taken by Christian theologians to refer to Jesus. But nevertheless the University provided for a course to teach the subject matter albeit the intent was to teach how to refute Judaic theologians. The University of Utrecht even more so became a center of criticism of Judaism. But even this controversial posture required study of the material and led to greater research into Judaica in both Holland and England, and via England to North America. [36]

Amsterdam emerged between 1600-1670 as a prototype of a modern western Judaic community. It would be exaggeration to say that Jews were fully equal citizens. They did not share in the political life of the city, but except for this they were treated under the law as Christians. Their educational endeavors were of the humanistic variety, their scholars had ongoing relationships with Christians, their lifestyle was acculturated, they travelled abroad and were influential in international trading and financial circles. Menasseh ben Israel was probably exceptional as a rabbi, but he certainly prefigured the modern rabbi and embodied all the acculturated traits already seen in a Farissol or a Modena. Furthermore, Amsterdam had a strong influence upon Hamburg and Menasseh upon England, and thus out of Amsterdam flowed the juices that lubricated the Judaic reformation and the acculturated Anglo Judaism. [37]

Withal, it should not be overlooked that religious life was long controlled by sefardic rabbis of Spanish-Portugese background. These people had a tendency to marry within their own families and to perpetuate communal power among themselves. At most they married among other Spanish-Portugese families and retained power within these circles. Some scholars regard this endogomous practice as having almost been an obsession with them. It was derived from the strong Catholic emphasis upon limpieza. This sixteenth century tendency to value so-called "pure blood" or a "purebred" stock in marriage was brought into Judaism by the erstwhile Marranos who were influenced by the Catholic policy of seeking undiluted "Old Christian" background before promoting a person within the church or state. [38] Consequently there was little mingling between the åshkenazim and sefardim, and the cultural advancement of sefardic Jews led them to a supercilious attitude of superiority over åshkenazim of German and Polish background. This separation continued everywhere, including North America, well into the twentieth century although there is some evidence of its coming to an end in western lands.

IV. Barukh Spinoza (1632-1677) [39]

A. Prefatory Comments

Some might question the inclusion of Barukh (Benedict) Spinoza in a survey of Judaism. But just as the early Christian teachers, emerging from their Judaic matrix were important for inclusion in Volume I in order to fully adumbrate interaction, parallels, and correlations between Judaism and Christianity, so too is it relevant to examine Spinoza at least cursorily. Whatever one's judgment will be on the question of including Spinoza in the pantheon of Judaic thought as has been to a small degree done with Philo, it is clear from an objective study of Spinoza's writings that he foreshadowed the modern Jew in more ways than a Farissol or a Delmedigo.

Although Spinoza was not a figure in Jewish philosophy per se he has been studied by Jewish philosophers and students of philosophy regularly in modern times, and has had an impact not only upon general European thought but also upon all modernist Judaic thought. Had he lived one century later he would have escaped the banishment imposed by his excommunication and would indeed have held an honored position in non-orthodox Judaic intellectual circles as have many other Judaic thinkers who did not believe in the doctrines of Judaism in the forms in which they had been articulated through the middle ages, and no longer practiced the rituals or observed the Sabbath and holy days in even a modified form.

B. Biographical Note

Barukh Spinoza was born into a former Spanish or Portugese Marrano family in Amsterdam where he studied under R. Saul Morteira at the Talmud Torah, and under R. Menasseh ben Israel. Spinoza early became drawn to broader intellectual vistas than were available to him in his Jewish education, and studied Latin in order to enter into the literature of the time. He was only twenty-four years old when his views on angels, the corporeality of God, and the immortality of the soul impelled the communal leaders to offer him the choice between a lifetime annuity of 1,000 florins to remain silent and to live outwardly in accordance with halakhah, or to face excommunication. We do not have a full picture of Spinoza's "heresy" in 1656 as the case file against him has not survived. But it appears that secular leaders, rather than the rabbis, were more concerned about the danger he constituted for the tranquility of the community in a Calvinist environment. Spinoza chose excommunication and demonstrated his alienation by altering his name to Benedict, the Latin for Barukh, "blessed." He left Amsterdam and lived in various rural areas until he settled in The Hague in 1677, where he died. As a lens polisher Spinoza earned a modest living and led a very austere, ascetic existence. [40]

Spinoza only published one book during his lifetime under his own name, and this was not one of the great works for which he earned historic fame. It was a book on Descartes. His famous **Tractatus Theologico-Politicus** was published in 1670 while he was alive, but only under the initials B.S. This was out of fear that its views would be proscribed by ecclesiastical and civic authorities who were regularly considering which books had to be prevented from publication or banned after publication. Spinoza's **Theologico-Politicus** was banned before publication and his views were protested by both church and state in Holland and England, and by Jews as well. His books were placed on the Catholic Index when they were posthumously published and were still there in 1948. [41]

Spinoza's independent religious position brought much calumny upon him throughout his life. The root of the problem was that his view of God led to the misconception of him as an atheist, and in that period of history an atheist was regarded in all branches of Judaism and Christianity as stepbrother to Satan. But after his death, the world moved into the modern era of freer thought, and conciliation with religious pluralism. Intellectual and scientific methodology applied, for example, to biblical studies led to conclusions similar to those of Spinoza. Within one hundred years of his death he was elevated to front rank by both gentiles and Jews as a saintly philosopher. He was brought back into the mainstream of European thought, and simultaneously to the attention of Jews in 1785 by the publication of an exposition of Spinoza along with a collection of letters written to Moses Mendelssohn. Nevertheless the time has not yet come when Spinoza has been admitted into the pantheon of Judaic thinkers. But in the light of the directions taken by modern Judaism Spinoza should be seen as a prototype of the naturalist believer and the advocate of a humanistic ethic unrelated to the symbolism of ritual. As distant as such a position is from the theologico-halakhic traditions that prevailed roughly from 70-1900, there has been no schism that has read such views out of Judaism. [42]

C. Aspects of Spinoza's Philosophy

This survey does not call for a comprehensive examination of Spinoza's philosophy. For one thing it is of a highly technical nature, and for another, especially the **Ethics** belongs more properly in a study of general philosophy. What concerns us here is limited to several highlights of his thought as they relate to his Judaic posture, his Christian thought, and the interaction between himself and others resulting from those views. What is emphasized here are those aspects of Spinoza's thought which clearly set him apart as a proto-modern Judaic thinker despite his own successful effort to transcend both Judaism and Christianity in his private life.

Spinoza labored under the impact of the new science, and under the new philosophy of René Descartes. He believed that nature operates in accordance with eternal laws, and since the human is part of nature he and she are bound by such immutable laws. But Spinoza was also extensively learned in medieval Jewish philosophy. The work of the medieval Judaic philosophers discussed in Volume II of this series, however, was directed at rationalizing and validating Judaism in terms of Greek or Arabic philosophy as the case might have been, or in altogether rejecting that pattern as did Yehudah Halevi. Spinoza had no interest in this process, but he had imbibed much from men like Crescas and Maimonides and used their systems in his own way. He believed that the natural powers of reason innate to all human beings are the sources of revelation, and that the conception of divine revelation as presented in scripture and rationalized by his Jewish and Christian predecessors was gratuitous. He asserted that to think in terms of the supernatural character of prophecy is beyond reason as much as to believe in miracles. Both prophecy and miracle as presented in scripture were for him impossible. God, he argued, does not reveal behavior patterns for humans to obey or disobey. Rather, for Spinoza what comes from God is reason and truth whereby a human understands which deeds are socially useful and good and which are socially evil. Thus, all of Spinoza's premises implied that there was no specific divine revelation of ethics and no possibility of the miraculous, the very heart of the Judaeo-Christian tradition. [43]

The God-idea propounded by Spinoza was undoubtedly the greatest stumbling block to his acceptance. This is not the place for an in-depth discussion of the Judaeo-Christian God concept and how Spinoza ran afoul of it. It must suffice only to indicate that Spinoza held that God is identical with the universe, God is what we call "nature," if by "nature" we understand all that exists both physical and non-physical, all moved by immutable laws having no external regulator or intelligence similar to the biblical God who stands outside His creation and outside of history. God, for Spinoza, as for Aristotle and Maimonides, was a causal principle, but Spinoza conceived this idea somewhat differently. God was not the first cause from which all other existence proceeded, but was rather a unifying principle of all laws of existence. These laws operate continuously and immutably. This did away with the concept of human free will as decisively as it eliminated the possibility of revelation and miracles. This was in consonance with the predestination and determinism of Calvinism even if out of tune with Roman Catholicism and Judaism. Thus, it would not be this negation of free will that would imperil Spinoza in Calvinist Amsterdam. But the rejection of revelation and miracles and the denial of a personal God who transcends, governs and shapes creation and human history would decisively alienate Spinoza in Amsterdam.

Spinoza maintained that the human state of blessedness or salvation does not require God's grace, but is attainable by human endeavor, specifically through liberating oneself from bondage to emotions. [45] For Spinoza reason was at the heart of the matter. It enabled the human to organize his life, to understand his capabilities and the ends which are possible for him to attain, and then to move in that direction. Like Socrates, Spinoza saw the inherent importance of humans knowing themselves. Spinoza's determinism did not imply that a human is a blind instrument of external forces. It only meant that each human is subject to the inexorable laws of nature. But it included the notion that as one discovers one's own nature one is capable of becoming intelligent, and gaining awareness of one's capability. One is then capable of harmonizing the conflicts one confronts in order to live a rational and virtuous life. [46]

For those to whom Spinoza's philosophy was too complex, and even enigmatic, his critique of the Bible was something that astonished them. Even if they were unable to follow his reasoning and understand his evidence, they were aware that he was exposing its defects. He was the first of major modern biblical critics who rejected Mosaic authorship of the Pentateuch and argued that many of the other books were not written by those to whom the books were attributed. But Spinoza went even further and argued that in reality the scriptural works before us are the highest attainment possible to the masses. They require folk belief or superstition because they have not attained the knowledge of God. Scripture, therefore, Spinoza believed was the product of popular religion, and although its ethical imperative is the highest attainable by the masses and therefore is an intrinsically valuable work the true philosopher or person who has attained knowledge of God stands beyond it. In consequence of this reasoning he maintained, as did some of the more radical Renaissance thinkers noted earlier, that mysteries and miracles, rites and incantations of liturgy, are all superstition rather than religion, and that superstition has its roots in fear. The rational, saved or blessed person knows that adverse events in nature are natural and are not portents of God's wrath. Thus, like many Renaissance predecessors and like many of the recently returned Marranos such as Uriel da Costa and his circle, with whose views Spinoza was most certainly familiar, he opposed the observance of ceremonial and rite. It was this rational, non-observant life-style that first brought him to the attention of Jewish communal leaders and led ultimately to his excommunication. From his belief that God was the sum-total of nature followed the conclusion that there was no supernatural realm and no transcendant supernatural being to whom the human must give obeisance. But Spinoza was not really a pantheist who argued that God is in all things. For Spinoza "Whatever is, is in God, and without God nothing can be, or be conceived." [47] This is more of what in current terminology is formulated as "panentheism."

Spinoza argued that the Judaic ceremonial practices were designed only for the order and tranquility of the Israelite-Judean kingdoms and were not applicable once the kingdoms were lost. Although he denied the rational possibility of revelation in the biblical sense, he turned to Isaiah and to Psalms as one of the earliest modern critics to argue that the ancient canonical preachers whom we call the prophets were opposed to the ceremonial rites, and taught that the will of God or the eternal divine and immutable law required only that humans live in virtue in order to establish and maintain a well-regulated society, or the state of blessedness. Spinoza cited Is. 1:16-17 " . . . cease to do evil, learn to do well; seek justice, relieve the oppressed . . . " as the climax of the prophetic assault upon the hypocrisy and corruption of the time (Is. 1:10-17). In the psalmist's words at Ps. 40:7-9 he found that God did not require cultic rites for human salvation: "Sacrifice and offering you did not desire . . . the whole-burnt offering and sin offering you did not request . . . " (Ps. 40:7). [48]

Spinoza was evenhanded. Just as he taught that Judaic ceremonial and cultic rite were primarily means to keep society regulated in obedience and conformity, so too were the Christian rites such as baptism, the Lord's Supper and the holy days and prayers. He doubted that these rites were instituted by Christ or his apostles, and postulated the idea that they were created by the early church as external signs for the member. Neither the Jewish nor the Christian rites, Spinoza argued, had any inherent sanctity nor were either of them significant for salvation. Although he had a high view of Christ as embodying universal wisdom and for promising spiritual reward as over the temporal reward of the Mosaic Torah, he argued that Christianity defended its cause by miracles and therefore turned a faith into superstition. [49]

There was considerable correspondence on these matters between Henry Oldenburg and Spinoza. [50] It appears that Oldenburg, a German theologian who travelled much on the continent met Spinoza in 1661. Following his assumption of the office of secretary of the prestigious Royal Society he inaugurated correspondence with all types of thinkers all over the continent. As has been noted by others in those days letters were like dissertations and functioned like scholarly journals do today. In this way Spinoza was also brought into wide-ranging contact with many philosophers and scholars. [51] As a believing Christian Oldenburg was seeking clarification from Spinoza on those matters which affect Christianity as fully as Judaism. Thus Spinoza regarded miracles and ignorance as synonymous, and if miracles were a sign of ignorance and superstition where does that leave Christian mystery in relation to Jesus both as it affects the incarnation and the resurrection? It is clear that Spinoza's philosophy of religion could not sit well in a believing Christian society. Although Spinoza wrote his **Theologico-Politicus** in an ambiguous way as if he were defending scripture against Jewish and Christian distortion his articulation of a critique of the Bible was clearly evident, and in this light it is understandable, even if not condonable, that the Jewish community ostracized him in order that they not bear him as an albatross. It also appears quite possible that Oldenburg, especially in his later years under the conservative Christian influence of Robert Boyle, the great scientist, hoped to convert Spinoza. [52]

It is likely that not all of Oldenburg's letters are preserved, and therefore difficult to ascertain whether he directly challenged Spinoza to become a Christian as Mendelssohn was later to be challenged. But we find that others certainly wrote Spinoza in this vein. A certain Albert Burgh, for example, a Calvinist who converted to Roman Catholicism after a period of addiction to the new science and philosophy, wrote him in 1675 that he ought to acknowledge his "most evil heresy, recover from the perversion of your nature, and be reconciled with the Church." [53] Burgh reflected a rather widespread impression of Spinoza. He lauded him as having "a mind adorned by God with brilliant gifts, and a lover of truth" but led astray by Satan. He deplored the fact that Spinoza had staked his eternal salvation on a chimerical philosophy, and the manner in which he had treated and rejected scripture as the word of God in his **Theologico-Politicus.** Burgh undoubtedly misunderstood Spinoza's acceptance of the historical fact of Christ's crucifixion, and therefore challenged him on the basis of "if you believe in Christ crucified." But Spinoza did not accept the christology anymore than he affirmed the revelation of Moses. Much of Burgh's letter is full of personal reviling vituperation against Spinoza to whom he refers, for example, as "wretched little man, vile worm of the earth . . . " guilty of "unspeakable blasphemy." He demands of Spinoza, "On what foundation does your bold, mad, pitiable and execrable arrogance rest?" We receive here the flavor of the alienation suffered by Spinoza. How prevalent such letters were is not the question, but the consciousness that Spinoza had that he was regarded as a heretic, an atheist, a perverted thinker and follower of Satan, could not have been other than disturbing. And yet in the twentieth century and even in the nineteenth century Spinoza would have been a highly respectable theologian, perhaps even, if he so chose, a theistic-humanist clergyperson in some branch of Judaism or Christianity.

Spinoza responded to this letter in a way that betrays some emotion. He asserted his belief "that holiness of life is not peculiar to the Roman Church" and called attention to all the just people among the Lutherans, Reformers, Mennonites and others. But he returned the vituperation in kind, calling Burgh insane, a brainless bewitched youth. Here Spinoza also reflected his bitterness over his excommunication. In responding to Burgh's arguments that the Catholic Church must be the true Church desired by God for it goes back to antiquity, possesses the word of God, has grown and prospered through uninterrupted succession of leadership, he referred to him as singing "the same old song of the Pharisees." Here Spinoza referred euphemistically to the Jews, pointing out that the "Pharisees" also claim antiquity, uninterrupted succession, survival by miracle against all vicissitudes, and growth, stability and solidity "in spite of the hostility of the heathen and the Christians . . . They declare with one voice that they have received their traditions from God Himself, and that they alone preserve the written and unwritten word of God . . . The miracles which they relate are enough to weary a thousand gossips." [54]

Spinoza argued both theologically and ethically in a way that was calculated to alienate him from both Judaic and Christian believers. He rejected theological and ethical principles taken for granted as religious virtues in Judaism and Christianity. Thus, he maintained, for example, in his **Ethics** that neither humility nor repentance were virtues. He said humility does not arise from reason, but is rather the product of the human's "contemplation of his own infirmities." Similarly he posited the idea that repentance does not arise from reason, but rather is the function of wretchedness brought on by the inability to live the virtuous life of reason. Nevertheless, Spinoza continued, it is better to live with humility and to practice repentance, as the prophets and saints urged, because people generally do not live under reason, and humility and repentance will therefore do more good than harm. [55]

Spinoza's appreciation of Jesus went far beyond that of any Jew previously. He wrote in Philonic terms that Wisdom is the Son of God, and this manifested itself in Jesus. But at the same time he was careful to add that this same " . . . Eternal Son of God . . . Eternal Wisdom of God . . . has manifested itself in all things and especially in the human mind . . . " He considered the Christian doctrine of incarnation and said that ideas related to the doctrine that God took upon himself human nature, "seem to me no less absurd than would a statement that a circle had taken upon itself the nature of a square." Nevertheless, in another letter, although he took the affirmation of the resurrection of Jesus in a spiritual sense he did concede that "God had specially manifested himself in Christ" and cited the Gospel of John as illustrating his view, that "the Word was made flesh." [56] That Spinoza was not subject to a confusion in his view of Jesus is clear from another letter in which he articulated his belief that the passion, death and burial of Jesus is to be taken literally. There Spinoza was clear. Jesus of Nazareth was a human figure and his fate as depicted in the gospels was to be taken as a historical event. But he continued to argue that the idea of the resurrection was spiritual, and that he understood it allegorically. [57]

Despite the excommunication Spinoza was apparently in correspondence with Isaac (Ishac) Orobio, referred to earlier, unless the name of the addressee should be Ostens. [58] Orobio or Ostens had received a vigorous critique of Spinoza's **Theologico-Politicus** and sent it on to Spinoza. Spinoza wrote him in 1671. [59] The critic accused Spinoza of atheism and of having cast off all religion. Spinoza pointed out that no atheist would argue as he does that the main objective of life is to acknowledge that the highest good is God, and to love him with a free mind is the greatest of virtues. Spinoza implied that the critic did not distinguish between religion and superstition, and argued that far from rejecting the need for commandments he believed that commandments are necessary, but should be observed neither out of fear of punishment nor out of expectation of reward. In the case of the latter, Spinoza indicated that when we seek reward for virtue it is not God we love but the object of our desire. [60]

Spinoza was not a humanist as that term is understood today, for he believed in, and used the term God. He was not what in current terminology would be considered a practicing Jew, and he was at no time a Christian. The closest Spinoza came to formal religion after his excommunication from Judaism was his association with a dissenting Calvinist movement called Collegiants who held private prayer-meetings and had no clergy, very similar to certain elements of Quakers. But actually there is no evidence that Spinoza did anything more with them than participate in a philosophy reading circle. In this group, at any rate, Spinoza enjoyed not only the company of highly intellectual people, but a group whose religion was more universalistic and unencumbered by the dogmatics that alienated Spinoza from both Judaism and Christianity.

In his religious perceptions Spinoza was a proto-modern Jew who had cast off the traditional theological doctrines related to supernatural religious thought as well as the ritualism. Such Jews are today legion, associated with the various Judaic religious denominations, even sometimes with the orthodox out of loyalty to the family heritage. But during the seventeenth century Spinoza was unique. His influence upon eighteenth century thinkers such as Moses Mendelssohn and twentieth century thinkers such as Mordecai M. Kaplan to name only two persons who have had a major impact upon contemporary Judaism has yet to be studied in depth. At a time when Leibnitz was becoming a leading philosophical force Moses Mendelssohn labored at bringing Spinoza back into the mainstream of philosophical credibility. He did this by seeking to relate Leibnitz to Spinoza, and was at work on this as early as the 1750's. In the 1770's he urged aspiring students of philosophy to study Spinoza and other thinkers despite their being considered Irrlehrer, "teachers of error." This is not to say that Mendelssohn agreed in all things with Spinoza. It is merely to draw attention to the fact that in a very real way Spinoza stands in the vanguard of modern Judaism. [62]

Spinoza was caught in a difficult situation in his day. As neither Jew nor Christian living in a Calvinist society at a time where Puritan England was emphasizing a Mosaic Commonwealth, Spinoza had to be circumspect. There is reason to believe, however, that he wrote his **Theologico-Politicus** with its critical evaluation of Moses and the ancient Israelite kingdom as a contribution to the debate over freedom of conscience, thought, and speech that were opposed to many conservative theologians and undermined by the encroachment of what Spinoza referred to in a letter as "the excessive authority and impudence of the preachers." [63]

Although he did not regard Muhammad with the same appreciation as he had for Jesus, Spinoza did believe in universal salvation for all, even as he specified, "Turks [Muslims] and other Gentiles, if they worship God by the exercise of justice and charity towards their neighbour . . . " [64] He apparently did not consider a reformed Judaism as any more attractive than a reformed Christianity and remained to the end of his life simply a Spinozist. Yet he reflected deeply upon the continued existence of Jews, and even after the Sabbatian fiasco he did not doubt the possibility that God might one day again elect Israel to function as a nation. All things, he argued, are possible "amid the changes to which human affairs are so liable . . . " and they might " . . . raise up their empire anew . . . " [65] It is possible for modern secularist Jewish thinkers to see in Spinoza a harbinger of their school of thought: that in the obsolescence of Judaism there remains the option of Jewish nationalism revived, and a society to be predicated upon cultural and ethical values devoid of the theological and cultic aspects of a formal religious faith.

Nevertheless, while Spinoza superficially appears to have lived without a formal religion after his excommunication it is also clear that he affirmed many of the doctrines of Judaism even if he had reconstructed them. He believed in a naturalist conception of God. He believed in creation in that he argued that all things that exist and all reality, had to have a cause and that God is the immediate cause of all things. As Spinoza phrased it, "whatsoever is conditioned to exist and act, has been thus conditioned by God." [66] He affirmed that God elected Israel, although like modern thinkers he also believed that God elects other people for their various purposes, "election" being the necessary process of nature which leads people to a particular pattern. Similarly his view of revelation did not coincide with the traditional doctrine, but Spinoza did believe that God stamped divine laws upon nature. In terms of human behavior Spinoza believed the individual acts out of reason and does not consciously follow a revealed precept, but love of virtue was part of the divine law. He also believed in a theory of immortality, although early in life he echoed Uriel da Costa and shocked his rabbinic mentors by arguing that nefesh in the Bible refers only to "life" or a living creature, and that there is no passage in scripture that teaches of an immortal soul separate from the body. What Spinoza ultimately clarified was that the mind is immortal: "the human mind cannot absolutely be destroyed with the body but there remains something which is eternal." The mind, he wrote, is "part of the infinite intellect of God." While he did not believe in a messianic figure he saw the possibility of a messianic age in which human reason has gained collective salvation. [67]

This is not to say that Spinoza, in his time, was unfairly treated when he was excommunicated, or that his theological constructs should be acceptable to traditional Judaism as it existed in seventeenth century Amsterdam. It is only to suggest that had Spinoza lived one hundred and fifty years later his fate would have been different. There are other scholars today who relate Spinoza's thought to medieval Jewish philosophy in which Spinoza was steeped, and another school which adjudges him a fullsome heretic with no saving virtue to be identified as a Jewish philosopher. [68] In any event it is difficult to reconstruct a certain picture of the odyssey of Barukh Spinoza from precocious rabbinical student to heretical outcast. It has been suggested that the immediate cause of Spinoza's rethinking his theology was an encounter with Isaac La Peyrère, a pioneer biblical critic who rejected Mosaic authorship of the Pentateuch, believed there were other branches of the human family before Adam, and that the Messiah was soon to come. [69] La Peyrère was active in Holland and Belgium in 1655-56, and Menasseh ben Israel, Spinoza's teacher, wrote a refutation of his ideas in 1656. [70] It can be conjectured, but no proof exists, that Spinoza met La Peyrère at that time. It seems surprising to some that if Spinoza had been influenced by La Peyrère that he did not adopt the latter's messianism which he predicated upon the divine role to be played by the French king. But while Spinoza might have given it some thought he could have set it aside in his writings which came after the Sabbatian disaster, and in any case might not have found that the messianic idea conformed to his religion of reason. It has been found that Spinoza's library contained both La Peyrère's work **The Prae-Adamitae**, and that of R. Menasseh. [71] It is a coincidence, but should not be surprising that Spinoza was excommunicated in 1656, while Menasseh ben Israel was out of Amsterdam. This forever leaves open the question whether the far more liberal and sophisticated R. Menasseh might not have held back Morteira and others from their drastic action.

On the one hand one might eschew any effort to "defend" Spinoza as a Jew and look upon him more productively as the rare person who transcended both Judaism and Christianity and pointed the way to universal religion. He went beyond the idea of dual covenant theology to the rarer atmosphere of no-covenant humanism. [72] But this is not to say Spinoza sought the overthrow of religion. He saw it as a valid and valuable instrument to help people to the rational salvation he espoused. [73] Nevertheless, in his very attempt to transcend the two religions Spinoza was caught in an insoluble dilemma. Although he accepted the historic Christian critique of Judaism and exalted Jesus above Moses, Christianity was appalled by his naturalistic deity and alienated by his rejection of incarnation and resurrection. As far as admitting him into the Judaic pantheon is concerned, a careful analysis of where Spinozism stands from a truly Judaic perspective has led to a manifold and harsh indictment drawn up by the modern Jewish philosopher Hermann Cohen. [74] Spinoza was accused of having taken the side of Christianity against Judaism, of considering Judaism carnal and particularistic, and Christianity spiritual and univeralistic, of relegating the Mosaic Torah to the service of the tribal interests of ancient Israel with no universal import, and of implying that in essence Judaism was a doctrine for one political state, the product entirely of human invention, despite his espousing the universalism of the prophetic teachings. But it cannot be overlooked that Spinoza's thought has been integrated into Judaism since the nineteenth century whether Spinoza has been given credit or not. As one philosopher has stated it, " . . . Modern Judaism is a synthesis between rabbinical Judaism and Spinoza." [75] One cannot overlook the reality that Spinoza's most vigorous critique of rabbinic Judaism of his time was directed at what is still Judaic orthodoxy, but that in his time he had no way of doing it within Judaism. He was essentially in variegated ways the first truly modern Jew in a more direct way than a Farissol, Modena or Delmedigo. Even his preference for aspects of Christianity could be asserted in the modern Judaic milieu without incurring the penalty of excommunication. It is non-Zionism alone which today leads to a milder form of ostracism, but no theological posture would be rejected as un-Jewish except among those same elements of what is today called orthodoxy, and which indeed was the object of Spinoza's critique.

In sum, Spinoza was the product of many forces. He received what was a seventeenth century Amsterdam orthodox Judaic education and lifestyle at home. Like many young rabbinical students who can testify to similar phenomena in their own lives in the twentieth century he encountered contrasting lifestyles and intellectual challenges both within and outside of Judaism. From rabbis of the time like Menasseh ben Israel he could be drawn to broader interests, to Latin, world literature and Christian writings. From his contemporaries, like his own family, returned Marranos, as exemplified by Uriel da Costa he could derive strong objections to ritualism and the general orientation of post-biblical Judaism. From his philosophical rationalism he might have drawn his opposition to revealed religion, and even from the pillar of today's "orthodoxy," Maimonides, he was able to derive his earliest critique of the traditional God-idea that was so encumbered with anthropomorphism. Recoiling from the excesses of Calvinism and Puritanism which exalted the law of Moses he might naturally denigrate the Mosaic contribution to human thought, and conscious of what both state control of religion had done to himself, and that in his case the doctrine that was kept pure by his expulsion was rabbinic Judaism, he tarred that with the brush of Pharisaism. If Spinoza was not a "Jewish" thinker in the seventeenth century, and even if his overall religious perspectives are still too radical for the twentieth century, one thing is nevertheless clear: in the twentieth century along with naturalists and humanists he would have stated his case within the Jewish community, would not have been excommunicated, and would have lived and died a Jew.

IV. Rabbi Menasseh ben Israel (1604-1657)

A. Prefatory Comments

R. Menasseh ben Israel was a quintessential seventeenth century Dutchman of Portugese extraction who saw himself as a Jew by faith. He looked upon Portugese as his mother tongue and himself as a Lisbonian. He never quite articulated such a philosophy, but it is clear from a letter he wrote, his acculturated tendencies to orient himself to the non-Jewish community, and his efforts to translate Hebraic materials into the Spanish and Portugese vernacular of the erstwhile Marrano community as well as to write in Latin. He served his entire career in Amsterdam and therefore belongs in this chapter as a major expression of the Dutch experience. But Menasseh also contributed importantly to the evolution of Anglo-Judaism and will, therefore, once again appear as a theme in the next chapter. Here I will briefly examine the man and his work and the intellectual-historical elements that led ultimately to his mission to England. [76]

B. The Man and His Work

R. Menasseh ben Israel was one of the most celebrated of all the significant figures that loomed on the Amsterdam horizon during the seventeenth century. He produced many scholarly and apologetic works in Spanish, not all of which have survived. It is doubly surprising to consider the importance of this man as a seventeenth century rabbi when one remembers that for over a century before his birth his family had been professing Christians in Portugal, since the massive compulsory conversion in 1497 referred to above. [77]

Menasseh's father, Joseph Dias, moved to Spain in 1580, was there arrested and tortured by the Inquisition on suspicion of being a judaizer, and finally left the country for the Portugese Madeira Islands where Menasseh was born in 1604. He was baptized at birth as Manuel Dias Soeiro (the last name being that of the godparents, the custom then being to adopt a surname other than the paternal line). From the Madeiras the family moved to France, and on to Holland. There all the males were circumcised and Manuel was renamed Menasseh, his father Joseph emulating the biblical Joseph's having named his son in that manner because, as he said, "God has made me forget my suffering" (Gen. 41:51). [78]

There were several important influences in Menasseh's early life including a scholar from Fez, a certain Isaac Uziel who was both a good talmudist and a vigorous moral purist. He also possessed knowledge of mathematics, poetry and grammar. [79] If the description of Judaic education in Amsterdam when Menasseh was a grown man is any indication of the system when he was a youngster or adolescent, he underwent very intensive training. Most especially in the upper grades they studied halakhah, talmud, grammar, and commentaries. They used the classical halakhic digests of Maimonides and Jacob ben Asher. Study hours were generally from eight to eleven in the morning, and from two to five in the afternoon. At home, especially when school was not in session, the students received additional private instruction in writing Spanish and Hebrew, and other secular subjects "each according to the parent's desire." [80] This is not as rigorous as what we noticed occurred in Italian yeshibot that were modelled after the Polish and older German academies. This in itself is evidence for the more acculturated pattern allowed in Amsterdam in order to provide time and energy for broader participation in the life around them.

Menasseh also came under the influence of Rabbi Saul Morteira who had studied under Leone da Modena in Venice and came to Amsterdam in 1616, and for half-a-century was a major influence there. He was Menasseh's teacher, later his colleague, and even survived him. [81] Menasseh was precocious and was a classmate of many older than himself, becoming a popular public speaker in Portugese by fifteen and writing a Hebrew grammar at seventeen. He began to teach children at that age, and with all these assets he soon emerged as the first major native rabbi to serve Amsterdam and begin the process of reducing reliance upon foreign rabbis. [82]

Menasseh ben Israel was a broad scholar if not a profound one, and a significant proto-modern personality who influenced the course of modern Judaism. There is no surviving teshubah (responsum) to indicate in what way he affected halakhah or theological presuppositions, but his important writings were studied in the eighteenth century, and these had their impact. This was certainly the case with Moses Mendelssohn who had read Menasseh early in life and then re-read him later in life and was moved to translate Menasseh's famous **Vindiciae Judaeorum (Judaism Vindicated)** into German. [83] As Moses Mendelssohn, scion of the ghetto, astonished people with his attainments in Germanic language and culture, so too Menasseh ben Israel appeared to be a prodigy to a Silesian visitor who had never before met a westernized Jew who could speak, write and publish in Latin. [84] Thus, purely aside from whatever influences the example of his life or his writings might have had on Mendelssohn, Menasseh ben Israel was already a pre-Mendelssohnian, westernized, acculturated proto-modern. And like Farissol, Modena, Delmedigo and others of their ilk, Menasseh must be given the appropriate credit for the transformation of inward-oriented medieval Judaism to outward-reaching contemporary Judaism.

Menasseh's interest was largely centered in the Bible although he studied and taught the Talmud, was proficient in mystical literature and philosophy, and extensively learned in many languages. He showed familiarity with the church fathers, Greek and Latin classics, Philo, and medical knowledge. [85] It was as a preacher, teacher and public leader, however, that he excelled. From 1626 he devoted himself to the publishing business in order to supplement his meager rabbinical earnings. He produced an index to the Midrash Rabbah in 1628, and established his reputation among scholars in 1632 with **Conciliador (Reconciler)**, which was soon translated into Latin. In this book Menasseh collected 180 discrepancies in the Pentateuch and reconciled them all. This process of harmonization of patent contradictions in Scripture is still a matter of great concern to biblical literalists, and in his day his work led Menasseh to his relationships with non-Jewish scholars. These relationships set in motion an entirely new direction in his life. [86]

Around 1640 Menasseh went through a period of conflict with the Jewish community when he was relegated to a subordinate position to that of his colleague Isaac Aboab who was a profounder talmudic scholar. In his frustration he planned to devote more time to trade and to settle in Pernambuco in Brazil where a growing Jewish community of Dutch and Marrano Jews flourished. From an exchange of letters between two of Menasseh's gentile friends, Gerhard Johann Vos and the jurist Hugo Grotius it appears they regretted Menasseh's plans, and Grotius even expressed surprise that the wealthy Jews of Amsterdam cannot arrange to make it possible for Menasseh to stay. As things turned out in 1642 Isaac Aboab was invited to become rabbi at Recife, Brazil, the first rabbi in the Americas, and Menasseh succeeded Aboab in Amsterdam. Two years later he became the head of a yeshibah established by Abraham and Isaac Pereria, two returned Marranos. [87]

As the fifth decade of the seventeenth century progressed, R. Menasseh ben Israel increasingly enjoyed a leading reputation as the representative Judaic scholar. His correspondence with gentile scholars was voluminous, and royal personages welcomed dedications of his books in their names. He was universally known and admired from Brazil to Sweden, and in almost every important center of culture in Europe. Delmedigo's Karaite friend, Zerah, reported having seen one of Menasseh's Latin writings in Vilna, and having a section of it translated into Polish. This inspired him to write this unusual rabbi in Amsterdam. [88] Menasseh virtually became the quintessential prototype of one form of modern rabbi: interpreter of Judaism to the non-Jewish society, participant in public affairs, congregational minister and sometimes, part-time academic.

Menasseh's role in the famous episode involving the returned Marrano Uriel da Costa is not clear. It has to be assumed that as a rabbi of a synagogue in Amsterdam Menasseh was an opponent of da Costa's views. But, on the other hand, since Menasseh had his own problems in 1640 when da Costa was being readmitted to the community after excommunication, the Ḥakham da Costa alluded to as having been instrumental in the harsh conditions imposed upon him could very well have been Morteira who was also later the rabbinical figure instrumental in banning Spinoza while Menasseh was in England. [89]

Like Renaissance Italian scholar-rabbis Menasseh ben Israel was involved as rabbi, teacher, and preacher, in interchange with gentile scholars, as a publisher, and sometimes involved in commercial trade. Withal he found time and energy to author a great flow of literary output and conduct his widespread correspondence. The Karaite Zeraḥ, as noted, wrote Menasseh among other reasons to request that he write for him a digest of the works of Philo, and to arrange the publication of Karaite works in Amsterdam. [90] For the most part Menasseh wrote his books in Spanish, Portugese and Latin, dedicated his works to non-Jews, and oriented them largely to the gentile reader. One historian has described some of his work as "anthological" in which he assembled a great array of sources that shed light on a theme. Yet, whatever differences there may be over Menasseh's originality and profundity as a scholar he has not always been given adequate recognition. His writings exhibit massive knowledge and extensive research in an endless array of works in an assortment of languages. In addition to the major works soon to be referred to Menasseh annotated what was by seventeenth century standards a critical edition of the Mishnah, published careful editions of the Bible, translated the prayerbook into Spanish and edited a collection of halakhah on shehitah (ritual slaughter) in Spanish. He also produced a large number of other works, some unpublished, including a concordance to the midrash and a bibliography of rabbinic literature. He refuted Isaac de la Peyrère's pre-Adamite work discussed earlier, wrote on Roman Catholicism and a number of other subjects, and translated a number of classical works into Spanish or Hebrew. Menasseh wrote on Josephus and projected a continuation of the latter's history down to his own time. [91]

Menasseh evidenced familiarity with the church fathers and medieval Christian theologians such as Albertus Magnus and Duns Scotus not to speak of Thomas Aquinas, with classical poets such as Vergil (Virgil) aside from Judaic philosophers, halakhists and commentators. This was forcefully evinced in his **Conciliador** of which three further volumes on the Former Prophets, Later Prophets and Writings followed the first volume on the Pentateuch in 1641, 1650 and 1651, respectively. But as universal as was Menasseh's erudition and his relationships, his biblical views were still constrained by a traditionalist literalism and, therefore, while the work might still be of value to fundamentalists it would hardly suit a modern Bible critic. [92]

It is perhaps of some interest, but nowhere commented upon, that Spinoza might have been aware of and influenced by Menasseh's accumulation of biblical discrepancies during his student days. In addition, Spinoza undoubtedly read his work on the Pentateuch and was his student when he published the next three volumes. It would be a matter of some irony if R. Menasseh, who reconciled all contradictions he gathered, left only the impression of contradiction with Spinoza who found the harmonizations unsound or unpersuasive, thus leading to Spinoza's becoming the first truly modern biblical critic, and thus, in turn, ultimately having partial influence upon his excommunication. Christian scholars were also impressed by the fact that **Conciliador** was free from any denigration of Christianity. This more open attitude of Menasseh to Christians was practiced also by dissenters and Karaites. This is seen, for example, in the fact that in 1643 when the Venetian rabbis banned a Karaite prayerbook Menasseh published a Karaite work in Amsterdam. [93]

Following the first volume of **Conciliador** Menasseh wrote a work on Creation (**De Creatione Problemata XXX; Thirty Problems on Creation**), and soon after one on resurrection (**De Resurrectione Mortuorum; On the Resurrection of the Dead**). The first was written to expound the Judaic anti-Aristotelian point of view upholding creation ex-nihilo (creation from nothing), and the latter was composed in order to refute one of the major tenets of the da Costa Marrano circle. It is undoubtedly the second part of the work which purports to discuss the method of resurrection unrelated to its christological connections that led to the book being placed on the Catholic Index in 1656 [94] After these works Menasseh published **De Termino Vitae (The Span of Life),** to deal with a problem that had been taken up by a number of Christian thinkers who later invited Menasseh to share his views on the question whether the span of human life is accidental or predetermined by a higher power. R. Menasseh's view was that the life span is not predetermined but rather depends upon one's bodily constitution, and environmental conditions. Like all these writings since **Conciliador** these works further established Menasseh as a leading Judaic authority among gentile scholars. He was widely read and enthusiastically approved. In this vein he also wrote **Of Human Frailty and the Impulse of Man to Sin** in which he opposed the Christian doctrine of original sin. He conceded, however, that the human is frail and is born with an impulse to sin. [95]

Within the Jewish community of returned Marranos there was a long-felt need for a halakhic digest in Portugese.

Menasseh supplied this with his **Thesouro dos Dinim (Treasury of Laws)**, which was published in two parts in 1645 and 1647. This reflected the versatility of Menasseh's intellectual interests. But soon after that his older son, Joseph, died and Menasseh fell to brooding over the question of immortality and resurrection anew. He then wrote a supplement to his previous Latin philosophical works on resurrection and sin, this time in Hebrew, entitled **Nishmat Ḥayyim (The Breath of Life)**. [96] In this work Menasseh expounded the view that the Judaic doctrine that the human is created in the image of God means that the human soul is endowed with divine properties, and that it can reenter its divine matrix through contemplation and piety. An interesting facet of this work, however, is that Menasseh here proved himself again typical of Italian Renaissance Judaic scholars. He revealed, on the one hand, a propensity for sound rational scholarship buttressed with many arguments and citations from the literature, and on the other hand, espoused a belief in demons and angels and the transmigration of souls, not to speak of placing a great amount of importance upon dreams. The surprise, however, need not be so great if we recall that Menasseh was a friend of Delmedigo, had a high regard for him and had read and published his works as he had read other Italian Renaissance works. So too later Moses Mendelssohn read both the Renaissance writers as well as Menasseh and Spinoza. [97]

In sum it might be said that if Menasseh did not make major original contributions to scholarship his wide-ranging scholarship and its uniqueness in its time allowed him at least to play the role of "apostle to the gentiles" as one historian who did not admire his scholarship has conceded. His work had extensive ramifications, and because of its encyclopedic nature, translation and composition in the vernacular, and palatable orientation acceptable to gentile scholars, it contributed to setting the stage for modern Judaic scholarship. [98]

If Menasseh ben Israel was an "apostle to the gentiles" he also had an interesting coterie of Judaic associates in Amsterdam, mostly former Marranos, and many of them, physicians. One of these, Ephraim Bueno (Bonus), was an intimate of Rembrandt Harmenzoon von Rijn. Bueno probably played a role not only in Rembrandt's interest in the Jewish community at Amsterdam and was a factor in the close relationship between Rembrandt and Menasseh, he was also the subject of the celebrated painting "The Jewish Doctor." The Jewish portraits Rembrandt painted constituted a high ratio of the total number of portraits he executed, and, in addition it has been estimated that he painted twenty pictures in the Jewish neighborhood of Amsterdam. Included in all these is the famous portrait of Menasseh which Rembrandt etched in 1636, and of which the original oil is no longer available. Rembrandt also supplied illustrations for one of Menasseh's last works. [99] Although his relationship with Rembrandt might have been sparked by a friend in his Jewish circle of associates, it was Menasseh's Christian friends and colleagues, however, who played the more important role in the ultimate direction of his life. He was appreciated and admired by them, and among them he had a ready audience full of curiosity about Judaism. Some might have taken the view of a professor of medicine at Leiden who held that Menasseh's only deficiency was his religion, and of another, the great theologian Gerhard Vos, who expressed it differently, but was candid to say, "I, for my part (and I would say this of few, not only of that sect, but of any other), consider him a man of true worth, albeit he lives in darkness," but all were in agreement that he was the quintessential seventeenth century Judaic scholar from whom much is to be learned despite his religious "darkness." [100] In his **Vindiciae Judaeorum**, written in England near the end of his life, Menasseh wrote that, "I have held friendship with many great men, and the wisest, and the most eminent of all Europe . . . " Some of these people came to hear him preach, others visited with him whenever they were in Amsterdam, but all of them maintained regular correspondence with him exchanging scientific letters with him that were often little less than treatises. How many of these would have hoped to witness his conversion to Christianity is difficult to ascertain. [101]

Among Menasseh's foremost admirers was the great jurist Hugo Grotius who maintained a regular correspondence with him through Gerhard Vos as intermediary. He met him through Vos, and when Grotius served as Swedish ambassador to Paris, he wrote to Vos that Menasseh was much read in Paris, and to Menasseh he wrote in 1639 that all lovers of learning would be grateful if he devoted himself to "unravelling the obscurities of the Law." [102] Other Christian friends of Menasseh were theologians, among them Simon Episcopius, formulator of the doctrine that goes by the name of "Arminianism" named for Jacobus Arminius who presented the Remonstrance in 1610 to which reference was made earlier. The Remonstrants of Menasseh's time advocated toleration of all religions and an end to persecution as a way to win people to a point of view. Similarly, Socinians who denied the trinity, were interested in Menasseh, but so were mainline Church people including Jesuits and Calvinists and English Puritans as will be seen later. [103] Possibly the greatest of Menasseh's Christian admirers was Johann Buxtorf the younger (1599-1664) who regarded Menasseh as the leading Judaic scholar of the time. [104] Mystics too were in communication with Menasseh, sometimes because of their interest in the second coming. One of these was Abraham von Frankenburg, a disciple of the mystic Jacob Boehme who believed that the true light would come from the Jews. Frankenburg and Menasseh had an intimate correspondence for years. Frankenburg also had a close relationship with a leader of a mystical group that expected the Jews soon to return to Palestine. Another messianist with whom Menasseh was in communication was Isaac de la Peyrère, mentioned previously, a virtual proto-Zionist who believed Jews would return to restore their nationhood in Palestine under the aegis of the French king before being converted to Christianity, and that subsequent to this all would be converted and Christianity would gain universal supremacy. [105]

By far the most interesting Christian friend and admirer, however, was Anna Maria von Schurman of Utrecht, a woman savant even more versatile than Menasseh in languages, erudite in kabalistic and rabbinic learning, and modern literature; she composed poetry and music and conducted a Hebrew correspondence with other women Hebraists. She was apparently friendly enough with Menasseh to have received as a gift from him an autographed copy of David Kimḥi's Hebrew grammar. Another woman with whom Menasseh had a prolonged relationship, in her case hoping for her patronage, which was satisfied only minimally, was Queen Christina of Sweden. [106]

C. Prelude to Menasseh's English Venture

English converts to Judaism lived in Amsterdam. These were exiles who took their enthusiastic Puritan devotion to the Old Testament most seriously. It is to be assumed that Menasseh had contact with these, and it is also known that he corresponded with English scholars, a fact of which he had himself written. His name and writings were referred to in English works. Thus, Menasseh's celebrity in England and his connection with the country went back to the turn of the decade, 1640, if not earlier. Otherwise it would have been unlikely that the Queen of England would have visited his synagogue in 1642. [107]

This connection, however, was considerably escalated in September, 1644, when a certain Antonio de Montezinos (Aaron Levi de Montezinos) returned to Amsterdam from South America where he told of a journey he took in what is now Ecuador. There, he claimed, he encountered a tribe deep in the interior beyond the great Cordillera mountains and a broad river, and discovered this tribe to be of the ancient Israelite tribe of Reuben, with the tribe of Joseph, according to them living on an island in the sea not too distant. We are told that his hosts recited the shemá (Deut. 6:4) for him in Hebrew to offer evidence of their origin. They asked Montezinos to send them twelve bearded men to teach them the art of Hebrew writing in order that they be able to reconnect themselves with all their traditional sources and with the Jewish people. They also assured him they were soon to emerge and to overcome all enemies, implying the messianic age was approaching. From his Indian guide, Francisco, Montezinos learned that this strange medley of alleged Israelites had established itself in that region as the result of many miraculous events, were badly treated by the Indians, but that supernatural miracles saved them. Subsequently, whenever the Indians tried to attack them, the Indians were defeated and ultimately their holy men became convinced that this mysterious tribe must be in possession of the true God and true religion, and that one day it will emerge to conquer the world. [108]

This incredible story told with manifold elaboration was accepted with naive credulity in Amsterdam where Montezinos offered an affidavit before R. Menasseh ben Israel for the truth of his account. As soon as this story spread over Europe, questions began to pour in upon Menasseh concerning the so-called "Lost Ten Tribes" of Israel. The legends concerning the fate of the northern kingdom of Israel after its defeat by Assyria were legion. Based upon the alleged evidence of scripture it was believed that it was entirely deported into the Assyrian hinterland whence it wandered to various countries. In consequence it has from time to time been identified as living isolated in Asia beyond the Sambatyon River, or as the inhabitants of various places on earth. These have been identified with the Falashas of Ethiopia, the Nestorians of Mesopotamia and the Afghans. Anglo-Saxons have at times claimed the honor, and the tribes have at different times been identified as segments of China, Japan and North and South American Indians. [109]

Biblical evidence offers no warrant for the mysterious disappearance of the erstwhile tribes of Israel. The canonical preachers, Ezekiel and Hosea, for example, at opposite ends of the chronological scale were aware of their continued existence, and saw them as quite nearby, known, and identifiable, ready to be reunited with Judahites. None of the canonical preachers intimated that these people were "lost," mysteriously concealed or would emerge only at the end of time. It is only logical to infer that the deported Israelites were also absorbed as were all other segments of Assyria by the Babylonian Empire, and when Judeans were deported by the Babylonians, Israelites and Judeans constituted two types of communities in Babylonia just as later Samaritans and Judeans did in Alexandria. Some of them probably went up with Zerubabel and might have objected to allowing Samaritans to assume the status of Israel since they had been intermingled with other tribes of Assyria. Rabbinic literature certainly reflects both in the name of R. Akiba and anonymously under the rubric aberim ("others") that the tribes were not "lost" but exiled, the latter specifically saying Lev. 26:38 "you shall be 'lost' does not mean literally 'lost.'" [110] In sum, many Israelites were joined together with Judeans both in Palestine and the diaspora, many others were mingled with Samaritans, and later in history many were assimilated into the spreading Christian, Islamic and Karaite movements. Yet the legend persisted that they existed somewhere as a "lost" entity, one day to be discovered, or to emerge, and to take on the conquering messianic mission. This legend, unhistorical, and unbiblical, was believed by large segments of Jews and Christians alike, and now surfaced as a fascinating harbinger of seventeenth century messianism.

Thomas Thorowgood, a friend of John Durie (Dury, 1596-1680) chaplain at The Hague, wrote a book called **Jews in America** in 1648. In it he tried to prove that the lost ten tribes were the Indians encountered in New England. He expounded on what he believed were similarities in customs, language and traditions. Thorowgood's theory was discussed and rejected by Sir Hamon L'Estrange in 1652. But Thorowgood had sent his book to John Durie in Amsterdam, who now recalled the South American phantasies of Montezinos and wrote to Menasseh ben Israel for more information. Menasseh sent him a copy of Montezinos' affidavit, and in this way his story became an appendix in Thorowgood's book in 1650. At the same time Menasseh entered into a correspondence with an English millenarian Nathaniel Holmes who believed the messianic advent was imminent and attempted to convert Menasseh. All of this influenced Menasseh to connect the Montezinos legend with the messianic age, arguing that if the dispersal of Israel would come to an end with the advent of the Messiah, and the lost ten tribes had surfaced in South America, then perhaps his millenarian Christian friends were correct that the messianic age is about to dawn. [111]

This led to Menasseh's Latin work in 1650 **Spes Israelis (The Hope of Israel).** This treatise propounded the theory that Israelites discovered America, having crossed the Bering Strait between Siberia and Alaska which was then still a landbridge between North America and Asia. The treatise fully expounded the question of the ten tribes and their expected emergence as that related to the messianic advent. Menasseh postulated that the tribes had been dispersed to Tartary and China, and from thence had gone on to America. They were followed by the Tartars who conquered and decimated them, only a remnant being left in the Cordilleras. Menasseh denied that the Indians were Israelites and argued that any similarities between Indian and Israelite culture and religion were the result of the conquerors adopting these from the conquered Israelites. He further argued that just as prophetic pronouncement of judgment and suffering had been fulfilled so is the time of prophetic hope about to dawn. He could point to the expulsion from Spain and most especially to ongoing persecution by the Inquisition and the Chmielnicki massacres as a prelude to hope. [112]

The book was written for the Englishman Dury and dedicated to the new Puritan government in London to whom Menasseh appealed for goodwill to worldwide Jewry. It was translated into Spanish, and soon into English by the Puritan scholar and publicist Moses Wall who rather produced a paraphrase than an exact translation from the Latin. It later appeared in twenty-six editions in six languages, diffused more widely than any contemporary Judaic writing, even having reposed in the library of, and presumably read by Benedict Spinoza. The crux of the book is in the dedication in which he envisioned the empathy of Puritanism for Israel, and he offered to travel to England to facilitate the great pre-messianic reconciliation. In effect, Menasseh saw English millenarianism and the Puritan Revolution as opportunities to link the consummation of the dispersal of Israel to resettlement in England, and understood that constitutionally there can be no guilt and no obligation upon the Puritan Parliament for the expulsion of the Jews perpetrated by Edward I in 1290. [113] A spate of messianic lost ten tribes literature in book and pamphlet form followed. This brought Menasseh into more contact with or to the notice of important Englishmen and served him well on the mission he soon undertook. The argument naturally went both ways, and a book called **Americans No Jews** also appeared.

Meanwhile the messianic ferment had been running hotly in France as well, as has been noted earlier relative to Isaac La Peyrère. But if the French messianists dreamed that the French king would do the Lord's work so too the Portugese dreamed that King Joas IV of Portugal (1640-1656) would lead the Jews back to the Holy Land. A Portugese Jesuit Antonio Vieira, confessor to the King met Menasseh in Amsterdam in 1647 and offered him such a proposition. The wealthy Portugese Jews in Holland were to help Portugal purchase back the areas Holland conquered from her in Brazil, in return for which the Portugese Jews or New Christians would be allowed to return to Portugal free of any recriminations from the Inquisition. The Portugese King would go on to conquer the Holy Land for the Jews and establish the "fifth monarchy" the one-thousand year messianic kingdom. These messianists believed in a two-messiah theory in which a Jewish national Messiah would arise along with Jesus' return, and the two entities would create the new so-called "Third Church." [114]

It was in this atmosphere that Menasseh began to make his plans to travel to England; he received a passport and welcomed the English ambassador to the synagogue with music and hymns. [115] It was with this rigorous call for the reinstitution of free domicile of Jews in England that Menasseh ben Israel became the proto-modern advocate of Jewish political liberty on a continent which had for so many centuries locked the Jew out of the body politic. Over one hundred years before the movement for Judaic emancipation in France and two centuries before the stirring struggle of Gabriel Riesser in Germany this Dutch rabbi fired the first salvos in Puritan England. It is to this chapter in the spread and evolution of modern Judaism that we now turn.

Chapter Six

JUDAISM RESTORED TO ENGLAND [1]

I. Introductory Comments

The English Reformation began with Henry VIII's marriage problems. He effected the separation of England from papal supremacy and reconstructed the religious institutions of England. His work was continued and escalated by his successor, Edward VI (1547-1553). After the interlude of the even shorter reign of Tudor Queen Mary, 1553-1558, also known to history as "Bloody Mary" for her thousands of executions of Protestants, heretics and dissenters, the work of Henry's Reformation was resumed and reached its peak under Queen Elizabeth I (1558-1603). [2] Erasmus was a major influence through his **Novum Testamentum.** Edward VI issued his **Injunctions** in 1547 consisting of a program of teachings to be carried out in the churches, and one of these was the required reading of Erasmus' **Paraphrases.** His **Enchiridion** had also been translated in 1533 and was widely used. [3]

The Elizabethan age, therefore, was already well-conditioned for humanism and classical propensities which came through in the writings of its foremost literary figure William Shakespeare (1564-1616). [4] It is not appropriate to consider him as either a Roman Catholic or a Puritan. He appears to have been born after the Catholic tide subsided and died before the Puritan flood engulfed the land. Shakespeare was a neutralist, akin to the earlier Erasmus. [5] Thus, he favored the use of epithets for God such as "heaven," or "eternal powers;" he rarely used the term "providence" in describing human destiny, although it does surface with a humanist tinge, for example in **Twelfth Night** in the line "Fate, show thy force . . . " and yet, while he used the term "fate" there is no real fatalism in Shakespeare's weltannschauung. There is, however, a decided ambivalence in Shakespeare when Brutus can put off "providence" in **Julius Caesar,** while in **Hamlet** he counterposed this with "there's a divinity that shapes our ends," and when he wrote, "In the great hand of God I stand" in **Macbeth.** Shakespeare was a theist, but the great Christian drama of salvation: the fall of Adam, incarnation, crucifixion, resurrection, and sacraments plays no role in his prolific literary compositions. And this, despite the fact that Elizabethan England was a time when all the doctrines and the sacraments were constantly before the public eye, enmeshed in ongoing religious strife. [6]

Basically, what was happening in the aftermath of the Renaissance was a religious tension in which, for example, in England at the end of the sixteenth century people were not merely Roman or Anglican, or even Puritan. There was an intelligentsia which questioned the veracity of the holy scripture, denied bodily resurrection, doubted creation ex-nihilo, immortality, and a real heaven and hell. [7] Beyond this many dissenters were becoming Judaic-like Sabbatarians and quasi-Jews. But even when religious enthusiasts did not go that far the intellectuals were obviously attracted to the denial of doctrines similar to those denied by the so-called Marrano "heretics" in Amsterdam. This reinforces the historical reality that long before the eighteenth century Judaic reformation, as a product of its time, Judaism was beset by the same religious tensions as affected Christianity. This was to be no less true in England than in Italy and Holland. In England, for example, Christopher Marlowe (1564-1593) never wrote of an afterlife, but reflected human free will. In **The Massacre of Paris** he attacked the murderers of Huguenots, in **The Jew of Malta** he had the Jewish character argue that the Jews were just as certain as the Christians that they had the ultimate truth. This attack upon the Roman Catholic Church along with negation of Calvinist predestination as well as the willingness to juxtapose the Jew and the Christian to the discredit of the Christian as Shakespeare did in **The Merchant of Venice**, all point to at least two things. First, the religious tensions within Christianity were leading to more humanistic thought, and second, a new and more open attitude to Jews was developing. Far from Shakespeare having been what some have called "anti-semitic," Shakespeare evinced empathy and understanding for the Jew. He cloaked his views in ambiguity, but this was typical of Renaissance writers, as noted earlier, and even of such daring philosophers as Spinoza. [8] Because Shakespeare has become controversial in some Judaic circles, a few comments are in order here.

II. A Shakespearean Digression

In the **Merchant of Venice** Shakespeare did not merely portray a vengeful Jew and the greed and contempt that went with the degradation of character in pursuit of the money-lending profession. He also portrayed Christians who enjoyed their Jew-baiting, and when Shakespeare reached the climax of the play, as one scholar has put it, Shylock became "the only one who has any dignity or depth of feeling." This play, in fact, has been seen as a turning-point for Shakespeare in which he began to exhibit empathy and compassion for all types of people. One critic has aptly put it that "The Jew fired Shakespeare's imagination and roused his sympathy as he wrote . . . " [9]

There has long been much debate over whether Shakespeare could have known any Jews. By implication those who deny him this opportunity on the basis of the expulsion of Jews from England in 1290, infer that Shakespeare misrepresented Jews, and simply drew on medieval anti-Jewish sentiment. Even one astute historian did a double-take within one paragraph when he wrote that Shakespeare created Shylock to be a villain but was overcome by sympathy and turned him into a human being. It is my suggestion that Shakespeare never intended to portray Shylock as a villain. He intended from the beginning to show that the Jewish money-lender was misunderstood. It should be recalled that, as indicated in Chapter Four above, sometimes Jews themselves, especially certain rabbis pronounced harsh judgment on money-lenders because in fact the unfortunate ethical aspects of a money-lender's career portrayed by Shakespeare were a reality. Whether Shakespeare ever met an actual person after whom Shylock is modelled cannot be determined, but that he had met Jews and possibly conversed with them and read about them and their religion in the light of Jewish-Christian mingling during that Renaissance aftermath, and especially Marrano mingling in London, is quite possible. Much speculation has been engaged in over whether Shakespeare visited Italy during the great plague of 1592-94 when the government prohibited all assemblies, including theatre within a seven-mile radius of London. This hypothesis places Shakespeare in Ferrara, Venice and Verona, in all of which places Shakespeare might have met Jews, and incidentally explains his knowledge of Italian culture reflected in several of his plays written after this period. [10] But it is not crucial that this be the case. For considering all the information now available for the relationship between Marranos and London and Bristol between 1550 and 1600 there need be no further discussion of whether Shakespeare could have known Jews. The absence of any direct autobiographical or biographical evidence for his association with Marranos or Jews is far from decisive. What is more significant is that during his lifetime they were subjects of discussion in London, grew in numbers, and were prominent in ruling circles. [11] One Elizabethan historian has aptly remarked that although Shakespeare's inner imagination was a dynamic creative force, this force operated within a real environment. Interestingly enough for our theme this historian concluded " . . . to no play are these observations more applicable than to **The Merchant of Venice.**" [12] It must be remembered that this play was written shortly after the celebrated trial of

Dr. Roderigo Lopez, the Queen's Jewish physician, who was unfortunately enmeshed in high-level political intrigue, and was executed in 1594. [13] The trial brought to the fore a number of plays which alluded to Lopez and contributed to the revival of Marlowe's **The Jew of Malta** which enjoyed a long run. Shakespeare probably then put himself to the task of writing **The Merchant of Venice.** As others have noted the truly most dynamic and dominating character in the play is Shylock, and not the love story which as one critic has said, "Shakespeare could turn out with his left hand at any time, but the character of Shylock and the disquieting thoughts he gives rise to" is what is memorable. [14] Few of Shakespeare's lines evoke the Renaissance spirit of humanist sympathy for the disadvantaged condition of oppressed groups as Shylock's speech:

> . . . hath not a Jew eyes? hath not a Jew hands, organs, dimensions, senses, affections, passions? fed with the same food, hurt with the same weapons, subject to the same diseases, healed by the same means, warmed and cooled by the same winter and summer as a Christian is? If you prick us do we not bleed? if you tickle us do we not laugh? if you poison us, do we not die? and if you wrong us, shall we not revenge? If we are like you in the rest, we will resemble you in that. . . The villainy you teach me I will execute . . . " [15]

It needs to be recalled that Queen Elizabeth did not believe the charges against Dr. Lopez. The latter was defended by the Queen's confidante Sir Robert Cecil, and in presenting the portrait of Shylock as misjudged and unfairly condemned Shakespeare might have reflected the Queen's sentiments toward Lopez. It might even have served as a stimulant to the emerging sentiment for allowing open residence for the Jews. Furthermore, it should also be borne in mind that those viewing **The Merchant** would not be misled to believe that Shylock's bond to take a pound of flesh from his debtor would be some kind of uniquely diabolical Jewish vengeance. The idea of a merchant, not always a Jew, making such a bond with a debtor with the latter committed to pay with part of his body if that became necessary was an oft-repeated medieval theme. In fact in one medieval play, **The Three Ladies of London,** the Jewish money-lender is wholly virtuous, surpassing his Christian debtor. [16]

Space does not permit a more exhaustive treatment of the Shakespeare question. A serious desideratum is an in-depth analysis of all the lines of Shylock and of the major Christian protagonists in the play for a reassessment of what Shakespeare really meant to say. I have here only very cursorily tried to adumbrate a revision of the view of the great bard, and to relate his play not to anti-Jewish sentiment but rather to the growing pro-Jewish sentiment of the turn of the sixteenth century. As an alert, observant Englishman Shakespeare was surely fully aware of the comings and goings of Marranos in trade and politics, and of the not-so-well-kept secret of Marrano synagogues. It has not been established that he was indeed the favorite of Queen Elizabeth, but it is likely that he would uphold her side in an important trial involving her own doctor, and in whose innocence she believed. [17] The year 1594 must have been traumatic for Elizabeth while all the publicity was given to Lopez as a traitor in league with England's mortal enemy, Spain, so soon after the great episode of the Spanish Armada of 1588 when England faced total eclipse at Spanish hands. Even Elizabeth could have been implicated in Lopez' dealings, and it was shortly thereafter, according to one historian that Shakespeare penned his line, "The mortal moon hath her eclipse endured," in reference to Queen Elizabeth. The Queen is seen by most Elizabethan scholars to be Cynthia, the chaste deity or "terrene moon" in the writings of the poets. [18] The poet who would exult in the Queen's passage from danger might also write a sympathetic play about another mistreated Jew as a statement on the injustice of the Lopez case. [19] The sentiment Shakespeare harbored for the Queen is brought out in his last play, Henry VIII, produced in 1612, in which he wrote of the christening of Princess Elizabeth. There in words ascribed to the Archbishop of Canterbury, Cranmer, he penned the tribute that tells of his high regard. Cranmer spoke of the infant princess in prophetic terms foretelling as by divine wisdom how great will be her reign. But this is the way Shakespeare ultimately assessed her after her reign. Resonant with biblical allusion he wrote of her as one who promises, "Upon this land a thousand thousand blessings, Which time shall bring to ripeness . . . In her days every man shall eat in safety, Under his own vine what he plants and sing the songs of peace to all his neighbors . . . " [20]

The debate about Shakespeare's attitude toward Jews is bound to continue, and opposition in some Jewish quarters to the reading and production of **The Merchant of Venice** in a free society is likely to remain on the agenda of "defense" organizations geared to oppose real or imagined anti-Jewishness. But some corrective is needed, and the play might be viewed from an entirely different perspective, as is here suggested. Furthermore, more consideration should be given to the general anti-alien sentiment in England at the dawn of the seventeenth century. An Italian publicist at the time had written, "It is easier to find flocks of white crows than one Englishman . . . who loves a foreigner." Such xenophobia was expressed against "Orientals" which at that time included the Mediterranean type, among whom were the sefardic Marranos. [21]

III. Judaism in England Prior to Menasseh

Jews were expelled from England in October, 1290, by personal royal decree of King Edward I. But there was probably never an extended period when a Jew, a Jewish convert to Christianity, or later a Marrano was not present in England, either as merchant, financial agent or traveller. Such people are known by name in every century. So certain is the record of sporadic residence of Jews in England that there exists a persistent tradition in Judaic and non-Judaic sources of a second expulsion by Edward III in 1358. Nevertheless it was only from around 1500 that the presence of Portugese "New Christians," or Marranos, who were of, or descended from, the generation of forced converts of 1496, became a permanent fixture in England. These included Jorge Anes who became the progenitor of a well-known family which, under the name of Ames, was distinguished for its participation in English public life. This group was closely connected with Marranos in Antwerp and was encouraged by Henry VIII. Henry interceded in 1532 to save a Jew from punishment for violating what was commonly believed to be a law prohibiting the open practice of Judaism. Alvares Lopez, a member of the family to which belonged Queen Elizabeth's physician, was the head of the secret synagogue that existed in his house. More of these new Christians made their way to England after the Inquisition became active in Portugal in 1537, and because the Spanish authorities cooperated with the Inquisition in Zeeland in the Netherlands, a previous haven for New Christians. By the 1550's the Portugese Marrano community in London is said to have reached the hundred mark. [22]

In the 1560's there surfaced a community in Bristol, then a major port and a natural magnet for the Marrano traders. Jewish religious worship was held regularly there, and a woman by the name of Beatrix Fernandes taught Judaic ritual observances and liturgy to new arrivals. She also conducted a communal Passover Seder in her home. They probably pre-dated the 1560's, but during those years Marranos in England still had to be circumspect, for at different times they were not only in fear of the applicability to them of Edward I's expulsion decree, but of the Inquisition, and of the personal zeal of Queen Mary after her accession to the throne, and prior to her dethronement by Elizabeth. [23] With the reign of Elizabeth I in 1558 this fear was removed, and the Marrano community flourished. Nevertheless, they remained under the influence of the fixed idea that still went unchallenged, that Edward I's expulsion decree was still valid, and so they retained their Marrano dissimulation. When a practicing Jew, Solomon Cormano, ambassador of the Turkish sultan, arrived in England armed with his diplomatic immunity, however, he needed Marranos for a minyan, the prayer quorum, and gathered Marranos to his house for open Judaic religious worship. Nevertheless, marriages and burials were still conducted according to the ritual of the Church of England, although there were Judaic marriage rites performed as well, and all London Marranos, for example, were buried side by side in what appears to have been a Judaically dedicated section of a church cemetery. [24]

The Elizabethan period was more amenable for Marranos. A Spanish prisoner of war was held in London in 1588 and learned about these New Christians. Later he gave a deposition to the Inquisition in which he was reported to have said, " . . . it is public and notorious in London, that by race they [the Portugese] are all Jews, and it is notorious that in their own homes they live as such, observing their Jewish rites; but publicly they attend Lutheran Churches and listen to the sermons, and take the bread and wine in the manner and form as do the other heretics . . . " The interesting thing here is not so much the description of the double life of Marranos known to us from so many other sources, but that when it was expedient the New Christians dissimulated in Protestant churches instead of Roman Catholic churches. The reason would be rather simple: in Elizabethan England they would want to ally themselves with Protestant opposition to Rome and Spain. [25]

Various factors led to a temporary demise of this Marrano community. First, Amsterdam arose as the great financial center of the world, and Holland liberated itself from Spain. The Portugese Marrano merchants were then more attracted to Holland, and this decimated the population in England. Second, some of the English Marranos such as the Ames family were absorbed into the general population, while others came into bitter conflict with one another and accused one another to the government as judaizers. Third, under James I harsh rules were promulgated against Jesuits, and since the Marranos posed as Portugese Catholics for the most part, they feared these laws would be applied against them, and some fled. This reduced community, in fact, did soon experience a mini-expulsion by James I in 1609. [26] This signalled the realization that the expulsion order of 1290 was considered valid, and Jewish residence in England continued to be precarious. Nevertheless, while there is a historical blank after 1609 it is to be supposed that Marranos remained there and others filtered back in, for a community is known to have flourished by 1630, was recognized to be such and was even headed by a certain Antonio Carvajal who is thought to have been a convert from Christianity to Judaism. The reign of Charles I seems to have been a time of expansion for the community. Carvajal conducted a synagogue in his home although at the same time the congregants also met as Roman Catholics at the Portugese Embassy. In Carvajal's community a born Jew, Simon de Caceres of Amsterdam lived an open Jewish life, and during the Cromwellian era offered to raise a Jewish army to help the English conquer Chile. With supporters of the new Puritan Commonwealth urging toleration of Christians and non-Christians alike the Marrano community was more emboldened to grow and to conduct Judaism in the open. [27]

Withal, the historical record shows that the first formal synagogue officially established in England since 1290 was in Creechurch Lane in London at the beginning of 1657. This was both the natural evolution of previous events, and the product of millenarian urgings that having Jews in England is necessary for the consummation of the millenium. The latter argued that only in this way will Jews be virtually spread to the "ends of the earth" as England was considered to be, and would be available for conversion in a friendly non-papal country. As early as 1606 a certain Leonard Busher had already written in this vein in his work entitled **Religions Peace**. [28]

This early synagogue was visited by Christians who have left written records of their visits, and their testimony offers us a rudimentary description of liturgical realities in English Judaism around 1660, or at least how Christians perceived these. A certain John Greenhalgh visited the synagogue in April 1662. [29] He had studied Hebrew in London with a Polish rabbi named Samuel Levi who invited him to attend Sabbath morning worship. Greenhalgh described the three-hour worship order, and about decorum he wrote much like others before him: " . . . what a strange, uncouth, foreign, and to me barbarous sight was there . . . for I saw no living soul, but all covered, hooded, guized, veiled Jews . . . " He described the talit and the style of the Jew's wearing it as a "veil cast over the high crown of his hat . . . covering the whole hat, the shoulders, arms, sides and back to the girdle place, nothing to be seen but a little of the face; . . . Their veils were all pure white, made of taffata or silk, though some few were of a stuff coarser than silk." He appears to have understood what he saw and heard, describing the physical details of the synagogue including the mehizah, a latticed partition that separated the women on one side of the synagogue. He described the Torah cabinet (Ark) as a high cupboard, and noted the brass candlesticks. Apparently the synagogue had lockers in which each member kept his talit and prayerbook. He also described the order of the shahrit (morning) liturgy beginning with the pesukei dezimrah, "the former part of the service which was a full hour long," and then the Torah reading which preceded the musaf (additional worship). He did not use Hebrew terms, nor did he worry about accuracy. He referred to "the priest" when he meant the rabbi, and spoke loosely of "five or six" people called to the Torah instead of the customary seven to the Torah and an eighth for the prophetic portion, the haftarah. Apparently the problem of conversation during worship was already endemic, as Greenhalgh tells how the parnas (whom he calls "chief ruler") "a big, black, fierce and stern man . . . when any left singing upon their books and talked . . . he did call aloud with a barbarous thundering voice, and knocked upon the high desk with his fist . . . " A curious reference he made was to stamping with their feet when they mentioned Edomites, Philistines or other enemies of David's or of Israel's when chanting the psalms of pesukei dezimrah (the preliminary psalms and hymns), a custom unknown to me. [30] The indecorous scene also seems unusual from what we know of later sefardic synagogues that appeared to have a greater sense of decorum than àshkenazic synagogues.

Greenhalgh apparently returned to the Synagogue for Purim and noted that "they use great knocking and stamping when Haman is named." We also learn from Greenhalgh incidentally that in the time of Oliver Cromwell they observed their Judaism so openly that they built sukot (booths) on the Thames to celebrate that festival. He informed us that there were over one-hundred people in the synagogue on the Sabbath morning he visited including a proselyte, and all [men] were "gentlemen . . . not one mechanic . . . most of them rich in apparel, divers with jewels glittering . . . several of them are comely, gallant, proper gentlemen." Interestingly, he described these Portugese Marranos as darker than Spaniards or Greeks. [31]

The diarist, Samuel Pepys, who had already once visited the synagogue for a memorial service for Antonio Carvajal in 1659, visited it for a Simḥat Torah service on October 14, 1663. He too described the "vayles," the women behind the lattice, and the bowing to the Torah scrolls. He described how the males said a berakhah before donning the talit and kissing it, while those who heard it responded amen. He wrote that the prayers were done entirely in Hebrew and "in a singing way." He described the hakafot, and a prayer for the King. And then Pepys emoted, "But, Lord! to see the disorder, laughing, sporting and no attention, but confusion in all their service, more like brutes than people who know the true God, would make a man forswear ever seeing them more . . . I never . . . could have imagined there had been any religion in the whole world so absurdly performed as this . . . " [32] This atmosphere in the synagogue has been a scandal to Christians through the centuries, and Jews appear oblivious to the spiritual problem involved, although it has much improved in the twentieth century. Where an emphasis upon decorum is made by rabbi or laypersons, however, many often react with the objection that that would be too "churchy."

This London community first organized itself as an open society of confessed Jews in 1656 and presented a petition to Oliver Cromwell's government at that time asking for the freedom to reside in England. As will be seen below Oliver Cromwell never took a formal position on the subject. But when the property of one of the Marranos was seized in 1656 on the grounds that he was a Spaniard, all the Jews argued they were Portugese Jews and not Spanish Catholics. The property was restored by the court, thus implying for the first time that judicially at least Jews could reside in England and that the decree of Edward I had no binding force. [33] Nevertheless, a community with formal regulations and an appointed ḥakham (a sefardic rabbi) was not organized until 1664. At that time there was opposition to it but the government of the restored monarch, Charles II, took no action to dissolve it. When another effort was made in 1673-1674 to indict the group for carrying on public worship on the basis that it was illegal to do so, they petitioned the King and he dismissed the indictment. Another effort was made in 1685 under an Elizabethan anti-papist law to compel the Jews to practice Christianity, but this time King James II dismissed the action and ordered that Jews be permitted to "quietly enjoy the free exercise of their religion." [34] James II (1685-1688) was continuing the benign policy of Charles II (1660-1685), and in 1688 he issued a new Declaration of Indulgence for religious freedom. This newly acquired status of the Jews was in no way affected by the revolution of 1688 and the accession of William and Mary of Orange. [35]

This progress was made in the face of older Stuart laws against "non-conformists," as they were termed. For example, the Act of Uniformity of 1662, and the Conventicle Act of 1670, which could have outlawed Judaism as effectively as Edward I had done in 1290, were never invoked against the Jews after 1685, and although the Toleration Act of 1688 was really designed to protect only Protestant Dissenters from older legislation designed to continue as anti-Catholic measures, and did not protect the Jews specifically, the Jews were no longer impeded in their full practice of Judaism. [36]

But while some historians have dated this new freedom for Judaism to Cromwell it is important to place the Menasseh-Cromwell episode in perspective. Oliver Cromwell did not allow the Jews to build a synagogue, or even to resettle in England officially, either at the time of the famous Whitehall Conference or later. As a matter of fact at that time a committee report was prepared but never formally presented to the Council that reflects a very medieval view on the subject: it is sinful to admit Jews to a Christian state as they might seduce the population to false religion; it is evil to allow a synagogue to exist in a Christian society; their marriage and divorce practices will serve as a degrading example to pious Christians, and since they discriminate against Christians in oaths and business they will hurt the natives in economic matters. Another group dissented from this position. This group argued that so long as they remain aliens and eligible for expulsion, do not dishonor Jesus or Christianity by word of deed, remain subject to English law and courts, and not their own, do not profane Sunday or have Christian servants, do not hold office or print anything offensive to Christianity in English, are warned of penalties should they proselytize a Christian, and do not attempt to prevent a fellow Jew from converting to Christianity, it should be permitted for them to settle in England. Here was simply a replay of typical medieval arrangements offered by others on the continent as was noted in Chapter Three above. [37] The ramifications of the inactivity of Cromwell and an assessment of the Menasseh-Cromwell interlude is reserved for a later section of this chapter.

Meanwhile, it should not be overlooked that Jewish "oratories" (chapels set aside for the private religious devotions) existed in Cromwell's era and went undisturbed. Menasseh ben Israel and other sefardic Jews in London presented a memorandum of gratitude to Oliver Cromwell on March 24, 1655 for allowing them to meet for their devotions, and asked that he issue such permission in writing for their future protection, as well as for the right to have a cemetery. Hitherto these Jews worshipped in the chapel of the Portugese or Spanish Embassy as the case might have been, as well as Judaically in private homes, the Embassy serving Roman Catholics as well. Everyone was obligated to attend some form of Christian worship, and Jews continued their dissimulation for some time. [38]

IV. The Millenarian Factor

Many an admirer of Oliver Cromwell, or of R. Menasseh ben Israel will be disappointed to know that the popular idea that these two men in an unusual alliance of Calvinist Puritan with proto-modern rabbi, contrived to undo the work of King Edward I and restore Judaism to England is not an accurate historical reality. Oliver Cromwell neither arranged the nullification of Edward's order of expulsion nor did he bring about legislation to certify the legality of the open practice of Judaism in England. R. Menasseh ben Israel, the apostle to the gentiles, who had great influence upon Christian scholars, contributed to the development of new and friendlier Christian attitudes toward Jews, and placed the toleration and acceptance of Jews and Judaism on the European agenda one and a half centuries before Napoleon, technically failed in his mission to England, although his aspirations were indirectly fulfilled, as will be seen.

Toleration of Judaism was slower in coming to England than to Holland because there were many that argued that diversity of religion in any given society is a curse and the work of Satan.

These believed that especially, as in England since the days of Henry VIII, the Chief of State was also the Head of Faith, it is not possible to maintain authentic political loyalty where one does not engage in religious conformity. Thus, the Puritan "Agreement of the People" in 1649 extended liberty of conscience only to all who professed Jesus, and even then was not always honored. Thus, Quakers, Roman Catholics and Unitarians were not included within the purview of this toleration, let alone Jews. [39]

Nevertheless there had been a long process at work of trying to have Jews readmitted to England with the right to live there openly as Jews. Much of this was the natural and perhaps sometimes unnatural outgrowth of the shift of England from Roman Catholicism and the subsequent emergence of Puritanism. But its roots are to be sought in Henry VIII. Those who had to deal with Henry's conflict over his marriage to Katharine of Arragon turned to Old Testament Hebrew in order to adjudicate between Lev. 18:16, the prohibition to marry one's brother's wife, and Deut. 25:5, the command concerning the levirate marriage. In 1530 Henry took the logical step and consulted Italian rabbinic opinions in Venice, Bologna and Rome. Richard Croke gathered rabbinic views for him and discovered that the levirate marriage was still practiced among the Jews of Rome, one case of which had just transpired. Traditionally, however, it was the unshoeing (ḥaliẓah) and not the marriage which took precedence, and Jewish scholars, therefore, encouraged Henry in his right to a divorce, the marriage having been inappropriate. Pope Paul III's physician, Jacob b. Samuel Martino (d. 1549) was a consultant in the matter. In any event it can be surmised that the regius chairs of Hebrew set up at Oxford and Cambridge in 1540 may be understood partly in the light of Henry's discovery of the importance of Hebraic studies in dealing with biblical matters. By 1545 the Hebraist at Oxford, Richard Bruern was listed as one of England's most notable scholars. In 1549 the Act of Uniformity authorized the use of Hebrew in private devotions. By 1597 the first product of Jewish scholarship ever published in England appeared, a book on the Torah. The decision of a classics-oriented monarch like James I to encourage the translation of the Old Testament by English scholars directly from the Hebrew was the culmination of three-quarters of a century of antecedent preparation. [40]

Collateral to the use of Hebraic studies in England was the publication of a great mass of eschatological literature. For example, Joseph Meade wrote **The Key to the Revelation,** a work decidedly influenced by rabbinic literature. The book contains an appendix, "The Opinions of the Learned Hebrews Concerning the Great Day of Judgment," in which Meade endeavored to show that he expressed the original Judaeo-Christian eschatological hope, and had not himself innovated. He argued that it is futile to attempt to convert Jews, for ultimately they will be called by divine vision and voice just as was St. Paul. The Jews who convert of their own accord before the call represent forerunners and prototypes. Others believed similarly that the conversion of the Jews will come naturally as a product of the eschaton, and will take place after the fall of Papal Rome, their conversion offering a sign of the Second Coming. [41]

This literature was very important in Puritan evolution for there was a significant millenarian segment in the movement which expected the messianic event in the immediate future. This in turn colored the opinion of many in reference to the role of the Jews and the importance of readmitting them to England. Perhaps the upsurge of millenarian literature can be dated to 1589 when Francis Kett was burned for claiming that Jews will be restored to Palestine by the human Jesus who will become God at the final resurrection in Jerusalem. This event turned many indifferent minds to eschatology. There was, of course, a long history in which Romans 11 and Revelation 16:2 were understood to mean that Jews will accept Jesus in the last days, and this faith in the inevitable conversion of the Jews along with economic factors related to international competition in trade played a leading role in the readmission debate during the 1650's. The millenarians believed that the Messiah will reign for 1000 years, having appropriated the idea from Judaic apocalyptic sources. Hellenistic Judaism had also given apocalyptic Christianity the idea that the world was destined to last seven millenia. Psalm 90:4, which reads, "To you, a thousand years are as but a single day," was repeated by II Peter 3:8, in the lines, "But there is one thing, my friends, that you must never forget: that with the Lord 'a day' can mean a thousand years 'and a thousand years is like a day.' " The author of the epistle went on to assure the reader that "the day of the Lord will come . . . the sky will vanish . . . the earth . . . will be burned up." (v. 10). The end-time apocalypse at Revelation 20 was also seen as teaching that the reign of Jesus will be for 1000 years. [42]

This was also the time when interest moved from the Old Testament and Hebraic studies to new considerations of such strictly Judaic observances as the Sabbath, and subsequently to the rise of a judaizing movement. It was with reference to these that James I himself, in his 1619 "A Meditation Upon the Lord's Prayer," cautioned people with a "domino theory" that being too Puritan leads one to trusting too much in one's private holy ghost, which will result in becoming a separatist or a member of some other radical sect such as the Anabaptists, and from these move further along until one ends up in the judaizing camps. [43]

Sir Thomas Sherley had written James I in 1607 of the

economic advantages that would accrue to England if he settled Jews in Ireland. Others such as John Weemse saw Jewish settlement as a prelude to their conversion to Christianity. At the same time opposition arose in reaction to the effort, and this is probably well illustrated by Henry Blount's work, **A Voyage Into the Levant** in which he spoke of Jews as mercurial, timid, possessive of a corrupt love of their private interest, given to cheating and commission of malicious deeds to one another, prone to wallow in dirt, swarthy of appearance, in general "the dregs of the people." [44] A great flow of literature followed during the 1640's and 1650's for and against the resettlement and toleration of Jews and Judaism, especially after the termination of press censorship with the Civil War. There were those who believed that although they must work for the conversion of "Papists, Jewes, Turks, Pagans, Heretiks, with all Infidels and misbelievers," they argued forcefully for their toleration. This school of thought suggested there was much to learn from Dutch toleration as well as, ironically, from papal toleration as practiced in Italy, and the argument often proceeded in logical sequence from all sorts of Christian non-conformists and dissenters to Jews. [45]

A spate of writings was produced between 1590 and 1608. Then an important one by Thomas Brightman appeared in 1616: **Revelation of Revelation.** In his work this influential thinker interpreted Rev. 16:12. The verse reads, "The sixth angel emptied his bowl over the great river Euphrates; all the water dried up so that a way was made for the kings of the east . . . " Brightman interpreted this to signify that there will take place an event parallel to the crossing of the sea on dry land during Israel's exodus from Egypt; and he saw the "kings of the east" as referring to the Jews. It was upon the shoulders of such writers that the aforementioned Joseph Meade as well as Sir Henry Finch stood. Finch expressed a proto-Zionism in **The World's Great Restauration or The Calling of the Jews,** which he prefaced with a dedication to Jews written in Hebrew accompanied by its English translation. In this preface he forecast that the Jews will gain Davidic supremacy and rule with great power. He alarmed the government. Finch's influence can be understood in the light of his important social standing, as author of a great treatise on common law, and a leading legal figure. He was, however, incarcerated and forced to recant. [46]

These English millenarians built upon a venerable tradition that began with an Italian monk, Joachim de Fioris in the twelfth century and passed on through the centuries to the reforming movements of Hussites and Anabaptists and on to Martin Bucer, who tried to convince Edward VI of this theory. The Chiliastic or thousand-year tradition is further traceable to hellenistic Judaism through II Peter 3:8 and the Epistle of Barnabas (15:3-8) to Irenaeus, who rabbinic-like declared that the true Sabbath of the righteous will be free of all earthly occupation and will enjoy a divinely-set table with all sorts of dishes. To this day the Jew who recites his prayers after meals on the Sabbath includes a line that signifies that the Sabbath is a foretaste of the millennium, and he prays, "May the merciful enable us to inherit the day that in its entirety will be a Sabbath and the rest of everlasting life." The Council of Ephesus in 431, however, condemned belief in a literal millennium as superstition, and defined the 1000-year reign of Jesus to be the span of the church on earth before the Second Coming. [47]

Reinterpretations of the millennial idea have arisen consistently in Christianity as in Judaism. And in 1566 the Second Helvetic Confession condemned ". . . the Jewish dreams that before the day of judgment there shall be a golden age in the earth, and that the godly shall possess the kingdoms of the world . . . " [48] It must be remembered that in his **De Civitate Dei (The City of God)** St. Augustine, who probably coined the term "millennarian" as a translation of "Chiliast," had already identified the millennial kingdom with the church as being free from seduction by the devil until the thousand years are over. He interpreted the one-thousand years of scripture (Rev. 20:1-6) to signify "forever," or as long as this world exists, that is, until the end of time. In this way he repudiated the idea of a physical existence after resurrection, and tried to separate the Christian spiritual kingdom from the Judaic this-worldly messianic kingdom, but to no avail. [49] Christian eschatology in its this-worldly millennarian form was alive and flourishing in the seventeenth century despite Augustine and the Second Helvetic Confession. And insofar as it referred to the Jews it taught the literal restoration of Jews in Palestine, and the likelihood that the proper meaning of Romans 11:25ff. is the reinstatement of Jews in the covenant. After 1599 a note in Protestant Bibles suggested that the biblical prophets assured the ultimate conversion of the Jews, and this note contributed to the diffusion of the idea that Jews will be restored to Palestine which is equally evident in prophetic teaching. A major thinker who moved all these ideas to the forefront was Heinrich Alsted (1588-1638), who carried forward complex mathematical exercises to conclude that the expected year of redemption was 1694. Others, however, had already predicted 1654, 1655 and 1656, all more pertinent to Menasseh ben Israel. As in the latter's case so too in the case of Christian millenarians the Thirty Years' War, and the persecution of Puritans parallel to the Chmielnicki outbreaks strongly influenced these messianic trends. Furthermore, the Christians increasingly adopted the rabbinic hermeneutical method of peshat, an unadorned literalist reading of texts of scripture, and the Judaic-type this-worldly kingdom of which they read in such church fathers as Irenaeus and Tertullian. [50]

When Finch had written, James I was not appreciative of the idea that a Jewish kingdom will gain supremacy ruling from Jerusalem, and was doubly alarmed that he not only had his hands full controlling dissenting Puritans, but was faced with the spectre of a new wave of semi-Jews arising out of the dissenting sects, and a new colony of dissenters to watch that had been implanted by the recent sailing of the Mayflower to what became New England. He objected to any hint that he was not already sovereign of the perfect theocracy and had no intention of paying homage to a Jewish king. The royal anger encouraged much other opposition and Finch's imprisonment was symbolic of the reaction to the pro-Jewish readmission school of thought. For Joseph Meade Paul prefigured the Jews and he drew up a list of ten parallels between Jews and Paul. Paul was the quintessential Jew who turned to Christ. Meade's thinking influenced the eschatological views of both John Milton and Sir Isaac Newton. Fifth Monarchy believers, basing themselves upon Dan. 2:44 which spoke of a fifth monarch arising after the failure of a sequence of four, and which they believed to be the eternal kingdom of Christ, were more extreme. They were looking forward to the overthrow of Daniel's Fourth Monarchy, which they took from Luther to be the papacy, and to the sudden conversion of the Jews. One of these interested millenarians was Nathaniel Holmes who corresponded with Menasseh. [51]

One thing all millenarians had in common was that the conversion of the Jews was an indispensable element for the realization of the Second Coming, but differed on whether the conversion would take place before or after the Second Coming, or before or after the restoration to Palestine. Another vital aspect of the thought of these millenarians was the conviction that England was chosen to lead Jews to salvation, just as we have seen both French and Portugese millenarians sought the same honor for their kings. Some Englishmen like John Sadler eventually occupied positions of power and were able to facilitate the Jewish readmission to England. Other millenarians believed that Charles II would be the messianic king, and that Jews will convert under his auspices. Various European monarchs were alternately nominated for the post. The coincidence of the Sabbatai Ẓvi messianic movement should not be overlooked, and millenarian support for it is clearly understandable. It has also been surmised that British interest in Zionism during the twentieth century was aroused by intellectual and spiritual progeny of seventeenth century millenarianism. There can be no doubt that the recent upsurge of enthusiasm and support for the State of Israel among right-wing fundamentalist groups, especially in the United States, is closely connected with their eschatological visions. The millenarians needed the Jews for the Second Coming, and because they needed all twelve tribes of Israel reunited as in Ezekiel's allegory of the two sticks (Ez. 37:15-22), they took the strong interest in the lost tribe issue referred to earlier. It was his contact with millenarians and interest in the lost tribe issue that inspired Menasseh's turning to England. Menasseh very brilliantly exploited the millenarian hope in an effort to bring about the formal, legal restoration of the Jewish right to live in England and openly practice Judaism there. [52]

Whatever the case may be in the twentieth century, it is clear as was recognized by Gershom Scholem, a modern Judaic scholar of mysticism and messianism, that the apocalyptic eschatological enthusiasm of millenarians was instrumental in bringing Jews to center stage and contributed in its own peculiar manner to the emancipation of the Jew. The Chmielnicki massacres of 1648 were seen by Jews as the "birthpangs" of the Messiah, and Christian millenariansim and Judaic messianism embraced. Scholem refers to Menasseh's **The Hope of Israel** and his interpretation of Dueteronomy 28:64 "And the Lord shall scatter you among all the people from one end of the earth [mikezeh haàrez] to the other," as signifying the indispensibility of Jews freely residing in England. He then adds, "Speculations of this kind [Menasseh's] incurred favor in chiliast circles. The copious literature on the subject created almost a pro-Jewish climate of opinion and some Christian circles in western Europe expected the imminent repentance of Israel and their acceptance of Jesus . . . " Menasseh related this verse in Deuteronomy to Daniel 12:7 which indicated that the completion of the dispersal is a precondition for redemption. [53]

Despite strong millenarian interest in the restoration of Judaism to England there was also strong opposition to it. Some, including the well-known Roger Williams of American fame, expected Jews to see the light once they were allowed to thrive in a friendly Christian society practicing Christian love. Before he set sail for the American colonies with his charter for Rhode Island in 1644 he wrote a tract arguing that Jews can be good citizens of England, and that the tribulations of the English Civil War were God's punishment for maltreatment of Jews in the past. But others were aghast at the idea that Judaism should be openly professed in England. [54] This same tension or ambivalence was reflected in Parliament, where in 1647 it was considered heresy and blasphemy to advocate toleration, and in 1648 Parliament was allocating thousands of pounds for Hebraic and rabbinic writings. John Selden (1584-1654), a leading jurist and Judaic scholar, had written a treatise as early as 1617 entitled **Treatise on the Jews of England.** As an orientalist he engaged in much rabbinic study and wrote a series of works between 1631-1653 which show acquaintance with the Old Testament and rabbinic literature, as well as Karaite literature. It was said of him that he acquired so much Judaic knowledge "such as has been acquired by few non-Israelites." It was John Selden now requesting Parliament's large outlays for Judaica volumes, and he expressed the belief that Jews were eligible for salvation just as they in turn profess the conviction that righteous gentiles are eligible for salvation. [55]

The climax of almost half-a-century of debate was about to occur. On December 25, 1648 the Cromwellian Council of War passed a toleration resolution to encompass "all Religions whatsoever, not excepting Turks, nor Papists, nor Jewes." This was followed on January 5, 1649 by the petition submitted by Joanna and her son Ebenezer Cartwright, English Baptists then living in Amsterdam, to readmit Jews in order to appease God's anger against England. [56] Nevertheless, the Agreement of the People entered into on January 15, 1649 included toleration only for those "who profess faith in God by Jesus Christ." The effort went on, and in 1652, on a visit to England Roger Williams renewed his appeal for the Jews arguing in Pauline style that their fall saved the gentiles, that refusal of toleration is unchristian, and that restoration in England will pacify God. The need for an English refuge was now intensifying as Iberian and Polish refugees increased after the heating up of the Portugese Inquisition in 1640 and the massive toll of the Chmielnicki massacres. Moses Wall, the friend of John Milton and translator of Menasseh ben Israel's **Hope of Israel** meanwhile calculated that 1655 will be the year for the seventh trumpet which ushers in the eschatological kingdom. [57]

It was into this milieu that Menasseh ben Israel intruded himself. A decade of discussion that had awakened in Menasseh the conviction that England is the Jew's last hope led him to the conviction that formal readmission and toleration of Jews is a possibility. He obliquely referred to this in his preface to **The Hope of Israel** in 1650, and he might have gone to England at that time had not political events resulted in a rupture between England and Holland.

V. The Mission of Menasseh

Menasseh shared in the millenarian spirit seeing it as kin to Jewish messianism. Messianism was strong among returned Marranos as noted earlier, and with the Thirty Years' War and the Chmielnicki massacres dislocating so much eastern European Judaic life, Menasseh was prone to see in millenarian arguments reinforcement for Judaic messianism. His work, **The Hope of Israel,** embodied all this. Thus when Menasseh received a millenarian tract dedicated to him by Paul Felgenhauer, a Bohemian mystic, he responded in the same spirit in February 1655. In this letter he reaffirmed that the signs as seen by millenarians are indeed in the Judaic tradition including: tumults, revolutions, cruel wars, the coming of Elijah, and the good news of Israel's revived kingdom spread over the whole earth, with all princes and people paying deference to it. [58]

The documents of the time show that Menasseh was first referred to in the English State Papers when a committee was appointed to peruse the question of giving him a pass, and evidence indicates that he received passes to England on several occasions from 1651-1653. The war with Holland 1652-1654, however, prevented the voyage. After the war his son Samuel and a Marrano Manuel Dormido of the famous Abravanel clan met with and petitioned Oliver Cromwell, but the Puritan leader insisted that so significant a question requires the presence of Menasseh himself. And thus, in October 1655 Menasseh arrived in London as guest of the Lord Protector, accompanied by three rabbis, one from Lublin, Poland to help him stress the urgency of the eastern Jewish problem. [59] Menasseh's arrival and the "Humble Address" which he presented to Oliver Cromwell led to the latter's convening a distinguished group of jurists and theologians in what is known historically as the Whitehall Conference. Menasseh asked forthrightly for "the free exercise of our religion, that we may have our Synagogue, and keep our own public worship . . . " The conference met five times. At its very first meeting on December 4, 1655, it decided the crucial question about Jews being so openly received in England, ruling that there is no law to prevent this, that the edict of 1290 was not an act of Parliament but a personal royal edict directed only against those particular Jews who, under the law of the time, belonged to King Edward I. The second question, however: under what conditions shall the Jews be readmitted, did not receive so felicitous and speedy a response, and became a matter of great debate all through 1656. No conclusions were reached at Whitehall on any day that the group met. [60] There were those who argued that Jews will debase the nation's morals. The Whitehall sessions brought forth William Prynne's **Short Demurrer to the Jews** offering vigorous opposition to readmission. Even Henry Jessey, a Baptist minister and scholar of Hebraica and rabbinics, who had long favored toleration modified his stand in the face of a great backlash and offered a compromise motion to admit Jews under very restrictive conditions. Cromwell, perhaps hoping to avoid such an adverse outcome, abruptly adjourned the conference with no vote taken. No decision was made at any subsequent meeting of the Council of State or any other body. Nevertheless, there remains an enigmatic entry in the diary of an important figure of the time, John Evelyn, who wrote on December 14, 1655 that he had visited the great philosopher Thomas Hobbes then in England, and seemingly irrelevantly added a sentence at the end of this entry, "Now were the Jews admitted." There was no further discussion, and his next entry was December 25. [61]

The problem was occasioned by the persuasive opposition. It argued that the opening of public synagogues was an evil, and was scandalous to other Christian churches, that Jews will probably not succumb to conversionist efforts, that they were lax in their matrimonial practices, and were not strict about the sanctity of oaths. [62] The millenarians were divided. There were those who argued that Romans 11:25ff. implied conversion of the Jews will take place by persuasion, and should therefore be welcomed to England and persuaded. Others argued that it will occur only by Grace, or after the miraculous appearance of Jesus in the heavens as he came personally to Paul, and the Jews should not be given the freedom of a Christian country before then. [63] In addition to the theological arguments about the inadequacy of Judaism, and the millenarian confusion over the sequence of the eschaton, there was also the understandable opposition of the merchants as a class who feared the competition of the internationally experienced Jewish merchants of Iberia, Holland and the east. Thus while Cromwell saw international Jewish trade as beneficial in English competition with Spain, Portugal and Holland, the merchants took the narrower view and saw it as detrimental to themselves. [64]

All the ferment of 1655-56 and Menasseh's lengthy stay in England resulted in nothing concrete. But Oliver Cromwell and his government did not prevent the continuing quiet immigration of Marranos into the country. [65] The Whitehall decision of December 4, 1655, that there was no law to prohibit Jewish residence in England was in itself a landmark, and thenceforward the English legal process ground regularly on securing the rights of Jews. In August 1656 R. Menasseh asked his Amsterdam community to send a Torah scroll for a London synagogue and negotiations were opened to secure a religious leader from Hamburg. Ultimately, R. Jacob Sasportas came from Holland as rabbi in 1663, and it is of considerable interest that it was Sasportas in England who was the lone rabbinic voice in Europe that totally rejected the messianic pretensions of Sabbatai Zvi in 1666.

Nevertheless, Menasseh's dreams had not been entirely futile. The pro-Judaic sentiment in England was too powerful, and too intensely fueled by religious enthusiasm to be of no avail. It is true that philo-Judaic elements caused backlash. In the years prior to Menasseh's mission various anti-Jewish slanders were concocted and were concretized in literature. Some were tales that were eventually passed down for generations. Some took on the aspect of history, when, for instance, the absurd rumor that the Jews were offering fabulous amounts of money to Cromwell's needy government for the purchase of St. Paul's Cathedral as a synagogue was reported in Venice in 1650 as a fact already accomplished. But in the end philo-Judaism, or as it is usually referred to, philo-semitism prevailed. Biblical orientation issued forth in a logical reversion on the part of some believers to the practices of the Old Testament, especially circumcision and the seventh-day Sabbath. From 1600 on one hears more and more about "Jewism," "Judaistic opinions" and judaizing. In 1612 two Arians died for their Judaistic monotheism, and subsequently people were imprisoned. Sometimes the culprits were freed from prison when they confessed their errors which the records show included such matters as the Jewish Sabbath and the dietary practices at least as advocated in scripture (Lev. 11). There was even some suggestion that a council or sanhedrin of seventy govern England, while others argued that worship should be conducted with the Hebrew text of the Old Testament. [66]

Henry VIII had established the Regius chairs of Hebrew at Oxford and Cambridge in 1540, and at the end of the century two converted Jews, Philip Ferdinand Polonus (1555-1599) and John Immanuel Tremellius (1510-1580) were teaching there, as did others. These men brought rabbinic commentary and post-biblical Judaism to Christian consciousness. Rabbinic scholarship was available to the translators of the Authorized Version of the Bible in 1611 (King James Version), both in books and through scholars. Many who were touched by all this, especially Protestants, moved from their Hebraic studies to a new examination of the ten commandments and on to concern about the true Sabbath. Both those who now advocated the seventh-day Sabbath, and those who only argued for a Judaic-type Sabbath on Sunday were stigmatized as judaizers. [67]

Among the major judaizers were the Traskites who took their name from John Traske (b. 1585) who in turn came under the influence of another prime judaizer, Hamlet Jackson who rejected the notion that the New Testament abrogated the Mosaic dispensation, and advocated biblical Sabbath and food practices. Traske converted enough people so as to alarm the authorities, and was charged with being "a very christened Jew, a Maran, the worst sort of Jews that is." Prison chastened Traske, and he recanted, but Jackson went to Amsterdam and there he and others joined the synagogue. It was these English judaizers, some of whom became outright Jews, and other radical Christians in London who were an initial factor in Manesseh's interest in England. Baptists like Henry Jessey were seventh-day observers, and it is known that Jessey, much interested in the millenarian question and the restoration of Judaism to England had received an autographed copy of Menasseh's **Hope of Israel.** So intense did the Sabbatarian movement become in England that after the restoration of the monarchy about two-hundred families are estimated to have migrated to the Rhineland. [68]

There were variegated judaizers, among them Levellers,

Quakers and messianists, and they included such disparate people as demented farmers who were planning to repeat Moses' miracle of the sea, and distinguished jurists such as Sir Henry Finch. But far more important were those who argued for toleration, and it was these who ultimately prevailed. The Baptist Leonard Busher's 1614 book **Religions Peace, or a Plea for Liberty of Conscience** was reprinted at a crucial time in 1646. This was the earliest published work in England calling for authentic religious liberty for all. He was followed by another Baptist, John Murton, in 1615, who saw religious liberty as assuring the same protection for Jews who should not any longer be subjected to persecution for their religion. Other such literature followed. It is evident from this record that the clear call to offer true religious freedom to Jews within a Christian society, that they be subjected neither to compulsory conversionism nor persecution for recalcitrance came in the English language, and in an English society which, in its American translation, was destined to become the greatest center of Judaism in history. The link between the English call and the American experience, already alluded to, was Roger Williams of Rhode Island. [69]

The millenarian and judaizing movements did not end with the passing from the scene of either Menasseh ben Israel or Oliver Cromwell. During the hectic messianic days of 1665-1666 when Sabbatai Zvi's movement was at its height English Jews were also caught up in it. But not only Jews were influenced. Certain Christian groups who believed in the imminence of the Day of Judgment were aroused by Sabbatianism. Quakerism had emerged from the Fifth Monarchy millenarian circle and at its outset was an intensely chiliastic movement. Christians regarded the advent of George Fox and his Quaker enthusiasts as reminiscent of the coterie of Sabbatian disciples. It was not lost on anyone that in 1657 the Quaker, James Naylor, had proclaimed himself King of Israel, firstborn of God and rode into the citadel of Quakerism, Bristol, with his callers crying hosanna. In 1666 a shipload of Quakers was reported to have sailed to the Holy Land "to behold the wonders of the Lord." [70] And when John Evelyn wrote the first book in English on Sabbatai Zvi he included a biographical sketch of James Naylor. This English consciousness of Sabbatai Zvi is further reflected by Samuel Pepys who recorded in his diary in February, 1666 that there was a Jew in London betting ten to one that "a certain person now at Smyrna" will be within two years recognized as "the true Messiah." The betting started in Hamburg, passed to the Jews of London and was picked up by Christians. [71]

V. The Aftermath to Menasseh's Mission

R. Menasseh ben Israel did not appear on the English scene in a vacuum, nor did he initiate the interchange between Judaism and Christianity in England. He was preceded by contacts with the English originating with men such as Leone da Modena. [72] Modena had been in communication with Sir Henry Wotton, the English ambassador at Venice, the jurist John Selden, and Sir William Boswell. He had written his **Rites and Ceremonies of the Jews** in honor of King James I, and this was translated into English by Edmund Chilmead in 1650. Even the celebrated Isaac Walton, author of the fishing classic, **The Compleat Angler** who also corresponded with Modena, frequently mentioned Jews and Judaism in his work, referring, for example, to the Jews making red caviar from carp because they did not eat sturgeon, which Walton still thought had no scales at any stage of its life. [73] Thus, in a very real sense Modena was a "preparer of the way" for R. Menasseh ben Israel.

Menasseh himself, however, had connections with England since 1642 at least when he welcomed the Prince of Orange and Queen Henrietta Maria of England, wife of Charles I, to his synagogue in Amsterdam. This evidently prepared Menasseh for a relationship with the royalists when he was simultaneously supported by Oliver Cromwell. In any event what played a more important role than this early contact with the royal family was the flow of literature that ensued during the seventeenth century, referred to earlier. This literature was concerned with Judaism, the lost ten tribes, messianism, and the readmission of Jews into England. Because some of this literature was inimical to Judaism and prejudiced the opportunity for readmission, Menasseh wrote his **Vindiciae Judaeorum** to deal with as he said in his sub-title, "reproaches cast on the Nation of the Jewes; wherein all objections are candidly, and yet fully cleared." This apologia for Judaism was largely a critique of the survey of Judaism written by Alexander Ross, who believed that diversity of religion results in malice, factionalism, treachery, innovations, "and many more mischiefs, which pull down the heavy judgment of God upon that State or Kingdom . . . " [74]

In his critique of Ross, Menasseh sought to refute the negative views of Ross on many themes, including the old blood libel, that Jews re-enacted their crucifixion of Jesus by killing a Christian each year and using the blood for passover ma𝗓ah and wine, the alenu prayer ("adoration") and a line in its older version that was said to excoriate Christianity, Judaic proselytization of Christians, use of an old amidah formula which cursed Christians in the synagogue, and discriminatory and dishonest Judaic business ethics, among many other liturgical and halakhic themes that Ross had cited in order to indicate Judaic perfidy.

Menasseh's work had an important influence in the stirrings of modernity on the continent and was brought into center stage by the German translation executed by Henrietta Herz. [75] The poet Southey had regarded this work as a "satisfactory refutation of the calumnies against the Jews, made by a liberal and learned man . . . " [76]

Menasseh's mission to England was an interlude. It did not establish Judaism in England which was already there, but as an intermediary he so energized it that it continued to expand despite the absence of formal approbation. He departed in 1657, Cromwell died in 1658, but Judaism remained permanently rooted in England.

For some time prior to the restoration of the monarchy Jews had negotiated with royalist supporters and with Charles II in Holland and France. The exiled king had seen economic advantages in promising them that there would be no impediment to their remaining in England under the monarchy. Thus, their numbers increased and they continued to hold open worship. An attempt was made to have Richard Cromwell, successor to Oliver, expel the Jews in 1658, and in 1659 Thomas Violet conspired to have Jews barred under various laws against non-conformists and Roman Catholics, but these efforts failed. After Charles II returned to the throne in 1660, the executors of Charles I were in turn executed, Oliver Cromwell was removed from Westminster Abbey and hanged, all legislation of the Protectorate and Commonwealth was nullified, but none of this affected the Jews. This was so despite the fact that the Puritans seen now as treasonous had been supporters of Jewish readmission and it was logical to consider Jews as in some way in league with the Puritan revolution and the regicides. A certain Thomas Violet attempted to make this connection in the public mind in 1660 by publishing a pamphlet, Petition Against the Jews and demanding that the King undo Cromwell's toleration which led to Jewish worship in London "to the great dishonor of Christianity and public scandal of the Protestant religion." Violet contrived a petition by the City of London to have the Jews expelled, but the Jews also petitioned the king. He referred both petitions to Parliament with a message to take under consideration legislation that will protect the burgeoning Judaic community. Parliament did nothing. This allowed the status quo to continue. [77]

Parliament escalated intolerance of all who did not adhere to the Church of England, but because Charles II came down on the side of toleration these laws were not strictly enforced. On March 15, 1672 the king issued a Declaration of Indulgence which suspended penal laws relating to non-conformists and allowed licensing of places of public worship other than the

Anglican churches with the sole exception of Roman Catholic places. The Declaration was cancelled in 1673, but nevertheless Judaism remained undisturbed. [78]

During the reign of Charles II there were in London two fully organized synagogues, one each for àshkkenazim and sefardim, each with a rabbi. Isaac Abendana translated the Mishna into Latin at Cambridge in 1673. There was still no Hebrew printing press at Cambridge, however, and since his manuscript called for much Hebrew intermixed with the Latin, it could not be printed. But the aborted effort indicates the beginning of Jewish religious scholarship on English soil soon after the emergence of the open Judaic community. [79] Hebrew type was soon brought to England and in 1695 and again in 1699 Abendana translated a prayerbook into English. [80]

The policies of Charles II were continued by James II (1685-1688) who issued a new Declaration of Indulgence in 1688 offering religious freedom for all. This policy was continued when William and Mary of Orange were brought to England to replace the Stuarts. [81] The new revolution unseating the Stuarts again caused international intrigues. Louis XIV of France supported the Stuarts and therefore William III of England insisted upon caution as to whom to admit to England. Travellers were carefully scrutinized and special passes were issued to allow travel to and from the continent. And yet the record shows that some Jews were admitted without passes because in the words of the English State Papers "They in no way disaffected to the Government," or were "poor Jews." The records indicate that Jews did much travel between England and Holland as well as Italy, the West Indies and New England. [82]

Population and economics are directly related to spiritual and intellectual progress, and by 1695 there were 850 Jews in London, constituted of both àshkenazim and sefardim. They lived intermingled with non-Jews, as a census taken by William III reveals. Many were prosperous and owned stock in the Bank of England after 1694. A Jew qualified for a governorship in 1701 when the records indicate that although less than one percent of the population of London, Jews were about eleven percent of the holders of the stock. [83] These statistics imply that the Jewish community was now prepared for religious resurgence. And indeed, it is clear that by 1700 the tragedy of 1290 had been undone. Not only had there been a long tradition of Judaic scholarship among Christians in England all through the centuries, with even what has been termed a "Maimonides circle" at Oxford, a theme to be explored further in the next chapter, but soon after the reestablishment of the Jews in reasonable numbers, the crystallization of communal life and stabilization of their economic life, Judaic scholarship by Jews began anew in England. It soon reached elevated heights, a matter, however, to remain for further discussion in Volume Four. [84]

There can be no doubt that although English Judaism existed before Menasseh's interest in England, its persistence and expansion was in large part a product of English respect for Menasseh. His writings had an unusual impact, and his persistence eventuated in the hitherto confused and concealed view that there really was no valid law in England to prevent Jews from residing there or Judaism from being practiced. As one historian has correctly surmised: if a law had been engineered by Cromwell to readmit Jews and for them to reestablish synagogues it would have been swept away by the Restoration. Providentially there was no law to be swept away, and Judaism flourished as a result of official silence and natural evolution. Basically Menasseh, for all his proto-modernity still had a somewhat medieval approach for the Jews: a special charter, special protection by the authorities, and a government overseer for the Jewish community. That he failed to attain his objectives was providential. The Jews melted into the non-conformist landscape. They became another religious community in a land learning to adjust to the tenuous peace between the established religion, the Church of England, juxtaposed to the non-conformist religions in a new kind of pluralistic society. [85]

England became the paradigm for Judaic freedom in all English-speaking societies and paved the way for the emergence of the greatest Judaic center in history in North America. Ultimately Judaic records in England credited Charles II with the resettlement, and to a degree this is accurate. But it was Cromwell's wise inaction that allowed Charles II the latitude to continue the status quo. In historical theory and evaluation the toleration engendered by this inaction of Oliver Cromwell's takes precedence over the later passivity of Charles II as an elemental factor in the revival of English Judaism. Menasseh became a legend among English Christians who, long after his death, perpetuated a mystique of a man of great virtue and profound knowledge. This mystique crossed the Atlantic where Menasseh and his writings enjoyed an unusual prominence in eighteenth century Harvard and Yale, and contributed to the unusual integration of Judaism into the American religious landscape. [86]

Chapter Seven

RELIGIONS IN TENSION

I. Prefatory Comments

Judaism and Christianity were in tension from the very beginning of the Christian movement within Judaism, and this tension escalated after the separation. After a long medieval status quo in this tension the attitudes of Humanism and their translation into the Reformation began to lead to a new assessment of the Jew, and in time to new opportunities for Judaism in western society. This did not heal the tension but began to transform its nature and effects. To understand the transformation that began in the fifteenth century and is still in progress, it is necessary to move through the medieval obscurantism and Christian efforts to submerge Judaism by the sheer weight of intellectual assault, when not employing secular brute force, and to rediscover the roots of modern Judaic-Christian dialogue and intellectual interchange. [1]

The persistence of anti-Judaism which began with the Epistle of Barnabas and continued on through patristic literature into the later middle ages was further enhanced by such significant thinkers as Robert Grosseteste, Vincent of Beauvais, Thomas Aquinas, Raymund Martini and Nicholas de Lyra. [2] Joining such personalities were Jews who possessed substantial knowledge of Judaism and who converted to Christianity. Possibly the earliest such scholar was Petrus Alphonsi (1062-1110), a physician, Moses, who became a Christian in 1106. He might have been the earliest polemicist of note, at least known to us, since patristic times, who attacked talmudic àgadah, and argued against what he considered "errors" of Jewish faith which he adduced from talmudic anthropomorphisms and other passages. [3]

A second major convert was Paul of Burgos (1350-1435), who wrote a comprehensive tract with Jn. 5:39 in mind, Scrutinium Scripturarum (Search the Scriptures). Paul became the archbishop of Burgos and was always zealous for the conversion of his correligionists. His widespread influence is indicated by the frequency with which he was referred to by Christian theologians in different lands for centuries. [4] This particular form of anti-Judaic polemic sought to establish the obsolescence and inadequacy of Judaism, as well as to validate the messiahship and divinity of Jesus, among other Christian doctrines, directly from the Old Testament, and eventually also from the kabalah. This style of teaching and debate proceeded without interruption for centuries.

A heightening of the interchange between Christian and Jewish thinkers can be dated to the refutation of the anti-talmudic diatribes of Johannes Pfefferkorn in the sixteenth century in the wake of the Renaissance and the Reformation. [5] Although such interchange has not yet attained the ideal pattern of theological and ecumenically oriented dialogue as late as the closing decades of the twentieth century, much progress can be documented. There still persists a relic of medieval apologetic and polemic. [6] Such medieval polemics were matched by Jewish apologists, some familiar with the New Testament, and many, such as Profiat Duran (Isaac ben Moses Efodi), ranging widely over theological themes sacred to Christians. [7]

II. Overview [8]

The earliest polemics between Christians and Jews are already found in the rabbinic literature with several exceptions of earlier Christian material. There is, for example, a record of a discussion between a Christian Jew, Jason, and an Alexandrian Jew, Papiscus. This is referred to in the ancient literature and was read and used by Celsus, a pagan philosopher in Rome, but is lost. It has been attributed to Ariston of Pella probably dating to about 135-140 A.D. Whatever its date and authorship, the little we have of it in citations by other writers offers examples of christological interpretation of Old Testament phrases. For example, the Hebrew "In the beginning" of Gen. 1:1, is interpreted to mean "by the son" although the process by which this came to be is not expounded for us. This interpretation later became quite common in Christian writings. This was soon followed by Saint Justin Martyr's **Dialogue With Trypho**, which is probably the best known apologetic work in Greek from the early Christian church. The best known similar work in Latin is that of the church father Tertullian (ca. 200), **Adversus Judaeos**, the first of many such works bearing the same title. These were followed by the homilies of Aphraates in Persia and by John Chrysostom's (347-407) **Homilies Against the Jews** (ca. 387-389). The last important specimen of this ancient approach was that of Isidore of Seville (560-636). Isidore presided over the Fourth Council of Toledo in 633 which prohibited converted Jews from returning to Judaism, and prohibited Jews from evangelizing Christians. But it also prohibited Christians from using compulsion to evangelize Jews. All of these works have several things in common. They defend Christian ideas of Jesus, assert a vigorous rejection of Judaism, and uphold the view that the Old Testament has been abrogated. [9]

A new group of writings arose in the later middle ages in which was evident the studies made in linguistic exegesis. Christian scholars felt it more imperative to study Judaic commentaries, especially the rabbinic literature, including the targums, midrashim and the talmuds, in order to refute Jewish scholars, and to support Christianity out of the Judaic sources. [10] Petrus Alfonsi was followed by the works of other converts to Christianity such as Abner of Burgos (1270-1348) known as Alphonso of Valladolid, and the aforementioned Paul of Burgos. [11]

Dominican monks were prominent in the effort to convert Jews, and in the fifteenth century Vicente Ferrer carried on an evangelical campaign in the synagogues of Spain holding a cross in one hand and a Torah in the other converting tens of thousands of Jews. He had an assistant by the name of Geronimo de Sante Fe who had once been Joshua ibn Vives al-Lorqui (Lorka). He was the chief Christian spokesman at a marathon disputation that took place at Tortosa between Jews and Christians and which lasted from February 1413 to November 1414. [12]

Geronimo is a paradigm of many features of the phenomenon we are here discussing. First, he was a Jew by birth. Second, he wrote treatises designed to prove out of Judaic sources that Christian doctrine was true. Third, he engaged in the typical form of medieval disputation in which the objective was not theological interchange, but theological triumph. Fourth, he evinced both courtesy and animosity toward the Judaic sources from which he drew. In **Concerning Jewish Errors Drawn From the Talmud** he made it his purpose to reveal what he termed "lying, foul, foolish and abominable quibbles, contrary to the law of God, to the law of nature and the written law" and saw his mandate from Pope Benedict XIII to be to show the world the specimens of abomination contained in the rabbinic writings. A comment made by a modern Christian scholar gives us a clear picture of Geronimo's writing as well as many others who came later and emulated him with terms of revilement, vituperation, and even profanity when discussing rabbinic sources. This scholar wrote, " . . . for our purpose it is not necessary to wade through the filth that Geronimo's . . . treatise contains." [13]

By far the greatest of earlier Christian medieval works on Judaism was that of Raymund Martini. [14] The second and third parts of his **Pugio Fidei** were devoted to Judaism. He cited the full range of ancient and medieval Judaic literature up to

his time including the recent scholars such as ibn Ezra and Maimonides, as well as the **Bereshit Rabbah** of R. Moses Hadarshan,
a work attributed to the eleventh century scholar of that name,
but generally unknown until very recently. [15] During the thirteenth century Dominicans supported an extensive program of
teaching Arabic and Hebrew to Dominican monks who would
then be able to read the sources of Islam and Judaism in the
original and argue with Muslims and Jews from their own sources.
One of the Dominicans thus educated was Raymund Martini.
Another was Paulus Christiani (d. 1274), a Jewish convert who
was a leading spokesman at the famous disputations at Barcelona
with the celebrated Naḥmanides, R. Moses ben Naḥman in 1263.
[16]

Our knowledge of Raymund Martini (1225-1284) is meagre.
Whether he was originally a Jew has not been verified. As a
member of a committee to censor the Talmud he protected it
from destruction. Martini was frequently accused in modern times
of forging alleged Judaic sources but the supposed forgeries
have since been found to be authentic. [17] Martini's work served
as a major reservoir of Judaic materials for centuries. The **Pugio**
became even more serviceable when Joseph Voisin edited it in
1651 and added a Prolegomenon consisting of a discussion of
the written and interpretive Torahs, an analysis of the Mishnah
and hermeneutics, Old Testament quotations that were interpreted
in a parallel way to Jewish usage in the New Testament, and
rabbinic parallels to the New Testament. Voisin also updated
the work with quotations from Maimonides, Albo and Azariah
dei Rossi. In this way **Pugio** became a major encyclopedic and
anthological work on Judaism of over seven-hundred pages. It
stands out as an unusual example of the sources available to
Christian scholars who began to turn to Judaica in the sixteenth
century in ever-increasing numbers. [18] But Martini too had
a vituperative touch. Thus, he referred to the rabbinic passages
he selected as "pearls from a great dung-heap." He entitled his
work **The Dagger** to indicate that this work will be the medium
through which the Christian can slice the divine bread of truth
to the Jews, or with which to destroy their falsehoods. [19]

Martini foreshadowed the sixteenth century Christian
Hebraists by understanding the importance of his using the Hebrew
text, and he took as his examples both Paul and St. Jerome who
used the Hebrew. Martini confined himself almost entirely to
midrash and talmudic àgadah in the Judaic literature other than
biblical literature and its commentaries, hardly touching upon
the halakhic material, a style later adopted by Reuchlin. It appears
that frequently Christian scholars were fascinated by the esoteric
elements of àgadah, and the mystical kabalistic lore, which suited
their theological interests more fully. Thus too Pico della Mirandola
took up kabalah as his major interest and used it in polemical

efforts. He argued that all christological ideas can be found therein, and Johann Reuchlin echoed his views. [20]

The Reformation stirred intensive efforts among Protestant scholars to do similar work to that of Martini, Pico and Reuchlin from a Protestant point of view. A major product of this new interest was the edition of the Hebrew text of the Mishnah brought out by Surenhusius between 1698-1703, along with a Latin translation, commentaries, notes and indices, a veritable proto-modern work of scholarship that facilitated Judaic studies. A new trend during the seventeenth century was that of including rabbinic materials and parallels in commentaries to the New Testament, an important example of which was **Mellificum Hebraicum,** published in 1649 by Christopher Cartwright covering the Old Testament Apocrypha and the New Testament. Such commentators owed a significant debt for their ability to execute such works to Johann Buxtorf the Elder whose work **Lexicon Chaldiaicum Talmudicum et Rabbinicum** was published by his son in 1640. This work incorporated the contributions of R. Nathan ben Yehiel's (d. 1106) **Aruk** and Elias Levita's **Meturgeman** of 1541. This period also saw the significant work of John Lightfoot (1602-1675), **Horae Hebraicae et Talmudicae** published between 1658-1678, including many glosses and excursi on rabbinic and New Testament parallels. The period was closed with what has been termed "a malignant book" written by Eisenmenger, **Entdekks Judenthum** in two volumes and published around 1700. This was a harsh attack on what Eisenmenger considered Jewish blasphemy against the Trinity and Mary, and all the errors, fables and absurdities as he termed them, allegedly in their own words. The eighteenth century, however, was less productive, and a more creative era arose during the nineteenth century. In the final analysis it must be conceded that even if some of the writing was unsavory, all of this early literature facilitated the modern scientific study of Judaism and led from an age of polemic and disputation to the interchange of Renaissance Italy and Holland on to the dialogues of the twentieth century. [21]

III. Christian Study of Judaica

A massive Hebraic-Judaic literature written by Christians existed by the middle of the sixteenth century. There were treatises that covered the Hebrew language, the Old Testament and rabbinics. Such efforts to incorporate Judaic data into Christian commentaries or Judaic perspectives into Christian writings began in the fourth century with Saint Jerome. [22]

Knowledge of Hebrew was rare before the Renaissance and Reformation turned the minds of Christian scholars back to classical and apostolic origins. The interest in Greek and Hebrew was intensified as was the interest in such classical works as that of Hermes Tresmegistus and those of the cult of Orpheus alongside the Old Testament. And out of these interests sprang Pico's intense romance with Judaic kabalah. It was his and Johann Reuchlin's interest in kabalah which had a large role in sending them to the study of Hebrew. Philological interests at the University of Alcala as well as among Polish and Lithuanian scholars influenced by Isaac Troki also contributed to the rise of Christian Hebraism. Pico was the first serious Christian student of Judaic kabalah. Pico espoused nine-hundred theses with which he challenged the scholars of Rome in 1486, thirteen of which were used against him in charges of heresy. In his defense he wrote his **Apology,** and in reference to the fifth thesis of the alleged thirteen heretical ones he wrote, "There is no science which can more firmly convince us of the divinity of Christ than Magic and Cabala." For Pico "magic" really signified natural science applied to discover the secrets of the universe, and "cabala" signified a metaphysical philosophy applying neo-Platonic principles to the Bible. In order to expand his capability in this latter field he studied Judaic mystical writings which were translated for him by a Jewish convert, Flavius Mithridates, and in his **Apology** he introduced Judaic kabalah to Christian scholars. Pico and Johannes Reuchlin found in kabalah all the major doctrines of Christianity: the trinity, incarnation, original sin, and atonement through Christ. [23]

Johann Reuchlin, a jurist, the celebrated personality of the Pfefferkorn incident, was the earliest major Christian Hebraist who not only taught Hebrew to others, but from 1510 he successfully campaigned for its introduction into universities. For although the Council of Vienna, 1311, recommended chairs in Hebrew for the universities very little had yet been done by the end of the fifteenth century. As a matter of curiosity even later it was often taught in centers in England and France where there were no Jews or a few Marranos since 1290 and 1394 respectively, and in Spain where there were no Jews since 1492 and where Marranos would be afraid to surface for the study of Hebrew. Frequently these studies were aided by converted Jews, and in the sixteenth century by the rising coterie of Christian Hebraists. [24] In 1492 Reuchlin studied under Frederick III's physician Jacob Yehiel of Loans and later from 1498-1500 he studied with the noted biblical commentator, Obadiah b. Jacob Sforno (1470-1550) at Rome. Sforno was then studying philosophy, mathematics, philology and medicine in Rome, and later settled in Bologna. His relationship to Reuchlin might be epitomized by his own commentary to Ex. 19:5 to which he appended Deut. 33:3 and argued that the Torah urges the Jew to love all humans, not only Jews, quite a step forward for that period of Jewish history. [25]

Reuchlin was less concerned for philology, rabbinic idiom and theology, concentrating mostly on the kabalistic esoterica. He was convinced that in numerology especially can the Christian mysteries be detected. In a mystical vein he wrote, "When reading Hebrew I seem to see God Himself speaking . . . And so I tremble in dread and terror, not however without some unspeakable joy . . . " He was convinced as were genuine Judaic kabalists that in his discovery of the true way to use words and manipulate letters of the alphabet one can effectively cure the sick, raise the dead, exorcise demons and perform many other miraculous feats. He believed that Plato and Pythagoras before him received knowledge from Jews, and drew the logical conclusion that all ultimate wisdom is concealed within the secrets of the Hebrew language. He had a special interest in divine names and he believed that the authentic pronunciation of Yhwh was known only to Moses, and that this tetragrammaton, the four-letter name contains the ground of all truth and reality, the secrets and mysteries of the four elements of nature, the four directions of the compass, and the four tones of the musical scale. How to harness this name was the problem as Reuchlin saw it. Ultimately Reuchlin produced a five-letter name, asserting that in the additional letter reposes the secret of all truth and salvation, and when added to the unpronounceable tetragrammaton, this letter energizes the four-letter name. This fifth letter he believed was the shin and Yhwh was thus transformed into Yehoshua or savior. [26]

Reuchlin's kabalistic interests also drove him to attempt to explain all the twenty-two letters of the alphabet, their numerical values and the mystical meanings implied therein. In a later work he turned to an intensive and concentrated effort to prove the trinity through kabalistic numerology. All of this was the product of Reuchlin's deep conviction of the truth of Christianity. But this conviction was coupled with an equally strong opinion that Christianity stemmed from Judaism, and that Judaism was God's primary revelation. He believed further that all religious, moral and scientific truth, even that of the Greeks, must have been channelled through Judaism. Consequently, the study of the original Hebrew and rabbinic sources was vital. He went to Tübingen which was already a famous university in 1481 but was not able there to attain an education in Hebrew. After his studies with Loans and Sforno he published his **Rudimenta Hebraica** in 1506, a work which opened the door to Hebraic study for Christians. But Reuchlin went on to publish two more works dealing with Hebrew grammar and biblical texts. All three books were guides for independent study of Hebrew by scholars who had no access to Jewish teachers. Reuchlin studied Rashi's commentary to the Bible and recognized the immense debt of Nicholas de Lyra to Rashi. He adjudged that if one struck out all of Rashi from de Lyra only a few pages would remain. Protestants were more inclined to the study of Hebrew for they were more interested in rabbinic exegesis than Catholics. The latter still relied on the Vulgate, reaffirming it even more vigorously after the Council of Trent. Centers arose at Basle, Paris and Zurich. Hebrew was on the curriculum also at Leipzig, Tübingen, Mainz and Heidelberg. And although Martin Luther urged the study of Hebrew at Wittenberg this city did not emerge as important a center as the others. [27]

As it turned out a Roman Catholic had published a Hebrew grammar before Reuchlin. This was Conrad Pellican (1478-1556), a Franciscan, who heard a Christian debater worsted by a Jew because he could not bring to bear the original Hebrew texts. This thought burdened him for years and he later studied Hebrew with a convert Matthew Adrian and published his grammar for Christian scholars in 1504. He can be claimed by Protestants, however, because he was deposed as a Franciscan monastery superior in 1526 for Protestant tendencies and fully identified with the Reformation when he accepted a call to teach Hebrew at Zurich for the Zwingli reformation group from 1526 until 1556. Pellican freely admited his debt to Rashi, and to both Joseph and David Kimḥi and Abraham ibn Ezra. [28]

Reuchlin's work, however, far surpassed that of Pellican. And Reuchlin's contribution to Christian Hebraism was immense, especially after he became embroiled in the celebrated Pfefferkorn episode. His partial victory in this battle with the Dominican Order facilitated the study of Hebrew at universities and the emerging interest in Judaic studies. The Jewish convert, a former butcher by name of Joseph, now Johann Pfefferkorn, was a protege of Dominicans. He won the support of the Emperor Maximilian to destroy all Hebrew writings in Frankfort and Cologne. He argued that Jewish possession of all these works is what impedes their conversion to Christianity and that post-biblical writings are inimical to the Pentateuch and Prophets. Pfefferkorn had already written two pamphlets in an unsuccessful effort to convert Jews in 1507 and 1508 in which he urged the German princes in whose lands Jews lived to compel them to attend church and to deprive them of all books except the Bible, and ridiculed Yom Kippur confessional rites. He also wrote a pamphlet against Jewish "perversion" of Passover which he considered should be observed appropriately as symbolic of Christianity. Reuchlin was enlisted as defense attorney, and he argued that Jews had a right to their religious works, and that these works were in no way harmful to Christianity. Pfefferkorn then published **Handspiegel, (Mirror)**, a slanderous work against Reuchlin, and the latter published **Augenspiegel (Eyeglass)** on the value of Judaic writings, upholding his previous views that Judaic works were in no way a threat to Christian faith and extensively refuting Pfefferkorn. Both sides wrote barrages of virulent letters and pamphlets over a period of several years. Ultimately the irritated Dominicans compelled Reuchlin to appear and defend himself against charges of heresy. Reuchlin was cleared of these charges by the presiding bishop of Speyer, whereupon the Dominicans appealed to Pope Leo X who was also then facing the challenge of Martin Luther's ninety-five theses. To help the Dominicans save face as the defenders of orthodoxy in an era when the papacy faced multiple attacks, the Pope in 1520 found **Augenspiegel** to be scandalous, the same year as Reuchlin was called to teach Greek and Hebrew at the University of Ingolstadt. This juxtaposition of events underscores the futility of the Dominican political victory in the face of a new era ushered in in large part by Johann Reuchlin in which the study of Judaica was legitimatized and expanded, contributing to the still-evolving modern concept of theological interchange. [29]

The important contribution made by these pioneer Christian Hebraists spotlighted in the Reuchlin-Dominican debate was the triumph of the humanistic method in the study of scripture. In a sense they were rejecting theological tradition in favor of the proto-modern textual analysis dependent upon knowledge of the classical languages. Taken one step further this implied that the content of faith can be determined only by scrutiny of the original text, and is not necessarily validated by tradition. This view was basically an onslaught upon ecclesiastical authority. [30] Its importance as a source of theological cleavage is as pertinent today as then, and in Judaism as in Christianity. When tradition is also believed to be the substance of divine revelation the challenge is even more confrontational. Cologne's desire, therefore, to silence Reuchlin, and Pellican's dismissal from his Franciscan monastery are understandable given the premise of an authoritarian posture in theology.

A vital element in the development of Hebraic and Judaic studies was the establishment of a printing press, which was done by Daniel Bomberg in Antwerp. There he published in 1517-18 the first **Mikraòt Gedolot,** the most accurate Hebrew text of the Bible then available with a full rendition of Aramaic targums then known and a great array of medieval Judaic commentaries and glosses. This was followed by the Babylonian and Palestinian Talmuds in 1523. Bomberg understood the importance of having Jewish scholars involved, and invited Elias Levita who had been born in South Germany, lived in Padua, then lived in Rome for thirteen years as tutor of Cardinal Egidio de Viterbo, whence he fled to Venice when Rome was sacked in 1527. It was in Rome and Venice that Levita produced his major works in linguistics and grammar, and the **Sefer Hazikhronot,** critical-historical essays on the masoretic text (the text as transmitted in Judaic tradition, masorah). It was in his other major work on masorology, **Masoret Hamasoret** in 1538 that he suggested a new theory: that vowel and punctuation marks were post-talmudic, and hence the key to understanding scripture through the proper reading of the text was not a matter of revelation but humanly conceived. It was in essence a strong argument against divine authorship of scripture and must in its starkest form also be seen as a prelude to Benedict Spinoza's higher critical theories. [31]

Levita's work underscores the fact that Judaism studied by Jews was not unaffected by Christian Hebraism which stimulated so many new developments. Similarly, Judaism studied by Christians did not leave Christianity unaffected insofar as its roots were in the Old Testament, and that theories touching upon revelation and authorship of scripture deeply affected Christian faith, even ultimately the christology. In this connection it must not be forgotten that since the earliest times church theologians interpreted the New Testament in the light of the Old Testament and read out of the Old Testament the advent of Jesus. [32] Indeed, one of the basic arguments during the sixteenth century for the study of Hebrew was to facilitate the discovery of the truth of the New Testament by studying the authentic text of the Old Testament in Hebrew. And yet ironically these same studies brought the theological authenticity of such interpretation into some degree of doubt if the Old Testament text as we have it was not the revealed text, but the product of post-talmudic masoretes. If the vowels and punctuation marks were not divinely revealed what guarantee is there that the consonants were? The very basis of revealed religion was at stake, and it was therefore no accident or mere whim that ecclesiastical authority was vigorously opposed to humanist methodology and to Christian Hebraism. Ultimately all factions made peace with modernist bibilical study although there remains much opposition to it in the ranks of that segment of Judaism termed "orthodox," and among fundamentalist Christians.

Another Hebrew press in Basle was sustained by the exceptional ability of Sebastian Münster (1488-1533). [33] Münster translated scriptural texts, and wrote grammars and dictionaries. In addition to his work in linguistics and lexicographies, he translated the entire Old Testament into Latin with annotations that included rabbinic material. His Latin translation of the Bible is intermediary between earlier Judaic exegesis and the future English translations of the Bible. [34] He also translated the Gospel of Matthew from Greek into Hebrew with annotations, and published ibn Ezra's commentary on the decalogue. He published Maimonides' well-known thirteen principles of faith enunciated in his **Commentary to the Mishnah,** but he erred in calling these a statement of "Pharisaic" religion. He also published Moses of Coucy's work on the so-called "six-hundred and thirteen" commandments, **Sefer Hamizvot Hagadol,** and the writings of Josephus. [35] Münster's motive in all of this was to enhance one's understanding of the matrix of the apostles. It must, of course, be forgiven such scholars as Münster who took it for granted that such medieval Jewish scholars as Moses of Coucy or Maimonides were expressing ideas of faith that were the same and the only option current in the environment of the apostles. Such anachronism was inevitable before the onset of the new historicism which was yet to come.

Münster worked with Bomberg's **Mikraòt Gedolot.** His notes also show that he used new editions of **Seder Òlam**, Yosippon, and other Hebraic works rapidly becoming available, including medieval commentaries and halakhic works. [36] Münster used Rashi, Kimḥi, Naḥmanides and ibn Ezra and studied with Elijah Levita, the important scholar of masoretic and targumic studies, and termed him the greatest Hebraist. Levita influenced Münster to rely upon targumic exegesis. Münster valued Jewish commentaries, used their hermeneutical rules, and followed R. Menaḥem di Recanti in paying careful attention to the masoretic trop (the musical accents) and the nikkud, (the punctuation symbols) to determine where to break phrases and sentences. He also used Talmud and midrash, many instances of which became widely circulated in later generations. [37]

Münster also translated works of Levita and much other halakhic and theological literature. A study of his Latin Bible has shown how he influenced future biblical translation including the King James Authorized Version. His work was largely based on showing the continuity between the Old and the New Testaments. After his first translation of the Bible he revised it and brought out a second, and a comparison of these show his growth in rabbinic knowledge. His translation was hailed as Hebraica Veritas, as providing a true translation of the Hebrew, and his work generally influenced Christian Hebraism for many generations. [38]

One of the men influenced by Münster was Phillipus Ferdinandus Polonus (b. 1555). He was born Jewish in Poland, was converted to Roman Catholicism, and then to Protestantism. [39] After leaving England he lived in Leiden, Holland where he was a teacher of Joseph Scaliger, the Dutch theologian. Through his influence on Scaliger and the Englishman John Selden, Polonus became an important link to seventeenth century Christian Hebraists, other Puritans, and to orientalists who had a common interest in offering freedom to the Jews of Holland and England. Only one of his works is extant, entitled **Haec Sunt Verba Dei (These are the Words of God).** In this work he provided an anthology, most especially a discussion of the celebrated so-called six-hundred and thirteen commandments. This was a methodological pattern through which many Christian scholars strived to present a quick and cursory review of Judaism. Polonus also used the Bomberg biblical text. Like Münster he presented a discussion of Maimonides' thirteen principles of the Judaic faith, and the thirteen hermeneutical rules of R. Ishmael. [40] Like Polonus there were other Jewish converts to Christianity who helped fertilize Christian study of Judaica, among them Antonius Margarita, the son of a rabbi in Regensburg. [41] Polonus also influenced the Englishmen Samuel

Purchas and John Selden. Purchas started an English version of the six-hundred and thirteen commandments in the seventeenth century. He did not finish the work, but did produce an English summary of the dietary practices. Similarly other English Puritans active in Judaic studies such as John Weemse and Thomas Godwin attempted partial presentations, while John Lightfoot chose to do so in his work on the tractate Ėruḃin. The most comprehensive work to affect England, however, was the previously mentioned **Historia de Riti Hebraici** of Leone da Modena after it was translated in 1650 by Edmund Chilmead. And there, too, we find a complete survey of dietary practices. [42]

Polonus also reflected the great Christian interest in kabalism which was discussed earlier. [43] He evinced enthusiasm for the secret meanings embodied in the letters of the alphabet, the numerological mysteries found in gematriot and notarikon, and re-wrote a sentence of Jacob ben Asher's comment on Genesis 1:1 which provided a word for each letter of bereshit "in the beginning." The Hebrew consonants of this word are: bet, resh, aleph, shin, yod, taf. Asheri sought to emphasize how the kabalistic techniques offer prescient insights. He read each letter as a word: the Hebrew bet of bereshit for barishonah, "in the beginning," the resh for ràah, "he saw," the aleph for ėlohim, "God," the shin for she'yisrael, "that Israel," the yod for yikablu, "will accept," the taf for Torah. He then translated the word as denoting "In the beginning God saw that Israel will accept the Torah." Polonus, applying the same technique sought to prove the christology by attributing to the same letters the following words, barishonah, ràah, ėlohim, sheyaḃȯ, Yeshu, tifartenu, "in the beginning God saw that Jesus our glory will come." In similar fashion Polonus and others critiqued the Judaic interpretations of scripture and replaced them with christological allusions. [44]

Michael Servetus has already been discussed earlier. [45] Servetus was knowledgeable of Judaic sources, and was influenced by these studies. In turn he contributed to future developments. He argued against the trinity by pointing out first, that there is no mention of it in the New Testament or the apostolic writings, and second, that Judaism had already provided such "modes" or "manifestations" to God represented by such terms as ElShaddai, Yahweh, Elohim, Shekhinah, and the like, without any of these implying separate "persons" or entities. He drew upon Judaic philosophers such as Isaac Arama, Maimonides and Philo to prove that "modes" of God do not mean "persons," and that while God appears and functions in variegated manifestations these are not perceived as separate "persons" and, therefore, do not support the Christian trinitarian concept. [46] Servetus also used the targums and argued that to understand the God-idea Christians must return to Judaic sources. Thus, in essence, Servetus worked in precisely the opposite direction of Pico and Reuchlin. While the latter labored at proving the trinity out of kabalah, Servetus sought to disprove it out of the targums and the philosophers. For Servetus the trinity signified "a three-fold invocation of the divine name." [47] Although there were already unitarian sectarians in Christendom, Servetus might be considered the father of modern Unitarianism in a formal sense. And it is of some curiosity that just as he was accused of judaizing, and even of being a Jew, and argued intensely against the trinity using many of the arguments used by Jewish polemicists, in modern times many Jews have found an alternative to both Judaism and Christianity in Unitarianism.

In Paul Fagius (1504-1549) we have another species of Christian scholar of Judaica. He rejected both Reuchlin's kabalism and Servetus' unitarianism. His interest in Judaica was to discover the matrix out of which Jesus and the apostles emerged. He was also concerned to explain the controversy over faith and works in the light of Christian origins and the significance of the sacraments or rituals of the New Testament. He was in the Calvinist tradition which emphasized the continuity between the Old Testament and the New Testament, and saw the Old Testament as a virtual blueprint for a covenanted society. He placed a strong emphasis upon Aramaic as the language of Jesus and the apostles, and argued that by understanding the Aramaic interpretation of scripture it will be easier to grasp how Jesus and the apostles understood the Old Testament. [48]

In 1542 Fagius wrote a work called **Hebrew Prayers** in which he discussed the berakhot, the prayers of thanksgiving known as birkhat hanehenin, "the berakhot in gratitude for benefits received," and the birkhat hamazon, the prayer of thanksgiving after meals, commonly called Grace After Meals. He provided a Hebrew text with a Latin translation, a comprehensive introduction and interpretive notes. He also included Christian parallels as, for example, in his discussion of the berakhot for bread and wine, he included a section on the Lord's Supper. Fagius' intent was to Christianize the Judaic ritual and thereby to demonstrate the meaning of the eucharist and how to conduct it. He hoped that by using the rituals of kiddush and hamoẓi at the Sabbath or Festival table he could bring Christians to visualize how Christ conducted the ritual of the Last Supper. [49]

In his publication of the Grace After Meals Fagius christianized the passages by inserting christological paraphrases. For example, in the second berakhah of Fagius' birkhat hamazon we read,

> We thank thee Lord our God for just as you have
> given a lovely and spacious land to our fathers as
> a heritage, so too have you given a spiritual land in
> heaven above on the merit and death of your first

> born son, the dear Jesus, messiah, our Lord, whom
> you sent to this world to forgive our sins . . .

Fagius goes on in the same vein, adding christological paraphrases throughout. Thus the opening portion of the first sentence of the third berakhah in Fagius' version reads as follows:

> Have mercy, Lord our God, on Israel your people, that
> is, on all the Christians who believe in the sent messiah
> who are Jerusalem . . . [50]

What Fagius did was quite in tradition with the early church which midrashized and Christianized Judaic prayers, as is found in **Apostolic Constitutions** and other early literature. [51] Fagius also wrote on Tobit, Ben Sira and Mishnah Abot to demonstrate the Christian development of ethics and piety out of its Judaic roots in the same manner as he illustrated Christian practice and liturgy out of their Jewish antecedents. He published a Latin translation and commentary to Abot, perhaps among the earliest of such Christian efforts to indicate the compatibility between rabbinic and apostolic thought. He frequently offered New Testament parallels in order to argue that the rabbis taught Christian values. [52] This reversed a historic tendency to slander the rabbis as teaching anti-Christian ideas. Fagius even found that the rabbinic maxim, "All is seen, freewill is granted, the world is ruled by goodness, and all is according to deeds" (M. Ab. 3:19), taught Protestant providence as the dynamics of human behavior. But this motif in Fagius was not unambiguous. He found sufficient material upon which to base a view that the rabbis also taught falsehood. [53]

Fagius thus represented an aspect of Renaissance and Reformation Christian study of Judaica which was distinct from triumphalist polemic, and rather sought to elucidate early christological interpretation of scripture from Judaic sources, and more, to establish the continuity of Christianity to Judaism. This facilitated the argument that Christian interpretation was implicit in Hebrew scripture from the beginning and that Jews were blind not to see this.

Fagius used Judaic sources prolifically. He wrote a book called the **Interpretation of the Words According to Literal Meaning,** expounding the rabbinic hermeneutical methodology of peshat, and drew upon both talmuds, targum, and medieval exegetes from Saadiah to David Kimḥi. Fagius' additional motive was to establish the correctness of Protestant theology over Greek philosophy in order to validate the Christian doctrine of creation ex nihilo which he argued was the special nuance of the Hebrew word barà, "to create." [54] In this work Fagius covered his Judaic tracks to avoid being condemned as a judaizer by stressing that the doctrine of the trinity is implicit in the use of plural èlohim for God both at Gen. 1:1, and when God speaks to His two divine partners, saying "let us make a human" (Gen. 1:26). He also connected this verse to the second account of creation where the Bible reads "And He fashioned a human," and the Hebrew word for "fashioned" vayizer, is spelled with two yods instead of one (Gen. 2:7). Fagius saw in this an allusion to the aeons of Christian thought, this carnal world in which the human lives until the eschaton and then the spiritual world, transformed by the second advent of Christ. It is interesting, however, that in adopting this midrashic approach to the text, Fagius drew upon Rashi who saw in the two yods the past and future without asserting any theological conclusions. [55] Furthermore, Fagius saw in the use of both terms, **Yhwh** and Èlohim "the Lord God" as creator of the human, an implication that two parts of the trinity, the father and the son are represented. The divine names as defined by the rabbis, yhwh (Lord) as compassion and èlohim (God) as authority, were seen to be the creators of the world and the human. The third partner of the trinity, the ruaḥ, the holy spirit, was represented by the nishmat ḥayyim, "the breath of life." This infused the human with vitality, and raised him to a level superior to that of the animal kingdom. [56]

In his exposition of Genesis 1-4, we also find an example of how frequently a Christian scholar might be aware of Judaic views that Jewish scholars are not aware of or have forgotten and the latter reject the Christian exposition as faulty. Thus Fagius understood that there is a Judaic view that the doubling of the terms mot tamut normally properly translated as "you shall surely die" implies the death of both body and soul, that is death in this world and annihilation in the next. One modern scholar has argued that this went against the grain of Hebrew linguistics, and that in pursuing that line of reasoning Fagius "was treading on thin ice." The fact is, however, that such exegesis is very old and is found in both Philo and rabbinic literature. This points up how important it is in theological interchange to prudently examine all possible sources before dismissing the Christian exposition of a Judaic view. We have seen how the charges against Raymund Martini for forgery were proven erroneous. Similarly the pejorative nature of some Christian exegesis provokes Jewish scholars to reject the substance along with the tone. But this is not an appropriate reaction. We will see below how even Menasseh ben Israel went aground upon the shoals of apologetics in seeking to refute Alexander Ross. [57]

The tendency for Christian writings to possess a pejorative tone and a negative evaluation of Judaism instead of containing a straightforward exposition of Christian doctrine and practice and how these relate to their Judaic antecedents was probably the major reason for the general failure of the Christian mission to the Jews. The sixteenth century Christian study of Judaica held promise, from a Christian evangelical standpoint, for a new climate that might facilitate conversion of the Jews. For now not only were Christian scholars restating certain Christian values in Judaic terms, but they were capable of presenting a Judaized Christianity or a Christianized Judaism to Jews as a first stage in their transformation into Christians. That they failed to materialize what from their standpoint was the inherent promise of their situation might be owing to the charges levelled against them of "judaizing." This compelled them to denounce Judaism and argue forcefully and pejoratively against the very Judaic sources that nurtured them, or to print supplementary works as conversionist polemics to cover their Judaic tracks.

An example of this type of supplementary tract is that of Sebastian Münster **Torat Hamashiah (The Torah of the Messiah)** published in 1537. [58] This contained a Hebrew translation of Matthew, the first such effort known, and also contained a treatise entitled, "This is the Holy Christian Faith" which explained Christianity and Judaism, and sought before Fagius to demonstrate the continuity of Christianity from Judaism. He stressed the monotheistic nature of the Christian God-concept by defining God in a paraphrase of the hymn Âdon Ôlam. [59] Münster gave an excellent exposition of the trinity as monotheistic by comparing the terms used for the trinity: father, son and holy spirit, to the unity of meaning in such Hebrew terms as ènosh, àdam and ìsh, all of which describe the same entity, the male person. [60] While neither this nor Münster's other material explaining the divine-human nature of Jesus and Jesus' role in his first advent ultimately affected many Jews, it is notable that it was all written in Hebrew and designed for Jewish readers.

In his exposition of Judaism Münster turned to Judaic liturgy. In this he exhibited an astute awareness that the theology of worship was the warp and woof of Judaic doctrine. [61] He argued for the incorporeality of God, largely paraphrasing the hymn Yigdal. [62] He was groping for a way to alleviate Judaic abhorrence with the idea that God became man, although the idea that God could be incarnate was definitely found in Judaic tradition. Münster need not have conceded that this was perceived as an impossibility and as a blasphemy. [63] Münster went on to discuss the significance of Torah and the nature of both the Messiah and the messianic age. He affirmed the restoration of Israel to its land, a human, Davidic messiah, and an ingathering of Jews from all corners of the world. Without doubt Münster's writings on this matter facilitated millenarian emphasis upon this ingathering and the discovery of the lost tribes which played such a role in the seventeenth century. Münster's emphasis throughout was on pre-talmudic Judaism in an apparent effort to delineate the continuity of interest between Judaism and its alternative, or its fulfillment,

Christianity. In this way Münster sought to point to the natural evolution of Judaism into Christianity and omitted a discussion of talmudic-medieval halakhic and àgadic development and kabalism. This omission was intended to deflect Christian critics who were harshest in their treatment of that material, and divert Jewish readers from apprehending the great gulf between that development of Judaism and its Christian offspring. [64]

Münster fell prey, however, to the traditional negative styles in the section of his work called "Some Answers to the Vanities and Errors of the Jews," in which he referred to those who charge that Christianity believes in "three gods" were "lying Jews." He defended the "death of God" as it occurred in the death of Jesus by arguing that when the body dies the soul lives on, and so too the human aspect of the divine-human compound in Jesus died, but not God. Münster also sought to discredit Judaic disbelief that the Messiah had already come by pointing to the wide array of contradictory views in rabbinic literature as to whether the Messiah will come when all are just or all are wicked, on where the Messiah is located before his appearance, whether all sacrifices or some, and which, will cease when the Messiah comes. In addition to the negatives in this section Münster added another section in which he was critical of Jewish avoidance of conversion. He gave various reasons for Jewish intransigence such as their condemning converts as "destroyed ones" (a literal meaning of meshumadim), their refusal to marry with converts, and their refusal to eat with them. In discussing the refusal to eat, he correctly noted that Jews will not use Christian butter, cheese, milk, or any food cooked by Christians. These items played a considerable role in medieval halakhah and continue as issues of debate in modern times between the so-called orthodox and other Jews. In this section he also fell back on such traditional epithets for the Jews as "depraved" and "corrupted." [65]

It appears that actually Münster's work **Torat Hamashiaḥ** was a compound of two separate treatises, one directed to Jews, the other to Christians. In the latter, Münster included his negative material in order to fend off charges of judaization. Thus, this section contained a full exposition of detailed Judaic ritual which Münster would not have had to write for Jews. Münster offered detailed descriptions of Purim, Hanukah, Sukot, the ritual of the lulab and etrog (palm branch and citron), the ceremony of bedikat ḥameẓ, removing the ḥameẓ on the fourteenth of Nisan, the use of tefilin (phylacteries) and talit (prayershawl). Obviously, this was designed to provide Christians with a better understanding of the Judaism around them, and at the same time to assure them of its error and redeem himself of charges of judaization. [66]

The pejorative in Münster grew with another treatise in 1539. This was called **Mashiaḥ** and consisted of a dialogue between a Christian and a Jew. Here Münster put into the mouth of the Christian the view that Jews have a peculiar color of face, "for you are black and ugly and not white as are other men." He went on to accuse the Jews of using their women as prostitutes to get what they want out of gentiles. The Christian clarified that this was a biological or genetic trait that went back to Abraham about whom we read that Pharoah treated Abraham well for Sarah's sake (Gen. 12:16). [67] The treatise goes on to describe the intense superstition of the Jews, although this is a rather curious criticism of Judaism in an age when Christians also believed in ghosts, demons, evil spirits, and the power of the devil, and it hardly seems possible that Münster was being anti-Jewish with these arguments. [68] It almost appears that Münster here was presenting a typical Christian position on Jews and even exaggerating it for effect, in order to make it seem quite as absurd as it really was. Once again, as noted earlier concerning Judaic writers, and even Spinoza, we must bear in mind the Renaissance habit of dissimulating in literature. Nevertheless, this is not to minimize the adverse effect that such writing might have on Jews, and the evil influence it might wield in the hands of readers even generations later.

When he became serious Münster addressed himself in the above dialogue to the question of why Jews do not believe that Jesus was the Messiah. The Jew responded that Jesus did not bring universal peace (Is. 2:4), Judaic restoration, as promised by all prophets, or the end of idol worship (Zekh. 14:9). Münster defended Christianity against the charge of idol-worship, but this was mere apologetic, for much of non-Christian, non-Islamic humanity was still involved in what Judaism would consider idol-worship. On the question of universal peace, Münster argued rather anemically that when Jesus came the pax Romana was in force, and it was his rejection by Jews that stirred up war again. Münster also used the rejection of Jesus to explain why Jews were not yet restored to their land. Münster thus had to explain Christian belief that there was continuing guilt for the rejection of Jesus, and not because the Jews had him crucified. But, based upon anti-Christian Judaic polemical works stretching over several centuries, he argued that the Jews crucify him over and over again by asserting that Jesus was a magician, that his crucifixion was appropriate for that reason, that his crucifixion was intended to prove a priori that he was not God, and that he was a wicked man who seduced the world. [69]

The only explanation possible for Münster's approach in this treatise, in the light of his great admiration for Judaic scholars which he expressed as late as 1546, is as an act of self-protection after Bucer's "Cassel Advice" and Luther's pamphlet against Sabbatarians in which he excoriated judaizers. The same thing was done by Paul Fagius in 1542. [70] Both were friends of Elijah Levita and immersed in Judaic studies. Both therefore used traditional pejorative material to ward off damaging allegations. Whether this brings into question their integrity as scholars, and whether they were in truth anti-Jewish will be a matter of differing opinion. Some scholars will maintain they lacked integrity and were basically anti-Jewish. [71] I would argue they were not anti-Jewish. Thus, a citation from **The Book of Faith** which both Münster and Fagius used urges Christians to speak with Jews " . . . with soothing and kind words . . . One should speak to the Jews with wisdom and gentleness." [72] Münster and Fagius tried to preserve their integrity as scholars of Judaica by furthering the possibility of Judaic studies and the interchange of theological knowledge such as they enjoyed with Levita. That this was not calculated to build better bridges appears true in retrospect. But nevertheless, their efforts mark at least a preliminary, if deficient, step in the first stage of transition to modern dialogue. Thus, in 1554, there appeared a conversionist tract written by John Emmanuel Tremelius without any pejorative remarks. He translated John Calvin's **Catechism** into Hebrew with a Hebrew introduction and called the work **Catechism of the Elect of God.** [73]

Another important aspect of sixteenth century Christian study of Judaica should not be overlooked. This is the study of targumic materials, which ultimately flowed into a significant aspect of New Testament studies. Although Martini used the targums in his **Pugio** at the end of the thirteenth century, little attention was paid to them until **Onkelos** was published in 1482, after which the Augustinian monk Aegidius became interested. Levita worked under his patronage in Rome in 1515. From that time forward interest in targums grew and many polyglot versions of texts were published, as were a large number of translations, and studies of the targumic language. Following Elias Levita's **Meturgeman,** the significant dictionary of J. Buxtorf, Sr., **Lexicon Chaldaicum** was written, and these works spurred seventeenth century studies. [74]

IV. The Seventeenth Century

Latin ceased being the international language during the seventeenth century, and scholars were in search for a universal language. Philosophers and philologists followed variegated courses but a consensus emerged for the idea that Hebrew was the original universal tongue, the lingua humana, spoken by God, and therefore by Adam and other humans before the tragedy of Babel (Gen. 11:9). Johann Reuchlin believed as early as 1508 that "God wished his secrets to be known to mortal man through Hebrew." The belief was also current that the language of eternity in heaven will be Hebrew, as was prefigured in the Greek version of Revelation when twenty-four elders and four beasts together use the Hebrew Amen and haleluyah (Rev. 19:1-8). It appeared logical that if Hebrew was used in heaven one ought to acquire the language on earth. On the other hand, the view that ultimately prevailed was that of Thomas Hobbes who negated Hebrew, Greek and Latin in favor of the modern vernaculars (at that time) such as French, Dutch and Spanish. [75]

Language scholars, however, believed that Judaic kabalah would lead them to a better understanding of the mysteries embedded in the divine Hebrew words, and so the quest for a lingua humana and the interest in kabalah fed upon one another. By the middle of the seventeenth century Lurianic kabalism was the primary expression of Jewish mystical theology, and was already seriously influencing Christian thought. [76] After Pico and Reuchlin the leading Christian kabalist was Jacob Boehme. The study of kabalism also spread to England where the linguistic philosopher John Wilkens expounded upon such central terminology as gematria (explaining a word by the numerical value of its letters), zeruf (the transposition of letters), notarikon (using each letter of a word as an abbreviation for a whole sentence), and the àtbash system, a code in which the àlef and the taf are transposed, as are the bet and shin, gimel and resh, and so on through the alphabet. Wilkens was an English representative of a school of thought which found that the word barà, to create, used at Gen. 1:1, signified the trinity. He took the letters bet, resh, àleph, as denoting ben, ruaḥ and àḇ, the son, the holy spirit and the father. The enthusiasm of Wilkens also infected other Englishmen including the poet John Milton, but ultimately by 1668 he had given up his zeal for Hebrew as the lingua humana. He is paradigmatic for the cooling off on this idea everywhere. [77]

The quest for Hebrew had its lasting impact upon English millenarians. Hebrew, the ten lost tribes, the expected end-time were all harnessed by Menasseh ben Israel. The Englishman Edward Brerewood, for example, offered a theory that the Indians in North and South America were an offshoot of Tartars who in turn were of the Israelites. He had them migrating from Asia over the land mass which joined Asia to North America. [78] This was an influential sixteenth-century view espoused by seventeenth century millenarians referred to in the previous chapter.

But more vital than these peripheral matters was the surge of biblicism represented by the translations of scripture on both the continent and in England. William Tyndale had already encountered opposition in 1530 among those who believed that if the lay people had the Bible in English they would all become heretics. Nevertheless, the drive for translation continued from Miles Coverdale who did not use the Hebrew and Greek texts, until the King James Authorized Version in 1611, which was based on the original Hebrew and Greek. [79] Interest in biblicism among such figures as John Selden, John Lightfoot, Edward Pococke (1604-1691) and John Milton, led to increased interest also in post-biblical Judaism and medieval Judaic commentaries. Milton's poetry is not only permeated by his Hebraism, but his translation of certain Psalms, and his "Paradise Lost" as well as his work in Christian theology, all point to his mastery of Judaic sources. Milton's tutor in Hebrew studies was William Chappel who also taught John Lightfoot. [80]

The interest in Judaism went further. Some adopted Judaic observances. Usually this took the form of adopting the seventh-day Sabbath. Very early on the Lollards, a reforming sect of the fifteenth century produced some who advocated the seventh-day Sabbath and abstention from pork. [81] In 1595 a certain minister, Nicholas Bound, wrote a book on the Sabbath question. In it he argued that the fourth of the ten commandments, to sanctify and observe the Sabbath day, was a perpetual obligation, albeit he regarded the complete Sabbath rest to have been transferred to Sunday. For Sunday observance he advocated total abstention from all forms of activity with a stringency that even went beyond that of Judaism. From this widespread introduction of the strict Sunday Sabbath arose the logical question: when, and by whose authority was the Sabbath changed from the seventh day hallowed by God, to the first day? Possibly influenced by continental groups that travelled the route from Wyclif to Huss to differentiated Protestant sectarianism, there arose the "Sabbatarian Dissenters" or "Seventh-Day Men." [82]

Another book was published on the Sabbath question by Theophilus Bradbourne in 1628. Its title, **A Defence of the Most Ancient and Sacred Ordinance of God, the Sabbath Day,** indicated its proposition. He argued that the only divinely hallowed day is Saturday, and all who violate it are sinners, the observance of Sunday being gratuitous for that is only a work-day. He argued that Sunday has no basis in scripture (Old and New Testaments) and its observance is superstition. [83] At first John Trask had observed the Judaic-style Sabbath on Sunday, but later transferred it to Saturday. It was at that time, close to the middle of the seventeenth century, that Sabbatarian churches began to multiply in England. By 1661, one of their ministers, John James, and his congregation were considered dangerous enough to king and country for him to be arrested and martyred. [84] This did not stop the movement. It flourished into the eighteenth century, and although it began to decline in England was exported to the United States where substantial numbers of Seventh Day Baptists and Seventh Day Adventists perpetuate the tradition.

Christian study of Judaica in the seventeenth century was given strong impetus by the millenarian movement. [85] Thus,

Joseph Mede's work **The Key of the Revelation** was extremely important and he influenced a host of seventeenth century writers including John Milton and Isaac Newton. It has been noted that those who believed that the Jews will be converted like Paul was, by a direct celestial vision, were able to study in Mede how Paul was the quintessential or typological Jew. Mede had elsewhere written of ten parallels between Paul and the Jews as a whole, including Paul's zeal for the halakhah, his obstinate opposition to Christianity prior to his conversion, and his conversion by miracle. He added that as Paul reproved Peter as a judaizer, so will the Jews reprove those who sit on the seat of Peter, the papacy, for its paganism. [86]

Working in the opposite direction, Christian study of Judaica stimulated the judaizing tendencies. These consistently cropped up in different countries and among various Christian groups. Thus, as early as the mid-sixteenth century, Richard Bruern (b. 1519), a leading Hebraist and teacher at Oxford, prayed like a Jew, and ate the paschal lamb on Maundy Thursday. Whether genuinely part of his eccentricity or not, he was later charged with both homosexuality and adultery and dismissed from Oxford. [87] Many other judaizers were imprisoned, and virtually persecuted all through this period. Some of the people who preached Judaism and observed Jewish practices actually became Jews. Among the punishments accorded to the aforementioned John Traske was the burning of a "J" on his forehead to brand him with his crime: Judaism. The Lord Chancellor spoke of how rapid had been the growth of his movement in a short time, and the Archbishop of Canterbury found it important enough to speak in the august chambers of the House of Commons of the inclination of some "to Judaisme, as the new sect of the Thraskites." There were even those who circumcized their children, and it was they who provided infusions for the seventh-day movement. [88]

Christian study of Judaism and Hebrew in England reached a crescendo in the seventeenth century. But it had a long tradition from much earlier times, long before millenarianism, sabbatarianism and judaizing became stylish. It was a respectable pursuit in the universities. Lady Jane Grey, Queen of England, was proficient in Hebrew early in the sixteenth century. She had corresponded in Hebrew with Conrad Pellican of Zurich. Fagius had been succeeded at Cambridge by Anthony Chevalier, author of a Hebrew grammar and tutor of Queen Elizabeth who in turn was an accomplished Hebraist. Many other female royal Hebraists lived in both England and on the continent. [89] The tradition went back even earlier. From the fourteenth century on, not long after the expulsion of the Jews from England there arose a "Maimonides circle" in England. [90] The fourteenth century translations of the work were used in the sixteenth and seventeenth centuries. The mathematician and philosopher at Oxford, Thomas Allen (1542-1632) owned a fourteenth century Maimonides manuscript with marginal and additional notes. This points up both the extent of study of Maimonides that went back to that early period, and the high quality of Judaic learning that flourished in Renaissance England. Maimonides study also went on among scholars on the continent. The Catholic scholar Gilbert Genebrard translated Maimonides' thirteen principles into Latin as did others. At that time too, Maimonides' **Sefer Hamadá** (**The Book of Knowledge**), the first book of his massive **Mishneh Torah** or **Yad Hahazakah** was translated by a certain Ralph Skynner who sent it to the well-known scholar, Bishop James Ussher (1580-1656) sometime before 1624. Ussher's correspondence contained much Judaica and in 1636 also revealed that he had already been reading Menasseh ben Israel. Skynner's letter to Ussher called Maimonides' works "the ocean of all Jewish learning," and in other letters his knowledge of Judaica and the ability to write Hebrew were fully illustrated. Ussher's collection of letters, in turn, indicated that Skynner, a scholar of both Mishnah and commentaries, was consulted for his knowledge of oriental languages, talmudics and medieval rabbinics. It is of some interest too that John Milton based his right to divorce his wife when she left him in 1643 upon Maimonides' **Hilkhot Gerushin (Halakhah of Divorce)**. [91]

In 1631 the section of **Mishneh Torah** entitled Hilkhot Teshubah (Halakhah of Repentance) was translated into Latin at Cambridge and entitled "The Penitential Canons of Maimonides." The orientalist Edward Pococke was friendly with Jews in Aleppo and Constantinople, and had served as Regius Professor of Hebrew at Oxford in 1648. He published **Porta Mosis** in 1655 which consisted of extracts from Maimonides' **Commentary on the Mishnah.** Another Maimonidian expert was Humphrey Prideaux (1648-1724) who was part of a Maimonides circle at Christ Church, Oxford, where portions of the **Mishnah Torah** were published in Latin around 1680. Johannes Buxtorf, Jr., who corresponded with Menasseh translated letters and responsa of Maimonides. These were only a few among many other scholars who found a fascination in the Judaic-rabbinic studies with the works of Maimonides. [92]

Space does not permit the kind of in-depth analysis I would prefer to offer of the Judaic materials produced in England. But I will provide a brief adumbration of at least one Christian scholar in England on the lines accorded earlier to other personalities. I have chosen Alexander Ross because his work was characteristic of the polemic of the opposition and was selected by Menasseh ben Israel as worthy of response. The interchange that resulted from the juxtaposition of Ross and Menasseh offers a window onto the transitional era in Judaeo-Christian dialogue. Menasseh was still a polemicist, often defensive and apologetic, but even at that was not far different from some Judaic polemicist-apologists of the twentieth century. The hallmark of their work is an effort to defend Judaism from calumny even where the critique is founded upon accurate Judaic sources. The Christian scholar often offers a critique of negative aspects of halakhah in Judaism in which he argues against what he considers crude minutiae of ritual or absurd ideas. This draws forth a defense. The argument is made that such crude rites or absurd ideas are not an aspect of Judaism. Quite often, however, as will be noted in Menasseh's case, the Christian scholar has accurately pinpointed a weak spot and was critical of Judaism on the basis of citations from within its own sources, or from observation of the behavior of some Jews toward Christians in social and business situations, and has not invented or forged a Judaic idea or text. In such instances, the Judaic scholar would have greater credibility if he approached the material more prudently and conceded that not every aspect of Judaism or the behavior of Jews is perfect. The unfortunate defensive tendency to establish the uniqueness and superiority of every facet of Jewish doctrine and practice, and to equate Judaic ethics with the behavior of Jews without discriminatory judgment remains a weakness in modern Judaic dialogue with Christian writings. It is legitimate for Judaic scholars to freely examine whether the apologies for Judaism such as that of Menasseh ben Israel on the threshold of the modern era were valid in every detail, or whether at certain points the critics had verifiable grounds for their strictures. [93]

V. Alexander Ross and Menasseh ben Israel

Alexander Ross published a survey of Judaism which went under the title of **A View of the Jewish Religion** in 1656. This was a reissue of the first section of Ross' earlier work **Pansebeia,** a disquisition on world religions. [94] Ross offered a relatively balanced picture of Judaism in contrast to the many pejorative pamphlets of the time. For example, Ross did not stigmatize his work with the conventional blood libel charge despite its being a current issue in anti-Jewish publications at the time. As late as 1648 a certain Thomas Calvert of York, well-read in Hebrew and a student of Judaic studies reissued the venerable libel that Jews crucified a Christian annually in order to use his blood in the Passover wine and mazah (unleavened wafer). [95] Calvert made no effort to reexamine the history of this charge in order to arrive at greater intellectual precision on the matter. Calvert translated the testimony of a certain Rabbi Samuel who became a convert to Judaism and in the course of his annotations he wrote of Jews, "So much are they bent to shed the blood of Christians . . . they add to that sinne to make it sweet and delectable that he who doth it is as if he had offered a Corban [a sacrifice] to the Lord . . . " and then described the alleged Jewish procedure of crucifying a Christian. [96] Menasseh responds to this charge in his **Vindiciae Judaeorum** with a number of arguments which are uneven in their accuracy or persuasiveness. But this is not the issue. Rather, the problem is that even in such a crucial slander, Menasseh has made some self-serving selections of the material in Maimonides' tenth chapter of his treatise, "Kings." [97]

Maimonides had extracted from rabbinic literature what he considered definitive halakhah, and one of the opinions he advocated was: if a gentile converted to Judaism he was unable ever to renounce his new faith. If he refused to remain a Jew he is eligible for capital punishment. It must be conceded that there is little to choose from between Maimonides and Torquemada on this subject. Furthermore, Maimonides drew an invidious distinction between crimes committed by a gentile against a gentile and those committed against a Jew. He stated that if a gentile embraced Judaism he is exempt from punishment for all the sins he committed before his conversion, even murder and adultery, provided these crimes were committed against a gentile. But if they had been committed against a Jew, he is to be put to death upon his conversion to Judaism. [98]

Medieval Hebraists had free access to such pronouncements, and clearly most especially in England where a circle of Maimonidian scholars existed, his views were undoubtedly widely available and widely discussed. As a matter of fact it would be of considerable interest to know whether the fascination with Maimonides was not to some degree attributable to the perception of him as an excellent primary source for all the negatives the scholars wanted to extract from Judaic halakhic and doctrinal materials. Maimonides was also the source for the opponents of readmission who argued that Jews would not treat Christians fairly in business. For Maimonides also selected as halakhah that in litigation between a gentile and a Jew, the Jew may use any means to win, either by choosing secular law in a case where he may lose in a rabbinic court, or the rabbinic court if his resort to these ancient privileges will be an advantage. Maimonides selected this halakhah despite the fact that it was only one opinion stated in the Talmud and was opposed by R. Akiba who argued that it is prohibited to cheat a gentile. And although Maimonides expressed the view that Christianity and Islam are monotheistic, he did not in this halakhic instance adopt the same magnanimity of another medieval commentator who annotated the talmudic text. In a marginal note the latter said that even the talmudic proponent of discrimination only meant that to be applied to barbarians, but not those who "live under the disciplined norms of religion," namely the Christians and Moslems among whom medieval Jews lived. [99]

Menasseh certainly had a difficult task to defend charges against so-called Judaic perfidy and anti-gentilism when Christian scholars, generally unfamiliar with the complex structure of talmudic literature and the less celebrated commentators were generally drawing their information from the scholar who was considered the leading halakhist of recent centuries and the greatest medieval Jewish mind. Menasseh also faced a difficult challenge in seeking to respond to a major charge often repeated by irate Christian scholars, namely, that Jews curse Christians in the synagogue. This engendered great emotionalism, and it was unfortunate that it was not regarded and dealt with by the Jews as an anachronism rather than a libel. For in truth the sources used by Christians accurately spoke of a liturgical formula used in the amidah, but which had long ago been eliminated from the text. They failed to check the seventeenth century liturgy, and Jews argued from its absence in the liturgy known to them that it never existed. Possibly they had no way of verifying it through ancient manuscripts, but they were imprudently hasty to assume that Christians had fabricated a slander.

Alexander Ross stated that in their prayers three times a day, Jews "utter an execrable prayer against all Christians and baptized Jews." Menasseh denied this and insisted that the prayer at issue contains only an attack on "minim, that is, Hereticks," referring to fellow-Jews. He then sought to counter it by citing an opposite type of prayer for the welfare and peace of the kingdoms in which Jews resided. At the same time he argued that Jews are always loyal citizens. [100] Menasseh provided what was until then a rare English translation of the prayer under consideration, one of the earliest English renditions of Judaic liturgy, the twelfth berakhah or paragraph of the amidah. His text is not in current vogue, nor for that matter has there ever been only one version of this paragraph. In fact Menasseh even brought to the reader's attention new versions arising in the seventeenth century. [101] The prayerbook used in England before 1290, compiled by Jacob ben Judah of London in 1287, had substantially the same text as that which stood behind Menasseh's translation. Menasseh was undoubtedly as innocent of dissimulation as a nineteenth century scholar who edited that early English prayerbook and referred to the paragraph under discussion as "the ancient form." [102]

The "curse" under consideration was the birkhat haminim, a formula aimed against Christians and introduced into the amidah by Gamaliel II at Yabneh. Alexander Ross was able to learn of this from three sources. The first was the Church Fathers, chiefly and perhaps originally from Justin Martyr who had argued with Trypho, "For in your synagogues you curse all those who through him [Jesus] have become Christians . . . " The second source was from later Christian critics who relied upon Justin. The third source might have been internal Judaic sources such as the talmudic reference to the formula and medieval manuscripts of the Siddur

of Amram Gaon. Even in the circumstance that the talmudic reference would be regarded as ambiguous because some censored
texts read zedokim (Sadducees) and others read minim which was
taken to be "heretics," and even if the Amram prayerbook were
scarce, there was a precise Judaic source in the **Maḥzor Vitry**. This
was a northern French compilation of the liturgy dating to the end
of the eleventh century and containing a censored line in the
twelfth paragraph with spaces where words were deleted. This pointed to the implication that the deleted words were offensive leading
to the supposition that minim was understood as Christians and
not heretics. There also existed a ninth century halakhic source
that attested to the fact that this anti-Christian paragraph had
been introduced into the liturgy after the rise of Christianity.
The way in which this was phrased was "after the incident,"
which was a code-word for the crucifixion, or more likely, the
establishment of Christianity following the War of 66-73. Although
the existence of such a paragraph was still denied in 1897, a
version of its ancient Palestinian text was discovered in 1898. [103]

Here we have an instance where both Christians and
Jews can be faulted. The Christians were correct as far as the
early Christian centuries were concerned, but at some indetermi-
nate juncture the text was censored and noẓrim was deleted.
Since the text was no longer available, Jews were able to feign
outrage by the charge, but Judaic scholars should have known
better, and probably did.

Similarly, Menasseh took Johannes Buxtorf to task for
saying in his **Biblia Rabbinica** of 1619 that the ălenu prayer,
a closing adoration of Judaic worship contained blasphemous
lines. Menasseh was able to reproduce the text in current use
to deny the existence of such lines. Once more an anachronism
was involved. Christian scholars might have seen the offending
lines in the prolific supply of liturgical manuscripts available
at Oxford and on the continent. But again, the offending line
had been deleted by the Christian censor. [104]

Alexander Ross dealt fully with the Jewish liturgy and
referred to both issues. He evinced a detailed grasp of the wide
spectrum of hilkhot tefilah, of both the content of the liturgy
and the prayer practices and procedures, down to the minutest
detail such as the admonition not to yawn during worship. The
unfortunate aspect of Ross' work was his occasional use of a
scornful tone in reference to minute details without seeking
to investigate what the cultural or psychological conditioning
behind these halakhic developments might have been. At times
Ross is even vituperative in traditional medieval style. [105]

The sources behind Alexander Ross cannot always be
determined with any certainty. He might have studied some Judaic

works in the original, the **Pugio,** John Selden's **Treatise on the Jews of England,** or any one of the many writings I have referred to earlier. Possibly he read Edmund Chilmead's translation of Modena's **Riti Ebraici.** He named Sebastian Münster, Johannes Buxtorf and Antonius Margarita as well as Judaic commentators such as ibn Ezra and David Kimḥi, among others. He rendered many liturgical passages in English quite accurately, but it is not known whether he was copying others' translations, translating from the Latin from such works as that of Fagius referred to earlier, or directly from the Hebrew. Thus, for example, we learn from John Evelyn's diary that in 1641 he met a Jew in Amsterdam who married a Kentish woman who affirmed Judaism. The man showed Evelyn "several books of their devotions which he had translated into English for the instruction of his wife," thus indicating that English translations of the liturgy were extant and available before 1650. [106]

Ross was one of those who replied with an unequivocal affirmative to the question whether conscientious princes may allow Jews to reside in their kingdoms. He advocated their segregation until they accept Christianity, but he espoused freedom of religious practice for them. He regarded them as essential to the Second Coming and suggested they be treated with kindness, never noticing the inherent contradiction between kindness and segregation. On one page, he denied they were part of the covenant of Abraham, and on the next he maintained they were still the covenant people. [107] Ross thus exhibited what might almost be hypothicated as a typical love-hate relationship these Christian scholars carried on with Jews and Judaism. At times they were enamored with Judaism but could not find sufficient love to tolerate real Jews in their environment. At times they despised Judaism, in Ross' words about Passover preparation, because it is a system in which the faithful are more careful "to wash the outside of the platter than to purge out the rapine and intemperance that is within," but advocated kindness and freedom to the real Jews in their midst. [108] This is a phenomenon which has also been seen in so noble a personage as John Milton who regarded Judaism as the chaff out of which was winnowed the Christian gospel, and wrote, "while we detest Judaism we know our selves commanded by St. Paul Rom. 11 to respect the Jews . . . " This did not preclude " . . . by all means to endeavor their conversion." [109] This love-hate relationship was archetypal for Christians, and went back to Saul-Paul who struggles with it in supreme agony in Romans 9-11. It is the product of the confrontation between parent and daughter, Judaism and Christianity, each staking out an exclusive claim of covenant and means of salvation. The love-hate relationship is destined to be smothered only when dual covenant theology will supersede mutual exclusivity.

The ambivalence of Ross is found throughout the genre

of Christian Judaica. On the one hand it transmitted Judaism relatively faithfully, and advocated gentleness for Jews, and on the other exploded in a great catharsis against Judaism and urged the suppression of the Jew. But Christian faith in the conversion of the Jews was so strong and fascination with the matrix of Christianity was so compulsive that Christian scholars of Judaica expended effort and time in the compilation and exposition of Judaic learning.

Ross attributed much of his knowledge to Buxtorf's **Synagoga Judaica.** [110] There, he said, he learned "many of their superstitions." An example he offered was the swinging of a cock around one's head on the day before Yom Kippur (Day of Atonement) as a vicarious atonement. He aptly attributed the custom as symbolizing that one "man" was substituted for the other because one form of the Hebrew for "cock" and "man" geber is the same. Here Ross was using philology, as many Christian Hebraists did as a means of clarifying the foundation of ritual observances. One modern critic has called this an example of Ross' "rags and tags." But in actuality this form of modern critique of Ross or other Christian scholars of Judaica is not warranted. The latter often rooted their scornful evaluations of the minutiae of Judaic ritual in authentic traditions. Thus the swinging of the cock, or kaparot as it is called (the ritual of atonement), was mentioned as early as the **Maḥzor Vitry** of the eleventh century, and was still found intact in the **Shulḥan Arukh** of the sixteenth century. Although it was frowned upon by the compiler, Joseph Karo, it was supported by Moses Isserles and other commentators. There was no dearth of earlier sources from which Ross' information could have been derived concerning kaparot along with a great array of other minutiae which were indeed superstitions and neither mandated by Judaic theology nor the classic structure of halakhah. [111]

While Menasseh ben Israel took strong exception to Ross' description of Purim as a "Bacchanal," as if it were a pagan wine-god festival the truth is unfortunately that in traditional Purim merry-making, much in imitation of the medieval European Christian carnival, there was a great deal of imbibing of alcoholic beverages. It was recommended that one drink so much that he will not be able to discern the difference between Mordecai and Haman. Customs that Ross recorded that might appear to modern Jews as being bizarre and not genuine, are confirmed by **Maḥzor Vitry.** [112]

Ross and others had exceptionally good opportunity to gain a detailed knowledge of Judaism because of the many works already referred to that preceded him which were expositions of the so-called six-hundred and thirteen commandments. This was a popular medium for presenting Judaism, and since it purported to describe each divine injunction, whether civil or criminal law, domestic relations or ritual practices, it is understandable why these avid students of Judaica acquired such extensive knowledge of both mandated halakhah and ongoing evolving folk-custom or superstition. Frequently scholars were selective. Thus Polonus discusses the "65th commandment" based upon Ex. 22:27, "you shall not revile judges, nor curse the prince of your people," and argued that it applied to non-Jews, a view with which Menasseh was in accord. As a matter of fact the first part of the verse had long ago been applied by both Philo and Josephus in accord with the Septuagint to foreign gods, a view recommended by Azariah dei Rossi in his discussion of Philo, and now adopted by Menasseh. This discussion led further into the complex question of whether Lev. 19:18, "you shall love your reah," means narrowly your "neighbor" and by implication your fellow-in-faith, or broadly, your fellow human. There were arguments for and against each view. One might select either tendency in both of these questions as in many other such ethical issues. [113]

Ross, along with the whole array of Christian scholars was thus subject to a particular flaw. They did not understand the complexities of rabbinic literature sufficiently to perceive that it was not monolithic, that the Talmud and midrashim were replete with diversity and that one may select one's preferences. They were insufficiently aware of how to ascertain whether a particular view represented consensus Judaism or was merely one supposition among many. Thus, Menasseh, while sometimes hasty to deny assertions made by Ross which were verifiable in Judaic sources, was nevertheless within the tradition in his apologia when he leaped over talmudic and medievalist discriminatory positions such as, for example, that of Maimonides, to recapture the striving for universalism that counterbalanced them. Menasseh was within his rights to reject Maimomides' view that limited the love command to one's brother in faith. Yet with a Maimonides circle having been active in England and his works considered of supreme importance his anti-gentile views would emerge in full view, and cause Judaism to bear the brunt of being antipathetic to Christians. [114]

VI. Dynamics of Christian Judaica

Their remains to be made a few comments on the dynamics of the study of Judaica and the Hebrew and Aramaic languages during the sixteenth and seventeenth centuries. Mention has been made of Elijah Levita's landmark work, **Massorah.** [115] Levita's thesis that the vowel points were late talmudic, dating to fifth century Tiberius had a delayed reaction. Only at the end of the sixteenth century did Roman Catholic polemicists argue that Protestants were running afoul of true faith by placing their trust in canonical scripture alone when that text cannot be considered a divine and infallible one. Since the Jews have invented the vowel points, they argued, they have by human devices corrupted the understanding of scripture for which one must rely solely upon Christian tradition that is embodied in the Roman Catholic Church. Contrary to Levita some Reformation apologists responded that the vowel points went back to Moses. [116]

The opponents of Levita could point to talmudic opinion that the points were Mosaic. Johannes Buxtorf, Sr., offered an alternative theory in a work of great erudition in which he placed the points with the so-called "men of the great assembly" which he identified as a council called by Ezra, and denominated the massoretes as editors and not innovators. [117] But Buxtorf's view solved nothing. It left the theory of human origin or the vowel points in place, and his precise scenario was in any case soon refuted. There remained two options in the Christian world: to accept the vowel points as divinely revealed with the consonants, or to concede their human origin and bring into question any interpretation of scripture not validated by the infallible teaching of the Church. What was often overlooked was that Levita had affirmed the belief that how to read the consonants was a carefully transmitted oral tradition before the massoretes invented the points, and that the massoretes simply invented the points to preserve the carefully preserved tradition of how Moses read the text. [118] Ultimately Christian debate dealt with this aspect of the problem, and Christian consensus emerged that despite the human invention of the vowel points, the reliability of revelation remained intact. [119]

This debate over vowel points reverting to a theory propounded by a Judaic scholar is but one small example of how Judaic studies intruded into Christianity and evoked polemics not only between Protestants and Catholics but also among Protestants. It is a symptom of the ever-presence of Judaism in Christian consciousness and the constant impact that Judaism has upon Christian self-perception and self-identity. It is a late medieval eruption of the darker side of the problem pointed to by Marcion almost a millenium and a half earlier when he urged Christians to jettison the Old Testament.

Another aspect of the dynamics of Christian Judaica is seen in the debate which emerged over the value of Judaic observance. As more and more Christian scholars and Jewish converts to Christianity wrote on Judaism, a negative evaluation of Judaic ritual observance emerged. This impelled Judaic response, the first major one being Modena's **Riti**, the next one being Menasseh's **Vindiciae**. This inaugurated a modern apologetic era in which Jewish scholars defensively portray Judaism as compatible with patriotism, slanted toward ecumenism and solicitous of gentile welfare. It was actually the great work of Buxtorf, Sr., the **Synagoga Judaica**, written in 1603 which caused misgivings in Modena and inspired him to write his **Riti.** Modena wrote a Christian friend that he had "the intention of refuting entirely that work of Buxtorf and of giving a true account of the fundamentals leaving out those items which have been considered by our own people as superstitions." Here we have an instance of a professed selectivity of sources to portray Judaism in a rational and gentle light as over against the critical Christian selectivity which often put forward unsavory aspects of folk superstition as representative of Judaism. [120]

Buxtorf's work was a monumental reprise of Jewish practice and doctrine. He was the greatest Protestant scholar of rabbinics at that time and wrote in German so that both Christians and Jews would be able to read the work. His intent was also to prove that Judaism was non-biblical, and by pointing out the worst features of folk custom he hoped to impress the reader whether Jewish or Christian with the idea that it is due to Jewish rejection of Christ that they are subject to such a degraded religion, and by implication the same would happen to papal Christians. Nevertheless, Buxtorf's manner of describing Judaism, despite its occasional tone of derision, was accurate. He remained loyal to actual texts, and in no way distorted them. He refrained from the use of the type of vituperation found in Luther, or of some of his contemporaries. What Buxtorf did was to include the unsavory aspects of ritual manifestly rooted in superstition, and what Modena did was to omit these. Buxtorf also exposed certain halakhot from the areas of commerce and finance that tended to discriminate against gentiles in order to bring into question whether Jews were capable of being patriotic citizens and whether they were, as those who opposed their freedom in Holland and England charged, misanthropes and xenophobic. These were ideas reinforced by many things said in medieval Judaic writings. Modena sought to show other sources that espoused equality for non-Jews in the practice of charity, and that special laws existed to discourage mistreating a non-Jew. He also tried to prove that Jews readily acculturate. But as noted earlier, it was difficult to overcome the negative impression conveyed by Maimonidian halakhah. Modena's efforts show a process that points up how when polemics are engaged in with design to triumph, rather than dialogue intended to empathize, both the critic and the apologist will equally be tendentious and unobjective in the strictest understanding of that term. [121]

A significant issue that aroused fervent Christian defense was that of the messiahship and sonship of Jesus. As has been seen, the worrisome nature of this problem for Christians ultimately impelled scholars to pursue kabalism as one more means of establishing the truth out of Judaism. It was very telling that Christian faith did not seem to suffice, and the faithful seemed compelled to seek verification in Judaism. An interesting less known work of this type is that of Philippe de Mornay (1549-1623), a Huguenot. [122] His intention was to refute all sorts of sects including, among others, atheists, Muslims and Jews. But he placed great store upon the common foundation upon which rests Judaism and Christianity, the Old Testament, and therefore was anxious to prove the roots of Christianity in Judaic scripture. Yet he went far beyond scripture and cited or alluded to many early rabbinic and medieval writings. Curiously the modern editor said nothing of the Judaic aspect of this interesting work, but there can be no doubt that Mornay's work highlights the tension in the heart of the Christian scholar. It also played a role as a source for seventeenth century writers on Judaism, including Alexander Ross whose own introduction to his work on Judaism has affinities with that of Mornay's. [123]

There was great ferment among Christian students of Judaica throughout the sixteenth and seventeenth centuries. This becomes evident from the letters of one such Christian scholar, Johannes Drusius (1550-1616), and those of his son who died at a very young age, Johannes Drusius, Jr. (1589-1609). Their correspondence was quite extensive and we find among the correspondents Johannes Buxtorf, Sr., and Joseph Scaliger. [124] The collaboration offered these Christian scholars by Jews, and this quest for the knowledge of Judaica in the original language were two sides of the same coin. It was part of a long tradition which went back to the earliest years of Christianity. Jewish scholars were empathetic to Christians seeking knowledge of Judaica despite their being here and there halakhic restrictions upon teaching Judaism to non-Jews. The line of tradition runs from Paul through St. Jerome to Nicholas de Lyra and on to the men of the Renaissance and Reformation. [125]

The attraction to knowledge of Judaica led, as we have seen to much judaizing in late medieval Europe from Bohemia to England. But such attraction for both pagans and Christians to Judaic observance went back to the earliest period of Christianity. People were interested in the special aspects of Judaism such as monotheism, the Sabbath, and even curiously, their dietary practices. At the same time they were repelled by what they considered Judaic aloofness in their refusal to marry with non-Jews. It has been aptly indicated by one scholar that "the roots of hate and love were the same," or as put by another, "antipathy and sympathy stood side by side." [126]

It must not be thought, however, that polemics were conducted only by Christians to discredit Judaism and convert

Jews. The scholarly world is familiar with a whole genre of literature that goes under the title of <u>Adversus Judaeos</u> or <u>Contra
Judaeos</u> in which Judaism is taken to task by Christian writers.
But anti-Christian polemics were extensively written by Judaic
scholars as well with the intention of discrediting Christianity.
A comprehensive study of this phenomenon juxtaposing the basically
fruitless endeavor of the mutual recriminations and refutations
of one another's traditions by Christian and Judaic scholars is
yet to be written. During the medieval period Judaic writers
handed out as bitterly as they received. Their anti-Christian assertions were as vituperative and aggressive as the Christian writers
who wrote on Judaica. Judaic efforts were not, publicly at least,
designed to convert Christians, but rather more to prevent Judaic
apostasy. As Christian writers attacked Judaic ritual superstition,
Judaic writers assaulted Christian irrationalism. As Christian
writers labored to prove the christology out of the Old Testament,
Judaic writers marshalled endless arguments to refute christological
concepts: the divinity of Jesus, the virgin birth and the resurrection. If Christian spiritual leaders from Paul to Luther and Calvin
were not always civil to Judaism, neither were the rabbis who
gathered the anti-Christian polemic always civil to Christianity.
[127]

The earliest comprehensive Judaic anti-Christian work
was that of an anonymous scholar, entitled **Sefer Niẓẓahon, (Book
of Polemic)**, which is dated to the thirteenth century and was
likely an anthological work that compiled many polemical arguments
circulating at the time, and included fresh material by the compiler.
[128] This is a paradigmatic work, and has a mate published in
the post Renaissance Reformation era, that of Isaac ben Abraham
(1533-1594) of Troki, Lithuania, author of **Hizuk Emunah (Faith
Strengthened)**. [129] These two works spanning the Middle Ages
attest to as highly systematic and sophisticated an anti-Christianity
literature as there was an anti-Judaism literature.

Modena's **Riti** and Menasseh's **Vindiciae** are a different
genre. They constitute apologetics without the refutational and
confrontational polemic. They usher in a new age wherein the
historical tensions might possibly be ameliorated. The two great
parallel traditions, Judaism and Christianity were in tension because
of the historic conflict raging since the first century. The strictures
against Judaism were based upon valid sources. Judaism was not
monolithic and possessed less than perfect opinions along with
alternate views on almost every subject. Judaism was not subject
to catechism, papacy, or authoritative hierarchy or authority
residing in the individual scholar's interpretation of the text and
contemporary need. His authority extended wherever constituents
accepted it, and rested upon his intellectual powers and persuasive
capacities. Therefore, when Menasseh rejected as invalid some
of the assertions of Christian critics he was on as slippery ground

as they were. They were correct insofar as they were able to verify their views in the primary sources. He was correct insofar as he was able to cite contrary views that were less stringent and tended toward the ecumenical. The critics were falling back on the harshest views of Judaic sources designed to oppose and distance an oppressor. Menasseh was moving forward into the future when ecumenical interchange could be conducted without the tension of medieval animosity. The critics failed to grasp the legitimacy of selectivity in Judaism, a failure often still pronounced in the twentieth century, a failure to be overcome only by extensive and intensive Judaic-Christian dialogue on theological and halakhic themes.

The dynamics of Christian study of Judaism and Judaic study of Christianity from the beginning until the end of the period under review in this volume (ca. 1650), were such as to perpetuate polemic and antipathy. This in turn concealed respect and genuine intellectual concern. The modern period has seen a shifting in these dynamics. Scholars of both faiths study both traditions as academic disciplines. What is now called for as a breach-healer is intellectual interchange of a high theological calibre which will search out the legitimacy of the dual claim to election and salvation; the wellsprings of covenant theology.

Chapter Eight

A BACKWARD GLANCE

We have now briefly surveyed the relationship with Judaism of the Renaissance and of that attitude toward life and the individual which we call Humanism. We have seen how it affected men who would otherwise have been conventional talmudists in Italy, such as Farissol, Modena, Azariah dei Rossi, Delmedigo and others. Humanism and the Renaissance impacted Judaic learning, religious life-style, and the degree of Judaic acculturation. The diffusion of the Italian Renaissance through Europe effected what one scholar has called the true Reformation of the sixteenth century, the Protestant and Catholic Reformations being secondary. [1] Whatever might be one's perspective on this matter regarding Christianity and European history, it is a certainty that the Renaissance was a major influence and catalyst in transforming medieval Judaism into modern Judaism. The cultural influences and the interaction with Christians similarly were factors that brought Judaic scholars to new approaches to writing history and expounding Judaism.

If anything stands out more than all else as a product of the confluence of Renaissance and Reformation in Judaic development it is the spur they gave to acculturation and accommodation of Judaism. Some have regarded the Renaissance to be the more potent force in turning western civilization toward modernity because under its teaching " . . . religion is not a doctrine leading to salvation along a path of definite ritual. It is a relation between man and higher powers which manifests itself in human behavior." [2] This attitude was accommodating to Judaism which had long emphasized observance of halakhah over creedal affirmation as central to salvation. But even more important, because it was a point of view that ultimately led to the separation of church and state and open-ended pluralistic societies it constituted a sea-change for the viability and acculturation of Judaism in modern times. The beginnings of that process are clearly evident in Italy, Holland and England. [3] The seeds sown by the Renaissance rabbis and scholars in these centers flowered in Germany during the eighteenth century and brought forth the Judaic reformation in the nineteenth.

The sympathy with which Judaism was able to get a hearing from a person in a Humanistic frame of mind is exemplified by Jean Bodin (1530-1596). Bodin wrote **Heptaplomeres** in 1593, in which he had seven people participate in a religious discussion. There were one each of Roman Catholic, Lutheran and Calvinist persuasion who argued their respective positions. A Christian convert to Islam refuted them, and a Judaic figure refuted all of them in turn. There was also present a person who espoused what was considered "natural religion" who owed loyalty to no dogma but centered his religion on morality as a product of reason, and finally a person who synthesized all of these positions. The book was considered dangerous to faith and not fully published until 1857.

Bodin portrayed the Jew and the Muslim as emphasizing such elements as might be identified with natural religion, and was most eloquent in his critique of traditional Christian doctrine. The leading dialogist in the book, furthermore, is a Jew named Salomo Barcassius, and one detects Bodin's solid knowledge of Judaica in Barcassius' talks. In contrast to the positions of both Luther and Erasmus who compared Catholic ritualism to Judaism, Bodin evinced greater insight when he had the Jew say, "Repentance and good deeds wash out sin better than sacrifices." This is an interesting allusion to the High Holy Day prayer which reads that "repentence, prayer and righteous deeds" annul the severe decree of annual judgment. But it is also a direct allusion to the view of Yohanan b. Zakkai, founder of rabbinic Judaism. [4]

The trend toward acculturation inspired by the Renaissance was such that David and Abraham Provenzalo of Mantua proposed a Judaic college in 1564. David was versed in Italian, Latin and Greek, was a friend of Azariah dei Rossi, and Abraham was versed in philosophy, medicine and other arts and sciences. The school was to be "dedicated to Torah and to the sciences," an unusual juxtaposition for Judaism. The letter outlining the plan makes a point to lament the ignorance of most Jews, and their isolation from the constantly growing wisdom in the humanities. Those Jews who were intellectually curious sought general learning in Christian universities and Judaic study was weakening. This school, therefore, was to provide a three to five year course in Torah, Bible commentaries, rabbinic doctrine, and observance, and to hold daily prayer while at the same time providing a full-scale general education. But this proposal was made as the Catholic reaction to the Protestant Reformation was under way, and never materialized. [5]

Venice provides a window to our theme. Venetian Jews

enjoyed a privileged life during the sixteenth century. Two major groups flourished: the German and Italian Jews called the "German Nation" and Spanish, Portugese and Levantine Jews, joined by an influx of Marranos after 1589 and known as the Ponentine Nation. Each group had its own agreement or <u>condotta</u> with the Venetian government. This underscores the well-known pluralism within Judaism that is axiomatic throughout history, and yet is repeatedly forgotten in evaluating the evolution of Judaism, or in expounding the nature of Judaism. [6]

Venetian Jews were largely bankers and international merchants. They were oriented to the culture of the upper classes, and lived a fully acculturated life. Their children were given the same education as the non-Jews received. It included the arts, languages, humanities, penmanship, elocution, all branches of mathematics and science, including astrology and medicine. Rabbis and Christian ecclesiastics freely mingled and discussed religion. Leone da Modena referred to the fact that all his days he flourished among Christian scholars and took every opportunity to read Italian, Spanish and Latin books on Judaism written by Christian scholars. His grandson Isaac Levita wrote that Leone was indeed better known among Christian scholars and in church and government circles than among Jews. He enjoyed not only intellectual and theological discourse with them but also like other Jews he joined with Christians in regattas and in gambling. The Jewish poet Sara Coppio Sullam conducted salons for cultured Jews and Christians prefiguring the similar activity of women in Mendelssohn's Germany over one hundred years later. She was well-versed in the New Testament and Josephus, and carried on a considerable correspondence with a Roman Catholic priest. [7]

Most important is how this serves as a microcosmic reflection of what was to come. This Italian phenomenon was the matrix out of which emerged similar developments in Amsterdam and Hamburg. These were pronouncedly affected by Venetian sefardic Judaism, and from those cities there radiated the German reforming tendencies in the eighteenth century that led to the reform movements of the nineteenth.

This acculturation was not limited to lifestyle, education and social relationships. It also tended to affect halakhah. It revived the ancient tendency toward leniency of which I have written elsewhere. Thus is was permitted to sail a gondola upon the Sabbath, headcovering was regarded as a mark of disrespect, tennis was played on the Sabbath, gentile wine was imbibed, gentile cheese was eaten, other aspects of dietary practices were relaxed, and Jews participated with Christians in Venetian carnivals despite the Christianized pagan origins and undertones of these events. [8] These are only a few examples reminiscent of the kind of acculturation witnessed in the hellenistic era, which once again surfaced in eighteenth century western Europe and has persisted to this day. But it underscores the prefiguration of the nineteenth century reforming movements.

This experience of Renaissance Italy and Holland whose product was diffused to England and Germany has been remarkably consistent for its occurrence in every age of Judaism. It was certainly a reality in biblical Israel, and is attested to fully in the hellenistic period, where Alexandria serves as a leading example. It was even true in Roman society from after the first century to the fifth, although one might have expected Judaism at that time to have rejected the conqueror's civilization. Antioch is as good a microcosm for the ancient Roman period as Venice for the Renaissance. [9]

What is also remarkably consistent is the emergence of judaizers. We have discussed this phenomenon during the gestation of the Reformation, and the manner in which it manifested itself in seventeenth century England. [10] But here too we have a long and recurring tradition. Since the earliest complaints voiced by Paul on how certain Christians seem not to be capable of liberating themselves from Judaic observances, there have been similar occurrences in various periods. Again we have an excellent microcosm in fourth century Antioch. There the problem was confronted and battled by a leading church father, John Chrysostom. He stated the basic problem that agonized Christian scholars for centuries, and might still perhaps inform the minds and strike terror to the hearts of those who see no legitimacy in Judaism. The problem as phrased by John Chrysostom was: "If the Jewish rites are holy and venerable, our way of life must be false." [11] At the same period St. Jerome met the problem head-on. Jews were prone to argue that Christians falsified scripture and do not use the Hebrew text, that in the Hebrew text they will not find the christology they pretend to extract from their Greek bibles. Jerome, therefore, decided that Christian response to Jewish challenge must be based upon the Hebrew text which Jews acknowledged to be authentic. But John Chrysostom did not know Hebrew, and it was because the Jews taunted him with the argument that scripture is their's and not the Christian's, and with this argument attracted many of his parishioners that he delivered his sermons against judaizers. At one point he even betrayed his mortal anguish with the cry, "This is the reason I hate the Jews, because they have the law and the prophets . . . " (Jud. 6:6, 1. 913). Many centuries later the Jews were still using the same taunt against Christians, and this brought forth a medieval floodtide of Christian study of Judaica which was the direct heir to the small trickle produced by Jerome. [12] This was a liberating phenomenon for both Jews and Christians, if not at its inception, then at its peak, the twentieth century.

From Jerome's **Vulgate** translated from the Hebrew in order to sharpen the polemic lance of Christendom to the development of Christian Hebraism in the sixteenth century was a giant step for Christian scholars. The motives might not yet have been refined, but the activity was a contributing factor in the integration of Judaic scholars into the university world. The process, long, and at times arduous, led to twentieth century altruistic study of Judaism by Christians, and of Christianity by Judaic scholars. As this process continues to unfold in disinterested scholarship the notion that dual covenant interchange is plausible will appear more regularly. Religious tensions that have persisted for near two thousand years will have opportunity to be dissipated and there will be real potential that in the third millenium of the siblings, Christianity and rabbinic Judaism, history will witness a reconciliation.

In various periods of the past Christians suffered degradations and depredations similar to those encountered by Jews. Pagans were as hostile to Christians at times as to Jews, and Jews were as hostile to Christians as the latter were to Jews. There were times when Christians were hostile to other Christians with the same vehemence and tenacity as to Jews. Such a situation arose in the Reformation period when an array of dissenting sects arose, some of them quite close to Judaism in a variety of ways. Antitrinitarians, for example, were the "Jews" of Christian Europe, and were detested. [13] Such groups embraced the Judaic theology of election and covenant with zeal, and justified their alienation and even their martyrdom with the argument that God wanted His true people to be separated from all the nations. Among such radicals, as for instance, the Czech Brethren in Moravia, there were conservatives who believed Christ came only to teach against hypocrisy and not to create a new moral law, while the minority seized upon Christ's teachings as implying the overthrow of the old ethic. These views also tended to influence whether a particular group espoused a just war theory as legitimized by Judaic tradition preserved by Jesus, or were opposed to all war as part of what they believed to be the new social program of Jesus. It must be noted here that we speak of a time when for a century, from the Peasants Revolt of 1525, cruelly opposed by Luther, to the end of the Thirty Year's War, there was over a century of mass killing of Christians by Christians. The question of a just war was not mere theologizing.

One must surmise that with the mass murder that has proceeded in the twentieth century since 1914, and the terror of nuclear holocaust peering into the eyes of every living human, the time when the question of just war as once again no mere theological curiosity is upon us. Neither Christianity nor Judaism has evolved an appropriate theology of war or of international violence that pertains to this unusual age. That this is a desideratum need not be argued. Discussion of this penetrating issue will be a matter of priority in Volume Five.

One of the themes of this volume as of the previous volumes is that Judaism tends to acculturate when not prevented from doing so by hostile forces. Jews do not by nature suffer from xenophobia nor are they genetically inclined to be alienated from the mainstream of society. At the same time, however, acculturation or assimilation does not lead to wholesale apostasy nor even to the undermining of Judaic learning and faith. It leads to the transformation of Judaism. This is perhaps well illustrated by the famous talmudic anecdote that when Moses was on his celestial visit to receive the Torah God showed him what R. Akiba will do with it, and Moses was unable to recognize it or to even grasp the discussion in Akiba's academy. [14] Tensions arise between the reforming elements and the traditionalists. The latter give birth to pietistic circles and react with halakhic stringency and rejection of general culture. These almost Hegelian processes in which a thesis is countered by an antithesis ultimately bringing forth a synthesis which constitutes a metamorphosis and radiates a new vision of Judaic religious society were clearly evident in the hellenistic-pharisaic tension, and were once again encountered in the Renaissance era as they are even more forcefully in the twentieth century. The evolution of Judaism is not that of a monolithic structure. It is not a single stream which flows on through history, nor even, to use the biblical image for wisdom, a tree, is Judaism to be seen as a single tree reaching toward the heavens. Judaism is a multiplicity of movements. The Torah may be seen as the original stream watering many tributaries, or as the sapling whose seeds have fallen all about and produced a cluster of trees. All of the tributaries are replenished by the same waters and all are Judaism. All of the trees in the cluster are nurtured by the same sapling and all are Judaism. Judaism becomes the end-product of the dialogue between the written word and the requirement of life, and because requirements vary the end-products will vary. Revelation requires commentary and the multiple commentaries are the reflections of variegated eras and societies. Each passing age creates new tradition that expands revelation, and in each passing age the new traditions are equally valid with their antecedents. [15]

This and the foregoing volumes have stressed that Judaism was never uniform, even when more or less homogeneous. Diversity is legitimate, pluralism does not offend authenticity, and contemporaneity is the word of God. Only the rejection of contemporary authority, refusal to accept pluralism, denial of the authenticity of diversity, and the call for uniformity in practice or belief, marks illegitimacy in Judaism. It is clear that judaizers were always attracted to Judaism despite, or perhaps because of the lack of a required creed or a mandated form of salvific ritual.

Judaism never rejected these judaizers and did not even press them to become full members of the faith with circumcision and by denial of Jesus. This is not to say that all Jews everywhere and in all periods subscribed to what is here averred. But it is to argue that this is the inner essence of Judaism, and is borne out in every era of its evolution. This basic quality of the all-embracing possibilities within Judaism was meticulously affirmed by a medieval rabbi Jacob ben Ephraim around the year 1000. He made the statement in reference to a sect called Isawites who believed in both Jesus and Muhammad as well as in a third charismatic figure, Abu Isa, from whom they derived their name. He said, "We, the Rabbanites, do not repel the Isawites, even though they ascribe prophetic power to those who were no prophets . . . because they agree with us about the festival calendar." [16]

Jacob ben Ephraim had his personal preferences. He identified a Jew by the calendar. But what is more important than his expectation that all those who observe the same festivals can be included in Judaism, is the fact that he did not make theology an issue. This opens other possibilities. Is it conceivable to reverse Jacob's construct? Can people observe the same theology on different occasions and be brothers and sisters in the same covenant? Is it possible to celebrate creation on Sunday as well as Saturday and thus legitimize both the Judaic and Christian holy days? Is it necessary to observe the outpouring of the holy spirit only on the day calculated by one group of Jews in ancient times, or can this outpouring be celebrated on both the Judaic Shabuot and the Christian Pentecost with the serious reflection that both outpourings are the climax of a profound bondage/crucifixion and a liberating redemption/resurrection?

These are only a few of the theological issues that will have to be reflected upon in the forthcoming volumes of this series as Judaism and Christianity begin in the eighteenth century to return full cycle to their first century interrelationships. Never since the first century did Jews and Christians live as closely and among one another, marry one another, study with one another, listen to one another in each other's houses of worship voluntarily and empathetically to the massive degree with which this is occurring in the twentieth century. And, given the premise that we will ward off the satanic onslaught of nuclear weaponry, what we decide is the word of God in coming decades, for good or ill, might conceivably determine the course of religious history for the twenty-first century, and certainly the course of Judaism and Christianity.

One final word must be noted. My advocacy of "dual covenant theology" which perceives of Judaism and Christianity under the image of parallel railway tracks leading to the same destination, the Kingdom of God, should not be understood as exclusionary.

There must be theological space for Islam and the eastern Asian religions. The complexity, however, of including in my discussion all of these profound human strivings for the universal Parent and their respective concepts of the redeeming Kingdom, by whatever name it might go, must await the preliminary amelioration of the Judaeo-Christian tension. Islam, Buddhism, Hinduism, Baha'i, Humanism and other spiritual expressions must also be understood as parallel railway tracks leading to the same destination as Judaism and Christianity. The perceptive and spiritually oriented person will not only meditate upon God's will for multiple tracks, each with appropriate space for independence and efficiency, but will also remember that such parallel lines meet in infinity. Since it is only God who is infinite, the implication is that these tracks will be reconciled in the Kingdom when the riders embrace in a universal faith.

ABBREVIATIONS

(Note: Only those abbreviations used in the text
and notes are listed.)

THE OLD TESTAMENT

(Order According to Masoretic Text)

O.T.	-	Old Testament	Jer.	-	Jeremiah
Gen.	-	Genesis	Ez.	-	Ezekiel
Ex.	-	Exodus	Hab.	-	Habakkuk
Lev.	-	Leviticus	Ps.	-	Psalms
Num.	-	Numbers	Prov.	-	Proverbs
Deut.	-	Deuteronomy	Dan.	-	Daniel
II Ki.	-	II Kings	LXX	-	Septuagint
Is.	-	Isaiah			

INTERTESTAMENTAL

II Esd. - II Esdras (IV Ezra)

Wisd. - Wisdom of Solomon

Test. XII Patr. - Testaments of
the Twelve Patriarchs

DEAD SEA SCROLLS

CDC - Zadokite Document
(Damascus Document)

IQH - Hodayot, Thanksgiving
Scroll

IQS - Manual of Discipline

THE NEW TESTAMENT

N.T.	-	New Testament	Rom.	-	Romans
Mt.	-	Matthew	I Cor.	-	I Corinthians
Lk.	-	Luke	Gal.	-	Galatians
Jn.	-	John	Rev.	-	Revelation

EXTRA CANONICAL CHRISTIAN WRITERS

D.	-	Justin Martyr's **Dialogue With Trypho**
Jud.	-	John Chrysostom, **Adversus Iudaeos**

PHILO

Alleg. Int.	-	Allegorical Interpretation
Plant.	-	On Noah's Work as a Planter
QG	-	Questions on Genesis
QE	-	Questions on Exodus

JOSEPHUS

Ant.	-	Antiquities
War	-	The Jewish War

THE TALMUD

(M or T before the name of a tractate in the text and notes signifies Mishnah and Tosefta respectively; B or P before the name of a tractate signifies Babylonian and Palestinian Talmud respectively; R preceding a name signifies Rabbi, with the exception of R. Travers Herford which is an initial. The works are listed alphabetically and not according to the order of the Talmud.)

THE TALMUD - cont'd.

Ab.	- Abot	Meg.	-	Megilah
Ab. de R. N.	- Abot de R. Nathan	Men.	-	Menahot
A.Z.	- Abodah Zarah	Pes.	-	Pesahim
B.K.	- Baba Kama	R.H.	-	Rosh Hashanah
Ber.	- Berakhot	San.	-	Sanhedrin
Er.	- Erubin	Shab.	-	Shabbat
Git.	- Gittin	Shek.	-	Shekalim
Hor.	- Horayot	Sot.	-	Sotah
Ket.	- Ketubot	Yeb.	-	Yebamot
Kid.	- Kiddushin	Yom.	-	Yoma
Mak.	- Makkot			

MIDRASHIM

Gen. R.	-	Genesis Rabbah
Ex. R.	-	Exodus Rabbah
Lev. R.	-	Leviticus Rabbah
Mekh.	-	Mekhilta de R. Ishmael to Exodus
PRE	-	Pirke de R. Eliezer
Sif. Num.	-	Sifre Numbers
Sif. Deut.	-	Sifre Deuteronomy

PERIODICALS and ANNUALS

AJS	-	Association for Jewish Studies Review
BJRL	-	Bulletin of the John Rylands Library
HBT	-	Horizons in Biblical Theology
HJ	-	Historica Judaica
HTR	-	Harvard Theological Review
HUCA	-	Hebrew Union College Annual
JJS	-	Journal of Jewish Studies

PERIODICALS and ANNUALS - cont'd.

JMRS	-	Journal of Medieval and Renaissance Studies
JQR	-	Jewish Quarterly Review
JSJ	-	Journal for the Study of Judaism
JSS	-	Jewish Social Studies
NTS	-	New Testament Studies
PAAJR	-	Proceedings of the American Academy of Jewish Research
REJ	-	Revue des Études Juives
SCH	-	Studies in Church History
SR	-	Studia Rosenthaliana
StR	-	Studies in the Renaissance

OTHER

BIB. ANT	-	The Biblical Antiquities of Philo
EJ	-	Encyclopedia Judaica
DNB	-	Dictionary of National Biography
Eng.	-	English
Gk.	-	Greek
JE	-	Jewish Encyclopedia
MJJSE	-	Miscellanies, Jewish Historical Society of England
TJHSE	-	Transactions, Jewish Historical Society of England

NOTES

Introduction

1. H. A. Enno Van Gelder, **The Two Reformations in the 16th Century**, trans. Jan F. Finlay (The Hague: 1961). See also Nicholas Wolterstorff, **Until Justice and Peace Embrace** (Grand Rapids, Mich.: 1983), 12, 182n15 for further references.

2. Van Gelder, 7, uses the dates 1450-1560 for his purposes of describing the transformation of religious thought. As will become evident in the following chapters the interplay of Renaissance and Humanism with Judaism continued well into the seventeenth century.

3. Jacob Burkhardt and William Dilthey are credited by Van Gelder, 9, with already bringing the attention of historians to this in Jacob Burkhardt, **Die Kultur der Renaissance in Italien,** 2 vols. (Leipzig: 1913); Jacob Burkhardt, **The Civilization of the Renaissance in Italy,** trans. S. G. C. Middlemore (New York: 1954); Wilhelm Dilthey, **Weltanschauung und Analyse des Menschen seit Renaissance und Reformation: Gesammelte Schriften** II (Leipzig-Berlin: 1921).

4. This will be discussed further in my forthcoming **Emergence of Contemporary Judaism,** vol. 5 (1987), where I will take up the twentieth century phenomena of Reconstructionism and Judaic Humanism

5. See Salo W. Baron, **A Social and Religious History of the Jews,** 18 vols. (Philadelphia-New York: 1952-1983); vol. XIII, 159. I accept the current view that the Renaissance was an evolving process that can be seen in motion since the twelfth century, although the earlier centuries cannot be discussed within the parameters of this volume, and in any case did not have the same interaction with Judaism as did the developments of the fifteenth century and later. On the significant interrelationship between the Renaissance and the Reformation, and the impact of Humanism in European civilization, see Van Gelder.

6. Van Gelder, 3.

7. See on this Phillip Sigal, **The Emergence of Contemporary Judaism,** vol. 2, **A Survey of Judaism from the 7th to the 17th Century** (Pittsburgh: 1977).

8. On the reformation see Van Gelder, 4f., and chapter three below. For Judaism see Chapters Two and Four especially, but further more extensively in forthcoming vol. 4.

9. For Spinoza see chapter five below. On the use of the term "prophets" see Phillip Sigal, **The Emergence of Contemporary Judaism,** vol. 1, **The Foundations of Judaism From Biblical Origins to the Sixth Century A.D.,** part one: **From
the Origins to the Separation of Christianity** (Pittsburgh: 1980), 38-46.

10. My two articles on dual covenant theology in HBT and in **The
Emergence of Contemporary Judaism,** vol. 1, **The Foundations of Judaism,** part
two, **Rabbinic Judaism** (Pittsburgh: 1980), Appendix C will be cited several times
in the course of this work. A more comprehensive discussion of this concept
and its ramifications for Judaism and Christianity will be undertaken in vol. 5.

Chapter One. **Reflections**

1. The vicissitudes of Greek at Cambridge and Oxford do not concern
us. Our interest for the purpose of this volume is in Hebrew. The Council of
Vienna resolved to establish a chair in Hebrew at Oxford in 1312, a resolution
fulfilled by Pope Clement V. Roger Bacon worked with Hebrew at Oxford, but
no real study of it was undertaken until after the establishment of the Regius
Professorship of 1546. See H. C. Porter, **Reformation and Reaction in Tudor Cambridge** (Cambridge: 1958), 51; Charles Edward Mallet, **A History of the University
of Oxford,** 2 vols. (New York: Longman's Green and Co., 1924), II, 71.

2. Israel Abrahams, "Pico Della Mirandola" HUCA Jub. vol. (1925),
327. Pico was also known as Count Giovanni Frederico.

3. Ibid., 318, 331. For Pico see further chapter 4.

4. See also Abrahams' discussion of this, ibid. See also George A.
Kohut, "Royal Hebraists," **Jewish Studies in Memory of Israel Abrahams** ed. George
Alexander Kohut (New York: 1927; rpt. Arno Press, 1980), 225.

5. H. A. Enno Van Gelder, **The Two Reformations in the 16th Century,**
134.

6. See Phillip Sigal, **The Emergence of Contemporary Judaism. A
Survey of Judaism From the Seventh to the Seventeenth Century** (Pittsburgh:
1977), chapter 10. The most intense period of kabalistic thought in Safed was
1540-1580.

7. Abrahams, op. cit., 325.

8. Ibid., 324.

9. Cited in the Hebrew by Kohut, op. cit., 237, n.7.

10. See my forthcoming **Emergence** vol. IV. A briefer survey is offered
in Phillip Sigal, **Judentum** (Stuttgart: 1984), chapters 6 and 7.

11. See Moshe Graupe, **Die Entstehung des Modernen Judentums** (Hamburg: 1969); in this intellectual and spiritual history of Judaism between 1650-1942, what the author terms a "Geistesgeschichte," Graupe reinforces my view, but I see it as having transpired as early as the sixteenth century. See e.g. his "Foreword," ix, in the English version, **The Rise of Modern Judaism**, trans. John Robinson (Huntington, N.Y.: 1978). Graupe, viii, claims that the only writer on the preEnlightenment period prior to himself that has grasped this need to revise our thinking on the subject was Azriel Shoḥet, **Im Hilufe Tekufot, Reshit Hahaskalah Beyahadut Germaneah** (Jerusalem: 1960). This orientation is also evident in Jakob Petuchowski, **The Theology of Haham David Nieto** (New York: 1970).

12. Gershom Scholem, **Messianic Idea in Judaism** (New York: 1971), 84, 140.

13. For the hellenistic precedent see Phillip Sigal, **The Emergence of Contemporary Judaism**, vol. I, pt. 1, **From Origins to the Rise and Separation of Christianity** (Pittsburgh: 1980), chapter 4.

14. See Petuchowski, **Theology**, xiv; xix, n.4.

15. Several available and accessible monographs are: E. Weil, **Elie Levita humaniste et massorète, 1469-1549** (Leiden: 1963); B. Netanyahu, **Don Isaac Abravanel: Statesman and Philosopher** (Philadelphia: 1953); Isaac Barzilay, **Yosef Shlomo Delmedigo, Yashar of Candia: His Life, Works and Times** (Leiden: 1974); David B. Ruderman, **The World of a Renaissance Jew. The Life and Thought of Abraham ben Mordecai Farissol** (Cincinnati: 1981).

16. For Tissard see M. E. Cosenza, **Biographical and Bibliographical Dictionary of the Italian Humanists and of the World of Classical Scholarship in Italy 1300-1800**, 6 vols. (Boston: 1962-1967), IV, 3418; and for Tissard on Farissol see Ruderman, op. cit., 98-106.

17. Ruderman, 104f.

18. Ruderman cites Tissard's views at 217, nn. 31-32.

19. Phillip Sigal, "Aspects of an Inquiry into Dual Covenant Theology," HBT 3 (1981), 181-209; and "Aspects of Dual Covenant Theology: Salvation," HBT, 5 (1983).

20. For the most recent study of the whole subject of Christian Hebraism, which will be discussed more broadly in chapter 7, see Jerome Friedman, **The Most Ancient Testimony** (Athens, Ohio: 1983).

21. Ibid., 2-3.

22. Ibid., 4.

234

23. Raphael Loewe, "Hebraists, Christians," _EJ_ (Jerusalem: 1971) vol. 8, 9-68.

24. Jerome Friedman, **Michael Servetus: A Case Study in Total Heresy** (Geneva: 1978); "Michael Servetus: The Case for a Jewish Christianity," _SCJ_, 4 (April, 1973), 87-110.

25. This will be more broadly discussed in my **Emergence** vol. 4, to be published in 1986. For background to elements of this approach of modern scholarship see Sigal, **Emergence,** vol. I, pt. 1, chapter 7, and note 19 above.

Chapter Two. The Impact of Medieval Humanism and the Renaissance

1. See in general Moses A. Shulvass, **The Jews in the World of the Renaissance,** trans. Elvin Kose (Leiden: 1973); Cecil Roth, **The Jews in the Renaissance** (Philadelphia: 1959); H. A. Van Gelder, **The Two Reformations in the Sixteenth Century,** op. cit., especially chapters I-II; Jacob Burckhardt, **Die Kultur der Renaissance in Italien,** op. cit.,; **The Civilization of the Renaissance in Italy,** trans. S. G. C. Middlemore, op. cit. The scope of this volume does not warrant a digression to review or critique the widely disparate views on how to define the terms "Renaissance" and "Humanism," or when precisely to place them chronologically. My use of the terms will be self-evident in the text, and the time-frame in this chapter is about 1450-1650. See also S. W. Baron, **A Social and Religious History of the Jews,** op. cit., vol. XIII, 159-205. On the problem of the usage of the terms "Humanism" and "Renaissance" see Baron, 389n2. Both Shulvass and Roth listed above concentrate on the Italian Renaissance, but in Jewish terms one must also consider the developments among Marranos in Spain who then travelled to other lands and had a considerable cultural influence. There were also significant developments in Holland and Germany. For a comprehensive bibliography see David Ruderman, **The World of a Renaissance Jew,** op. cit., 239-256. Additional select, but far from exhaustive recommendations for this chapter follow: **Jewish Medieval and Renaissance Studies,** ed. A. Altmann (Cambridge, Mass.: 1967); I. Barzilay, **Between Reason and Faith: Anti-Rationalism in Italian Jewish Thought** (1250-1650) (The Hague-Paris: 1967); J. L. Blau, **The Christian Interpretation of the Cabala in the Renaissance** (New York: 1955); B. Netanyahu, **The Marranos of Spain from the Late Fourteenth to the Early Sixteenth Century** (New York: 1966). Although Roth's work, **Renaissance,** cited above is inadequately documented, the bibliographical notes, 337-340, are useful. Furthermore, general histories of medieval times should be consulted, such as **The Cambridge Medieval History,** as well as histories of the major countries under consideration such as Italy, Holland, France, and England. Other useful bibliography and periodical literature will be cited in the notes, and can be found in the bibliographies offered by the cited authors.

2. Van Gelder, 15.

3. Gen. R. 9:7.

4. Van Gelder, 17. Lucretius was a poet-philosopher who lived 98-55 B.C.

5. Ibid., 20.

6. Ibid., 25.

7. Cited by Van Gelder, 26. The translation is at n. 4. See Gen. R. 22:6 for a rabbinic view that God gave humans the ability to overcome the evil impulse (Gen. 4:7).

8. See rabbinic anthologies and theologies such as A. Cohen, **Everyman's Talmud** (New York: 1949), chapter 3; Claude G. Montefiore and Herbert Loewe, **A Rabbinic Anthology** (London: 1938) chapter 11; Kaufman Kohler, **Jewish Theology** (New York: 1918), part II; Samuel S. Cohon, **Jewish Theology** (Assen: 1971), section 3; Solomon Schechter, **Some Aspects of Rabbinic Theology** (London: 1909).

9. B. Ber. 33b. The doctrine of free will was always part of Jewish theology, and distinguished it from such Reformation theologians as John Calvin. Cf. Gen. R. 21:5.

10. Cited in translation by Van Gelder, 28n1, from Ficino's **Epistolae.**

11. M. Ab. 4:1.

12. Van Gelder, 42f.

13. Leone Ebreo, Don Judah Abravanel, a physician and poet, was a son of the famous Don Isaac Abravanel who left Spain in 1492. See Roth, **Renaissance,** 128-136, and bibliography on 349f.

14. Baron, **History,** XIII, 193f., 201; Shulvass, 148-158; Van Gelder, 59f. See further on Leone da Modena, chapter four below.

15. See **Leone Ebreo. Dialoghi d'Amore. Hebraische Gedichte,** ed. Carl Gebhardt (Heidelberg: 1929), including a good introduction.

16. Baron, 194.

17. Van Gelder, 67f.

18. Ibid., 69f.

19. See below especially chapter four.

20. Van Gelder, 74f.; Hubert Jedin, **Ecumenical Councils of the Catholic Church**, trans. Ernest Graf (New York: 1960), 138-141; H. J. Schroeder, **Disciplinary Decrees of the General Councils** (New York: 1937), 480-509, 630-649; **Conciliorum Oecumenicorum Decreta**, ed. Josepho Alberigo et al. (Freiburg, Germany: 1962), 569-631. For a translation of extracts from the bull on false religion see Schroeder, 487f. Not only was it intended to seriously curtail and bring under surveillance the study of philosophy, but students were to be placed under very careful scrutiny. The objective was to have them properly honor church attendance, mass, and vespers, and to beware of blasphemy against God, Jesus or Mary; see 495ff.

21. Charges of judaizing persisted throughout the sixteenth century, and will be discussed more fully in various contexts below.

22. Schroeder, ibid., 498, par. 10. Along these lines the Church also condemned books being translated from other languages, including Hebrew, that were held to contain "errors," and "teachings contrary to the Christian religion." At that time the celebrated censorship system in which the official imprimatur had to be placed upon a book before it was allowed to be printed was introduced; see 504.

23. For the changes in art styles reflecting the changes in religious belief and practice see Van Gelder, op. cit., 79-105; Erwin Panofsky, **Studies in Iconology** (New York: 1939), 40-66; see also for general developments, Robert Ergang, **The Renaissance** (London, New York: 1967), 41f.; 153-199; 386-408.

24. Van Gelder, 85. At 90f. Van Gelder also reviews the paintings of Titian (1477-1576) from this perspective. For a more comprehensive study of Titian see Erwin Panofsky, **Problems in Titian, Mostly Iconographic** (New York: 1969). Panofsky, 112, points out, for example, how Titian reflects the change of the meaning of nudity in Renaissance art. From its general negative medieval sense of carnal pleasure it came to represent feminine beauty, friendship, and other positive ideas; see also his **Studies**, 154ff., figures 109-111.

25. Van Gelder, 92-97.

26. Jedin, **Ecumenical Councils**, 154-186; **Conciliorum**, 633-775; Herbert Jedin, **Geschichte des Konzils von Trient**, 4 vols. (Freiburg, Germany: 1951-1978); **A History of the Council of Trent**, trans. Dom Ernest Graf, 2 vols. (St. Louis, Missouri: 1957-1961); Martin Chemnitz, **Examination of the Council of Trent**, trans. Fred Kramer, 2 vols. (St. Louis, Missouri: 1971); H. J. Schroeder, **Canons and Decrees of the Council of Trent** (St. Louis, Missouri: 1950); this work also contains the Latin texts of the canons and decrees issued at Trent, 281-578. See further, chapter 3.

27. Van Gelder, chapters IV-V.

28. Ibid., 116.

29. Ibid., 121f. See Sigal, **Emergence** II, chapters 9 and 11.

30. Van Gelder, 122f.

31. Cited ibid., 127.

32. See further on this relevant matter in **Emergence**, vol. IV. See also Phillip Sigal, **Judentum**, op. cit., chapter 7.

33. Van Gelder, 130.

34. Select bibliography for the student to peruse in addition to the works mentioned in the notes below, include Margaret Mann Phillips, **Erasmus and the Northern Renaissance** (London: 1967); Lemuel Flores Ignacio, **The Life and Thought of Desiderius Erasmus and His Influence on the Reformation** (Indianapolis: 1960); John C. Olin, **Six Essays on Erasmus and a Translation of Erasmus' Letter to Carondelet**, 1523 (New York: 1979); Louis Bouyer, **Erasmus and the Humanist Experiment**, trans. Francis X. Murphy (London: 1959); **The First Tome or Volume of the Paraphrase upon the Newe Testamente** (1548), Facsimile Reproduction, "Introduction" John N. Wall, Jr. (Delman, New York: Scholars' Facsimiles and Reprints, 1975); C. A. L. Jarrott "Erasmus' Biblical Humanism" **Studies in the Renaissance**, 17 (1970), 119-152; **Christian Humanism and the Reformation** with Beatus Rhenanus, **The Life of Erasmus**, ed. John C. Olin (New York: 1965). See also below, chapter three, for further references relevant to Luther, Calvin and other Reformation theologians and influences.

35. Phillips, op. cit., 5f.

36. For a brief and accessible analysis of Erasmus' views see Van Gelder, chap. IV, and bibliography at n.34 above.

37. Gal. 2:16. See my paper to be published in the Proceedings of the annual meeting of the Calvin Studies Society held at Calvin Theological Seminary, Grand Rapids, May 1983: "The Law in Calvin's and Luther's Commentary to Galatians."

38. **The First Tome**, 4-5; cited by Roland Bainton, "The Paraphrases of Erasmus," **Archiv für Reformationsgeschichte**, 57 (1966), 67, from "anonymous."

39. **The First Tome**, 16ff.

238

40. Although Paul was certainly interested in the centrality of righteous behavior, Erasmus in no way adapted Paul's major theological orientation to the death of Jesus. See **The First Tome**, 20; James 2:14; Phillips op. cit., 51; Olin, **Essays**, 9. Erasmus cites James several times in his **Enchiridion**. See **The Enchiridion**, trans. Ford Lewis Battles in **Advocates of Reform From Wyclif to Erasmus**, ed. Matthew Spinka, The Library of Christian Classics, ed. John Baillie et al., vol. XIV (London: 1953), 295-379; bibliography, 382; his view of Jewish externalism is here expressed at 335 in his "Fifth Rule," and again at 340f. Erasmus often, in fact, charges Christianity in his time, with being a kind of Judaism in the sense of emphasizing mystery and ritual, as Battles points out, 340n2. Erasmus accuses the sacerdotal orders of being "full of Jewish superstitions;" see Battles, 346.

41. Battles, 378. Cf. also Erasmus' "Letter to Paul Volz" August 14, 1518, trans. John Olin, in **Christian Humanism**, ed. Olin, 107-133, at 125-129.

42. It is also of more than passing interest that Erasmus described Christianity as the progeny of Christ, and the synagogue of Moses pejoratively by analogy to David and Bath Sheba. See his "Letter to Martin Dorp," May, 1515, trans. John W. Bush and Martin Feeny, in Olin, op. cit., 51-91, at 76.

43. Van Gelder, 152f. Note that Erasmus' view of grace is very Judaic, as in the idea that "he who comes to purify himself, help is given him" at B. Shab. 104a. But Erasmus fails to grasp both this element in Judaism, and that he was in accord with Judaism that opera ceremonalia (ceremonial works, that is, ritual) are inadequate, and that opera moralia (moral deeds) are essential. Erasmus, however, is correct in not including the notion that the latter are un-necessary as long as one has the former, as being a "Jewish" idea, of which error Martin Luther was guilty. Contrary to Luther, Erasmus correctly understood that Paul never condoned the idea that moral practices are unavailing or even that Judaism taught that notion, Paul's emphasis only having been that cultic acts were no longer availing for salvation. See Van Gelder, 154n4.

44. See n. 43. Further, Prov. 10:25 refers to the righteous persons as the foundation of the world. In a variety of talmudic sources 30, 45 and 36 righteous men in each generation sustain the world. In the Jewish conception, however, the righteous men did not sustain the world by a predetermined way of life centered in vows, seclusion, and a consistent round of prayer and other duties, but rather by acts of love performed in the give and take of the hard, real world. See Gershom Scholem, "The Tradition of the Thirty-Six Hidden Just Men," trans. Michael A. Meyer, in **The Messianic Idea in Judaism**, 251-256. As for original sin, Judaism emphasized that Adam's sin brought evil and mortality into the world but did not regard it as so in-bred that it cannot be surmounted by the human will to do good.

45. **Enchiridion,** trans. Battles, "Twentieth Rule," 370f.; n. 49. This idea was also in harmony with certain Jewish Humanistic thinkers, such as Raphael Norzi whose dates are unknown, but who was either a young contemporary of Erasmus, or lived soon after him. See below section V and nn. 145-147.

46. Van Gelder, 161f.

47. Ibid., 173f.

48. Concerning modern branches of Judaism see vol. IV, forthcoming.

49. Van Gelder, 174f.

50. See above, section I. As Baron, XIII, 169 indicates, disputations and polemics continued, but there were many new dialogues engaged in as academic exercises.

51. Salo W. Baron, **History** XIII, 159f. For Marranos see chapter 56 and **Emergence** II, 129-135, notes at 467-470, and under index entry "Marrano, Marranism." See also Netanyahu, **The Marranos of Spain;** Cecil Roth, **A History of the Marranos** (New York: 1974).

52. Alexander Marx, **Studies in Jewish History and Booklore** (New York: 1944). The rabbinic Bible, **Mikraòt Gedolot,** containing the full text of the Old Testament, Aramaic Targums, notes and a number of commentaries was published by Daniel Bomberg in 1518, again in 1525, and by Johannes Buxtorf, at Basel 1618-19. See further on Bomberg's work, Frank Rosenthal, "The Study of the Hebrew Bible in Sixteenth-Century Italy" **Studies in the Renaissance,** I (1954), 81-91, 84f.; Baron, XIII, 168-171.

53. Baron, op. cit., 160f. For further bibliography on Christian interest in Judaic studies see Baron, vol. VI, 462f., nn. 51-52; 466f., n. 58; Friedman, **Ancient Testimony,** 7f., nn. 4, 6. On Nicholas de Lyra and his role in the transmission of rabbinic commentary see Herman Hailperin, **Rashi and the Christian Scholars** (Pittsburgh: 1963). See also George F. Moore, "Christian Writers on Judaism" HTR, 14 (1921), 197-254; and further discussion below, chapter 7.

54. Rosenthal, op. cit., 85f.

55. Ibid., 89; J. Levi, **Elia Levita und seine Leistungen als Grammatiker** (Breslau: 1888), 24ff.; see also in general the more recent study of Levita, Gérard E. Weil, **Elie Lévita** op. cit.

56. Rosenthal, 90f.

57. Baron, XIII, 161f. The large numbers of medieval Hebraists are computed by various scholars: ibid., 392n4. See above, chap. 1n23. See also below, chap. seven.

58. Baron, 164.

59. Ibid., 167; 396n9.

60. Gershom Scholem, **Kabbalah** (New York: 1974), 196-201; see also the interesting discussion of Pico's **Heptaplus** and his emphasis upon the centrality of Moses in his kabalistic system, in Raymond B. Waddington, "The Sun at the Center: Structure as Meaning in Pico della Mirandola's **Heptaplus**," JMRS vol. 3, No. 1 (1973), 69-86, especially 74-86.

61. Baron, XIII, 174.

62. Ibid., 176; for a short sketch of Reubeni and Molkho see Abba Hillel Silver, **A History of Messianic Speculation in Israel**, rpt. (Boston: 1959), 145-150. For the sefirot see Scholem, **Kabbalah**, 96-117, and passim.

63. Scholem, 197. Moncada was also known as Flavius Mithridates.

64. Baron, XIII, 179ff.; 405nn22-23. Johannes Reuchlin, for example, used kabalist speculation on the names of God to lead up to manifestation of Jesus. He argued that in the first period God revealed Himself as Shaddai, later to Moses as Yhwh, and finally in the period of redemption, Christian era, He revealed Himself as Yhwh plus the letter shin which signified logos. See chap. seven below, and n. 26 there. See Scholem, **Kabbalah**, 198; Friedman, **Ancient Testimony**, chap. four; F. Secret, **Les Kabbalistes Chrétiens De La Renaissance** (Paris: 1964).

65. Heinrich Graetz, **Geschichte der Juden von den ältesten Zeiten bis auf die Gegenwart** (Leipsig: 1907), IX, 63-195; 477ff., n. 2; **History of the Jews** (Philadelphia: 1894), IV, 422-476; Baron, XIII, 182ff.; 406n24. See further on Reuchlin in chaps. three and seven below.

66. Baron, ibid.

67. This is not to be confused with a convert of the same name who was burned at the stake in 1514. For a brief sketch of Asher Lämmlein see Silver, **Messianic Speculation**, 143-145. He appeared in Istria, Italy, in 1502, to announce the coming of the Messiah.

68. Baron, XIII, 186ff. For Pfefferkorn see also chap. seven below.

69. Reuchlin's statement is cited in English by Baron, XIII, 188, and is given from Reuchlin's **Memorandum** reproduced in his **Der Augenspiegel** (Tübingen: 1511); see Baron, 408n30; Graetz, **History**, IV, 442f. See also Friedman, **Ancient Testimony**, 26ff., on the Reuchlin-Pfefferkorn matter. See also S. A. Hirsch, "Johann Reuchlin, The Father of the Study of Hebrew Among Christians," JQR, 8 (1896), 445-470.

70. Graetz, ibid., 453ff.

71. Ibid., 456ff., 468.

72. Baron, XIII, 190f.

73. Salo Baron, "An Italian Responsium by R. Abraham Graziano," **Studies in Jewish Bibliography, History and Literature in Honor of I. Edward Kiev**, ed. Charles Berlin (New York: 1971), 122-137 [Hebrew]. See n. 13 above for Leone Ebreo.

74. Baron, **History**, XIII, 196f. See further, Section VI below.

75. Sebastian Franck, **Sechshundert dreyzehn Gebot und Verbot der Juden** (Ulm: 1537). In his brief discussion of Franck, Salo Baron, **History**, XIII, 199, here evinces a misunderstanding of New Testament matters. He asserts that Franck took a cue from Luke to argue that God will punish Jews for their sins more than the heathen, instead of tending to "the more Judaeo-Christian oriented Matthew and Mark." The fact is that Luke is more Judaic than Mark, and sometimes more accurate or detailed than Matthew. But this point is irrelevant, for if Franck tended to the more Judaeo-Christian views of Matthew at any rate, he would still be able to follow Luke, as all had a cue to take from Amos (3:2).

76. Cecil Roth, **The History of the Jews of Italy** (Philadelphia: 1946), 294ff. Roth believes the term ghetto is derived from the sections in Venice known as Ghetto Nuovo ("new foundry") and Ghetto Vecchio ("old foundry"). Jews were first compelled to reside in a section of the city to be completely sealed off from the rest of the city in 1516, and to be so constrained there as to have nobody enter or leave between sunset and sunrise. See ibid., 186. For a brief description of ghetto life see Roth, 353-406. A major weakness of Roth's volume is the absence of references and bibliography.

77. Pope Paul IV did not introduce the ghetto in 1555. He only institutionalized what was already a reality as a Jewish "quarter" in certain European cities. Thus in 1460, after an anti-Jewish riot in the Jewish quarter of Avignon the authorities limited the size of the quarter to two streets; it was surrounded by walls and had three points of access to the rest of the city, all locked after dark. See Ruderman, **The World of A Renaissance Jew**, 6. See P. Prévot, **Histoire du ghetto d'Avignon** (Avignon: 1975).

Notes to pp. 19-21

78. Roth, **Italy,** 328.

79. Ibid., 193-227. Shulvass, **Jews in the World of the Renaissance,** 163.

80. See, for example, a discussion of the educational endeavors of Abraham ben Mordecai Farissol of Ferrara by Ruderman, **The World of the Renaissance Jew,** 15-18. See also Alexander Marx, "Glimpses of the Life of an Italian Rabbi of the First Half of the Sixteenth Century (David Ibn Yaḥya)" <u>HUCA</u>, 1 (1924), 605-616; also his "R. Joseph D'Arli as Teacher and Head of an Academy in Siena," **Louis Ginzberg Jubilee Volume,** Hebrew Section, ed. Alexander Marx et al. (New York: 1945-6), 271-304. As will be discussed in my **Emergence** vol. four, Jewish reformation leaders in Germany like Herz Wessely and Moses Mendelssohn were influenced by Renaissance figures in their approach to Jewish learning. See also, chap. four below.

81. Roth, **Italy,** 195, misconstrues this art as "incongruity" resulting from the artist's ignorance. But it was only eastern Jewry that customarily wore Islamic-style turbans. Scholars as late as the seventeenth century defended the bareheadedness even during the performance of sacred ritual. More will be written of this in reference to the rise of Reform Judaism in **Emergence** IV. Meanwhile, see **Emergence** II, 318f., 330, 550n21. See also n. 87 below; Shulvass, 75f. Regarding Cellini see **Autobiography of Benvenuto Cellini,** trans. John Addington Symonds (New York: n.d.), where he tells that he worked as a goldsmith and draughtsman for a Jew named Graziado in Bologna (p. 16).

82. See Israel Adler, "The Rise of Art Music in the Italian Ghetto," **Jewish Medieval and Renaissance Studies,** ed. Alexander Altmann (Cambridge, Mass.: 1966) for a brief summary of Jewish activity in the field of music in Italy during the Renaissance, 327-332, and bibliographical references throughout the notes there. See Roth, **Renaissance,** 274-304. See n. 103 below.

83. Benvenuto Cellini, op. cit., 16.

84. Shulvass, op. cit., 172-182. For Renaissance social life see also Immanuel of Rome, **Maḥbarot Immanuel,** ed. A. M. Haberman (Tel-Aviv: 1950); **Sippur David Hareubeni,** ed. A. Z. Aescoly (Jerusalem: 1940); **Zaḥut Bediḥuta Dekiddushin,** ed. Jefim Schirmann (Jerusalem: 1946); Azariah dei Rossi, **Meor Enayim,** ed. I. A. Benjacob (Vilna: 1865). On gambling see Leona da Modena, **Sefer Chaje Jehuda,** ed. Abraham Kahanna (Kiev: 1911); Louis Finkelstein, **Jewish Self Government in the Middle Ages** (New York: 1964), 291, which describes regulation of gambling taken at Forli, Italy in 1418; Roth, **Renaissance,** 20f.

85. Judaic response to emancipation was different in post-Czarist Russia since the situation of religion was in a different condition in the Soviet Union. This will be discussed in **Emergence** IV.

86. Shulvass, 184-189, 197f. **Responsum of Maharam of Padua** (Venice: 1550), No. 76; Finkelstein, op. cit., 286; Roth, **Italy**, 201.

87. Shulvass, 187n7; Isaac Rivkind, "A Responsum of Leo da Modena on Bareheadedness," **Ginzberg Jubilee Volume** II, 412-421; see also **Responsa of Rabbi Joseph Colon** (Warsaw: 1884), Nos. 88, 149. See n. 81 above. Da Modena surveyed extensive sources on the subject of bareheadedness, and among his strictures he pointed out that the practice of bareheadedness is not an imitation of Christians and hence not a violation of Lev. 18:3. He argued that it reverts to the secular symbol of respect in the Graeco-Roman civilization, and as a result was applied as a form of respect at pagan worship long before the rise of Christianity (Rivkind, 407; and see n. 11 there). Nevertheless, he added, the custom of bareheadedness became the halakhah of Paul for Christianity, at I Cor. 11:3-7. Da Modena raises the question whether Paul continued what I term a proto-rabbinic halakhah, or was in fact uprooting the proto-rabbinic halakhah requiring one to cover the head. Rivkind maintains, 408n15, that the latter was the case, thus implying that the obligation to cover the head in Judaism was pre-Christian. Other Jewish scholars with whom I concur, have maintained the reverse, that Paul was in effect continuing the Judaic custom of bareheadedness for men. See Rivkind, 422f. Modena argued for leniency in the matter, and among other things, he wrote that Lev. 18:3 does not apply to bareheadedness, citing an array of scholars who did not believe it to be obligatory for a Jew to cover his head. He approvingly cited the contemporary responsum of R. Solomon Luria (No. 72), author of **Ḥokhmat Shelomoh**, whom he describes as a "great and awesome man among all the men of Poland and Germany." Luria's responsum permitted bareheadedness at all times, even when praying, reciting God's name, reciting <u>berakhot</u> or the shema, when eating and drinking, and studying religious books (cited by Rivkind, 420ff.). But Luria cautioned people to comply with the growing custom of covering the head lest they be considered irreverent. This responsum is available in abridged form in English in Simon Hurwitz, **The Responsa of Solomon Luria** (New York: n.d.), 109ff. A fuller discussion of the question will be offered in **Emergence** IV, in the more relevant context of nineteenth century change. On the question of dress see Roth, **Italy**, 213f.

88. Burckhardt, **Die Kultur der Renaissance** II, 116, wrote "<u>zum Ver-ständnis der höheren Geselligkeit der Renaissance ist endlich wesentlich, zu wissen, das das Weib dem Manne gleich geachtet wurde,</u>" ("In order to understand this higher social environment of the Renaissance it is ultimately important to know that the woman was regarded as equal with the man"). While Burckhardt does not adequately document this sweeping statement, it may with caution be taken to refer at a minimum to the social life as it applied to leisure, entertainment, and education. See also the more accessible English translation by Middlemore, **The Civilization of the Renaissance**, 292ff.

89. Cited by Adler, "Rise," 357.

244

90. Shulvass, 168f., 229n1, 281f. see also Roth, **Italy**, 214f.

91. Ibid., 161, 163f.; on R. Gershom see **Emergence** II. The sefirah period is the forty-nine day span from the second day of Passover to Pentecost. Sources for sefirah halakhah are quite obscure. Thus, the prohibition of marriage during the period is only known since the eleventh century, and this source cites a tradition which stemmed from Hai Gaon (d. 1038). One might assume the ban went back to the tenth century and possibly the ninth. But it is not found in the Talmud, and is therefore post-talmudic. Similarly the other quasi-mourning customs associated with the sefirah period and practiced by those who style themselves "orthodox," are of much later provenance and of insubstantial rationale. Usually the reason given for the semi-mourning to be practiced is the death of Rabbi Akiba's disciples at this season (B. Yeb. 62b). Just as the sefirah restrictions are not known until medieval times, so too relaxation from them on lag beomer, the thirty-third day of the seven-week count from the bringing of the first ōmer (sheaf) of grain (Lev. 23:15) is only known since the twelfth century. See **Tur** Orah Hayyim 493 where R. Zerakhiah b. Isaac Halevi Gerondi (d. 1186) is cited, and the commentary to B. Yeb. 62b by R. Menahem Meiri (d. 1306), which elevates lag beomer into a festive day, a development which subsequently escalated. See also R. Joseph Karo, **Shulhan Arukh** Orah Hayyim 493 which details lag beomer halakhah and custom. It is also clear there, however, from the widely differing views of Moses Isserles in his glosses to Karo, that halakhah and minhag (custom) differed radically between sefardi and ashkenazi Jews.

For prevalent licentiousness among Jews in Renaissance Italy, see Roth, **Italy**, 211f.

92. Ibid. 217f.; for Colon see p. 220. Most scholars consider the dates of Messer Leon as uncertain. See on this Isaac Rabinowitz, "A Rectification of the Date of Judah Messer Leon's Death," **Studies in Jewish Bibliography**, 399-406. Rabinowitz concludes that Messer Leon died in 1499.

93. See Levi ben Gershon, **Milhamot Adonay** (Leipzig: 1866), 172-74. For general introduction to Gersonides see Isaac Husik, **A History of Medieval Jewish Philosophy** (Philadelphia: 1948), chap. XV.

94. Actually Bertinoro wrote his commentary in Jerusalem. On the influence of printing, see Roth, **Italy**, 222-227; see also 397ff. Lampronti was the author of a highly significant rabbinic-theological encyclopedia, **Pahad Yizhak**, containing thousands of halakhic opinions, a virtual monument to Italian learning. An interesting sidelight on R. Meir Katzenellenbogen was his use of the civil date in many responsa, something not done by other scholars. He did not oppose the reading of Jonah on Yom Kippur afternoon in Greek at Candia, Crete (see his Responsum No. 78). For Isserles, see Sigal, **Emergence** II, 321f. For responsa by forty sixteenth century Italian rabbis, see **Responsa Mattanot Beadam**, ed. Yacov Boksenboim (Tel Aviv: 1983).

95. Roth, **Italy,** 361ff.; Shulvass, 203-206.

96. Shulvass, 205, cited from Leon da Modena, **Historia de gli Riti Hebraici, The History of the Rites, Customs and Manner of Life of the Present Jews Throughout the World in Italian by Leon Modena a Rabbi in Venice,** trans. Edmund Chilmead (London: 1650), Pt. I, chap. 11, par. 6.

97. This has been adequately delineated throughout **Emergence** vols. I and II.

98. For a discussion of the efforts to organize a general Italian Jewish structure, and in the absence of that, regional communal organizations, see Shulvass, 83-113. See also Louis Finkelstein, **Self-Government,** 82-95, 265-315.

99. Shulvass, 97.

100. Ibid., 99. "Chief rabbis" are functionaries appointed by the secular government, and are not invested with such powers by any doctrine or halakhah of Judaism. Thus in Renaissance Italy there was a "chief rabbi" in Sicily. Sometimes a "regional rabbi" was appointed, but this was in no way a centralized authority imposed upon other rabbis or communities. Compliance with his decisions was voluntary. See Shulvass, 100. Regional organizations are discussed ibid., 101-113. Shulvass' discussion relies heavily upon Isaiah Sonne. "The Waad Kelali in Italy as the Prototype of the Council of the Four Provinces in Poland" **Hatekufah** 32-33 (1948), 617-689, and upon a variety of sources listed in the footnotes to Shulvass, 101-113, including the Responsa of Rabbi Isaac ben Sheshet Perfet and of Rabbi Joseph Colon. On the question of "chief rabbi," see **Emergence** II, 3, 227, 257, 465.

101. See Shulvass, 109; R. Judah Minz, one of the illustrious rabbis of the late fifteenth and early sixteenth centuries, gathered "sages and men of affairs" at Padua in 1509 at which he managed to have certain ordinances related to matrimony agreed upon, as well as general support for his rabbinical school. This only points to the great influence of Judah Minz and to no real "chief rabbinate" that could govern all religious matters and enforce uniformity over any broad region. As a matter of fact this effort at Padua was a strike for independence from a more general organization of communities in the Republic of Venice.

102. Joseph Reider, "Non-Jewish Motives in the Ornament of Early Hebrew Books," **Studies in Early Jewish Bibliography** (New York: 1929), 150-159.

103. See Adler, "The Rise of Art Music," 333-360 for musical developments from about 1550-1650, when the ghetto was enforced and Jews were restricted from participating in the general cultural life. For a general study of Jewish art music prior to Emancipation see I. Adler, **La Pratique musicale savante des quelques communautés juives en Europe aux XVII et XVIII siècles** (Paris-Hague:

1966). The dates of Salamone Dei Rossi are uncertain, but he published prolifically between 1589-1628.

104. R. Katzenellenbogen was cited in "The Rise," 334n57. For cities that practiced art music, see Adler, passim; on the size of choirs, Adler, 356. De Fano is cited by Adler, 330, from a lost work. See also Leon Modena's responsa **Zikne Yehudah,** ed. S. Simonsohn (Jerusalem: 1955-56), No. 6.

105. Excerpts of the text of Modena's responsum are cited by Adler, ibid, 336f. Ên kelohenu is a hymn sung near the close of sabbath and festival prayers; alenu, also known in English as the Adoration is the closing prayer at all worship occasions, expressing the eschatological hope of the advent of the Kingship of God; adon olam and yigdal are closing hymns for sabbath and festival worship.

106. Adler, 340.

107. The invocation to both maarib and shahrit, daily as well as sabbath and festivals.

108. An evening prayer for peaceful sleep and healing awakening, recited at maarib or before retiring.

109. Adler, 355.

110. See n. 105.

111. Adler, "Rise," 349-360; see especially 353ff. Sporadic comments in the Talmud were often used by medieval scholars as sources for the prohibition not only of instrumental music, but also of vocal music. B. Sot. 48a, "the ear listening to song shall be extirpated" was one such. Another, B. Git. 7a opined that there was no difference between vocal and instrumental music, but did permit singing at worship. See Maimonides, **Mishneh Torah** Taan. 5:14. Alfasi **Responsa** (Leghorn: 1781), No. 281, had prohibited applying Arabic tunes to prayers, and this prohibition was extended later to all gentile music. Music will be discussed more extensively in **Emergence** IV. See also, Phillip Sigal, "The Organ and Jewish Worship," Conservative Judaism, XVII (Spring-Summer, 1963), 93-105.

112. Cited by Adler, "Rise," 357.

113. Roth, **Italy,** 390ff. On art and the second commandment see **Emergence** I, pt. 1, pp. 21, 62n27; pt. 2, pp. 74-76, 101f.; 111, 159, 224, 260; and more fully in **Emergence** IV.

114. Roth, **Renaissance,** 191ff., 354. On the subject of art and Jewish artists over the ages, see F. Landsberger, **A History of Jewish Art** (Cincinnati: 1946).

115. Roth, ibid., 392ff.

116. Ibid., 394-406.

117. Ibid., 397. Roth also names others who came later, such as Raphael Rabeni, Jacob Saraval, and Isaac Cardoso.

118. See below, chapters on Holland and England.

119. See **Emergence** II, chap. 10.

120. For Shabbatai Zevi see **Emergence** II, 303-310, and the comprehensive biography, Gershom G. Scholem, **Sabbatai Sevi** (Princeton, N.J.: 1973).

121. Roth, **Italy**, 403ff. This post-Sabbatian era and the ramifications of it had variegated influences upon the rise of modern Judaism. See **Emergence** IV.

122. See Moses Hayyim Luzzatto, **Mesilat Yesharim**, trans. Mordecai M. Kaplan, (Philadelphia: 1948). **Mesilat Yesharim** became the basic text of the nineteenth century musar (moralist) movement, which prevailed in many of the non-hasidic yeshibot into the twentieth century. This will be discussed in **Emergence** IV.

123. The rabbinic saying was that of R. Pinhas ben Yair, found at B. A.Z. 20b; P. Shek. 6a; M. Sot. 9:15. The text as given by Luzzatto in his "Author's Preface," ed. Kaplan, p. 9, lines 1-8, is unlike that cited at B. A.Z. 20b, somewhat closer to Alfasi's loc. cit. 6a, but not quite, nor is it similar to any version in the standard texts; it also appears that the commentator R. Hananel operated with another text. It must, therefore, be from a textual variant available to Luzzatto. I have not attempted to trace this as it is not germane to our theme here. On kabalism, see **Emergence** II, chap. 10, and bibliography there.

124. Shulvass, 169f.; Alexander Marx, "Rabbi Joseph D'Arli as Teacher and Head of an Academy in Siena," **Ginzberg Jubilee Volume**, II, 271-304. Marx surveyed and dated a number of Italian scholars and provided a birdseye view of the curriculum at Siena from a sixteenth century letter of R. Joseph Arli. See 284f. The following discussion of the yeshibah curriculum in our text is based upon the letter of R. Joseph. As Marx noted, the schedule is probably an over-generalization, perhaps even a bit of exaggeration for public relations reasons, for it manifestly leaves an inadequate amount of time for sleep or rest, and hardly any time at all for private matters. In my own youth once the student had completed high school and was in the bet midrash level at Mesivta Torah Vodaath in Brooklyn during the 1940's we rose for morning worship which took place at 7 A.M., breakfast at 8 A.M., the morning study session at 9 A.M. to 1 P.M. Lunch followed, and an afternoon study session resumed after 2 P.M.

minḥah worship. This session closed at 5 P.M. Dinner was at 6 P.M., followed by an evening session which lasted until 10 P.M. and was closed with maárib.

125. See further on this **Emergence** IV.

126. This is not to deny the hardships often suffered as a result of the many wars fought in Italy, or from sporadic local persecution such as the expulsion from Naples in 1540, and finally the burden of the ghetto. But none of this in any way approximated the massive humiliation and large-scale expulsion endured by Jews in the Franco-German and Spanish environments 1200-1500.

127. Roth, **Italy,** 209; Alexander Marx, "Glimpses of the Life of an Italian Rabbi," 605-624. Marx published a 1538 Ms. by R. David ibn Yaḥyah of Naples. Among other interesting items it informs us that by then Italian rabbis were paid salaries (606). But see below.

128. Marx, ibid., 612ff.

129. Ibid., 615.

130. Shulvass, op. cit., 77f.

131. Ibid., 78f. See also the strictures of Abraham Farissol of Ferrara to be discussed in chap. 4, in Ruderman, **Renaissance Jew,** 15f. The same negative attitude was taken by communities living in the Islamic sphere according to Saul Lieberman, **Yemenite Midrashim** (Jerusalem: 1940), 26ff.

132. Shulvass, 79f. The Italian term for sexton was sometimes sagrestano and sometimes manigliore (in Sicily). The shoḥet was known as sciattatore, scammatore and sagatino.

133. Ibid., 74f. Synagogues in Italy were usually known as bet keneset in Hebrew and sinagoga in Italian, but also as moschetta, a mosque, a residue of Islamic influence in southern Italy.

134. That different synagogues served the needs of varying ethnic groups when they gathered in a large urban center such as Jerusalem is evident, for example, from Acts 6:8 which refers to a Greek-speaking synagogue as a separate entity. See also P. Meg. 73d for an Alexandrian synagogue in Jerusalem, and B. Meg. 26a for "Tarsians."

135. Shulvass, op. cit., 192; Cecil Roth, **History of the Jews in Venice** (Philadelphia: 1930), 141.

136. Shulvass, 75f.

137. Ibid., 199f., 201.

138. Ibid., 200f.

139. See N. Porges, "Elie Capsali Et Sa Chronique De Venise" REJ 77 (1923), 20-40; 78 (1924), 15-34; and 79 (1924), 28-60 for the Hebrew account of Capsali's history of Venice. It is from the original Hebrew, p. 51, that the quotation here is taken. More will be said of Capsali in chap. 4.

140. See Shulvass, 282f.; Ruderman, **Renaissance Jew,** 57-84; select midrashim on mysterion are at Tanhuma (Warsaw: 1910), Vayera 1:5 (p. 25a); Ki Tissa 34 (p. 127a); **Pesikta Rabbati,** trans. William G. Braude (New Haven-London: 1968), I, 5:1. See also David Kaufmann, "Elia Menahem Chalfan On Jews Teaching Hebrew to Non-Jews," JQR 9 (1897), 500-508. Halfon's (Chalfan) responsum written in Venice, 1544 was here published in the original for the first time, 503-508. In it Halfon upholds the permissibility to teach Hebrew but prohibits the teaching of tradition. He does not adequately deal with all the talmudic examples of where ancient rabbis engaged in the teaching of post-scriptural tradition to gentiles.

141. For Jewish-Christian debates during the Middle Ages see J. Rosenthal, "The Anti-Christian Polemical Literature Until the End of the Eighteenth Century" [Hebrew], Areshet 2 (1960), 130-179; 3 (1961), 433-439. As for the Magen Avraham, there are difficulties in any attempt to make a technical study of it since the complete text has never been published, and a proper study of all its extant manuscripts has not been made; see Ruderman, 64-68. On the subject of earlier medieval polemic and debate see also Salo Baron, **History,** vol. IX, chap. 39, and the bibliographical references in his notes, 287-307. See further chap. 4 on Abraham Farissol, and chap. 7 below.

142. Shulvass, 209; on Azariah, n. 9.

143. Ibid., 210f.

144. Ibid., 212. The shomrim laboker received their name from Ps. 130:6. Their aim was to hasten the coming of the Messiah by emphasizing midnight prayer, and specifically to direct this prayer to the redemption of Israel. The name of this society is also sometimes given as meirei hashahar, "awakeners of the dawn."

145. Hyman G. Enelow, "Raphael Norzi: A Rabbi of the Renaissance," HUCA, Jubilee Vol., (1925). See further on Norzi's thought in the context of other thinkers, below, chap. 4.

146. This is found in Raphael Norzi, **Seah Soleth [A Measure of Fine Flour]** (Venice: 1579), 1f. See Enelow, 338ff.

147. Enelow, 373ff. See earlier in this chapter on Erasmus, and n. 45 above.

148. David Kaufman, "The Dispute About the Sermons of David Del Bene of Mantua" JQR 8 (1895-6), 513-524. An old ban on pagan and secular teachings in the synagogue issued by the fourteenth century scholar, R. Solomon ibn Aderet was being violated here.

149. Ibid., 513. There were a number of Sfornos who were scholars and these should not be confused. Israel Sforno used his son Obadiah, a Venetian talmudist, to help recruit the excommunicating rabbis, but this Obadiah should not be confused with Obadiah b. Jacob, 1470-1550, the celebrated biblical exegete who also taught Hebrew to Johann Reuchlin. On Reuchlin see above III, A and further in chaps. 3 and 7.

150. Ibid., 515.

151. Ibid., 516.

152. For the geonic time see my **Emergence** II, 25f. For the nineteenth century see the forthcoming vol. IV.

153. See further chap. 4 below.

154. The modern reader should not confuse this **Tanya** with the modern **Tanya**, a philosophical ḥasidic work of the first Rabbi of the ḥasidic line of Luba-vitch, Shneur Zalman of Ladi, on whom see further, **Emergence** IV.

155. Shulvass, op. cit. 268f. On French and German Judaism see, **Emergence** II, chaps. 7 and 9.

156. Shulvass, 273ff. Attention was paid to Hebrew grammar, unlike the neglect of it in Germany; effort was made to study history and become ac-quainted with ancient society, including its mythology, and knowledge of Greek and Latin; they studied Philo and Josephus, and included general history, philosophy and geography in their purview, as well as medicine and other sciences. See Shulvass, 285-323, and chap. 4 below.

157. In his commentary to M. Abot, **Naḥalat Abot** 6:1, Don Isaac Abravanel wrote that there was indiscriminate ordination in Italy. Shulvass, 276. See Aaron Rothkoff, **Bernard Revel** (Philadelphia: 1972), 14, as cited from Hutchins Hapgood, **The Spirit of the Ghetto** (New York: 1909), 62.

158. Shulvass, 284f.

159. Ibid., 328-332.

160. Jews were not as addicted as gentiles to astrology, but nevertheless did engage in it, and many took very seriously the notion that the stars governed human destiny. As noted earlier, for example, Raphael Norzi believed in the impact of the constellations upon life.

161. The example of the double marriage ceremony is at Shulvass, 330, and n. 2 for references. For demons see 332.

162. Ibid., 201f.

163. Ibid., 331.

164. Ibid., 331f.

165. Ibid., 200.

166. Cited by Shulvass, 200, from Archivolti's **Mayyan Ganim** (Venice: 1553), 22a. The Shakespearean picture of Shylock in **The Merchant of Venice** might not at all be an exaggerated stereotype of an Italian Jewish moneylender in the sixteenth century.

167. Shulvass, 197.

168. Ibid., 334. My own view of Solomon is rather less sanguinary. I maintain that he was a rather inept monarch in his foreign policy, crude and insensitive in his domestic policies, and religiously and morally corrupt as is seen in his manifold marriages and his concessions to his wives' idolatries. Solomon was responsible for the secession of Israel from the United Kingdom and consequently for the weakening and ultimate destruction of both petty kingdoms. His reign was the watershed of Israelite/Judean history. From that point on, with minor exceptions it was all downhill until the Romans vanquished Jerusalem in 70 A.D.

169. Ibid., 335ff.

170. Ibid., 344.

171. Cited by Adler, "Art Music," 361. Adler points out that the state of synagogue music during the sixteenth century is not yet as fully documented as desirable, but that seventeenth and eighteenth century documentation indicates the spread and continuity of the practice.

172. Adler, 362f. On the Counter-Reformation see chap. 3 below.

173. Ibid., 363; similarly, as Adler concedes, 364n147, that art music was practiced in Mantua about 1605, but the ghetto was not established until

between 1610-1612. To argue that "the process of segregation . . . was already well advanced" does not justify the theory that art music in the synagogue was the product of the inward-turning occasioned by the segregation encouraged by the Counter-Reformation. As he has himself recognized, documentation for the sixteenth century is sparse, and art music might have been introduced in Mantua, and elsewhere much earlier, just as it was in Padua.

174. Shulvass, op. cit., 346-359.

Chapter Three. Reformation and Counter-Reformation

1. The bibliography on the Reformation is massive and need; not be reproduced here. A few selected works will provide the reader with general background. Among them: Enno Van Gelder, **The Two Reformations** (see above, Introduction, n. 1); Roland H. Bainton, **The Reformation of the Sixteenth Century** (Boston: 1956); James Mackinnon, **Luther and the Reformation,** 4 vols. (New York: 1962); Robert Herndon Fife, **The Revolt of Martin Luther** (New York: 1957); **The New Cambridge Modern History,** Vol. II, **The Reformation,** ed. G. R. Elton (Cambridge: 1958) especially chaps. 3, 4, 7; T. H. L. Parker, **John Calvin: A Biography** (Philadelphia: 1973); Paul Henry, **The Life and Times of John Calvin,** 2 vols. (New York: 1853); Hugh Y. Reyburn, **John Calvin** (London-New York-Toronto: 1914). See also Salo Baron, "Protestant Reformation" in his **History,** vol. XIII, 206-296, with the prolific references provided in his notes, 415-463. See especially the bibliographical works cited at 415n4. See also H. H. Ben-Sasson, "The Reformation in Contemporary Jewish Eyes" **Proceedings of the Israel Academy of the Sciences and Humanities** 4 (1970), 239-326 [English]; 62-116 [Hebrew].

2. Baron, **History** XIII, 416, end n. 4.

3. Bainton, **Reformation,** 3.

4. Ernst Troeltsch, **Protestantism and Progress,** trans. W. Montgomery (New York: 1912), 65f.

5. Ibid., in general chaps. 4 and 5.

6. Van Gelder, 127 appears to use Colet as the early influence.

7. Ibid., 130f.

8. See Sigal, **Emergence** II, chap. 8 for the early Judaic community in England; Baron, XIII, 209f.; 416n5. Special note should be taken of Baron's statement ". . . a collaborative effort between a Wyclif expert and a student of Judaism might indeed yield some worthwhile new insights." See also Bainton, op. cit., 19f.

9. Cecil Roth, **The Jews of Medieval Oxford** (Oxford: 1951), 134f., 167f.; Sigal, **Emergence** II, 228ff.

10. Baron, XIII, 209f.; 416n5; see n. 8 above.

11. Fife, **Martin Luther,** 464. Luther took care in a letter to George Spalatin, written January 14, 1520, to deny that he or his ancestry were Bohemian. See **Luther's Works,** ed. Helmut T. Lehmann, Vol. 48. **Letters,** ed. and trans. Gott-fried G. Krodel (Philadelphia: 1963), 143-148. For some reason Fife dates this letter to January 10. See also Baron, 212, 214.

12. Baron, 213f.

13. Van Gelder, 204ff.; 209ff. For the mastery of the evil yeẓer or the inclination to sin, see Gen 4:7; Gen. R. 22:6.

14. Van Gelder, 223.

15. Ibid., 221f.

16. Ibid., 230. For a correction of Luther's view of Paul's discussion of "works of the law" erga nomou see Sigal, **Emergence** I, 415f. and notes; and my paper delivered at the Fourth Colloquium, Calvin Studies Society, May 5, 1983, at Calvin Theological Seminary, Grand Rapids, "Luther and Calvin on Law and Gospel in their Galatians Commentaries" to be published in the Proceedings of the Society. On Luther and Erasmus see Mackinnon, **Luther** III, 224-273.

17. Bainton, 23.

18. The details of Luther's life follow Fife (n. 1 above).

19. Ibid., 10ff., with citations from Luther's **Table Talk.**

20. Ibid., 55f.; 423-435.

21. Van Gelder, 231, 234.

22. Ibid., 235. For a similar situation obtaining for John Calvin, see 268.

23. Ibid., 236ff.; for Calvin see below; for the yeẓers and the ability to choose, or free will in Judaism, see Deut. 30:15-19; Jer. 21:8; **Sifre Deuteronomy,** ed. Louis Finkelstein (New York: 1969), 53-54; M. Ab. 3:19. The prolific references to the doctrine of free will in Judaism need not be multiplied here. Apocryphal, rabbinic and medieval philosophical literature are replete with sayings attesting to the all-pervasive nature of the concept in Judaism by the time of the Protestant

Reformation. See Solomon Schechter, **Aspects of Rabbinic Theology** (London: 1909), 264-292.

24. Van Gelder, 186-192.

25. Ibid., 194-204.

26. Baron, XIII, 218. In one of his virulent outbursts against the Catholic Church Luther said, "If I had been a Jew and had seen such dolts and blockheads govern and teach the Christian faith, I would sooner have become a hog than a Christian." See his "That Jesus Christ Was Born a Jew" trans. Walter I. Brandt, **Luther's Works,** op. cit., vol. 45, pp. 195-229; the quotation cited is on 200. It is in the light of this tendency on the part of Luther to speak in virulent hyperbole that some of his more vituperative remarks aimed at Jews should be seen and not summarily adjudged "anti-semitism" of a crasser nature. The second quotation cited in the text is at 229.

27. Martin Luther, "A Sincere Admonition by Martin Luther To All Christians To Guard Against Insurrection and Rebellion," trans. W. A. Lambert, Rev. Walter I. Brandt, **Works,** op. cit., 45, 51-74. On the date of the pamphlet see Brandt, 56; the quotation cited is at 63.

28. Ibid., 63. Luther used Deut. 16:20 ẓedek ẓedek tirdof "you shall pursue justice," the repetition of the Hebrew representing the emphatic, or justice in its fullest sense. Luther took this to mean, "that which is just, ẓedek, you shall pursue justly," and he did not consider insurrection a just method. While this is a midrashic exegesis it is within reason and within the spirit of the verse. He also used Deut. 32:35 which clearly leaves all retribution to God.

29. On the rising of the peasants see Mackinnon, III, 188-210. Under Luther's inspiration there ensued a ravaging of the peasants, and Luther forgot Deut. 32:35 (see n. 28). Luther's anti-peasant posture eventually slowed the spread of Lutheranism among the common people, and the fear of further revolution induced Lutheran princes to consolidate absolutism.

30. On this see below chap. 6.

31. Baron, XIII, 220ff.; on Nicholas de Lyra see Hailperin, **Rashi,** 135-246. That Luther discussed texts with Jews is clear from his own testimony in "On the Jews and their Lies," trans. Martin H. Bertram, **The Christian Society** IV, ed. Franklin Sherman, **Luther's Works,** vol. 47, p. 191, and n. 63, where he reported discussions with three learned Jews. Cf. also a sermon of 1526, in **D. Martin Luther's Werke,** vol. 20, ed. Paul Pietsch (Weimar: 1904), 569f.

32. Baron, XIII, 223ff. It should be pointed out that no direct line ought to be drawn between Nazism and Luther simply because W. Linden compiled

Luther's anti-Jewish statements in **Luther Kampfschriften gegen das Judentum.** (Baron, 428n24, writes "not surprisingly, Luther's violent anti-Jewish diatribes greatly appealed to modern German anti-semites . . . "). On Josel of Rosheim see Selma Stern, **Josel of Rosheim,** trans Gertrude Hirschler (Philadelphia: 1965); on the Jewish condition in Germany in the sixteenth century see Wilhelm Maurer, "Die Zeit der Reformation," Karl Heinrich Rengstorf, Siegfried von Kortzfleish, eds. **Kirche und Synagoge, Handbuch zur Geschichte von Christen und Juden Darstellung mit Quellen** I, (Stuttgart: 1968), 363-375.

33. "Against the Sabbatarians: Letter to a Good Friend," trans. Martin H. Bertram, **The Christian Society** IV, **Luther's Works,** Vol. 47, pp. 57-98; "On the Jews and their Lies," op. cit., 121-306. It is difficult to date precisely when Luther turned against Jews, but by 1537 we find that he refused to help Josel of Rosheim come to Saxony to plead against the elector's edicts to ban Jewish residence and travel in Saxony. In 1543 he also published another anti-Judaic tractate "On the Ineffable Name."

34. Bertram, "The Sabbatarians," 59f. For Luther's contacts with Jewish scholars see n. 31 above. See in general for Jewish relations with reformation trends, Louis I. Newman, **Jewish Influence on Christian Reform Movements** (New York: 1925).

35. **Works,** vol. 47, p. 62. In 1523, in "That Jesus Christ Was Born A Jew" Luther sympathized with the Jews and blamed Christians for forcing them into usury by not allowing them normal business and human fellowship. See ibid., vol. 45, p. 229. In "On the Jews," ibid., vol. 47, pp. 272ff. he argued that the Jews suck the marrow of Christian bones and get rich on Christian sweat and blood by means of their usury and then the lords take the money from the Jews. At this time he evinced no further empathy as he did earlier for one of the causes of their historic role in the practice of usury.

36. Ibid., vol. 47, pp. 121-306 (n. 32 above); see 123f.

37. Ibid, 126f.; 137; 253. See also Newman, op. cit. 628. Osiander wrote a pamphlet to defend Jews against the charge of ritual murder. Luther's special invective for the rabbis whom he regarded as distorting all scriptural understanding for Jews for all time is well-exemplified in his commentary to Genesis. See **Lectures on Genesis,** trans. George V. Schick, et al., ed. Jaroslav Pelikan, Walter Hansen, **Luther's Works,** vols. 1-8, (St. Louis: 1958-1966). See also Arnold Ages, "Luther and the Rabbis," <u>JQR</u>, 58 (1967-68), 63-68.

38. See **Lectures,** passim.

39. **Lectures,** vol. 1, pp. 3, 169, 227; even where he does not denigrate them he rejects the rabbis' exegesis because they lack understanding of the text and "torture" a passage (ibid., 295); or make "presumptuous fabrications," vol.

8, pp. 88f. This type of critique continues through all eight volumes and requires no further documentation here. On James see **D. Martin Luthers Werke. Tischreden,** vol. 5. "Introduction," Karl Drescher, items 5974, 414; 5443, 157; 5854, 382. Here he writes "Ich werde ein mal mit dem Jekel den offen hitzen." "One time I would like to heat the oven with Jimmy." See also Frans Mussner, **Der Jakobusbrief** (Freiburg-Basel-Wien: 1981), 42-47. These table talks took place contemporaneously with the lectures on Genesis. For Sebastian Muenster see chap. 7 below. A comparative study of Luther and rabbinics will yield more than one Ph.D. dissertation.

40. Sigal, **Emergence** II, 258ff., 270ff., and notes with bibliography at 511n79; 528n44. See especially Guido Kisch, **The Jews in Medieval Germany: A Study of their Legal and Social Status** (Chicago: 1949).

41. Bertram, "On the Jews," in **Luther's Works,** vol. 47, p. 129. See also Stern, **Josel,** 165, 183. For Bucer see further chap. IV, B2 below.

42. Sigal, **Emergence** II, 463n66.

43. "On the Jews," op. cit., 267-292. At 292 we find Luther calling the most uncivilized barbarites "mercy," a cure to be administered like a physician proceeds in a case of gangrene, and then reversing himself to admonish the rulers not to be merciful. The tone of the words used by Luther raise serious questions about the psychological state in which he found himself when he wrote this treatise.

44. Armas K. E. Holmio, **The Lutheran Reformation and the Jews** (Hancock, Mich.: 1949), 65f.

45. See n. 26 above.

46. Holmio, 99f.

47. "On the Jews," 137; Luther wrote: " . . . since I learned that these miserable and accursed people do not cease to lure to themselves even us . . . I have published this little book so that I might be found among those who opposed such poisonous activities . . . " See also Holmio, 110f. Holmio, 113ff. also points out the interesting fact that Luther's attacks on Jews for usury were dependent upon his traditional attitudes in the matter, nor realizing that both the Roman Catholic and other Protestant thinkers including Calvin were accepting a "just price" theory for taking "profit" for the use of money, the usual amount being five per-cent. Christian thinkers also seemed to miss the fact that some Jewish exegetes and halakhic authorities were opposed to usury on the grounds that it was banned by Ps. 15:5, that the one who "dwells with God" is one who does not lend out his money at usurious rates, and that this indeed even includes not to do so to pagans. In the Christian era Christians were considered monotheists and so the ban on usury would apply to them. See B. Mak. 24a.

48. Holmio, 123f.

49. "The Licentiate Examination of Heinrich Schmedenstede," trans. Lewis W. Spitz, **Works**, vol. 34, p. 317; see n. 21 for a story about a preacher in Kalenberg burning a statue of James to heat a room for the background to Luther's remarks. See n. 39 above.

50. Bainton, **Reformation,** 77.

51. See the relevant volumes of Baron's **History.** See also for a survey of anti-Jewish feeling in fifteenth century pre-Reformation Germany, E. G. Gudda, **Social Conflicts in Medieval German Poetry** (Berkeley, Calif.: 1934), chs. 9-12.

52. For Melanchthon see Baron, vol. XIII, 229-232. For Osiander see ibid., 232. For Levita see chap. 2 above. See also Stern, **Josel,** for the Brandenburg matter, 171f.

53. Baron, XIII, 233f.

54. Friedman, **The Most Ancient Testimony,** 31ff.; Baron XIII, 235-239. For Zwingli see also Newman, **Jewish Influence,** 454-510; Bainton, op. cit. 80-94.

55. Bainton, 89.

56. Baron, XIII, 241f., 435n41. See also John W. Kleiner, **The Attitude of the Strassbourg Reformers Toward Jews and Judaism,** Dissertation, Temple University (Philadelphia: 1978), 181-266; W. J. Nottingham, **The Social Ethics of Martin Bucer,** Dissertation, Columbia University (New York: 1962), 236ff. See also Stern, **Josel,** 170-174. For a detailed discussion of the whole Bucer matter see Kleiner, 208-260.

57. Kleiner, 193-197, 204f. **The Dialogi** was published at Augsburg, 1535, but the Cassel Advice or **Ratschlag** was more extensive.

58. Deut. 28:43f. reads, "The alien in your midst will rise even higher above you, while you will descend even lower. He will lend to you but you will not lend to him. He will be the head and you will be the tail." Bucer's argument reflecting wrath over the institution maintained by Jews and in more recent times known as "the shabbas goy," the gentile who does tasks forbidden to the Jew on the Sabbath, was most unfortunate. The irony is that this was not truly permitted in classical rabbinic Judaism and should never have been practiced. The principle was amirah lenakhri shebut, a word to a gentile [to ask one to perform a task forbidden to a Jew on the Sabbath] is a rabbinic interdiction." See B. Shab. 150a; Er. 67b-68a; Git. 8b, and parallels. This rule is implied at M. Shab. 16:6, that one does not ask a gentile to perform a forbidden act although if he is doing so a Jew need not ask him not to since the gentile is not obligated to the Sabbath.

59. Cited by Kleiner, 227.

60. Ibid., 233f.

61. Neither the Hebrew nor the German originals survive.

62. Stern, op. cit. 215f.

63. Baron, XIII, 240f.; for Capito see also Kleiner, 63-104; for Josel's experience with Luther, see Stern, op. cit., 159f. For Capito and Hebrew see Kleiner, 63, 71ff.

64. Capito's attitude to Judaism and Jews is mainly evident in his **Hexemeron Dei** (Strasbourg: 1539); Kleiner, 75-81. The quotation from Capito is cited by Kleiner, 82.

65. On Hedio see Kleiner, 105-137.

66. Baron, **History** XIII, 238, 433f., n. 37.

67. For a brief survey of Anabaptism see Bainton, **Reformation,** 95-109. The so-called Anabaptist movement consisted of widely diverse groups. Their main common thread was their opposition to infant baptism.

68. Baron, XIII, 242-247, 438f., n. 45; 463n103. The statement by Mantz is cited at **Luther's Works,** vol. 46, 90n13, by Robert C. Schultz who edited and annotated Luther's "Whether Soldiers Too, Can Be Saved," 93-137, in which Luther defended the legitimacy of a military career for a Christian as divinely ordained to punish evil and preserve peace; he compared the soldier who does his work correctly to a physician who amputates a limb to save the whole body. (p. 96).

69. Gershom Scholem, **Sabbatai Zevi,** 99ff., 100n170. For the Augsburg Confession see **The Book of Concord,** trans. and ed. Theodore G. Tappert (Philadelphia: 1959), 38f.

70. Baron, XIII, 249. See also Silver, **Messianic Speculation,** 143-145. A brief review of medieval calculators of the year of Messiah is found ibid., 116-143, and offers a glimpse of the intensity of messianic fervor at the time, exacerbated by the expulsion from Spain in 1492, and reaching an apex with Shabbatai Zvi in the mid-seventeenth century.

71. Silver, 114, 145-150. For Joseph Karo see **Emergence** II, 105, 204, 276, 319-324. See also Stern, **Josel,** 131-137. Josel opposed Molkho's idea of persuading the Emperor Charles V to a Jewish-Christian crusade against the Turks to liberate Palestine. Josel was not messianically inclined, rejecting all

mystical calculations and predictions. He also thought it impolitic to aggravate the Turks who had recently granted refuge to the victims of the Spanish expulsion.

72. See G. H. Williams, **The Radical Reformation** (Philadelphia: 1962).

73. See Haim Hillel Ben-Sasson, "Jews and Christian Sectarians: Existential Similarity and Dialectical Tensions in Sixteenth-Century Moravia and Poland-Lithuania," Viator 4 (1973), 369-385.

74. Ibid., 370n5; 371. Arians were a new effulgence of the old early Christian movement begun by Arius ca. 320. Anabaptists were slaughtered by the thousands, and like medieval Jews they composed many a chronicle and hymn of martyrology. See examples in translation, Bainton, 102-104.

75. Ben-Sasson, 375. Ganz' Hebrew text is cited in n. 22. But see Baron, XIII, 250-258 for the political vicissitudes Jews encountered in Protestant areas in the aftermath of the early Reformation, and under Roman Catholicism, 258-267.

76. Ben-Sasson, 377, 380ff.

77. Ibid., 382, texts cited from Rabbi Haim Löw, brother of R. Judah, at nn. 50, 51.

78. Ibid., 383n55.

79. The bibliography both of John Calvin's writings and on John Calvin's life and thoughts is massive, and no effort is made here to be exhaustive. The following brief selection might, however, be of some value for background to Calvin and Calvinism. Bibliographical studies of literature on Calvin are listed in Baron, XIII, 456n86. For proper understanding of Calvin's outlook and his theology one must consult his major works, **Institution of the Christian Religion**, trans. Ford Lewis Battles (Atlanta: 1975); **Commentaries**, trans. and ed. by various scholars, 22 vols. rpt. (Grand Rapids, Mich.: 1979). See also Jules Bonnet, **Letters of John Calvin**. 2 vols. (Edinburgh: 1855-1857); Williston Walker, **John Calvin** (New York: 1969). R. N. Carew Hunt, **Calvin** (London: 1933); and n. 1 above.

80. The meaning of the term Huguenot used for French Calvinists is obscure. On Calvin see Parker, **John Calvin** (n. 1 above), Appendix 2, 162-165; 32f.; Baron, XIII, 279f.

81. Van Gelder, **Two Reformations**, 271f.

82. Ibid. chaps. 8-10.

83. Ibid., 313f. For the Jewish view of imitatio dei see, for example,

Mekhilta de R. Ishmael, ed. Jacob Z. Lauterbach, 3 vols. (Philadelphia: 1949), II, 25.

84. Van Gelder, 315, and n. 2; see M. Ab. 2:4. On divine grace granted to aid free will in Judaism see Philo, **On Drunkenness** 36 (145); Sigal, **Emergence** I, 320f., and rabbinic sources listed at 370f., n. 126.

85. For Farissol see chap. 4. Calvin's visit to Ferrara is mentioned by Henry, **Life and Times** (see n. 1), I, 99ff. For his humanist education I have also relied upon the unpublished paper, Ford L. Battles, "Calvin's Humanistic Education" given at a Colloquium at the Pittsburgh Theological Seminary in 1976.

86. Jules Bonnet, **Letters** I, 416f., and n. 1; I, 443.

87. Baron, **History** XIII, 280f., 456n86; Salo Baron, "John Calvin and the Jews," **Ancient and Medieval Jewish History** ed. Leon A. Feldman (New Brunswick, N.J.: 1972), 338-352. There Baron suggests, 548n1, that a careful study of Calvin's sermons might yield more information on Calvin's attitudes; but a great number of his sermons have been lost.

88. This commentary is cited rather misleadingly by Baron, ibid., 339. Baron fails to take account of Calvin's equal negativism toward the papacy in the same commentary, and quite incidentally, Baron erroneously attaches it to the words of v. 5, "abundance of the sea and wealth of nations." See John Calvin, **Commentary on the Book of the Prophet Isaiah,** trans. William Pringle, 4 vols. (Grand Rapids, Mich.: 1948), IV, 281.

89. Calvin, **Commentary Is.,** II, 320-324; the quotation is cited from his comment to Is. 29:13, p. 324.

90. Ibid., III, 467. The scope of this chapter does not allow for a more comprehensive examination of Calvin's commentaries. It must suffice here to suggest that the numerous negative references to Jews are basically theologically oriented with a view to stressing that only conversion to Christianity can redeem Jews from their darkness and misery. These comments and glosses are not programmatic on how Christians ought to treat Jews in the contemporary world. On the subject of Judaic sources behind Calvin's commentaries, see T. H. L. Parker, **Supplementa Calviniana** (London: 1962), 18ff.

91. Baron, "Calvin," 339.

92. See IV, B above for Bucer.

93. Ford Battles, "Introduction," **Institution,** xxiv. See Benoit Girardin, **Rhetorique et Theologique Calvin** (Paris: 1979), 254-265, for observations on rabbinic rhetoric in Calvin's commentaries. For background on this subject see

David Daube, "Rabbinic Methods of Interpretation and Hellenistic Rhetoric," HUCA 22 (1949), 239-264.

94. Calvin's remark on Luther's liturgy is cited by Baron, "Calvin," 550n11. For Servetus see Friedman, **Ancient Testimony,** chap. 3; Jerome Friedman, **Michael Servetus: A Case Study in Total Heresy** (Geneva: 1978). More will be said of Servetus in chap. 7 in the discussion of Christian Hebraism. See also Roland H. Bainton, **Hunted Heretic: the Life and Death of Servetus, 1511-1553** (Boston: 1953). See also Newman, **Jewish Influences,** 511f.

95. Parker, op. cit., 118.

96. See Friedman, **Case Study** (see n. 94), 83-87; Jerome Friedman, **The Theology of Optimism,** Dissertation, University of Wisconsin (Madison: 1971), 266-276.

97. Friedman, **Case Study,** 9, 103-112, 121-132.

98. The question of multiple manifestations of God need not be documented here. The reader can pursue this in my **Emergence** I and II, under shekhinah and bat kol, and in II, chap. 10 on kabalism.

99. Israel Bettan, "The Sermons of Isaac Arama," HUCA 12-13 (1937-38), 538-634. See. 586.

100. Ibid., 587f., n. 6.

101. Ibid., 622.

102. Ibid., 622ff

103. Ibid., 633f.

104. Friedman, **Ancient Testimony,** 59, 62-67; Servetus had easy access to targums because by that time they were widely diffused by the **Complutensian Polyglot Bible** of 1514-1517. See also E. M. Wilbur, **The Two Treatises of Servetus on the Trinity** (Cambridge: 1932). This includes the first English translation of the treatise **On the Errors of the Trinity** and **Dialogues On The Trinity.** Wilbur suggests Servetus might have coined the term "trinity" to describe the orthodox belief in a triune deity. See 54f., and n. 9, for the shifting use of the word, from being used for antitrinitarians as a term of opprobrium until they were finally renamed "unitarians." For Paul Fagius see chap. 7 below.

105. Friedman, **Case Study,** 132, uses the term "distortion" for Servetus' method, and writes that Servetus " . . . totally misunderstood the essence of

262

Jewish tradition." The material examined by Friedman does not sustain such a charge. See also Friedman, **Optimism**, 299-313.

106. Cited by Baron, **History** XIII, 283f. See also Baron, "Calvin," 341; Newman, op. cit., 588ff. For Servetus' last words at the stake, reasserting faith in Jesus, but condemning trinitarianism see Roland H. Bainton, **Michael Servet. Heretique et Martyr** (Geneva: 1953), 128, cited from a letter to Calvin.

107. Baron, "Calvin," 343.

108. Again, as noted earlier, it is important to take careful stock of Calvin's biblical commentaries in seeking to assess his attitude to Jews and Judaism. But at the same time it is necessary to distinguish between his pejorative attitude to Jews of the biblical milieu and to those of his own time before issuing a blanket indictment of anti-semitism. In this connection one might examine his commentary, e.g., to Is. 38:8; 48:21; Obad. vv 19f.; Mic. 5:1-2 and throughout. The commentary to Genesis at 1:26, e.g., shows that he is aware of rabbinic ăgadah even when he rejects it. Unless one is reading the Latin, however, it is important to carefully scrutinize the different translations. For example, where Baron, "Calvin," 343 translates an anti-rabbinic comment as "This is the result not merely of their ignorance but of their audacity . . . " Pringle, op. cit., III, 490 translates, "and they do this, not through ignorance, but through presumption . . . " which somewhat softens Calvin's tone.

109. See his commentary on Romans 11:28-32.

110. Baron, "Calvin," 346; **History** XIII, 461n97; 457n86.

111. Stern, **Josel**, 138ff.

112. Baron, "Calvin," 347ff.; **History** XIII, 462n100.

113. Baron, "Calvin," 349. See also **Concerning Heretics**. Records of Civilization, Vol. XXII, ed. Roland H. Bainton (New York: 1935).

114. Baron, "Calvin," 349f. In this matter Calvin's **Institution** must be carefully studied. See further below.

115. On the role of Protestantism in the formation of western individualism and democracy see Salo W. Baron, "Protestant Individualism," **Modern Nationalism and Religion** (New York: 1947); **History** XIII, 292ff.

116. Walker, **John Calvin**, 391f.; Reyburn, **John Calvin**, 248.

117. **Institution**, I, A. 1, ed. Battles, 20.

118. Ibid. I, B. 2, p. 21. This Calvinist view of original sin is not in accord with Judaism. In Judaism Gen. 6:5, that the human is persistently immersed in evil, and Gen. 8:21, that the human inclination is evil from his earliest days, are balanced by Gen. 4:7, where God tells Cain that although sin crouches at the door, he is capable of mastering it. The dual nature of God's justice and mercy is found many times in rabbinic literature. See for example, Gen. R. 12:15; 33:3. It is predicated upon the Old Testament, where see such verses as Gen. 18:25; Ex. 34:6-7. See also Gen. R. 21:5.

119. Perhaps the best known and most explicit statement on this is at B. Ber. 33b, "All is in the hands of heaven except for the reverence of heaven." "Heaven" is here an epithetical circumlocution for God, and reverence implies doing His will. The maxim therefore asserts that if providence governs the condition of human life, the human nevertheless has freedom of choice in his obedience to God's will. Furthermore, from that theological perspective doing God's will and suffering in this world were not contradictory phenomena. Salvation was of the next world, and hence if providence seemed to mire the righteous in a sorrowful condition of life that did not mean that the continued life of righteousness will not bring salvation in eternal life. See, for example, Sif. Deut. 53.

120. M. Ab. 3:19 is perhaps the most explicit statement that encompasses all these related questions, the reconcilability of justice and mercy, and providence and free will. This is either a maxim by R. Akiba, as is implied by the sequence in which it is found, or anonymous. In any event, it states: "All is seen, but the right to act is granted; the world is judged by goodness, but all is in accord with the deed." Texts vary here. Some read "All is in accord with the preponderance of the deed," that is, whether good or evil outweigh, and some read "not in accord with the deed," that is, but rather simply by goodness, while others read as I have translated "all is in accord with the deed." The Hebrew texts would be: lefee hamaaseh; lo lefee hamaaseh; lefee rob hamaaseh. Cf. Rom. 11:22 where God's judgment is according to their works, lefee hamaaseh. For my reading of lefee hamaaseh see Charles Taylor, **Sayings of the Jewish Fathers** (Cambridge: 1897), text section, 20, 3:24. Regarding God's knowledge of human action it is better to speak of "knowledge" rather than the conventional "foreknowledge." The concept signifies: God knows all that occurs but does not intrude upon human freedom. It is His knowledge rather than His foreknowledge that should give humans pause to consider, for related to His knowledge of human action is the belief in reward and punishment.

121. **Institution,** I, B, 3, pp. 21f.

122. Ibid., I, C, 4, pp. 22f.

123. Ibid., I, D, 6, pp. 24f. See Jn. 3:16-20; I Jn. 5:11-12.

Notes to pp. 68-71

124. Ibid., I, E, 14, pp. 32f.

125. Ibid.

126. Ibid., 15, p. 33.

127. Ibid., I, F, 25, p. 39.

128. Ibid., I, H, 33, p. 49. On the attitudes of Jesus and Paul toward the Torah or nomos see **Emergence** I, pt. 1, chap. 7.

129. On grace in Judaism: P. Kid. 61d; Ex. R. 45:6. See also my paper, "Luther and Calvin on Law and Gospel" (n. 16 above). See also below on the Council of Trent and the doctrine of free will.

130. Bainton, **The Reformation,** 118-122.

131. **Institution,** II, B, 22, p. 79.

132. M. San. 10:1. See n. 129. See also, for example, Yoḥanan ben Zakkai's concern on his deathbed that he have grace to supplement his inadequate deeds in order to experience salvation (B. Ber. 28b).

133. B. Shab. 31a; Mak. 24a; San. 81a. On the 613 commandments see **Emergence** II, 162f., 202, 483n48, 499n24. See also ibid., 404 for the passage from B. San. 81a expressing Gamaliel's concern about the weight of good deeds required for salvation and how his colleagues assured him that Ez. 18:5-9 does not require that a person live by all the items on the roster, but by any one of the items. Similarly sages are reported at B. Mak. 24a to interpret Ps. 15:5 "he who does these [the virtues of vv. 2-4] shall not slip forever," as meaning any one of these. They derive it by the hermeneutical rule gezerah shavah, analogy, from Lev. 18:24, where kol ēleh can only mean "any one of these" and not "all of these." This view was upheld by Moses Maimonides in **Commentary to the Mishnah** Mak. 3:16. See also Schechter's discussion of salvation in **Aspects of Rabbinic Theology,** 164ff., 182, 189.

134. **Emergence** I, pt. 1, 415-422.

135. Calvin is correct in **Institution** I, F, 25, that some Jewish sages (whom he mistakenly terms "Pharisees") were of the opinion that anyone who refrains from an overt violation of the precepts of the Torah might be eligible for salvation, that is, they advocated a theory of "negative righteousness." But these sayings can be balanced by others that reject the view, a fact that Calvin omitted. See, for example, M. Mak. 3:15; B. Kid. 39b; P. Kid. 61d; Sif. Deut. 286. And against these, B. Kid. 31b; P. Kid. 61d; B.A.Z. 18b-19a.

136. See e.g. Mekh, ed. Lauterbach, III, 200, that observing the sabbath is giving witness that God is the creator.

137. Select bibliography on the Catholic Reformation: Henri Daniel-Rops, **The Catholic Reformation,** trans. John Warrington (London: 1963); John C. Olin, **The Catholic Reformation** (New York-London: 1969); Frederick C. Church, **The Italian Reformers** (New York: 1932).

138. Baron, **History,** XIV, 3f. Daniel-Rops, 1ff. See also Olin, "Introduction."

139. Olin, "Introduction," xxiiff.

140. Ibid., xxvf.

141. Ibid., 1-15; an illustrative sermon of 1495 is published at 4-15.

142. Ibid., 16-26.

143. Ibid., 40-53.

144. The bull is reproduced by Olin, 56-64. The quotation is from pt. III, sec. 10, p. 64.

145. Ibid., 118-127.

146. Baron, **History,** XIV, 6ff.

147. Olin, 183f.

148. This report is given by Olin, 186-197; the quotation is at 187.

149. Ibid., 188-197.

150. Ibid., 198-211.

151. See Olin, 198n1, for bibliography.

152. Ibid., 209f.

153. Much of what we know about Romano (Giovanni Battista Eliano) is derived from his own **Autobiography** where he revealed that he was involved in the censorship of Jewish books. See Baron, **History,** XIV, 304n8.

154. Baron, **History,** XIV, 10f. On Laynez and his elevation to the papacy see Baron, 304f., n. 9, where he indicates that it has not yet been verified.

Notes to pp. 75-78

155. Ibid., 15f. On <u>limpieza</u> see also Roth, **Marranos**, 74ff.

156. Selected bibliography on the Council of Trent: Daniel-Rops, op. cit., ch. 2; **Canons and Decrees of the Council of Trent**, trans. H. J. Schroeder (London: 1950); Martin Chemnitz, **Examination of the Council of Trent**, trans. Fred Kramer, 2 vols. (St. Louis, Mo: 1971); Herbert Jedin, **Geschichte des Konzils von Trient**, 4 vols. (Freiburg: 1951-1975); **A History of the Council of Trent**, trans. Ernest Graf, 2 vols. (St. Louis, Mo.: 1957-1961); Baron, **History**, XIV, 17-25.

157. For the papal bull in translation see Schroeder, op. cit., 1-10; the Latin text is at 281-289.

158. Cited by Daniel-Rops, 67.

159. Ibid., 66.

160. Ibid., 73ff.

161. Ibid., 85ff. On the Index see Baron, **History**, XIV, 22f.

162. Kenneth R. Stow, **Catholic Thought and Papal Jewry Policy 1555-1593** (New York: 1977), 3. The bull's title is taken from its opening words "since it is absurd . . . " A very clear picture of the status of Jews during the sixteenth century is given by Marquardus de Susannis, **De Judaeis,** a legal tract of 1558 containing one hundred and fifty laws and canons with four hundred interpretations from one hundred commentators. See Stow, xiif.

163. Baron, **History**, XIV, 29f. See also **The Jew in the Medieval World,** ed. Jacob R. Marcus (New York: 1978), 170ff., where he cites Joseph hakohen, **Emek Habaka** (1575).

164. Cited by Stow, ibid., 6.

165. See also Rom. 9:6-13. Paul's midrash was adopted by the author of the Epistle of Barnabas 13, and this became a characteristic feature of early Christian theology. Paul's notion that Ishmael "persecuted" Isaac is derived from targumic interpretation of Gen. 21:9.

166. Daniel-Rops, 89, 95ff. My theological exposition emphasizes the Jewish view as basically being the tension between God's expectation and human fulfillment, the product of human moral deficiency. This leaves a gap which is filled by grace. Thus, human free will and effort mingle with God's compassion to allow for salvation. See above my comments on free will contra Calvin, and references, nn. 118, 119, 120, 129, 132. At the sixth session of the Council in January 1547 a decree was formulated restating that while all labored under the defect of original sin and neither Jews by Torah nor gentiles by natural

moral law can save themselves from it, free will has not been extinguished. See Schroeder, op. cit., 29f., and for the Latin text, 308f. See also canons 5 and 9 at 43, that anyone who says free will has been destroyed by Adam's sin is anathema; Latin texts, 321.

167. Daniel-Rops, 108ff.

168. Pius V reissued cum nimis and broadened its range in his bull **Romanus Pontifex** in 1566, and reinforced that with another bull, cum nos nuper in 1567 and created a centralized office to supervise enforcement in the hands of the head of the department which oversaw conversion. See Stow, 17f., 25.

169. Baron, **History**, XIV, 18; Daniel-Rops, 134ff.

170. See n. 163.

171. See W. Bacher, "The Sabbatarians of Hungary," JQR 2 (1890), 465-493. In Russia Sobotniki belonged to a sect known as Molokani or "Milk-Drinkers." These practiced circumcision. See Bacher, 466f. Bacher's article relies upon Herman Sternberg, **History of the Jews in Poland** (Leipzig: 1878).

172. Bacher, 467.

173. Ibid., 469ff.

174. For the Hungarian sect, Bacher follows the work of Samuel Kohn, **The Sabbatarians. Their History, Theology and Literature** (Budapest: 1890), written in Hungarian.

175. Bacher, 471f.

176. Ibid., 473f. Gospel of Thomas 27 reads in Thomas Lambdin's translation, "If you do not observe the Sabbath as a Sabbath you will not see the Father." See **The Nag Hammadi Library**, ed. James M. Robinson (New York-London: 1977), 121.

177. See further in Bacher, 474ff. A more detailed investigation than was done by Bacher is a desideratum.

178. In this connection the reader might consult my article on Dual Covenant Theology referred to earlier, HBT 3 (1981), and another article on this subject in HBT, 5, p. 1-48, (1983).

Chapter Four. **Proto-Modernity in Italy**

1. See Michael A. Meyer, **The Origins of the Modern Jew** (Detroit: 1967), 132ff. The changes effected by Israel Jacobson will more fully be explored in the forthcoming **Emergence** IV.

2. Meyer, ibid., 9 uses this time framework. In the light of what I present here he missed the mark in saying, "Modern Jewish history in its intellectual aspect begins with these years" (p. 9).

3. See David Ruderman, **The World of a Renaissance Jew,** op. cit. My account of Farissol is indebted to Ruderman's exhaustive treatment.

4. C. W. Previté-Orton, **The Shorter Cambridge Medieval History,** 2 vols. (Cambridge: 1952), II, 835ff.; 953-962.

5. Ruderman, op. cit., 4-6.

6. Ibid., 10-17; 26-30. Farissol adapted the curriculum reflected at M. Ab. 5:24; this called for the study of scripture at five years of age, Mishnah at ten, and Talmud at fifteen.

7. This is recorded by François Tissard in his section De Judacorum ritibus compendium which tells of Farissol and Ferrara, and is attached to his **Grammatica Hebraica et Graeca** (Paris: 1508); cited by Ruderman, 101. N. Porges, "Die Anfangsgründe der hebräischen und griechischen Grammatik des Franciscus Tissardus," **Festschrift Professor David Simonsens** (Copenhagen: 1923), 172-87, contains a German summary of Tissard's Latin work. For Pepys see chap. 6 below.

8. On Farissol's interchange with Christian scholars see Ruderman, chaps. 5 to 7, pp. 57-97. The **Magen Avraham** has never been published in its entirety. See D. S. Löwinger, "Selections from **Sefer Magen Avraham** of Abraham Farissol" [Hebrew] **Hazofeh Lehokhmat Yisrael** 12 (1928), 277-297; "Recherches sur l'oeuvre apologetique d'Abraham Farissol," REJ, 105 (1940), 23-52.

9. Ruderman, 72-74.

10. Ibid., 37-40. Mercurio adopted his name from the Roman god who was identified with Hermes, thus signalling his opposition to traditional Christianity.

11. On the Hermetic tradition see **Hermetica,** ed. and trans. Walter Scott, 4 vols. (Oxford: 1924). The fourth volume was completed by A. S. Ferguson. See also F. A. Yates, **Giordano Bruno and the Hermetic Tradition** (Chicago-London: 1964); D. P. Walker, **Spiritual and Demonic Magic from Ficino to Campanella** (London: 1958); W. Schumaker, **The Occult Sciences in the Renaissance: A Study**

in **Intellectual Patterns** (Berkeley-Los Angeles-London: 1972). A very exhaustive study of Hermetic literature can be found in R. P. Festugière, **La revelation d'Hermes Trismegiste**, 4 vols. (Paris: 1944). On what has been said in our text regarding Hermes Trismegistus see Scott, "Introduction," 5f.; Yates, 2f.

12. Yates, op. cit., 6ff. On the historicity of Hermes Trismegistus see, for example, Augustine, **The City of God,** ed. Marcus Dods, 2 vols. (Edinburgh: 1871), XVIII, 39, ed. Dods, II, 266. Clement of Alexandria refers to forty-two books by Hermes on philosophy, the stars, medicine, and religious hymns, but these books are distinct from the corpus we know, although Renaissance thinkers believed that the **Corpus Hermeticum** they had in Marsilio Ficino's translation was the sacred library described by Clement as possessed and used by the Egyptian priests. See Yates, 11ff. Ficino had given the general title of <u>Pimander</u> (<u>Poimandres</u>), taken from the beginning of the first of the treatises to all fourteen he translated.

13. On the Hermetic magical tradition see Yates, 44-61. On the astral effluvia described in the Asclepius, one of the branches of the **Corpus Hermeticum,** see Yates, 45.

14. Scott, 8.

15. Ibid., 12f. Scott places full emphasis upon Platonic origins for certain ideas that could as easily have come from the intensive hellenistic Judaic milieu in which Hermetic ideas arose. Philo was widely read in Egypt and just as he is found in patristic literature it is logical to assume he was an influence upon Hermetic literature. Furthermore, the gnosticism of the Hermetic treatises which rests upon a Judaic background is a further element that intrudes itself into the Hermetic literature.

16. John G. Gager, **Moses in Greco-Roman Paganism** (Nashville-New York: 1972), 77; see also 148ff. for similar titles of treatises attributed to Moses and Hermes.

17. Ibid., 17, 31ff. Scott originally held the view I have expressed here, that the design portrays the sequence Moses to Hermes to Plato and others, but later relented. See p. 31n1. I read no persuasive reason to change this interpretation. The beardless man, indeed, could represent all philosophers since Pythagoras, even including, or specifically including Ficino who now hands down the Hermetica in Latin for a new era.

18. See chap. 7 below; Ruderman, 38, 188n14. See also G. Scholem, **Kabbalah** (New York: 1974), 23-30 on <u>Sefer Yeẓirah</u>. Scholem, 26 refers to presently unknown "introductions" to earliest texts to which Lazarelli might have been referring. That those Judaic mystics believed in the possibility of vivifying a new creation is borne out at B. San. 65b where R. Ḥanina and R. Hoshaiah

of the fourth century used <u>Sefer Yezirah</u> to create a three-year old calf which they then consumed, perhaps in a festive ritual meal, 27.

   19. Ruderman, 204n30.

   20. It is not germane to our chapter to discuss here the vigorous debates among scholars as to when Farissol had his interchanges which stand in the background of **Magen Avraham,** or when he actually wrote the work. See Ruderman, 63f., 200n47, 67f., 201f., nn. 78-79. Isaac Troki, **Ḥizzuk Emunah,** trans. Moes Mocatta (rpt. New York: 1970). See further on Troki, chap. 7 below.

   21. See L. Thorndike, **A History of Magic and Experimental Science,** 8 vols. (New York: 1923-58); "The True Place of Astrology in the History of Science," <u>Isis,</u> 46 (1955), 273-278; H. Kocher, **Science and Religion in Elizabethan England** (San Marino, California: 1953), and for problems faced by Christianity, 215-224.

   22. Ruderman, op. cit., 124-130, p. 126. For the problems of astrology in Judaism in the earlier period see Alexander Marx, "The Correspondence Between the Rabbis of Southern France and Maimonides on Astrology," <u>HUCA</u> 3 (1926), 311-342.

   23. See **Magen Avraham,** chap. 8; Ruderman, 75.

   24. The promise of material reward permeates the Old Testament. See e.g., Deut. 11:13-15; Lev. 26:3-6.

   25. Ruderman, 75. See Wisd. 5:5, 15; 3:1-6, which conceives of immortality as limited to the righteous. See also Wisd. 2:23f. where immortality is described as the very essence of the human being in God's image.

   26. <u>PRE</u> 34; B. R. H. 24b; Shab. 152b; Sif. Num. 40, 139; Aḅ. de R. N. A. 12. The early provenance of the rabbinic idea that the souls of the righteous survive in heaven to await resurrection is seen in the fact that Josephus was able to write of this idea confident that his readers would be familiar with it. See Josephus, **War** III, 8.5 (374).

   27. Ruderman, 76.

   28. This matter is discussed in the twenty-sixth chapter of **Magen Avraham.** See also Ruderman, 77f. and the Hebrew quotation cited at 206n47.

   29. Ruderman, 80-84. See J. B. Roberts, **The Old Testament Texts and Versions** (Cardiff: 1951). See also further below, chap. 7.

30. Ruderman, 43-51. The Pico circle, especially Mithridates was using Raymund Martini's (1228-1281) **Pugio Fidei** which for a long time was accused of containing Martini's personal forgeries of non-existent Judaic materials, but which have been proven not to be forgeries. See Sigal, **Emergence** II, 121f. See also Saul Lieberman, "Raymund Martini and His Alleged Forgeries," **Texts and Studies** (New York: 1974), 286. Ruderman seems not to have noticed the Lieberman material and raises no question concerning Farissol's historic error.

31. Ruderman, 51.

32. See n. 7 above.

33. Ruderman, 98-105. On the matter of using gentiles on the Sabbath see my comments in chap. 3 and n. 58 there.

34. See Louis Finkelstein, **Jewish Self-Government in the Middle Ages,** 302.

35. Ruderman, 111-116. See also Natanyahu, **The Marranos,** 80-134. More will be said of the Marrano influence on Judaism in the next chapter.

36. Ruderman, 121. I would not agree with Ruderman that Farissol was oblivious of Copernicus.

37. Ibid., 137-143.

38. See Charles Berlin, "A Sixteenth-Century Hebrew Chronicle of the Ottoman Empire: **The Seder Eliyahu Zuta** of Elijah Capsali and its Message," **Studies in Jewish Bibliography,** ed. Charles Berlin, 21-44. See also **De Vita et Scripta Eliae Kapsalii (Likutim Shonim Misefer Deve Eliayahu)** ed. Moses Lattes (Padua: 1869; rpt. Jerualsem 1967-8). See also Barzilay, **Delmedigo,** 9; **Seder Eliahu Zuta of Rabbi Eliahu Capsali,** The Ottomon Section, ed. Aryeh Shmuelovitz; The Spanish-Venetian Section, ed. Shlomo Simonsohn, Meir Benayahu, 3 vols. (Tel Aviv: 1975-1983); Meir Benayahu, **Rabbi Eliahu Capsali of Crete** (Tel Aviv: 1983).

39. On Delmedigo see below.

40. **Divre Hayamin** and **Sifre Eliyahu Zuta** respectively.

41. Berlin, op. cit., 22.

42. For a brief sketch of Jewish historiography in the Renaissance, which, however, does not discuss Capsali, see Shulvass, **Renaissance,** 295-309.

43. Josephus, **Ant.** I, 3.9 (108); II, 16.5 (348).

44. Berlin, 29f.

45. See N. Porges, "Elie Capsali" REJ 77 (1923), 20-40; 78 (1924), 15-34; the Hebrew account is at REJ, 79 (1924), 28-60.

46. Barzilay, **Delmedigo**, 18.

47. Ibid., 26, 36. For Moses Capsali see also H. Rabinowicz, "Joseph Colon and Moses Capsali" JQR, 47 (1957), 336-344; for the quotation see 336, and n. 2. See also S. Assaf, "Responsa and Letters of Moses Capsali," Sinai III (1939), 155, where he writes "the minhagim [customs] and fences of our early ancestors shall remain in place . . . "

48. Rabinowicz, 341.

48. See Salo W. Baron, "Azariah de' Rossi: A Biographical Sketch;" "Azariah de' Rossi's Attitude to Life;" "Azariah de' Rossi's Historical Method," **History and Jewish Historians**, ed. Arthur Hertzberg, Leon A. Feldman, (Philadelphia: 1964), 167-239.

50. For "Letter of Aristeas" see **Aristeas to Philocrates**, ed. and trans. Moses Hadas (New York: 1951).

51. Baron, "Attitude to Life," op. cit., 174; "A Biographical Sketch," op. cit., 167, 170; "Historical Method," 215. See also Ralph Marcus, "A 16th Century Hebrew Critique of Philo," HUCA, 21 (1948), 29-71, for dei Rossi's critique of Philo. Dei Rossi faulted Philo for deviating from Palestinian halakhah without realizing that he often verified earlier halakhah, and that his so-called "deviations" evinced the type of pluralism dei Rossi was unable to grasp. See text below, and n. 78.

52. Ibid., 171, 405n4.

53. Ibid., 171f.

54. Ibid., 172f.

55. The line was always very fine, and often depended upon who possessed police power rather than upon a fixed creed or halakhah. The wide diversity in both halakhah and precisely what are the fundamental doctrines of Judaism, was demonstrated in **Emergence** I and II; and is also alluded to for Renaissance Italy in chap. 2 above.

56. Baron, "Attitude," 175f., 406nn4-6. For dei Rossi on Philo see Ralph Marcus, "A 16th Century Hebrew Critique of Philo" (n. 51 above); see also Baron, 222f.

57. Ibid. 176f.

58. Ibid., 177f.

59. Ibid., 178f. For demons in the halakhah see Joseph Karo, **Shulḥan Arukh** Yoreh Deah 179, the halakhah concerning magical divination. See 179:10, 19.

60. Baron, ibid., 179.

61. Ibid., 180f.

62. Ibid., 185; 413f., n. 61. Baron attributes dei Rossi's aggressive note on Hebrew language to refutation of the opposing view expressed, for example, by Gianozzo Manetti (1396-1459) who maintained that all languages and their scripts were invented as humans sought to communicate with one another. But Baron was surely aware that much closer in time to dei Rossi the view prevailed that Hebrew was the original human language. See further on this in chap. 6 below.

63. See Sigal, **Emergence** I, pt. 1, pp. 180f., 182ff, and nn. 116, 119. See also n. 16 above.

64. Baron, "Attitude," 186f.

65. The entire fifty-fifth chapter of **Mᵉor Ĕynaim** is devoted to the subject of national and international peace. Jeremiah's letter, the basis of Jewish loyalty to the land of their residence and to pray for peace, is at Jer. 29:4-7; Is. 2:4; cf. M. Aḥ. 3:2.

66. On Menasseh see the next chapter. For Baron's review of Azariah's discussion of loyalty to existent governments and his political science in general see "Attitude," 188ff.

67. See Baron, 191. His comment on Jerome is cited at 435n128.

68. See Baron, "Azariah de' Rossi's Historical Method," **History and Jewish Historians,** 227ff. A partial listing of the scholars used only in his treatment of Philo is given by Marcus, op. cit., 33ff.

69. Baron, "Attitude," 192f.; **Mᵉor Ĕynaim,** chap. 2 is devoted to this question. See also Baron, "Historical Method," 227. Zacuto's bitterness stemmed from his having been a victim of the 1492 expulsion from Spain, a tragedy he was unable to transcend in his scholarship.

70. Baron, "Attitude," 194f. On Moses Mendelssohn see **Emergence** IV.

274

71. Chap. 28 of Mĕor Eynaim deals with the question of halakhah.

72. Dei Rossi could easily fall back for his theory of the equality of all religious deeds upon M. Ab. 2:1. For Karaites see **Emergence** II, chap. 4. The quotation is cited by Baron, 426n35.

73. Baron, "Attitude," 198.

74. See Baron, "Historical Method," 206.

75. Ibid., 207, 423n4.

76. Ibid., 216f.

77. Ibid., 218f.; the first quotation is cited at 430n73, the second at 219. For variations on the story of Titus and the gnat see Gen. R. 10:7; Lev. R. 22:3; B. Git. 56b; PRE 49; Dei Rossi's treatment of this legend is translated and published in Michael Meyer, **Ideas of Jewish History** (New York: 1974), 117–121.

78. Baron, "Historical Method," 432n96. It is to dei Rossi that we owe the Hebraic name Yedidiah for Philo. See Marcus, "16th Century Critique," 30. The quotation in the text is as given by Baron; but see also Marcus, p. 58. Philo is discussed in chaps. 3, 4–6 of Ĭmrei Binah, the third section of Mĕor Ĕynaim.

79. For Philo see **Emergence** I, chap. 6, and bibliography there. See also Guido Kisch, "Pseudo-Philo's **Liber Antiquitatum Biblicarum** Postlegomena to the New Edition," HUCA, 23 pt. II (1950–51), 81–93; especially 85–91. For the order of the commandments see **Bib. Ant.** 11:10f.; Philo, **Decalogue**, 24 (122).

80. Marcus, op. cit., 29f.

81. Ibid., 37f. This comes at the very end of dei Rossi's discussion of Philo in chap. 6 of **Imrei Binah.**

82. Marcus, 38–42. Believing that the pseudo-Philonic **Biblical Antiquities of Philo** were indeed written by Philo, as everyone did at that time, dei Rossi also critiques that work, "proves" Philo's authorship, and approves the work as containing nothing "crooked or perverse" from the standpoint of the Torah. See Marcus, 42ff. See **Emergence** I, 361n98; **The Biblical Antiquities of Philo** trans. M. R. James, Prolegomenon, Louis H. Feldman (New York: 1971).

83. Marcus, 44ff.

84. Ibid.

85. Ibid., 48ff.

86. Ibid., 50ff.

87. The quotation is cited by Marcus, 51. But see my discussion of Philo's halakhah in **Emergence** I, pt. 1, 314-318.

88. Marcus, 51-55. For the quotation see 58.

89. Baron, "Historical Method," 223f. See Sigal, **Emergence** II: for geonim, chaps. 2 and 3 for tosafists; chap. 7 for Jacob b. Asher, 313f.; for Karo and Isserles, chap. 11.

90. Baron, op. cit., 435n123.

91. Graetz, **History of the Jews** IV, 614.

92. This is written in conscious rejection of the views of Hiram Peri (Heinz Pflaum), "Leon Ebreo, Renaissance Philosopher," **Studies in Jewish Thought. An Anthology of German Jewish Scholarship**, ed. Alfred Jospe (Detroit: 1981), 270-280; see 270f.

93. Ibid., see also Bernhard Zimmels, **Leo Hebraeus ein judischer Philo-soph der Renaissance** (Breslau: 1886).

94. For Portaleone see David Kaufmann, "Leone De Sommi Portaleone (1527-92)," JQR, 10 (1897-8), 445-461; 450; 453n1; 454.

95. An important primary source is Modena's autobiographical journal Ḥayyeh Yehudah ed. A. Kahana (Kiev: 1911); **Leo Modena's Briefe und Schriftstücke** ed. Ludwig Blau (Budapest: 1905-6). Much work has been done in recent times on Leone da Modena and the bibliography at this time is relatively extensive. The following are only a few select items of interest: Ellis Rivkin, **Leon de Modene and the Kol Sakhal** (Cincinnati: 1952); "The Sermons of Leon of Modena" HUCA, 23 (1950-51), pt. II, 295-317; Cecil Roth, "Leon de Modene, see **Riti Ebraici** et le saint-office a Venise," REJ, 87 (1929), 83-88; "Leone da Modena and the Christian Hebraists of His Age," **Jewish Studies in Memory of Israel Abrahams**, op. cit., 384-401; Isaiah Soone, "Leon Modena and the Da Costa Circle in Amsterdam," HUCA, 21 (1948), 1-28; and further references in the notes that follow. The controversy referred to in the text was over whether Modena wrote the text **Kol Sakhal** as a devious way to express his own concealed heresies.

96. Cecil Roth, "Modena and the Christian Hebraists," 384.

97. Modena's tragedies included the death of two sons and a daughter, the disappearance in Brazil of a third son, a dissolute, the widowing of his second

daughter and mental breakdown of his wife. See **A Treasury of Jewish Letters,** ed. Franz Kobler (Towbridge, England: 1952), II, 412. See also Rivkin, **Leon,** 42ff., and n. 58; Cecil Roth, **Renaissance,** 27, 36. Gambling was undoubtedly the reason why a historian such as Roth inappropriately used such subjective value terms as "scapegrace" and "wayward" in describing Modena.

98. Roth, "Christian Hebraists," 388ff. See also Cecil Roth, "Leon of Modena and England," TJHSE, 11 (1928). See also Kobler, op. cit., II, 422ff., for letters from Modena to De La Pause, and especially one of 1640 in which he appealed to him for financial help and expressed his willingness to "spend that little time he has before him in the service of the Lord and then in yours" (426). Modena's economic situation must always have been precarious as the rabbinate at the time enjoyed very limited financial security, a relatively low social status and shrinking authority. Those who were supported by patrons were in better condition, and this is apparently what Modena hoped for from his erstwhile pupil, the bishop. See a recent study of the rabbinate, Reuven Bonfil, **The Rabbinate in Renaissance Italy [Harabanut Beitalyah Bitekufat Harenasans]** (Jerusalem: 1979). Bonfil overemphasizes Italian Jewish "cultural" and "national" "feeling" and "pride" as factors which brought changes in the late sixteenth century leading Jews away from the Renaissance synthesis. Factors that deserve more consideration were the natural religious retrenchment of the traditionalist rabbis seeking to overcome growing dissent and laxity in ritual observance, the reduction of opportunities to acculturate instigated by the Catholic Reformation and the reinvigoration of the Inquisition and censorship, and the shift of the pendulum to east European leadership.

99. Roth, "Christian Hebraists," 390.

100. Ibid., 391n25, cited from a letter written by Modena, and which is published on 399f. For Menasseh see chap. 5. On Jesus and the question of Pharisees see my **Emergence** I, pt. 1, chap. 7; I, pt. 2, chapter I. Jesus was indeed a proto-rabbi but not a Pharisee, and Pharisees were similar to Essenes.

101. Roth, 392n31; 398f. Buxtorf lived from 1564-1629, wrote his work in German in 1603. It was translated into Latin in 1641 by his son, Johannes Buxtorf the Younger. He also enlarged it in 1661. It was in his autobiography that Modena indicated he wrote the **Riti** primarily in response to an English friend who requested it for James I of England (1603-25). Leone da Modena, **Historia de' Riti Hebraici** (Venice: 1638); see chap. 2 n. 96 above.

102. On Catholic censorship see William Popper, **The Censorship of Hebrew Books** (New York: 1899); see also Mark R. Cohen, "Leone da Modena's Riti: A Seventeenth-Century Plea for Social Toleration of Jews," JSS, 34 (1972), 287-321; see 287n3; Blau, **Modena's Briefe;** letter no. 193, among others discusses the **Riti.**

103. Graetz, **History**, V, 65-67, 71-74; Graetz exaggerated, however, at p. 71, when he wrote that, ". . . he was forced to admit one thing and another in Judaism to be defective and ridiculous . . ." and that in **Riti** he, ". . . like Ham, uncovered his father's nakedness." (See Gen. 9:22f.).

104. Cohen, op. cit., 298.

105. See Cohen, 298f., and "Appendix," 320f., for a brief catalog of some of the items criticized or ridiculed by Buxtorf and minimized or omitted from Modena's published version of **Riti**. See further 299ff. Modena's Italian letter is reproduced in translation by Kobler, op. cit., II, 426f.

106. Roth, TJHSE, 11, pp. 211f.; see also Cecil Roth, "Leone da Modena and His English Correspondents," TJHSE, 17, pp. 39-43; see pp. 40ff. See also **Anglo-Jewish Letters** (1158-1917), ed. Cecil Roth (London: 1938), 44ff. Modena did not publish the **Riti** for many years because of the constraints of censorship by the Inquisition. Modena's passage concerning his fears is published in translation from his Ḥayye Yehudah **(The Life of Judah)** at Marcus, **The Jew in the Medieval World**, 406-408.

107. Roth, TJHSE, 11, pp. 214ff., nn. 9-10.

108. Thomas Coryat, **Crudities** (Glasgow: 1905), I, 370-376; see Roth, TJHSE, 11, pp. 217-221.

109. Rivkin, **Leon**, 47f.

110. Ibid., 52f. The **Toledot Yeshu** might be as old as the fifth century. See Hugh J. Schonfield, **According to the Hebrews** (London: 1937).

111. See Isaac Rivkind, "The Responsum of R. Judah Aryeh Modena on Bareheadedness," **Ginzberg Jubilee Volume** II, 401-423. Modena's responsum taken from his collection, **Zikne Yehudah** is reproduced at 412-420. See at 416, ". . . There is not even one [scholar] who says it [bareheadedness] should be prohibited, and now I will argue directly to them that even from the standpoint that it is midat ḥasidut, a measure of piety to restrain from anything which is disrespectful, for us Italians there is no need for such restraint, for it is necessary to understand the words of the rabbis according to place, time and person, and if not so then we will become toward their words heretics like the Karaites toward the written Torah. For there is no end to the matters that we find were forbidden for them which have become permitted with the passage of time and change of place . . . and for us Italians who dress differently and allow our hair to grow long and have the custom of doffing the hat . . . " bareheadedness is a mark of respect. See further on this question, Vol. IV relative to modern Judaism. Modena years later incorporated into his manuscript the responsum of R. Solomon Luria, the great Polish halakhist which agreed entirely with Modena's.

Modena's responsum on music in the synagogue was published with his introduction to Solomon Rossi's **HaShirim asher Lishelomah** in 1623. See Rivkin, **Leon,** 57; see also Kobler, op. cit., II, 416-419 for a translation of Modena's letter commending Rossi's work to the Jewish public. See also Alfred Einstein, "Salamone Rossi As Composer of Madrigals," HUCA, 23, pt. 2 (1950-51), 383-396.

112. Rivkind, 412. See M. Ber. 5:1. R. Solomon Luria had, however, supported continuing the new custom of covering the head to avoid communal friction and loss of credibility from some scholars among the pious masses. Thus his views were ambivalent and did not serve to avert the ultimate antagonism which emerged when reformers bared their heads.

113. Ibid., 419.

114. Rivkin, **Leon,** 68-75. For Karaism see Sigal, **Emergence** II, chap. 4. More will be said of so-called Marrano "heresy" and Uriel da Costa in chap. 5. That the person being refuted in **Magen Vezinnah** was Uriel da Costa is indicated by Rivkin, 108.

115. Rivkin, 78, citing Modena's **Ari Nohem,** 50f.

116. See Rivkin, 80-95. Many scholars have accused Modena himself of having written **Kol Sakhal** and have argued that it exposes his true views while his pro-rabbinic views were a cover-up. See Rivkin, 98f., and n. 224 for references. Early modern scholars who attributed the work to Modena were Isaac Samuel Reggio, **Behinat Hakabalah** (Gorizia: 1852); Abraham Geiger, **Leon da Modena** (Breslau: 1856). Unfortunately Rivkin's zeal to save the honor of Leone da Modena led him at times to indulge in a rather rude and offensive critique of Reggio and Geiger. Isaiah Sonne more recently argued that da Costa wrote **Kol Sakhal;** see Sonne, "Leon Modena and the Da Costa Circle in Amsterdam," HUCA, 21 (1948), 1-28. See also his earlier "Da Costa Studies," JQR 22 (1932), 247-293. For Uriel da Costa and heresy see further chap. 5 below. More recently Isaac Barzilay upheld the older notion that Modena wrote the work and that it reflects the Renaissance literary style of concealing contrary views within the same work. See Isaac Barzilay, "Finalizing An Issue: Modena's Authorship of the Qol Sakhal," **Salo Wittmayer Baron Jubilee Volume,** ed. Saul Lieberman, 3 vols. (New York-London: 1974), 135-166. Barzilay used the sermons collected in Modena's **Midbar Yehudah** and other writings to argue Modena's authorship of **Kol Sakhal,** 149-165. To the question of whether Modena was "heretical," if it be true that he wrote **Kol Sakhal** it is best said that his writings in general, like those of Delmedigo reflect the inner tension of being proto-modern in a medieval milieu. Furthermore the notion of heresy simply does not apply in a pluralistic religion such as Judaism.

117. See further my forthcoming vol. IV.

118. Surveyed by Rivkin, 81-83.

119. Ibid., 85f. For Jesus see **Emergence** I, pt. 1, chap. 7; for Pharisees and rabbis see **Emergence** I, pt. 2, chap. 1. Rabbinic ritualism also multiplied in the late first century and second century in polemic with rising Christianity in an effort to differentiate the two. When two religions share as much theology and morality as Judaism and Christianity, ritual and sacrament become the major instruments of individuation.

120. Rivkin, 87-94, 125, 127f., for a brief survey of the material that follows in my text. See also Sigal, **Emergence** II, chap. 11, for "Judaism Circa 1650." Although **Kol Sakhal** was written before 1650, and possibly around 1620, for Modena claimed he received it in 1622 (see Sonne, 2), all of the critique of rabbinism received in the text can be clearly understood in the light of Judaism as it was then practiced. My date of 1650 is only a terminal date. That style of traditionalism and most of its content was in place before 1500. As a point in fact Modena claimed that **Kol Sakhal** was written in 1500 by a Spanish Jew, and one must allow for the possibility that Modena had his facts correct. Should that be so it would reflect how constant was the Karaite spirit within rabbinism, although the new critics did not opt to join Karaism but rather to reform rabbinism. The Averroeistic tendencies in Spain, the Pico circle in Italy, the growing restiveness among returning Marranos all allow for the plausibility that the views of **Kol Sakhal** could have a strong following in the early sixteenth century. The extensive and often vituperative critique of rabbinism found in **Kol Sakhal** indicates that the anti-rabbinic campaign often conducted by Christians and Jewish apostates in that era could have originated within Judaism, and therefore should not necessarily be considered "anti-semitism" as that term is used in modern times. It cannot be claimed, for example, that Luther read **Kol Sakhal**, but if it were actually written close to 1500 there is every possibility that its contents were described to him and influenced his own attacks upon rabbinism. On kaparot see **Shulḥan Arukh** Ŏraḥ Ḥayyim 605:1 where Karo urged that minhag be abandoned while Isserles upheld it. Cf. **Emergence** II, 347.

121. See Rivkin, "The Sermons," 295 (n. 95 above). These sermons are collected as **Midbar Yehudah** (Venice: 1602).

122. Ibid., 297f.

123. B. Shab. 21b.

124. Ibid.; cf. B. Ber. 28a; Yom. 12f, 73a; Meg. 9b, 21b; Hor. 12b; Men. 39b, 99b. For the Sukot offerings see Num. 29:12-38.

125. Rivkin, op. cit., 306. It might be of interest to the modern reader, and in order at this juncture to refer to the well-known question of whether one places and kindles the Ḥanukah lights from left to right or right to left,

Notes to pp. 113-115

a minutia of observance that arouses some concern among the pious. See **Shulḥan Arukh** Oraḥ Ḥayyim 676:5 to place right to left and kindle left to right. There are other views depending upon whether one follows the custom of the Rhineland or of Austria. These customs are brought together and briefly reviewed by Shlomo Yosef Zevin **Hamoâdim Behalakhah** (Tel Aviv: 1955), 171. The matter should be set to rest: there is no halakhic requirement either way, and the obvious proof of that is that the matter did not seem important enough for Bet Shammai and Bet Hillel to discuss when they discussed whether to progress from one to eight or diminish from eight to one.

126. Barzilay, "Finalizing an Issue," 149; Alexander Altman, "Ars Rhetorica as Reflected in Some Jewish Figures of the Italian Renaissance," **Essays in Jewish Intellectual History** (Hanover, New Hampshire-London: 1981), 97-118. For Moscato see 112-117. Moscato's sermons are collected as **Nefuẓot Yehudah** (Lemberg: 1850). There is a monograph on Moscato: Abba Apfelbaum, **Sefer Toledot HaGaon Rabbi Yehuda Moscato** (Drohobicz: 1900). See also Israel Bettan, "The Sermons of Azariah Figo," HUCA, 7 (1930), 457-495; 467ff. for comments on Moscato.

127. Israel Bettan, "The Sermons of Azariah Figo." Seventy-six sermons are collected in **Binah Laltim** (Lemberg: 1797).

128. Bettan, "Figo," 468f.

129. Israel Bettan, "The Sermons of Isaac Arama," HUCA, 12-13 (1937-38), 583-634. See 586f., nn. 2-3; 594f., 622f., 626f. For the mussar movement, see **Emergence** IV.

130. Gamaliel's formula: M. Pes. 10:5. See Bettan, 587f., n. 6.

131. Rivkin, "Sermons," 315f.

132. Isaac Barzilay, **Yoseph Shlomo Delmedigo,** (chap. 1, n. 15). For Jewish life in Crete (Candia) see Elias S. Artom, Humbertus M. D. Cassuto, **Taqqanoth Candia V'Zikhronotêah** (Jerusalem: 1943); Louis Finkelstein, **Self-Government,** 82-85; 265-280; Joshua Starr, "Jewish Life in Crete Under the Rule of Venice," PAAJR, 12 (1942), 59-114. See also the bibliography in Barzilay, 342-357. The name Yashar was composed of the acronym Y(oseph) Sh(lomo) Rophê (physician; del medico or del medigo). Barzilay, 1-4, 24; for the Thirty Year's War see Baron, **History,** XIV, 224-294. For the Chmielnicki massacres see Max L. Margolis, Alexander Marx, **A History of the Jewish People** (Philadelphia: 1953), 551-557. These historical events will be discussed in **Emergence** IV, when the pre-modern developments in Germany and Poland will be treated. See also Bernard D. Weinryb, **The Jews of Poland** (Philadelphia: 1982), 181-205.

133. For non-Jewish Humanists and the occult see such general works as cited at n. 21 above. See, e.g., Thorndike, **History of Magic,** V, chap. 10. Yashar's works referred to in the text are **Maṣref Laḥokhmah** and **Novloth Ḥokhmah.** See also Barzilay, **Delmedigo** 260f. where he cites Yashar's belief that the saving factor in his life was his birth under the constellation of Mercury. Barzilay comes close to self-contradiction when, on the one hand, he asserts of Yashar "his open rejection of demons," and on the other hand, quotes Yashar to the effect that he never saw any demons and cannot speak of them so ". . . I do not want categorically to deny their existence . . ."; 265ff.

134. Barzilay, 18f. "Shibah worship" is the holding of daily worship in the house of a deceased or a mourner for seven days of mourning following the death of a next of kin. Select relevant takanot as published by Cassuto are Numbers 3, 18, 30, 82, 106. Literary activity is attested to in Vatican library manuscript lists for the sixteenth century. See Barzilay, 20ff.; 22n6.

135. Ibid., 27, 30f., 41, 43, 48.

136. Ibid., 50, 66f.

137. Ibid., 69, 72, 77, and n. 1, 78ff., 82, 85.

138. Ibid., 271; Barzilay's brief discussion of Yashar's attitude toward the Bible is at 299-304; toward the Talmud and rabbinic Judaism, 305-314.

139. Ibid., 300ff. Averroes was the Arabian commentator of Aristotle and it was his version of Aristotle that prevailed during those late medieval centuries. His views brought into question creation ex nihilo, free will and individual immortality, all important elements of Roman Catholic Christianity and Judaism. There were other implications to Averroism that cast doubt upon the doctrine of reward and punishment, providence, the efficacy of prayer and so forth, all stemming from his popularizing of Aristotle. The interested student can pursue this in works on general philosophy. In Jewish philosophy Averroes is referred to numerous times in passing, e.g., Isaac Husik, **A History of Medieval Jewish Philosophy** (Philadelphia: 1948), 306-336, passim.

140. Uriel da Costa returned to Amsterdam from Hamburg in 1618 either before or after his public excommunication in Venice. Delmedigo was in Amsterdam sometime before 1630, after which he settled in Frankfurt. See chap. 5 for da Costa.

141. See Altmann, **Moses Mendelssohn** (Philadelphia: 1973), 33ff., and the useful index entry, "Spinoza." More will be said of these influences upon Mendelssohn and modern Judaism in vol. IV.

142. Barzilay, 306n5, 309.

Notes to pp. 119-122

143. See Jacob Mann, **Texts and Studies,** 2 vols. (New York: 1972), II, 675-680. Karaite letters incorporated by Delmedigo in his correspondence are given by Mann, II, 1185-1187.

144. More will be said of this in vol. IV.

145. Barzilay, 315-322.

146. Ibid., 316.

147. At Mann, op. cit., 1226ff., there is a copy of a letter from Zeraḥ to Menasseh ben Israel referring to **Sefer Elim** whose title page tells that it was published in Amsterdam by Menasseh ben Israel; see n. 359. In that letter, 1227f., he mentions that Delmedigo translated Philo into Hebrew but that the copy was stolen and he expressed the hope that Menasseh will do it since nobody in his land can translate Latin into Hebrew.

Chapter Five. **The Dutch Experience**

1. See Sigal, **Emergence,** II, chap. 11.

2. Tycho Brahe and Johann Kepler were celebrated astronomers, and ultimately became major contributors to our modern understanding of the laws of planetary motion. See Graupe, **The Rise of Modern Judaism,** op. cit., 29f.

3. **Die Statuten der Drei Gemeinden Altona Hamburg, Wandsbek,** ed. and trans. Heinz M. Graupe, 2v. (Hamburg: 1973), no. 34 of Altona and no. 89 of Wandsbek.

4. See Graupe, **Modern Judaism,** 41-49; Ellis Rivkin, **Leon Da Modena and the Kol Sakhal,** 1-17; Cecil Roth, **Marranos,** 195-251. In reference to the Marrano question it is inappropriate to refer to them in terms of "seventeenth century heresy," as so many historians are wont to do. They had philosophical and theological opinions that often varied with traditional concepts and a non-rabbinically oriented approach to ritual practice. In an age of pluralistic religion their views would not necessarily have been "heresy."

5. Roth, op. cit., 5.

6. See **Emergence** II, 129-135; 467-470 nn. 82-94; Roth, 19. On the general conversion of Portugese Jews as a separate matter after 1492, see Roth, **Marranos,** chap. 3. Roth discusses the religion of the Marranos in chap. 7, 168-194. For meanings of the term "marrano" see Roth, 28, and Sigal, ibid.,

467 n. 85. See also H. P. Salomon, "The 'De Pinto' Manuscript," SR, 9 No. 1 (January, 1975), 1-9; the translation of the Portugese Ms is at 10-45, the Portugese text is published at 45-62.

7. Roth, 170f.

8. Ibid., 174f, 390 n. 1; see also Y. Kaplan, "The Portugese Jews in Amsterdam: From Forced Conversion to a Return to Judaism," SR, 15 (1980-81), 41f.

9. Roth, 176ff.

10. Ibid., 181ff.

11. Ibid., 190f.

12. Graupe, **Modern Judaism**, 43ff.

13. Rivkin, Leon, 3, 5, 6, and n. 1. See Immanuel Aboab, **Nomologia** (Amsterdam: 1628), dicussed by Rivkin, 12f. For conversos in France after 1550 see Salomon, 'De Pinto,' SR, 9, 4.

14. See **Emergence** II, 243, 468f. n. 90; 508f. n. 65; Y. Kaplan, "The Portugese Jews in Amsterdam," 37.

15. James C. Boyajian, "The New Christians Reconsidered: Evidence From Lisbon's Portugese Bankers, 1497-1647," SR, 13 (1979), 129-156; 129f. On limpieza see previous chapter. See also H. P. Salomon, "Haham Saul Levi Morteira en de Portugeese Nieuw-Christenen,," SR, 10 (1976), 127; "The 'De Pinto' Ms., op. cit., 39. See also I. J. Revah, "Les Marranos," REJ, 18 (1959-60), 29-77.

16. Boyajian, 132ff.

17. See e.g., the arguments by Boyajian regarding the Pinto family, 152ff. The arguments Boyajian makes concerning the discontinuity of the Judaic heritage among conversos in the dilution of what he calls the "Semitic clans" and "irrelevance of racial heritage" are irrelevant. What stands out is that the conversos were unaware of their faith, and indeed had engaged in much exogamy along with endogomy, in order to survive by establishing alliances with powerful Old Christian groups. But this does not prove they had not preserved their distinctive crypto-Judaism; they were therefore still aware of their remote origin, and for whatever reason, many sought to return during the sixteenth and seventeenth centuries. Their very unawareness of rabbinic Judaism would naturally contribute to their producing a disproportionate segment of so-called heretics.

284

18. Kaplan, "Portugese Jews in Amsterdam," 38ff., 41f. The idea that when Jews, "Israel," are in a state of sin they remain "Israel" in its theological significance is at B. San. 44a. Cf. also Sif. Deut. 308 that they remain "God's sons" even when in a state of sin.

19. Kaplan, 43f.

20. Salomon, 'De Pinto,' 5.

21. Cited by Kaplan, 49ff.

22. Rivkin, op. cit., 9f. A Hebrew version of these theses is published in Carl Gebhardt, **Uriel da Costa** (Amsterdam: 1922), 3-10'; the Portugese version is at 22-32; da Costa was refuted by Samuel da Silva; see ibid., 159f. The Venetian ban is cited by Rivkin, 13ff. See Gebhardt, 153.

23. The rabbi cited was Jacob b. Samuel Chagiz, **Halakhot Ketanot** (Venice: 1704), responsum No. 7; cited by Rivkin, 16. See further Rivkin, 16 nn. 11-16 for references. Menasseh ben Israel's anti-heresy writings are discussed in Cecil Roth, **A Life of Menasseh ben Israel** (Philadelphia: 1934), 87-100.

24. The student should consult general histories of Holland and Spain for background. For the Dutch experience as it relates to the Jews, the focus of this chapter, it is of interest to peruse J. S. Fishman, "Discovering and Utilizing Sources for the History of the Jews of the Netherlands," SR, 15 (1980-81), 75-84. See Baron, **History**, XV, chap. 1; Cecil Roth, **Marranos**, chap. 9; and for readers of Dutch attention should be given to H. J. Koenen, **Geschiedenis des Joden in Nederland** (Utrecht: 1843); J. Meijer, **Zij Lieten Hun Sporen Achtes** (Utrecht: 1964). See Roth, **Marranos**, 236f. for early settlement in Antwerp; Baron, **History**, XV, 5f; the documents cited by Baron indicate there was confusion over whether they were still Marranos or open Jews, the former mocking Catholicism, or the latter stirring dissent; see also 7, 11, 14.

25. Baron, **History**, 16f, 37f. Arminians were sixteenth century followers of Arminius (Harmensen) who rejected Calvinist predestination and believed in freewill. The term "Remonstrants" was derived from the "Remonstrance" or formal document expounding the differences between Arminians and Calvinists presented to the government of Holland in 1610. Erasmus is cited by Baron, **History**, 16; see also 384 n. 18 for sources.

26. Baron, **History**, 17, 19f. See also Graetz, **History**, IV, 673. This William of Orange is not to be confused with the celebrated William of Orange who became King of England in 1688 after the flight of James II. For the far-reaching socio-economic development of the Marranos/Sefardim in Holland and their impact upon Spanish power and Dutch power in the international arena see Jonathan Israel, "Spain and the Dutch Sephardim, 1609-1660," SR, 12 (1978), 1-61.

27. The early history of Dutch Judaism is still shrouded in a mist. See some useful bibliographical references in Baron, **History**, XV, 387f. n. 27; see also 389 n. 29, for other difficulties in ascertaining information about Amsterdam's early Jewish settlement because of the aliases under which names appear as a result of the mixed use of Portugese and Hebrew names. Aliases were used by returned Marranos also in order to protect relatives in Spain who went by the true family name. See a report by the Spanish consul in Amsterdam, 1655, at Baron, **History**, 58, and 405 n. 69. See also Roth, **Marranos**, 241f. For Spinoza see below. For socio-economic developments, not germane to the major interest of this chapter, see Baron, **History**, XV, 41-54. See also Daniel M. Swetchinski, "Kinship and Commerce: The Foundations of Portugese Jewish Life in Seventeenth-Century Holland," SR, 15 (1980-81), 52-74.

28. See Baron, **History**, 25ff; on Grotius' competence with Judaica see further in chap. 7 below; and see A. W. Rosenberg, "Hugo Grotius as Hebraist," SR, 12 (1978), 62-90.

29. Baron, **History**, 28f., 32, 38f.; Grotius, curiously, had suggested that the Talmud not be printed in Holland, but since this type of censorship was too "papal" and affected Protestants, the Dutch Reformed Church would not favor it, and in 1644-48 an unexpurgated edition of the Talmud was published in Amsterdam (31f.). See also Arthur Löwenstamm, "Hugo Grotius' Stellung zum Judentum," **Festschrift zum 75 Jährigen Bestehn des Jüdisch Theologischen Seminars,** 2v. (Breslau: 1929), 295-302.

30. Baron, **History**, 39ff.; 395 n. 46. See also J. Meijer, "Hugo Grotius' **Remonstrantie**," JSS, 17 (1955).

31. Baron, **History**, 392 n. 35. For a discussion of the ambiguities and evolution of Jewish civic rights in Amsterdam, see Baron, **History**, 30f., 33f., and notes at 393; for the change from corporate to individual status, see 72. See also Roth, **Marranos**, 242f.

32. Roth, 247f.; Baron, **History**, XV, 55, 65f.; Graetz, **History**, IV, 681ff.

33. Baron, **History**, 34; Moshe Carmilly-Weinberger, **Censorship and Freedom of Expression in Jewish History** (New York: 1977), 47f. But see further below.

34. Roth, **Marranos**, 249f. See **Emergence** II, 303-310, for Shabtai Zvi; see 543 n. 74 for bibliography, 546 n. 95 for the title-page messianic announcements in Amsterdam.

35. Baron, **History**, XV, 60, 405 n. 71; 62f., 406 n. 74.

Notes to pp. 132-135

36. See further on Menasseh below, Section V; see Baron, **History,** 63ff.

37. On communal organization, synagogue structure and community life in the fully developed Amsterdam Jewish community later in the seventeenth century see Kenneth R. Scholberg, "Miguel De Barrios and the Amsterdam Sephardic Community," JQR, 53 No. 2 (1962), 120-159.

38. Scholberg, 156f.; and see n. 104.

39. This is by no means a full bibliography, but within various works further bibliographical material is available. See: **Improvement of the Understanding, Ethics and Correspondence of Benedict De Spinoza,** trans. R. H. M. Elwes (New York: 1936; **The Chief Works of Benedict De Spinoza,** trans. R. H. M. Elwes, 2v. (New York: 1951); **The Correspondence of Spinoza,** trans. and ed. A. Wolf (London: 1928); Harry Austryn Wolfson, **The Philosophy of Spinoza,** 2v. in one (Cambridge, MA: 1948); Leon Roth, **Spinoza, Descartes and Maimonides** (New York: 1963); **The Philosophy of Spinoza,** ed. Joseph Ratner (New York: 1927); **Spinoza,** ed. Marjorie Grene (Garden City, N.Y.: 1973); Leo Strauss, **Spinoza's Critique of Religion,** trans. E. M. Sinclair (New York: 1965); **Baruch Spinoza, The Ethics and Selected Letters,** trans. Samuel Shirley, ed. Seymour Feldman (Indianapolis-Cambridge: 1982). See also Graetz, **History,** Vol. V, 87-109; K. Klatzkin, **Baruch Spinoza: Life, Works, System** [Hebrew] 2nd ed. (Tel Aviv: 1954). Spinoza's completed works include his **Theologico-political Treatise,** published in 1670, and **Ethics,** 1675. Other works: his earliest, **Short Treatise on God, Man and His Well-Being; The Improvement of Understanding** and **Political Treatise,** were left incomplete. Spinoza's works are available in the original in **Spinoza Opera,** ed. Carl Gebhardt, 4v. (Heidelberg: 1925).

40. Ratner, op. cit., xv f.; **Benedict De Spinoza,** trans. Elwes, "Introduction," Frank Sewall, vii. See also Asa Kasher, Shlomo Biderman, "When Was Spinoza Banned?" SR, 12 (No. 1, July 1978), 108-110. See also Kasher, Biderman, "Spinoza's Excommunication," **Special Colloquium in Memory of Baruch de Spinoza,** February 21, 1977 [Hebrew] (Tel Aviv: 1977), 31-58, for question of respective roles of rabbis and secular leaders. Carmilly-Weinberger, op. cit., 228 n. 43 indicates there were copies of the ban of Spinoza extant, but is not clear whether this included a full record of his case delineating the explicit reasons for the ban.

41. Ratner, xix; Carmilly-Weinberger, 47-49.

42. The branch of Judaism that today goes by the name of Reconstructionism is certainly Spinozistic in many ways. These contemporary developments will be discussed in Vol. IV. The excommunication of Mordecai Kaplan during the 1940's by a small group of zealots in New York had absolutely no effect upon his functioning as a professor at a rabbinical seminary, as a rabbi and leading figure of Judaic religious life.

The partial rehabilitation of Spinoza in 1785 was largely due to Moses Mendelssohn, and especially to F. H. Jacobi, **On the Doctrine of Spinoza in Letters to Herr Moses Mendelssohn;** see Leo Strauss, **Spinoza's Critique,** 16; Altmann, **Moses Mendelssohn,** 638-653.

43. For a brief summary of Spinoza's philosophy see Ratner, op. cit., xxvii-lxx; see also Julius Guttman, **Philosophies of Judaism,** trans. David Silverman (Philadelphia: 1964), 265-285; for revelation see 281ff. On the Judaic medieval philosophers see Sigal, **Emergence** II, chap. 6.

44. Ratner, xxxiii.

45. Ibid., xlix.

46. Ibid., lix ff.

47. Ibid., lxii f.; lxvii; see also Elwes, **Improvement,** 49; the quotation is from Proposition XV of Spinoza's **Ethics.** See also Spinoza's letter of November, 1675 to Henry Oldenburg in Elwes, 302ff. where Spinoza articulates the idea that God is the immanent cause of all things, "all things are in God, and move in God." See also Guttman, 285.

48. Spinoza, "Of the Ceremonial Law," **Tractatus Theologico-Politicus,** chap. 5; see the selections in Ratner, 88-102.

49. Ratner, ibid., 95f.; see also Elwes, **Improvement,** Letter XXI, from Spinoza to Oldenburg, 302f.

50. See the selection of letters in Elwes, op. cit., 279-313; but see more especially the collection of the Spinoza-Oldenburg correspondence and annotations in **The Correspondence of Spinoza,** ed. A. Wolf. The letters are not segregated in one segment of the book, but are clearly listed in the Contents. In all, Wolf published eighty-five letters to and from Spinoza. Many others have been lost, but it is conjectured that some will yet turn up in private collections. The letters are extremely significant for a proper appreciation of Spinoza's views presented in a non-technical format. See Wolf, 64-69.

51. Wolf, 34f.

52. Ibid., 37f.

53. Ibid., Letter LXVII, 309-324. The quotations cited from Wolf's translation of an original Latin letter are found at 313, 314. The letter aside from being rude and offensive, is intensely evangelical seeking to convince Spinoza of the infallible truth of orthodox Catholicism.

Notes to pp. 139-141

54. Ibid., Letter LXXVI, 350-355; the quotations are on p. 353. Wolf, 475, suggests that the term "Pharisees" to designate the post-talmudic advocates of ritualism was introduced by Uriel da Costa. There can be no doubt that the knowledge of the dissenting views of da Costa and other Marranos discussed earlier played a role in Spinoza's intellectual maturation although da Costa had committed suicide in 1640. See further below on the question of immortality.

55. Propositions LIII and LIV of his **Ethics,** IV; see Elwes, op. cit., 227f.

56. Wolf, op. cit., Letter XXI, 303; Letter XXIII, 308.

57. Ibid., Letter XXV, 311.

58. See Section II above for Orobio. See n. 59 on question of addressee.

59. Wolf, op. cit., Letter XLIX, 369-374. It should be noted here that Wolf, op. cit., 239-254 published the letter to which this letter to Orobio was a response. Wolf, however, published it as a letter from a certain Lambert De Velthuysen to a Collegiant associate of Spinoza's, Jacob Ostens, and published Spinoza's reply as a letter to Ostens, not Orobio. Neither Elwes nor Wolf discuss the matter to explain why each believes the letter went to a different person. It is logical that the addressee was Ostens and that Orobio would not have been in touch with Spinoza. There appears no other evidence for letters to or from Jews, although in truth there might have been and were lost, or even deliberately destroyed because of Spinoza's state of excommunication.

60. Wolf, ibid., 372. Here Spinoza was evidently under the influence of M. Ab. 1:3. The mishnaic pericope of Antigonus is a saying which ends with "but let the reverence [morā] of heaven be upon you." If one translates morā as "fear" as some do one misses Antigonus' point. Yirā in the context of piety before God should be translated "reverence" or "awe" and understood in the deeper spiritual sense of love and piety rather than fear.

61. Wolf, op. cit., 49.

62. Altmann, **Moses Mendelssohn,** 33f. Altmann unfortunately and erroneously referred to Spinoza's "apostasy" which Mendelssohn was determined to avoid. But Spinoza was never an apostate. More on the relationship of Spinoza to Moses Mendelssohn will be presented in forthcoming **Emergence** IV. See also Altmann, 50-55. At 285 Altmann translates Mendelssohn's term Irrlehrer as "heretical doctrine," but I rather think that Mendelssohn simply meant "error." On some disagreements between Mendelssohn and Spinoza see, for example, 686ff.

63. Wolf, Letter XXX, 205f.; 419 n. to 206, 1. 17.

64. Ibid., Letter XLIII, 259.

65. This comes from the end of the third chapter of Spinoza's **Theo-logico-Politicus.**

66. **Ethics** I, Proposition 28; the translation in the text is by Elwes, op. cit., 62; see Wolfson, **Spinoza** II, 143. Cf. also **Ethics** I, Proposition 25 at Elwes, 61.

67. **Ethics,** II, Prop. XI, Corollary; cited by Elwes, op. cit., 87; V, Prop. XXIII, ibid, 266; see also Wolfson, II, 323, 324; on revelation, Wolfson, II, 325f.; for the goal of Spinoza's rational religion, Wolfson, II, 328f.

68. See, for example, Wolfson, op. cit., and Leon Roth, **Spinoza, Descartes and Maimonides.** For a critique of these views see Richard H. Popkin, "Spinoza and La Peyrère," **Spinoza: New Perspectives,** ed. Robert Shahan, J. I. Biro (Norman, Oklahoma: 1978), 177-195.

69. See Popkin, op. cit., 182ff.; Ira Robinson, "Isaac de la "Peyrère and the Recall of the Jews," JSS, 40 (1978), 117-130.

70. Richard Popkin, "Menasseh ben Israel and Isaac La Peyrère" SR, 8 (1974), 59-63.

71. Popkin, "Spinoza," 189.

72. For dual covenant theology see Sigal, **Emergence** I, Pt. 2, Appendix C, 287-296, and "Aspects of an Inquiry into Dual Covenant Theology," HBT, 3 (1981), 181-209.

73. Strauss, **Spinoza's Critique,** 17.

74. Ibid., 18ff.

75. Ibid., 27.

76. See Cecil Roth, **A Life of Menasseh ben Israel;** M. Kayserling, "Menasseh ben Israel: sein Leben und Wirken," **Jahrbuch für die Geschichte der Juden und das Judenthums,** II (1861); "The Life and Labors of Menasseh ben Israel," trans. F. de Sola Mendes, **Miscellany of Hebrew Literature,** II (1877); Lucien Wolf, **Menasseh ben Israel's Mission to Oliver Cromwell** (London: 1901); see further bibliography in Roth, op. cit., 291-307, and the references that will be cited below, as well as the section on R. Menasseh in chap. 6 below. The letter referred to in the text is at Kobler, op. cit., II, 505.

77. Roth, **Menasseh,** chap. 1.

Notes to pp. 145-148

78. What little is known of the family history is reviewed briefly by Roth, chap. 2, and basically derived from Menasseh's own books, **De Termino Vitae** and **Conciliador**. See Roth, Additional Note, 28ff.

79. Roth, **Menasseh**, 23f.

80. Ibid, 20f. cited at length from the preface of Sabbatai Bass' **Sefer Sifthe Yeshenim.**

81. Roth, 24f.

82. Ibid., 26f.; 32f.

83. Altmann, **Mendelssohn,** 463f. This will be dealt with more fully in **Emergence,** IV. Mendelssohn did not always agree with Menasseh, and others repudiated Menasseh's defensive and apologetic view of Judaism; see Altmann, 497f. But this does not change the reality of Menasseh's influence upon Mendelssohn. See further on **Vindiciae Judaeorum,** chap. 6 below.

84. Roth, **Menasseh,** 158ff.

85. Ibid., 40ff.

86. Ibid., 43f., 86f.; the index to Midrash Rabbah is called Peneh Rabbah. Menasseh described his daily activities of teaching, serving as rabbinic guide to his congregation, working in his publishing business, meeting, advising and carrying on intellectual discourse with a great variety of people, and responding to four to six letters a week. See his letter to a Marrano, Manuel Villareal, January 1648, at Kobler, op. cit., II, 503-507.

87. Roth, **Manasseh,** 50f., 57ff., 61ff.

88. See Mann, **Texts,** II, 730; see below, n. 90. The Latin work referred to could be any one of Menasseh's early works, but quite possibly **Conciliador** which gained wide currency. This is referred to in the letter, 1226, lines 7-9 as possessed by the nobleman Christopher Radziwill.

89. Roth, **Menasseh,** 71ff.

90. Ibid., 84ff.; see also Barzilay, **Delmedigo,** 74; note 2 provides an incorrect reference to Mann, **Texts,** probably a typographical error. See end of this note for correct reference. For some strange reason Roth omits Menasseh's knowledge of Philo, or Zerah's contact with him, but that might be because the Genizah documents upon which this information is based were not known to Roth. See Jacob Mann, **Texts,** II, 730f.; No. 134, 1225-1228, 1228 lines 1-4.

91. Roth, **Menasseh,** 103f. H. Graetz, **History,** V. 20, wrote that the Christian scholars of his time "overestimated" Menasseh ben Israel.

92. Roth, 88f.

93. Ibid., 90; on the Karaite work see 82, 319 n. 10.

94. Ibid., 91ff.

95. Ibid., 95ff. Menasseh was unable to escape either Adam's easy fall, or Gen. 6:5 and 8:21. See also Ab. de R. N. A, 16 on the idea that the inclination to evil, yezer hara enters the human in the embryonic state. Cf. Solomon Schechter, **Some Aspects of Rabbinic Theology** (New York: 1936), 253, and 242-263 generally.

96. Roth, 100ff. The Thesaurus of halakhah was reprinted many times and was used as late as the twentieth century. **Nishmat Ḥayyim** was published at Amsterdam, 1651.

97. Roth, 98ff.; on Delmedigo's relationship with Menasseh see 132ff.

98. Ibid., 106f.

99. Ibid., chap. 7; on Bueno as subject of the painting, 117; see also 168f., and 329 n. 39. Roth gives 1654 as the year of Rembrandt's etching of Menasseh, but others argue for 1636; see on this Franz Landsberger, **Rembrandt, the Jews and the Bible,** trans. Felix N. Gerson (Philadelphia: 1962), 51, 178f. n. 18; for the etching of Menasseh, plate 12, p. 50; for Bueno see 35f., 40, 47ff. See also 96ff.

100. Roth, **Menasseh,** cited at 121 from a collection of Vos' letters. It was one of Vos' sons, Dionysius (Denis) who translated Menasseh's **Conciliador,** Part I into Latin; see 144; he would ultimately have done all four volumes as each appeared, but died at age 22 soon after the first was published.

101. Roth, 140ff., and chap. 8, in general.

102. Ibid., 146ff.

103. Ibid., 156f.; Graetz, **History,** V, 22.

104. Roth, 165.

105. Ibid., 158ff., 161f.; see 327 n. 27 for reference to the revival of the notion that the French king would lead the Jews back to Palestine in 1806 during Napoleon's interest both in the middle east and in convoking a sanhe-

drin to deal with the question of Jewish emancipation. See further on these matters and their impact upon Judaism, **Emergence**, IV.

106. Roth, 165f. On Menasseh's relationship with Queen Christina of Sweden see 169ff.

107. Ibid., 187f. The public figure John Evelyn visited the synagogue and cemetery in Amsterdam in August 1641. See **The Diary of John Evelyn**, ed. E. S. DeBeer, 6v. (Oxford: 1955), II, 42f.

108. Ibid., 176-181.

109. See Albert M. Hyamson, "The Lost Tribes and the Return of the Jews to England," TJHSE, 5 (1908). See William Rosenau, "Ezekiel 37:15-28. What Happened to the Ten Tribes," HUCA, Jubilee Volume (1925), 79-88. A listing of theories is provided by Joseph Jacobs, "Tribes, Lost Ten," JE, Vol. 12, 249-253. See also the comprehensive work, Allen H. Godbey, **The Lost Tribes, A Myth** (Durham, N.C.: 1930), especially chap. 1 for the theories developed concerning the tribes.

110. II Ki. 17:24-32; Rosenau, "Ezekiel," 81ff. It is conjectural whether Deutero-Isaiah refers to Judah poetically or to Israel factually, at Is. 49:6, or by parallelism of Jacob and Israel to both. It is to be recalled that Tobit is identified as of Naphtali although the book and its event occurred long after the deportation. As late as the first-second century R. Akiba understood that Israelites were somewhere in Media, not "lost." See **Sifra d'be Rab**, ed. I. H. Weiss (New York: 1946), 112b. The Jewish legends about the Sambatyon River beyond which Israelites were said to dwell and which no human can cross were brought into European consciousness by the historian Joseph ben Gorion (Yosippon) who was widely read in Europe for post-biblical Jewish history, especially after he was translated by Peter Morwyng in 1558. Menasseh believed in the Sambatyon legends. See Hyamson, "Lost Tribes," 120-129. For a brief discussion of the Sambatyon legend see Aaron Rothkoff, "Sambatyon," EJ, 14, pp. 762-764.

111. Roth, op. cit., 181ff. Hyamson, op. cit., 136ff.

112. Hyamson, 140.

113. Roth, 186, 331 n. 5. See Graetz, **History**, V, 30f. See also Godbey, op. cit., 3; Roth, 189f. See Sigal, **Emergence** II, chap. 8; Graetz, op. cit., 33.

114. See A. J. Saraiva, "Antonio Vieira, Menasseh ben Israel et le Cinquieme Empire," SR, 6, No. 1 (1972), 25-57. See also Richard H. Popkin, "Menasseh ben Israel and Isaac La Peyrère," op. cit., (n. 70 above).

115. Graetz, op. cit., 34.

Chapter Six. Judaism Restored to England

1. The bibliography for this chapter is massive. The following is only a select group of books to provide the reader first with some background to Tudor and Stuart English history and second, in a general way with matters related to the restoration of Judaism in England. More relevant references will be found in succeeding notes, and in the bibliographies included in the works cited. **English Historical Documents**, General Editor David C. Douglas, 12 vols. (London: 1953-1977); see Vol. II for 1603-1660, ed. Mary Coate; Albert Frederick Pollard, **The History of England From the Accession of Edward VI to the Death of Elizabeth 1547-1603** (New York: 1969), which is Vol. VI of **Political History of England**, ed. William Hunt, Reginald L. Poole, 12 vols. (rpt. New York: 1969); F. C. Montague, **The History of England From the Accession of James I to the Restoration** (New York: 1969), Vol. VII **Political History** cited; Richard Lodge, **The History of England From the Restoration to the Death of William III 1660-1702** (London: 1969), Vol. VIII of **Political History** cited; George W. O. Woodward, **Reformation and Resurgence 1485-1603** (London: 1963); Geoffrey Rudolph Elton, **Reform and Reformation England 1509-1558** (Cambridge, Mass.: 1977); Barry Coward, **The Stuart Age--A History of England 1603-1714** (London-New York: 1980); George M. Trevelyan, **England Under the Stuarts** (London: 1930), Vol. V of **A History of England**, ed. Sir Charles Oman, 8 vols. (London: 1905-1934); Lucien Wolf, "Jews in Elizabethan England," TJHSE, 11 (1928), 1-91; "Crypto-Jews Under the Commonwealth," TJHSE, 1 (1895), 55-88; "The Jewry of the Restoration 1660-1664." TJHSE, 5 (1908), 5-33; **Manesseh Ben Israel's Mission to Cromwell**, ed. Lucien Wolf (London: 1901); Cecil Roth, "New Light on the Resettlement," TJHSE, 11 (1928), 112-142; **A History of the Jews in England** (2nd ed. Oxford: 1949); the articles on Leone da Modena's relationship with England, cited in chap. 4 at nn. 95, 98. Alfred Rubens, "Portrait of Anglo-Jewry 1655-1836," TJHSE, 19 (1960), 13-52; A. S. Diamond, "The Cemetery of the Resettlement," TJHSE, 19 (1960), 163-190; Menasseh ben Israel, **The Hope of Israel**, ed. Moses Wall (2nd ed., London: 1652); **Vindiciae Judaeorum** (London: 1656), rpt. ed. Lucien Wolf (London: 1901); David S. Katz, **Philo-Semitism and the Readmission of the Jews to England 1603-1655** (Oxford: 1982); see also the bibliography by Katz, ibid., 245-271. **Three Centuries of Anglo-Jewish History**, ed. V. D. Lipman (London: 1961); Raphael Loewe, "Jewish Scholarship in England," **Three Centuries** op. cit., 125-148; I. Baroway, "Toward Understanding Tudor-Jacobean Hebrew Studies," JSS, 18 (1956), 3-24; P. Collinson, "The Beginnings of English Sabbatarianism," SCH, 1 (1964), 207-221; Albert M. Hyamson, **The Sephardim of England** (London: 1951); Salo Baron, **History**, XV, 125-160.

2. Van Gelder, **Two Reformations**, 328. It is not possible here to enter into the complex questions relative to Henry VIII's marriages. It is known, however, that Jews were involved in consultations regarding the Judaic halakhah on the matter. For example, in a letter dated January 30, 1530, Modena Rabbi Jacob Raphael Peglione wrote to a representative of the English ambassador in Italy that a priest had inquired of him how to interpret Lev. 18:16, not to sexually

Notes to pp. 157-160

violate a sister-in-law in the light of Deut. 25:5 to marry the widowed sister-in-law in the levirate arrangement, in reference to Henry VIII's desire for a divorce in 1530. R. Peglione noted that Henry VIII engaged in levirate marriage and his union should be treated as a legitimate marriage. See **Anglo-Jewish Letters (1158–1917)**, ed. Cecil Roth, (London: 1938).

3. Ibid., 329f. For Erasmus see chap. 3 above.

4. For Shakespeare see A. L. Rowse, **William Shakespeare, A Biography** (New York-Evanston: 1963); S. Schoenbaum, **William Shakespeare, A Compact Documentary Life** (New York: 1977); F. E. Halliday, **The Life of Shakespeare** (London: 1961).

5. Van Gelder, 349.

6. Ibid., 351-358. See William Shakespeare, **Twelfth Night**, Act 1, Scene 5, line 331; **Julius Caesar**, Act 5, Scene 2, lines 106-8; **Hamlet**, Act 5, Scene 2, lines 9-11; **Macbeth**, Act 2, Scene 3, line 137.

7. Van Gelder, 380.

8. This is not the place for a fuller discussion of a much rehashed and misunderstood subject, "Shakespeare and the Jews." But it is clear from a proper reading of the **Merchant** that Shakespeare was empathetic, not negative. Thus, for example, at Act 1, Scene 3, when Shylock described the humiliating treatment accorded him by Antonio, Shakespeare was presenting the worst side of Christian hypocrisy toward the Jew.

9. Halliday, **William Shakespeare**, 130ff.

10. See Rowse, **William Shakespeare**, 229; Schoenbaum, **Documentary Life**, 169ff.; 337 n. 19.

11. For example, a letter is published in Roth, **Letters**, op. cit., 27ff., from a returned Marrano, Solomon aben Ayish, Duke of Mitylene, to Queen Elizabeth from Constantinople dated July 28, 1592. He was Alvaro Mendes, who helped fashion an alliance between England and Turkey which contributed to stemming King Philip of Spain. It was his agent, Cormano, who will be referred to below. See also Wolf, TJHSE, 11, 67f.

12. Rowse, **William Shakespeare**, 227.

13. Roth, **Jews of England**, 140ff., 143.

14. Rowse, 229. Rowse draws attention to the fact that at **Merchant** Act IV, Scene 1, Shakespeare plays with the word "wolf," its Latin form, lupus

reminding the play-goer of Lopez. This is doubted but not rejected by Geoffrey Bullough in **Narrative and Dramatic Sources of Shakespeare**, ed. G. Bullough, 6 vols. (London-New York: 1964), I, 445. See especially Gratiano's lines, " . . . thy currish spirit/ Governed a wolf, who, hanged for human slaughter/ Even from the gallows did his fell soul fleet . . . Infused itself in thee; for thy desires are wolfish . . . "

15. **Merchant**, Act III, Scene 1.

16. Bullough, 446f., 450. See in general, 446-462. Bullough is one of that school of thought who views Shakespeare's intent as anti-Jewish. He argues, 455, that Marlowe and Shakespeare, when expressing mutual blame between Christians and Jews each was not "so much seeking sympathy for his Jew as explaining the depth of his hatred." Salo Baron also views "Shylock" as anti-Jewish. See his extensive references and bibliography, **History** XV, 435ff. n. 70.

17. On whether Elizabeth admired Shakespeare publicly: Schoenbaum, 204, who rejects any evidence for it.

18. Sonnet 107; see Rowse, op. cit., 181ff. The sonnets are numbered differently in various collections. See e.g., **Sonnets, The New Temple Shakespeare**, ed. M. R. Ridley, (London: 1944), x-xiv; in this collection the sonnet referred to is No. 97.

19. I therefore reject Roth's more negative view, that Shakespeare's Shylock "clearly reflected in its cruder facets the popular abhorrence of the new Judas [Lopez] and his machinations." First, the play was produced two or more years later; second, although there is Judas-allusion in it, people who viewed the play might have been quite aware that Elizabeth did not regard Lopez as a Judas. See Roth, **Jews of England**, 144. As a matter of fact, Roth recognizes Elizabeth's treatment accorded the widow of this so-called Judas was "generous," 143 n. 2, and this reinforces the idea that Sir Robert Cecil led a pro-Lopez faction with which Shakespeare might easily have identified himself.

20. **Henry VIII**, Act IV, Scene IV. See Rowse, op. cit., 437f., 442f.

21. See Baron, XV, 134f. where is found the citation from the Italian publicist cited in the text; see also 438 n. 72.

22. See Sigal, **Emergence** II, Chapter Eight. Hyamson, **The Sephardim**, 4f.; see Roth, op. cit., 132f., 140f. See also Lucien Wolf, "Jews in Elizabethan England," RJHSE, 11, 2f., n. 4; 3f.

23. Hyamson, 6f. "Bloody" Queen Mary was the daughter of Henry VIII and Katherine of Aragon, a devout Catholic who tried to undo Henry's reform of the church and secession from papal supremacy as well as all the supporting legislation of her half-brother Edward VI who reigned from 1547-1553.

Notes to pp. 163-166

24. Ibid., 7f.

25. Wolf, op. cit., 7f., 19; see substantiating documents at 33-91. Probably the Jews participated in Calvinist churches rather than Lutheran ones, a distinction which might have been unclear to the Spanish prisoner.

26. H. S. Q. Henriques, "The Jews and the English Law," JQR, 17 (1905), 203-237, 236; Roth, **Jews of England,** 144 n. 3, 280 n. VI (e).

27. Hyamson, 9, 10ff.; Lionel Abrahams, "Menasseh ben Israel's Mission to Oliver Cromwell," JQR, 14 (1901-2), 1-25, p. 6.

28. Hyamson, 14; Wilfred S. Samuel, "The Jewish Oratories of Cromwellian London," MJHSE, Part III (1937), 46-55; Herman Adler, "A Homage to Menasseh ben Israel," TJHSE, 1 (1895), 25-54; p. 47. See also Abrahams, op. cit., 10f. More will be said below of the literary role of millenarians in the restoration of Judaism to England.

29. Greenhalgh's description is in a letter he wrote to a friend dated April 22, 1662, cited extensively by Hyamson, 15-19; see also H. S. Q. Henriques, "The Jews," JQR, 17 p. 206.

30. Hyamson, 18.

31. Ibid., 19. See also W. S. Samuel, "The First London Synagogue of the Resettlement," TJHSE, 10 (1924), 1-147; Appendix I, 49-58 for Greenhalgh's description of his visit to the synagogue.

32. Ibid., 20f. See **The Diary of Samuel Pepys,** transcribed by Mynors Bright, ed. Henry B. Wheatley, 10 vols. (New York: 1942), Vol. 4, 293f., entry of October 14, 1663; see also **The Diary of Samuel Pepys,** ed. Robert Latham and William Matthews (Berkeley and Los Angeles: 1971), Vol. 4, 334f. See also Wilfred S. Samuel, "Carvajal and Pepys," MJHSE, Part II (1935), 24-29. Pepys' December 3, 1659 visit to the synagogue long went unnoticed because he had not yet begun his diary. On that day, however, he wrote a letter describing the visit, and was very careful to say he went only "for observation's sake" to obviate any charge that he was a judaizer.

33. Abrahams, "Menasseh," op. cit., JQR, 14 p. 20f.

34. Henriques, "The Jews," JQR, 12 p. 664; Vol. 14, 653ff., Vol. 17, 210f. During the reign of Charles II at least 70 people gained the right to citizenship (17, p. 213), and 34 others during the reign of James II (219), and these people were given the right to take oaths on the Old Testament alone, or to alter the time of a court case if it occurred on the Sabbath (213).

35. Henriques, JQR, 17 pp. 215, 219.

36. Henriques, "The Jews," JQR, 14 p. 670; Vol. 13, 280ff.

37. Ibid., JQR, 16 pp. 333ff., 343f. Henriques argued that Cromwell did nothing during his regime to change or improve the status of Jews, but allowed the Jews already there to remain. See also Wilbur Cortez Abbot, **The Writings and Speeches of Oliver Cromwell**, 4 vols. (Cambridge: 1937-1947), IV, 54.

38. On the cemetery, see D. Bueno De Mesquita, "The Historical Associations of the Ancient Burial-Ground of the Sephardic Jews, TJHSE, 10 (1924), 225-254. See also W. S. Samuel, "First London Synagogue," TJHSE, 10, pp. 47ff., 50ff., 54 n. 20. See also Lucien Wolf, "Crypto Jews," TJHSE,1 pp. 55-75; see Abbot, III, 669.

39. Katz, **Philo-Semitism and Readmission** (see n. 1), 162.

40. John Fines, "Judaizing in the Period of the English Reformation," TJHSE, 21 (1967), 323-326; Roth, **Jews of England**, 145ff. For Christian Hebraism see chap. 7 below. See E. N. Adler, "Auto De Fe and Jew," JQR, 14 (1902), 698f. Regarding Henry VIII see also Friedmann, **Ancient Testimony**, 22, and n. 2 above. The advice received by Henry from Judaic scholars was evidently not consistent and only exacerbated his problem.

41. See R. G. Clause, "The Rebirth of Millenarianism," **Puritans, The Millenium and the Future of Israel**, ed. Peter Toon (Cambridge-London: 1970), 60; Katz, op. cit., 93f. See also in general on this subject, P. Christianson, **Reformers and Babylon** (Toronto: 1978).

42. Franz Kobler, "Sir Henry Finch (1558-1625) and the First English Advocates of the Restoration of the Jews to Palestine," TJHSE, 16 (1952), 101-120; see 102ff.; 105f. The word "millenarian" (a believer in the one-thousand year reign of the Messiah) is from the Latin translation, miliarii of the Greek chilioi, "one-thousand," for which reason these people are also called "chiliasts."

43. More will be said about the judaizing movement in chap. 7. See Katz, 26.

44. H. Blount, **A Voyage Into the Levant** (2nd ed. London: 1636); see Katz, op. cit., 164ff.; 168f. See also E. R. Samuel, " 'Sir Thomas Shirley's Project for Jews'--The Earliest Known Proposal for the Resettlement," TJHSE, 24 (1974), 195-197.

45. Katz, 172f.

46. Kobler, 107; Katz, 95ff. See also Kobler, 112, 115f., 118.

47. See Toon, op. cit., 14. For the Judaic "Grace After Meals," see any standard prayerbook. **In Daily Prayer Book,** ed. Philip Birnbaum (New York: 1949), the line is found in Hebrew at 767, in English, 768. For Hussites, Anabaptists and Bucer see chap. 3 above. For how Paul Fagius christianized the Grace After Meals see below in chap. 7.

48. See **The Creeds of Christendom,** ed. Philip Schaff, 3 vols. (New York: 1877), Vol. III, chap. XI, Latin text, 254-258; see par. 14, 257, "Damnamus praeterea Judaica somnia . . . " and the English version at 853.

49. Augustine, **City of God,** ed. Dods, II,: 356-360. See n. 42 above.

50. Toon, 19, 45, 47, 55. Katz, 99, 103.

51. Kobler, op. cit., 118; Clause in Toon, op. cit., 61f. n. 21. Katz, 89, 98f.

52. Katz, 103, 107ff., 120-124. See also Nahum Sokolow, **History of Zionism,** 1600-1918, 2 vols. (London: 1919), I, 21-54 as a representative Zionist historian who traces the origins of British interest in Zionism to the seventeenth century. At II, 207f., Appendix XXVI, Sokolow offers the title page of Sir Henry Finch's **The World's Great Restauration and The Calling of the Jews,** and in other appendices he offers extracts of literary works of the period.

53. Scholem, **Sabbatai Zevi,** 88-93; 339. From Abraham ibn Ezra to Isaac Abravanel, about 1100-1500 at least, the Hebrew term <u>kezeh haárez,</u> "end of the earth," signified England, being a literal translation of the French name for England, <u>Angle-terre.</u> See Roth, **Menasseh,** 207. See also Cecil Roth, "New Light," (n. 1), 113f., with documents reproduced at 136-142. Menasseh's interest in the juxtaposition of Dan. 12:7 and Deut. 28:64 is at **Vindiciae,** vii, 37. Dan. 12:7 speaks of the time when the end-time wonders will take place as being when "he who crushes the power of the holy people meets his end." This was taken to mean when the Jewish exile ends upon the consummation of the dispersion.

54. Katz, 172, 173f., 187. See also Toon, 115f.

55. Ibid., 174ff.; **Table Talk of John Selden,** ed. F. Pollock (London: 1927), 54, 123. See also <u>DNB,</u> ed. Lesslie Stephen, Sidney Lee (London: 1908), XVI, 1150-1162.

56. Katz, 177f.; Toon, 116. **The Cartwright Petition,** Facsimile Reproduction, Introduction by Nat Shmulowitz (San Francisco: 1941). The Cartwright petition contained two major errors. One was that it attributed the expulsion of the Jews from England to King Richard II who reigned a full century later than Edward I, and considered them banished by a "Statute of Banishment" when in fact it was by a royal edict. The very fact that there was no statute allowed Oliver

Cromwell so much flexibility. I have not found that historians have drawn attention to the anachronism of Richard II. It may be, however, that the Cartwrights had in mind an anti-heretical statute enacted by Richard II in 1381 and confused that with the expulsion decree of 1290. See also Roth, **Menasseh**, 199, 334 n. 23. The date of the petition is often given as 1648 because of confusion of the old numbering and new dating. Under the old system, March 25 was regarded as the end of the year so dates between January 1 and March 25 are often misdated to the previous year.

57.   Katz, 181, 187; Toon, 119. See Rev. 11:15f.

58.   Kobler, **Letters**, II, 511-514. See generally, Roth, **Jews of England**, 149-172.

59.   Lucien Wolf, **Mission**, xxxvii n. 4. Roth, op, cit., 339f., n. 1, argues that the three rabbis accompanying Menasseh are not substantiated by any source, and are simply repeated from historian to historian. See also Adler, "A Homage," TJHSE, 1 43f.; related documents are found at 45-54.

60.   An important primary source for Whitehall is England's **Calendar of State Papers, Domestic** 1655-56. The decision to convene Whitehall is at 23. Roth, "New Light": this article uses the official "Publick Intelligencer," No. 10, as its source. As late as December 31 it was said "the Jews, we hear, will be admitted by way of conniving, though the generality oppose," (46). See also Abbot, **Cromwell**, IV, 18f.; 34-36; 51-55.

61.   Roth, **Menasseh**, 245-247; 345 n. 24. Wolf, op. cit., LXXXIVf. Jessey wrote an eye-witness account of the Whitehall Conference in 1656. See Katz, op. cit., 213. The negative proceedings at Whitehall were also monitored by Francesco Salvetti, envoy of the Grand Duke of Tuscany, whose reports make it clear that Whitehall would produce no decision. See Roth, "New Light," 128-133.

62.   Roth, **Menasseh**, 244. The argument about oaths was undoubtedly framed by Judaica scholars who were aware of the kol nidre prayer and misunderstood its intent. See on this, **Emergence** II, 348f., 558 nn. 59-60. The argument about matrimonial laxity might have had reference to the halakhah still allowing four wives to sefardim who never accepted the ban on polygamy and possibly also the more liberal halakhah of divorce than that of Christianity (ibid., 244-247; 378-382), the levirate marriage (ibid., 527 n. 37) and other such practices. As was seen in the previous chapter, Menasseh wrote his tract, **Vindiciae Judaeorum**, in 1656 in England to offer an apologia for Judaism, but in the 1650's those opposed to Judaic toleration in England had many negative sources to draw from. See further on Christian Hebraism and the study of Judaism, Chapter Seven below, where Menasseh's work will be further discussed. See **The Diary of John Evelyn**, ed. William Bray, 2 vols. (Akron, Ohio: 1901), I, 307; thus, it seems although the position taken in the text is that no decision was made by Cromwell or his

300

Notes to pp. 176-179

government, Evelyn is telling us something important that should cause us to qualify our view. Perhaps Cromwell then imparted secretly to some confidantes that he wanted no formal decision but will allow Jews to enter and practice Judaism unhindered. See also **The Diary of John Evelyn**, ed. DeBeer, where "Now were the Jewes admitted" is given as of Dec. 9, at Vol. III, 163.

63. Toon, 124.

64. Wolf, op. cit., XXIXf.; Robert S. Paul, "Oliver Cromwell and the Jews." London Jewish Chronicle, January 27, 1956.

65. See Section III above.

66. Roth, **Jews of England**, 149, 281 nn. VII, a, b. See David S. Katz, "Edmund Gayton's Anti-Jewish Poem Addressed to Menasseh Ben Israel, 1656," JQR, 71 (1981), 239-250; Katz, 244, quotes the English royalist residing in Venice who told the Doge that "the church of St. Paul, comparable with St. Peter's at Rome, remains desolate and is said to have been sold to the Jews as a synagogue."

67. Katz, **Philo-Semitism**, 10ff. See also P. Collinson, "English Sabbatarianism," SCH, 1, pp. 210ff.

68. Katz, 18ff., 23ff., 32f., 33 nn. 116-120, for further bibliography.

69. Roth, **Jews of England**, 150f. For a history of freedom of religion in England see W. K. Jordan, **Development of Relgious Toleration in England**, 4 vols. (London: 1932-1940).

70. Scholem, **Sabbati Ẓevi**, 101, 547f. n. 202.

71. Ibid., 548f. n. 204. See also Michael McKeon, "Sabbatai Sevi in England," AJS, 2 (1977), 131-169; **The Diary of Samuel Pepys**, ed. Wheatley, Vol. 7, 42f.

72. For Modena see chap. 4 above, and next note.

73. See **Anglo-Jewish Letters**, 44-46; Roth, "Leon da Modena and England," 224. During the twentieth century when halakhic authorities of the Conservative movement learned that at one stage of its development the sturgeon did have scales they permitted sturgeon to those who observe the dietary practices.

74. A facsimile of the title page to a pamphlet written by Menasseh in honor of the occasion of the English Queen's visit was published by E. N. Adler, "A Letter of Menasseh ben Israel," JQR, 16 (1904), 562-572. See facing 563. See further on Ross in chap. 7 where I will expand upon Menasseh's reply as

a paradigm of the modern Judaic critique of Christian scholars as over against medieval polemic, but will also substantiate Alexander Ross' material in the face of Menasseh's critique. See Roth, **Menasseh**, 261ff.; Katz, 161.

75. Roth, ibid., 263f. All the items mentioned in the text may be pursued further in **Emergence** I and II and in the readings suggested in the notes there. For example, on the blood libel, also termed "blood accusation" or "ritual murder," see **Emergence** II, 226, 513 nn. 6-7; for alenu, I, Pt. 1, pp. 445f., 502; Pt. 2, pp. 147, 188; amidah, II, 45-48; I, Pt. 1, and Pt. 2, with index entry "ami-dah;" for the anti-Christian liturgical formula in the amidah, the birkhat haminim, see I, Pt 1, pp. 391, 429, 431, 444, 492f., 502; Pt. 2, pp. 23. 45f., 148, 244.

76. Cited at Roth, **Menasseh**, 348 n. 12.

77. Roth, **Menasseh**, 276ff.; Henriques, "Jews and the English Law," JQR, 16, pp. 631ff.; Wolf, "Jewry of the Restoration,' TJHSE, 5, pp. 14f.; 16; perti-nent documents at 28f., 29f.

78. Henriques, ibid., 643f., 647.

79. See I. Abrahams, "Note on Isaac Abendana," TJHSE, 10 (1924), 221-224; Wolf, op. cit., 10f.

80. Cecil Roth, "Gemaliel ben Pedahzur and his Prayer Book," MJHSE, Pt. 2 (1935), 1-8; p. 1.

81. Henriques, "Jews," JQR, 17, pp. 215ff., 219. For general historical background on the events in England see bibliography at n. 1 above.

82. See I. Abrahams, "Passes Issued to Jews in the Period 1689-1696," MJHSE, Pt. 1 (1925), xxiv-xxxiii.

83. Arthur P. Arnold, "A List of Jews and their Households in London," MJHSE, Pt. 6 (1962), 73-141; see 73ff.; J. A. Guiseppe, "Sephardi Jews and the Early Years of the Bank of England," TJHSE, 19 (1960), 53-63; see 53.

84. See S. Levy, "English Students of Maimonides," MJHSE, Pt. 4 (1942), 61-84; see 68f.

85. Roth, **Menasseh**, 282f.

86. Ibid., 286f., 352 n. 13, citing the **Diaries of Ezra Stiles**. There were, on the other hand, Jewish savants such as E. N. Adler who tried to debunk Menasseh. See his publication of one of Menasseh's Spanish letters with Spanish translation, **Letter**, op. cit., (n. 74 above), 566-572; p. 565: " . . . He [Menasseh] strikes one as snobbish and mercenary . . . " This latter point is rather a harsh

judgment as anyone familiar with Menasseh's ongoing straitened circumstances, the penury of his last years and the destitution of his widow and surviving daughter, hardly point to a mercenary personality who would have engaged only in trade and finance rather than interfaith relations and scholarship. What Menasseh hoped for and expressed in that letter (see ibid., 572) was the economic independence "to serve my friends, with more liberality and satisfaction," referring to his Christian colleagues with whom he corresponded and had extensive intellectual and theological interchange.

Chapter Seven. **Religions in Tension**

1. Sigal, **Emergence** I, Pt. 1, chap. 7; see further **Emergence** II, index entry "Christians, Christianity;" "Christian Judaism;" "Christology," "Church, Church Councils;" "Innocent III." Baron, **History,** IX, chap. 39.

2. Baron, IX, 101. I prefer the term "anti-Judaism" to that of Baron's more conventional "anti-Jewish." On Barnabas and the Church Fathers see Sigal, **Emergence** I, Pt. 1, 435, 441f. See also Baron 288ff., n. 4, for a review of some of the literature, and bibliographies containing listings. A less well known figure but not less influential was Raymond Lull (1266-1315), a very prolific writer who wrote several tracts on Judaism. See also A. L. Williams, **Adversus Judaeos** (Cambridge: 1935), 256ff. For de Lyra see Williams, 408-415. Despite his indebtedness to the biblical commentary of R. Solomon ben Isaac (Rashi), Nicholas de Lyra wrote tracts against Judaism, and even appended them to his biblical commentary. It is possible that Raymund Martini had been born a Jew and was referred to as a Jew and a rabbi in the fifteenth century by Paul of Burgos. His great work **Pugio Fidei (Dagger of the Faith)** was written in 1278. Much controversy surrounded the authenticity of his work, but see Sigal, **Emergence** II, 121f., 463n66; see also Williams, 249n4. See further below.

3. Williams, 233-240. See also Baron, IX, 102f.; and see the listing of other Jewish converts who were polemicists against Judaism, 292f. n. 6.

4. Paul of Burgos was Solomon Halevi, and was known as Pablo de Santa Maria. See Williams, 267-276. Jn. 5:39 reads "Search the scripture for in them you think you have eternal life, and it is they which bear witness concerning me."

5. Baron, **History**, XIII, 182-191. See also Chapters Two and Three above.

6. The focus of the discussion here must be on the period no later than the end of the seventeenth century. For the eighteenth century to the present see the forthcoming Volume IV.

7. An outline of the twelve chapters of Duran's **Kelimat Hagoyim** (**Shame of the Gentiles**) is offered by Baron, IX, 103f. At 293ff. n. 7, Baron provides a considerable list of Jewish apologists and bibliographical information from Jacob ben Reuben ca. 1170, to Abraham ben Mordecai Farissol (Perizol) in the sixteenth century. For Farissol see Chapter Four above. A good bibliography of this juxtaposed polemical and apologetic literature is in Hebrew by J. Rosenthal, "Anti-Christian Polemic From its Beginnings to the End of the Eighteenth Century" in **Areshet**, Volumes II, III and IV.

8. The following is by no means an exhaustive bibliography but will allow the interested reader to pursue the subject more deeply, and there encounter more extensive bibliography. George Foote Moore, "Christian Writers on Judaism," HTR, 14 (1921), 197-254; Ludwig Blau, "Polemics and Polemical Literature," JE, X, 102-109; Raphael Loewe, "The Medieval Christian Hebraists of England," HUCA, 28 (1957), 205-252. For cursory discussions of a substantial list of writers see Williams, op. cit., and n. 9 below.

9. R. Travers Herford, **Christianity in the Talmud and Midrash** (Clifton, N.J.: 1966); Moore, op. cit., 197ff. Isidore's work was entitled **De Fide Catholica ex Veteri et Novo Testamento Contra Judaeos.** See Origen, **Contra Celsum,** trans. Henry Chadwick (London-Cambridge: 1980). For a brief discussion of the dialogue between Jason and Papiscus see Williams, 28ff. My own guess on how Gen. 1:1 came to refer to the son of God is that the term rḗshit, was taken as analogous to Gen. 49:3 where Jacob refers to Reuben as his rḗshit, first manifestation of his reproductive energies, bearing in mind that the theory was common that Jesus was the logos, and the logos was God's medium of creation and firstborn son in Philonic terms; see On Husbandry 12 (51). For a discussion of Tertullian's work see Williams, 43-52. Aphraates is discussed by Williams at 95-102. Chrysostom is discussed at 132-140. For Chrysostom see also Robert L. Wilken, **John Chrysostom and the Jews** (London-Berkeley: 1983). For Isidore of Seville see Williams, 216ff.; see also a summary of Isidore's **Contra Judaeos** 282-292. Williams, 217 expresses the notion that Isodore's work became a basic resource for many other writings into modern times.

10. Moore, op. cit., 210f.

11. For Abner of Burgos, Williams, 259f.; see also n. 4 above.

12. Williams, 261f.; Moore, 211n21.

13. Williams, 266.

14. See n. 2 above.

15. See n. 2; Moore, 204.

Notes to pp. 186-189

16. Williams, 243f. Naḥmanides wrote a Hebrew account of this debate, edited and published by Moritz Steinschneider, **Sefer Vikuaḥ haRamban** (Berlin: 1860); see also I. Loeb's article on this disputation in REJ, 15 (1887), 1-8; Solomon Schechter, **Studies in Judaism,** First Series (Philadelphia: 1911), 103-107.

17. See n. 2 above.

18. Martini had not only translated many texts but also printed them in Hebrew. Voisin did the same. Thus, select original Hebrew texts were available to scholars who did not have access to the rabbinic writings. See Moore, 208f.

19. Williams, 250. A brief summary of the **Pugio** is offered by Williams, 251-254.

20. Moore, 210f. For Pico and Reuchlin see above, Chapter Two.

21. Moore, 216f. On Eisenmenger see ibid., 213f.

22. Jerome Friedman, **Ancient Testimony,** 12ff.; H. Hailperin, "Jewish Influence on Christian Biblical Scholars in the Middle Ages," HJ, 4 (1942); "The Hebrew Heritage of Medieval Biblical Scholarship," HJ, 5 (1943); L. Geiger, **Das Studium der Hebräische Sprache in Deutschland vom Ende des 15 biz zur mitte des 16 Jahrhunderts** (Breslau: 1870). For further bibliography see Friedman, op. cit., 266-275. See also Jerome Friedman, "Sixteenth Century Christian-Hebraica: Scripture and the Renaissance Myth of the Past," SCJ, 11 (1980), 67-85.

23. Abrahams, "Pico," 320-325; see also Charles E. Trinkaus, **In Our Image and Likeness,** 2 vols. (London: 1970), for a discussion of Pico. For Reuchlin, see Max Brod, **Johann Reuchlin: Sein Leben und Sein Kampf** (Stuttgart: 1965). See also Friedman, "Scripture and the Renaissance," 66f., and bibliography at n. 1; see also 77; Isaac Troki will be discussed further as part of the Polish scene in **Emergence IV.**

24. See S. A. Hirsch, "Johann Reuchlin," JQR, 8, p. 467; "John Pfeffer-korn and the Battle of the Books," JQR, 4 (1891-2), 256-288.

25. Friedman, **Ancient,** 24, 28f.; Obadiah Sforno should not be confused with Obadiah b. Israel Sforno, a Venetian Talmudist of the 16th-17th centuries. Ex. 19:5 records God's affirmation that Israel is His elect people, and Deut. 33:3 refers to God's love for all nations. Sforno deduces from the latter that Jews too are to love all nations as they act out their mission of God's elect.

26. Friedman, **Ancient,** 74-77; this kabalistic endeavor is critiqued by Friedman, 78-81, but this material is not relevant to our purposes. The most obvious error made by Reuchlin was in reading Jesus' name Y e h o Sh u a h inserting the shin into Yhwh, for Yehoshuaᶜ, "the lord is the savior" is not spelled

with a hey at the end, but with an eyein, and Yhwh ends with a hey. For the citation from Reuchlin see Friedman, "Scripture," 84, where a letter by Reuchlin written 1510 is referred to.

27. Hirsch, "Johann Reuchlin," 452, 458ff., 461; Friedman, **Ancient Testimony,** 24f, 30f., 33f. For a discussion of medieval universities see Hastings Rashdall, **The Universities of Europe in the Middle Ages,** 2 vols. (Oxford: 1895); see also Martin Luther, **Works,** vol. 48, p. 63, in a letter to George Spalatin, May 18, 1518: " . . . that you become concerned for establishment of a chair in Greek and a chair in Hebrew."

28. Friedman, op. cit., 31f.

29. Ibid., 26ff.; see also Charles G. Nauert, "The Clash of Humanists and Scholastics: an Approach to Pre-Reformation Controversies." SCJ, 4 (1973), 1-18; Hirsch, "John Pfefferkorn," 261ff., 280ff. See also Kleiner, **Strasbourg Reformers,** 45-62 on Reuchlin-Pfefferkorn controversy; for a letter by Reuchlin to Pope Leo X's physician to intercede on his behalf in order to have his trial in his own diocese and in a papal court rather than by the Dominicans, see **The Jew in the Medieval World,** 159-164.

30. Nauert, 13ff.

31. Friedman, op. cit., 36-42.

32. See for example a discussion of aspects of this problem in Leonhard Goppelt, **Typos,** trans. Donald H. Madvig (Grand Rapids, Mich.: 1982), 2ff.

33. Erwin, I. J. Rosenthal, "Sebastian Muenster's Knowledge and Use of Jewish Exegesis," **Essays Presented to J. H. Hertz,** ed. I. Epstein, E. Levine and C. Roth (London: 1942), 351-369; Friedman, op. cit., 45-49. See also Erwin Rosenthal, "Rashi and the English Bible," BJRL, (April, 1940), 138-167, also found in his **Studia Semitica** (Cambridge: 1971), I, 56-85.

34. Rosenthal, "Rashi," 7f, 11f.

35. See in general the articles at n. 33.

36. Rosenthal, "Muenster," 352.

37. Ibid., 353ff.; 357f. n. 26; 362f.

38. Rosenthal, "Rashi," 16-26.

39. Siegfried Stein, "Phillipus Ferdinandus Polonus," **Essays Presented to J. H. Hertz,** 397-412.

40. Such expositions of Judaism were written by Paulus Riccius in Italy, also a Jewish convert, and Genebrardus, a Frenchman. Cf. Stein, 400, 406, 408f., 411. For R. Ishmael, see **Emergence** I, Pt. 2, p. 88n17.

41. Stein, 401. Other converts active among Christian scholars were Victor de Carben and Conradus Huserus.

42. Ibid., 405f. Purchas wrote **Pilgrimage;** Weemse wrote **The Christian Synagogue;** Godwin wrote **Moses and Aron.**

43. See Chapters Two and Four above.

44. Stein, 410f. For R. Jacob b. Asher see **Emergence** II, 313f. For gematriot and notarikon, see Section IV below.

45. Chapter Three above; see references and bibliography there; see also Friedman, **Ancient Testimony,** 59-69.

46. Friedman, 62-67. For Arama, see Bettan, "The Sermons of Isaac Arama," op. cit.

47. Servetus is cited by Friedman, 64.

48. Friedman, 99-118; see 100ff. For Fagius, see also Kleiner, op. cit., 138-180.

49. Friedman, 102f. Friedman does not offer the Latin, to which I have not had independent access, and so it is not clear to me whether it was Fagius or Friedman who was wrong in translating the berakhah for bread as "who creates the fruit of the earth," as Friedman renders it. The vegetable blessing, "fruit of the earth" has the word "create" [borĕ], but the formula for bread does not. The question is whether Fagius had erred in the hamozi formula for bread, or Friedman erred in reproducing Fagius.

50. The italics in the text constitute the paraphrased material. For Grace After Meals, see any standard comprehensive Jewish prayerbook, e.g., **Hasidur Hashalem, Daily Prayerbook,** trans. Philip Birnbaum (New York: 1949), 759-769 (Hebrew), 760-770 (English); the Hebrew original and the English translation of the second berakhah cited in the text are found at 761, 762 respectively; the fourth berakhah begins at 763 and 764 respectively. The Grace is more conveniently cited according to berakhot, for it consists of four berakhot which are not coextensive with paragraphs. See also Friedman, **Ancient Testimony,** 104, where he reproduced from Paul Fagius, **Precationes Hebraicae quibus in Solemnioribus Festis Iudaei** (ISNY: 1542), B3-B4.

51. See Phillip Sigal, "Early Christian and Rabbinical Liturgical Affinities: Exploring Liturgical Acculturation," NTS, 30 (1984), 63-90.

52. Since Fagius such parallels have been discovered in even greater numbers and along with parallels there are also many allusions. See e.g., Lk. 10:39, "And she had a sister called Mary who also sat at Jesus' feet and heard his word," and M. Ab. 1:4, " . . . Yosi ben Yoezer said, 'let your house be a gathering place for sages and dust yourself at their feet . . . " [i.e., sit at their feet as a disciple]; cf. Acts 22:3 where Paul said he was "brought up at the feet of Gamaliel," "let your house be wide open . . . " Fagius also saw at Mt. 15:13 " . . . every plant which my father has not planted shall be rooted up" as a metaphor for the same idea as Gamaliel phrased at Acts 5:38-39, that any counsel which is not of God will come to nought; both are parallels to M. Ab. 4:14, 5:20; see Mt. 18:20 "wherever two or three have gathered in my name there I will be in their midst," and M. Ab. 3:3; 3:7.

53. Friedman, 114f. The Hebrew zafoo, usually translated "foreseen" is to be correctly understood as "seen" that is, God knows all that occurs as the human choice is made, and hence the human is subject to judgment, which is kindly, for God considers the deed. See also Charles Taylor, **Sayings of the Jewish Fathers,** 2 vols. (Cambridge: 1897), I, 59n38 to Ab. 3:24 as Taylor numbers the text.

54. Friedman, 148.

55. Ibid., 152f. Rashi based himself upon Gen. R. 14:5 where the midrash takes the two yods to signify two creations, that of this world and that of the future world, that is, of the resurrection.

56. Friedman, 154. On use of divine names see Gen. R. 12:15; Ex. R. 3:6; Sif. Deut. 27; Sigal, **Emergence** I, Pt. 2, pp. 118, 181n41. Philo at **On Abraham** 24 (121) and **Plant.** 20 (86) reverses the rabbinic definitions and takes kyrios (Yhwh) for justice and theos (elohim) for mercy. It is conceivable that Philo represents the older view. The differences would take us too far afield here. See N. A. Dahl, Alan F. Segal, "Philo and the Rabbis on the Names of God," JSJ, 9 (June, 1978), 1-28.

57. Friedman, 158, fell into the error of rejecting Fagius' view that Jewish scholars so interpreted mot tamut regardless of linguistics. Midrash does not consider linguistic science. For rabbinic and Philonic sources for this, see my **Emergence** I, Pt. 1, pp. 325f., 374f. n. 143. See also my article, "An Inquiry Into Aspects of Judaism in Justin's Dialogue with Trypho," Abr-Nahrain, XVIII (1978-79), 74-100, for another example of a Christian scholar who was inappropriately rejected as lacking adequate knowledge of Judaism.

58. Friedman, 215-234.

Notes to pp. 198-201

59. For Ádon Ólam see **Daily Prayerbook,** op. cit., 10 (Hebrew), 11 (English.

60. Friedman, 217.

61. See on this my **Emergence** II, Chapter Three.

62. **Prayerbook,** 11-13 (Hebrew), 12-14 (English).

63. See my comments on incarnation at "Inquiry Into Dual Covenant Theology," HBT, (1981), 199, 208nn73-74.

64. Friedman, 222f. takes a partially different and at times more critical approach to Münster's omission of post-biblical Judaism. For example, he argued that it represented "a bias that conceived of Judaism as an ancient religion with little change in the period after Christ's coming (223). It is inconceivable that Münster thought this in the light of his comprehensive knowledge of Judaism.

65. Friedman, 225f. See B. San 96b-99a for a sampling of the diversity of views. See the citation from a treatise called **Book of Faith** on why Jews eschew conversion at Friedman, 247ff. This treatise was used by both Fagius and Münster. The halakhic matters concerning food and usury in this passage are accurate, and were selected from older sources for inclusion in the **Shulḥan Arukh,** on which work see **Emergence** II, Chapter Eleven. Cf. Shulhan Arukh Yoreh Deáh 152; Maimonides **Mishneh Torah** Forbidden Foods, 3:14-24; cf. Yoreh Deáh 112-115 for complex of halakhah related to foods of non-Jews, including bread, cheese, milk, cooked foods; ibid. 118 for meat; 123 for wine.

66. Friedman, 231ff.

67. Ibid., 235f.

68. Ibid., 237, does not appear to notice this discrepancy.

69. Ibid., 238f. See below for anti-Christian Judaic polemic.

70. Ibid., 243f. See above.

71. Friedman so argues, ibid., 249f.

72. Ibid., 249.

73. Ibid., 250.

74. A brief survey of targumic studies in our period is offered by Martin McNamara, **The New Testament and the Palestinian Targum** (Rome: 1966), 7-14.

75. See Katz, **Philo-Semitism,** Chapter Two; for citation from Reuchlin, Friedman, "Scripture," 84, and n. 50, from a letter published in **Briefwechsel,** ed. L. Geiger (Tübingen: 1875), No. 102, p. 105. See also W. J. Allen, "Ancient Ideas On the Origin and Development of Language," Transactions of the Philosophical Society (1948), 35-60. See also Katz. 63-68. Hebrew-philes could have inferred that the celestial language is Hebrew. Is. 6 where we also have heavenly creatures praising God in Hebrew in the thrice-holy formula, kadosh, kadosh, kadosh, "holy, holy, holy, is the Lord of Hosts."

76. Katz, 70f.; Scholem, **Sabbatai Ṣevi,** 25; see also Scholem, **Kabbalah,** 196-201; J. L. Blau, **The Christian Interpretation of Cabala in the Renaissance** (Port Washington, New York: 1965).

77. Katz, 76-83. See also M. L. Bailey, **Milton and Jacob Boehme** (New York: 1914).

78. Katz, 152ff., citing Edward Brerewood, **Enquiries Touching the Diversity of Languages and Religions** (London: 1614), 94-97. See Chapter Six above for the ten tribes issue. The entire matter reverts to II. Ki. 17:6 which simply states that the king of Assyria captured Shomron (Samaria), and took "Israel" captive to Assyria, settling them in places called Ḥelaḥ, Ḥabor, on the river Gozen and in the cities of Media (cf. II Ki. 18:10f.). This is amplified at II Esd. (IV Ezra) 13:40-47. The seer had a dream in which he saw a man who emerged out of the sea. A multitude of men made war upon him and he annihilated them by a stream of fiery sparks that he blew from his mouth, and after that he called to himself a great peaceable multitude (II Esd. 13:1-13). The seer prayed to the Most High for an explanation of the dream and the Most High interpreted it. In reference to the peaceable multitude the Most High told him these people were the Israelites led into captivity by Shalmaneser, King of Assyria. Thus far the author alludes to II Ki. 17:6. But then he goes on to amplify: they decided to migrate beyond Assyria to uninhabited lands in order to separate from the heathen and observe God's word which they had violated in Israel. They travelled to a region called Arzareth where they dwell until the eschaton (II Esd. 13:40-47). It has been surmised that "Arzareth" represents ereẓ aḥeret, "another land," as at Deut. 29:25-28, which verses are applied to the ten tribes at M. San. 10:3; cf. B. San. 110b. See **The Apocrypha and Pseudepigrapha,** ed. R. H. Charles, 2 vols. (Oxford: 1913), II, 619, note to v. 45. See also I and II Esdras, trans. Jacob M. Myers, **The Anchor Bible,** Vol. 42 (New York: 1974), 306, 311f. At M. San. 10:3 the text refers to variegated views on certain sinners who will not attain salvation in olam haba. Among these it lists the ten tribes and says "they are not destined to return." This is not necessarily a negation of their eligibility for salvation except indirectly: if they will never "return," this implies they will also not be known in the resurrected state in olam haba. We have here a view that the rediscovery of the lost tribes is unnecessary for the coming of the millenium. This was the view of R. Akiba, based upon Deut. 29:27, that they are cast away to "another land, as at this day," that is, just as they are lost this day they will be lost forever. R. Eliezer

differed and said that just as the day begins in darkness and turns light, the ten tribes will enjoy the future light. So too Josephus, **Ant.** XI, 5, 2 (133) located myriads of Israelites "whose number cannot be ascertained" beyond the Euphrates, probably signifying such vast hinterland stretches as Afghanistan and China. See also J. Trachtenberg, **The Devil and the Jews** (Philadelphia: 1961), Chapter Two.

79. Baron, **History,** XV, 141f. See also 441ff., nn. 80-81. See on the Bible in general, **The Cambridge History of the Bible. The West From the Reformation to the Present Day,** ed. S. L. Greenslade (Cambridge: 1963). For the development of the English Bible, see Chapter Four. On efforts to translate into English before the Reformation and the emergence of John Wyclif's translation see **The Cambridge History of the Bible. The West From the Fathers to the Reformation** ed. G. W. H. Lampe, 2 vols. (Cambridge: 1969), II, 362-415.

80. Baron, 143f.; see for Milton, Kitty Cohen, **The Throne and the Chariot** (The Hague-Paris: 1975) and her bibliography, 173-181; 13n35; Harold Fisch, **Jerusalem and Albion: The Hebraic Factor in Seventeenth Century Literature** (New York: 1964).

81. W. E. Mellone, "Seventh-Day Christians," JQR, 10 (1898), 404-429; John Fines, "Judaizing," TJHSE, 21, pp. 323, 326, and notes.

82. Mellone, "Seventh-Day Christians," 409ff. On the change of the Sabbath day in Christianity, see Samuel Bacchiocchi, **From Sabbath to Sunday** (Rome: 1977); **From Sabbath to Lord's Day,** ed. D. A. Carson (Grand Rapids, Mich.: 1982).

83. Mellone, 411.

84. Ibid., 418-425.

85. See Chapter Six above.

86. R. G. Clouse, "The Rebirth of Millenarianism," **Puritans,** ed. Toon, 60f., n. 21.

87. Fines, op. cit., 324f.

88. See Chapter Six above; Henry E. I. Phillips, "An Early Stuart Judaizing Sect," TJHSE, 15 (1950), 63-72; see 67, 72n23.

89. George Alexander Kohut, "Royal Hebraists," **Studies in Memory of Israel Abrahams,** 225f., 227, 229f. See also Cohen, **Throne,** 13n35.

90. S. Levy, "English Students of Maimonides," MJHSE, Part IV (1942), 61-84; Jacob I. Dienstag, "Christian Translators of Maimonides' **Mishneh Torah** Into Latin," **Salo W. Baron Jubilee Volume** I, 287-309.

91. Levy, 61-66; Dienstag, 288n6, 300; a list of Christian Maimonides scholars with biographical annotations is given by Dienstag at 289-308, but many are later than the period covered by this chapter.

92. Levy, 67ff., 70-74; Dienstag, 290.

93. See for example my article on Justin, n. 57 above. See also my article, "Responding to Christologies," Jewish Spectator, Vol. 46 (Winter, 1981), 31-34.

94. Alexander Ross, **Pansebeia: A View of all Religions in the World** (London: 1653). The discussion in this chapter is based upon the sixth edition available in the Rare Book Room of the University of Pittsburgh Hillman Library. There is no volume entitled **A View of the Jewish Religion** in Ross' official bibliography. For Ross' bibliography see G. A. Aitken, "Alexander Ross," DNB ed. Leslie Stephen and Sidney Lee (London: 1908-1971), XVII, 251f.

95. There is a brief review of some reappearances of the charge in England between 1290 and 1656 in Lucien Wolf, **Menasseh Ben Israel's Mission,** 165f. William Prynne, writing his **Short Demurrer to the Jews** was honest enough to reject the charge in 1656.

96. Thomas Calvert, "Diatribe of the Jews' Estate," **The Blessed Jew of Marocco.** There is a British Museum Ms. a copy of this dated July 25, 1649, cited by Wolf, op. cit., 166. For the blood libel in England see Joseph Jacobs "Little St. Hugh of Lincoln," TJHSE, 1 (1895), 89-114; original documents from the account of Matthew of Paris, records of trials of Jews and ballads in French and English are at 115-132. See also Menasseh, **Vindiciae,** 119f.

97. Menasseh ben Israel, **Vindiciae Judaeorum,** rpt. Wolf, op. cit., 107. The most accessible edition of Maimonides for the average reader is **The Code of Maimonides** published as part of the Yale Judaica Series; see Sigal, **Emergence,** Vol. II, 161-184.

98. Maimonides, **Mishneh Torah,** Kings 10:3f.; cf. B. Yeb. 47b; Ket. 11a.

99. Maimonides, op. cit., 10:12; cf. B. B. K. 113a; Git. 61a, 62a; Sif. Deut. 16; see also **Shittah Mekubezet** I, marginal note to B. B. K., ibid.

100. Ross, op. cit., 29-33; Menasseh, **Vindiciae,** 125ff.

101. The relevant passage of the version offered by Menasseh, ibid., 126, reads: "For Apostates [meshumadim] let there be no hope, let all Hereticks [minim] be destroyed . . . , " and he argued, citing Maimonides that apostates and heretics are renegade Jews and cannot refer to people of other faiths. Cf. Maimonides, **Mishneh Torah,** Tefilah 2. The current version reads "For slanderers

[lamalshinim] let there be no hope, may all evil perish instantly . . . " See **Prayerbook**, 87 (Hebrew), 88 (English).

102. David Kaufman, "The Prayerbook According to the Ritual of England Before 1290," _JQR_, 4 (1892); **Contributions to the Scientific Study of the Jewish Liturgy**, ed. Jakob Petuchowski (New York: 1970), 459-502; see 481, 467.

103. Saint Justin Martyr, **The Dialogue With Trypho**, trans. A. Lukyn Williams (London: 1930); see **Dialogue**, 96. The talmudic text is at B. Ber. 28b. See also Sigal, **Emergence** I, Pt. 1, 429, 431, 444; 492f., n. 152; 502n196; Pt. 2, pp. 45f., n 83; 148, 244. **Halakhot Gedolot**, ed. Ezriel Hildesheimer (Jerusalem: 1971), 54; **Maḥzor Vitry**, Oxford Ms. ed. S. Hurwitz (Berlin: 1899); Solomon Schechter, "Genizah Specimens," _JQR_, 10, (1898); **Contributions to Scientific Study**, 373. This find in the Cairo Genizah proved beyond doubt that patristic charges had been correct. The text reads, "Let there be no hope for apostates, may the presumptuous kingdom be speedily uprooted, in our day, and may the noẓrim [followers of the man of Nazareth, Christians] and sectarians rapidly perish . . . " Here noẓrim was specifically used and minim retained. The various terms used indicate the prayer was against renegade Jews, the Roman overlord, Christians, and other sectarians of whom there was a plethora in the first century. The unfortunate blitheness with which Jews approached this subject is illustrated by Wolf's note to Menasseh's third section of **Vindiciae** in 1901, three years after the discovery by a fellow Englishman, Solomon Schechter, where he wrote, "The subject matter of this section, the alleged cursing of gentiles is, like the Blood Accusation, an obstinate delusion of anti-semites." See Wolf, op. cit., 168. Actually as late as 1426 a Ms. of **Seder Rabbi Amram**, Codex 1095 of the Bodleian Library, still carried the term noẓrim. See **Seder R. Amram Gaon**, Pt. 1, trans. David Hedegard (Lund: 1951), xxi.

104. The ẻlenu is at **Prayerbook**, op. cit., 135, 137 (Hebrew); 136, 138 (English). The offending passage had read (in italics) " . . . who has not made us like the families of the earth [gentiles] . . . for they worship air and emptiness and pray to a god who cannot save, while we bend the knee, worship and give thanks to the king of the king of kings . . . " Menasseh, op. cit., 136f.

105. Ross, 30f. Cf. the notes of Tosafot to B. Ber. 2a. An especially abusive section of Ross' work is at 37-42.

106. See Sir Edward Frye, "John Selden," _DNB_, XVII, 1150-1162; IV, 257f.; VI, 945b; S. Singer, "Early Translations and Translators of the Jewish Liturgy in England," _TJHSE_, 3 (1901), 39f.; "The Earliest Jewish Prayers for the Sovereign," _TJHSE_, 9 (1920), 104. Roth, "Leone da Modena and England," 206. For Modena, see Chapter Four above. John Evelyn, **Diary**, ed. DeBeer, II, 54f. For the plethora of Mss. available to English and other scholars in the Abbeys, and at Oxford, see Herman Gollancz, "Anglo-Judaica," _TJHSE_, 6 (1912), 57ff. Ross provided some of his sources at the end of his treatise. See also on Mornay, below, and nn. 122-123.

107. Ross, 38-41.

108. Ibid., 36.

109. Cited by Cohen, op. cit., 15f. from Milton's <u>Articles of Peace</u> found in **Complete Prose Works of John Milton** ed. Dom. M. Wolfe, et. al., 4 vols. (New Haven: 1953-1966), III, 326n79.

110. Ross, 48.

111. For Karo, Isserles, etc., see **Emergence** II, Chapter Eleven. For <u>kaparot</u> see ibid., 346f.; **Shulḥan Arukh** Oraḥ Ḥayyim 606:1ff. For **Maḥzor Vitry** see ibid., 36, 93f., and above n. 103. See also Rashi's commentary to B. Shab. 81b; he cites earlier geonim on a <u>kaparot</u> ritual which was somewhat different: a planting set in a pot turned around the head seven times on the day before Rosh Hashanah and the formula "this instead of this, this is in place of me, my substitute" was recited. It was then thrown into a river.

112. For medieval Purim see **Emergence** II, 357ff.; Ross, 51, 54ff. See also Louis Rabinowitz, **Social Life of the Jews of Northern France** (New York: 1972), 190ff.

113. For the broader view, see e.g., Azariah dei Rossi, **Meor Eynayim**, Part I, 100, cited by Stein, "Polonus," 402. See also Philo, **Special Laws** I, 9 (53); Josephus, **Ant.** IV, 8, 10 (207); **Against Apion**, II, 32 (237). Tanaitic literature had much earlier extended Jewish ethics to encompass the non-Jew in many directions, and although the circumstances of continuing conflict and antipathy often impelled Jewish exegetes to take anti-Christian positions others transmuted these into anti-heathen positions not applicable to Christian monotheists. See on this the theme of Christian-Jewish relations to be discussed further in Volume IV.

114. See, for example, Moses Maimonides, **The Commandments**, trans. Charles Chavel (London-New York: 1967), 221. See also Maimonides, **Mishneh Torah**, (Judges), Mourning 14:1, where he interprets Lev. 19:18 "you shall love your neighbor as yourself" to mean "what you would have others do unto you do unto him who is your brother in the Torah and in the performance of the commandments." Cf., however, an opposite view, requiring equal treatment for gentiles in matters of social concern at B. Git. 61a; T. Git. 3:18. Maimonides concedes this halakhah at ibid. 14:12. In sum there is much ambiguity in the halakhah and this did not help the reputation of Judaism.

115. See above. See also Christian D. Ginzburg, **The Massoreth Ha-Massoreth of Elias Levita** (1867; rpt. New York: 1968), 45-48; Richard A. Muller, "The Debate Over the Vowel Points and the Crisis in Orthodox Hermeneutics," <u>JMRS</u>, 10 (Spring, 1980), 53-72.

314

116. Muller, 55f., n. 9.

117. Ibid., 58f. For "men of great assembly" see **Emergence** I, Pt. 2, 18f., 20, and nn. 38f.

118. Muller, 60f.

119. Ibid., 70f.

120. Cohen, **Riti**, JSS, 34, p. 293; see also Roth, "Leon da Modena and Christian Hebraists," op. cit., 392; the letter is published at 395.

121. Cohen, 294f., see n. 34. I would differ here with Cohen's strictures that imply Buxtorf was not basically objective. For an analysis of both Buxtorf and the **Riti** as anti-Buxtorf polemic see Cohen, 296-314. See also Jacob Katz, **Exclusiveness and Tolerance** (Oxford: 1961), Chapters 1-5.

122. Philippe de Mornay, **A Woorke Concerning the Trewnesse of the Christian Religion**, trans. Sir Philip Sidney, Arthur Golding, Scholars Facsimile Reproduction, Introduction, F. J. Syphen (New York: 1976).

123. See his "Preface to the Reader." Although he confines himself in most of the book to biblical citations, and paraphrases and quotations from pagan and patristic authors, from Chapter 27 on he begins to refer to rabbinic sources and steps up his rabbinic material from that point on, citing various midrashim, including Rabbah, Mekhilta, Tanhuma, the Talmud, Maimonides, R. Moses Hadarshan, and Seder Ōlam Zuta, in addition to Philo and Josephus. A proper analysis of Mornay's work in relation to sixteenth century Puritan Judaica would be fruitful in a history of religions context tracing this aspect of Judaic-Christian interchange.

124. L. Fuks, "Het Hebreeuwse Brievenboek van Johannes Drusius Jr." SR, 3 (January, 1969), 1-52.

125. See for the later period, Eric Zimmer, "Jewish and Christian Hebraist Collaboration in Sixteenth Century Germany," JQR, 71 (October, 1980), 69-88; for the earlier period see Herman Hailperin, **Rashi**, op. cit.

126. See, for example, for the situation in Antioch as early as the first century, Robert L. Wilken, **John Chrysostom and the Jews** (Berkeley-London: 1983), 38ff. See further, Chapter Eight below.

127. See A. L. Williams, **Adversus Judaeos**, op. cit.; B. Blumenkranz, **Les Auteurs Chrétiens Latins du Moyen Age sur le Juifs et le Judaisme** (Paris: 1963). I am not aware of works of the same extent and quality surveying Judaic anti-Christian writings although there are many articles and monographs that deal with limited themes or writings. See the translator's brief Introduction to **The**

Jewish Christian Debate in the High Middle Ages, A Critical Edition of the Niẓẓahon Vetus, trans. David Berger (Philadelphia: 1979), 3-37. Judaic anti-Christian literature is scarce before the twelfth century because: a) the material in the rabbinic literature has been censored; b) little Judaic literature of the early Middle Ages has been preserved to our present knowledge, although this does not preclude a great genizah (repository) find being discovered akin to the one found in Egypt in 1896; see Berger, op. cit. 7f., and his references at nn. 10, 12. See also E. I. J. Rosenthal, "Anti-Christian Polemic in Medieval Bible Commentaries," JSS, 11 (1960), 115-135. See also Oliver Shaw Rankin, **Jewish Religious Polemic** (Edinburgh: 1956); on church and synagogue as symbols in art and literature see Wolfgang S. Seiferth, **Synagogue and Church,** trans. Lee Chadeayne and Paul Gottwald (New York: 1970), 153-162. See also Daniel J. Lasker, **Jewish Philosophical Polemics Against Christianity in the Middle Ages** (New York: 1977); see 13-20 for a listing of some major Judaic polemical works from the 12th to the 18th century.

128. Berger, 32f., 35f., n. 100.

129. Isaac ben Abraham Troki, **Ḥizuk Emunah,** trans. Moses Mocatta (New York: 1970). This book will be discussed further in dealing with eastern Europe in **Emergence,** Vol. IV. In Volume V, I will discuss more extensively the question of Christian-Jewish polemic and dialogue as background to a new approach to ecumenical interchange.

Chapter Eight. A Backward Glance

1. Van Gelder, op. cit., 399f.

2. Ibid., 400f.

3. In the interest of economy of space the post-Puritan, post-Menasseh process in England will be taken up in Volume Four where the earliest figure of importance, Ḥakham David Nieto will be discussed.

4. Van Gelder, 393-399; the citation is at 398. See any High Holy Day Prayerbook at the Unetanah Tokef prayer, e.g., Maḥzor for Rosh Hashanah and Yom Kippur, ed. Jules Harlow (New York: 1972), 242 (Hebrew) 243 (English); see also Ab. d. R. N. A, 4; for Yoḥanan ben Zakkai see Sigal, **Emergence** I, Pt. 2, pp. 20-28; 32n22; 43 nn. 76-77, and passim. For Bodin see R. Chauviré, **Colloque de Jean Bodin des Secrets Cachez des Choses Sublimes entre Sept Sçavans qui sont de Differens Sentimens** (Paris: 1914); Solomon Pines, "The Jewish Religion After the Destruction of Temple and State: The View of Bodin and Spinoza," **Studies in Jewish Religious and Intellectual History,** ed. Siegfried Stein, Raphael Loewe (University, Alabama: 1979), 215-234.

316

5. See on this Chapter Four above; see also Simḥa Assaf, **Mekorot Letole-dot Haḥinukh** (Tel Aviv: 1930), II, 117-119 for the Hebrew text of the proposal.

6. Rivkin, **Leon da Modena and Kol Sakhal**, Chapter Two; see 18ff. See also in general Cecil Roth, **The History of the Jews of Venice** (Philadelphia: 1932). The term "Ponentine" had reference to their origin in the West (Latin, ponens, west).

7. Rivkin, 24n26; 25n27; 26f. nn. 30-32; 37n48; Roth, "Leone da Modena and Christian Hebraists," 399f.; "Leone da Modena and England," 208ff.

8. On leniency see Phillip Sigal, **New Dimensions in Judaism** (Jericho, New York: 1972), index entries "Leniency, Liberalism," especially 75-78, 202-204; **Emergence** I, Pt. 2, pp. 41ff., 55f., 58ff. 90f. nn. 25-26. See Rivkin, 36n46. These halakhot are discussed at: a) Modena's **Pahad Yiẓhak**, the word "sefinah" (boat); b. Modena's responsum on bareheadedness and carnivals, **Ginzberg Jubilee Volume** op. cit.; c) Isaac Rivkind, "Responsum of Moses Provencal on Ball Playing" Tarbiz, 4 (1933), 373-376; R. W. Henderson, "Moses Provencal on Tennis," JQR, 26 (1935), 1-6; Provencal, however, opposed games being played while the sermon was preached! For the questions of wine and cheese see: Modena, **Riti**, Pt. 2, Chap. 8; Samuel Aboab, **Deḇar Shmuel**, responsum 8.

9. Sigal, **Emergence** I, Pt. 1, Chapter Four, for hellenistic era. See also Wilken, **John Chrysostom**, Chapter Two for the Jews of Antioch.

10. See above, Chapters Three and Six.

11. Wilken, 68-79. See **Patrologia Graeca**, ed. J. P. Migne (Paris: 1844-), Vol. 48 for John Chrysostom's eight sermons against judaizers, **Adversus Iudaeos**; see Jud. 1:6, 1. 852. An accessible English translation of Chrysostom's sermon is **Saint John Chrysostom, Discourses Against Judaizing Christians**, trans. Paul W. Harkins, **(The Fathers of the Church)** ed. Hermigild Dressler, et. al. (Washington, D.C.: 1977), Vol. 68.

12. Wilken, 81ff. See also H. H. Ben-Sasson, "Jewish Christian Disputation in the Setting of Humanism and Reformation in the German Empire," HTR, 59 (1966), 369-390; see 382, and for Hebrew text of such a challenge, n. 51.

13. See above, Chapter Three; for millenarians and judaizers, Chapter Six. See also for a specific element of this phenomenon, H. H. Ben-Sasson, "Jews and Christian Sectarians: Existential Similarity and Dialectical Tensions in Sixteenth-Century Moravia and Polish Lithuania," Viator, 4 (1973), 369-385.

14. B. Men. 29b.

15. There is an interesting essay on this theme although rather limited in scope: Gershom Scholem, "Revelation and Tradition as Religious Categories in Judaism," **The Messianic Idea in Judaism** (New York: 1971), 282-303.

16. The quotation is cited by Louis Ginzberg, **An Unknown Jewish Sect** (New York: 1976), 105; cf. Wilken, op. cit., 92.

BIBLIOGRAPHY

The following is not a comprehensive reading list or guide to research materials. It contains most of the works referred to in the notes, and some which are not referred to but are useful for the period under discussion. The reader is also urged to use the bibliographies in Volumes I and II of this series. The notes contain references to numerous primary and secondary sources not listed here for which the author index might be helpful. The notes also list other bibliographies contained in the volumes cited. These may all be consulted with advantage. Periodical literature is scattered in a wide variety of journals and only a relatively small selection of articles has been listed here. Primary classical rabbinic and medieval halakhic literature have not been listed with a few exceptions. Unless otherwise indicated in the notes Babylonian and Palestinian talmudic material and commentaries thereon have been cited by pagination according to the edition published by Shulsinger Brothers, New York (1948); Midrash Rabbah texts from the standard edition published by Grossman and Weisberg (New York: 1951); the editions of all midrashic collections are given in the notes when first cited; the edition of Abot de Rabbi Nathan of Solomon Schechter (rpt. New York: 1945); and Mishnah Abot of Charles Taylor (Cambridge: 1897) or R. Travers Herford (New York: 1945). Aside from Abot the mishnaic texts cited are from the edition of Philip Blackman (London: 1951-1956), and Toseftà from M. Zukermandel (Jerusalem: 1963). The biblical text is that of **Biblia Hebraica** ed. Rudolf Kittel (Stuttgart: 1952). The Greek edition used for Philo and Josephus is the Loeb Classical Library, and the LXX is that published by Bagster and Sons (London: n.d.).

Abbot, Wilbur Cortez. **The Writings and Speeches of Oliver Cromwell.** 4 vols. Cambridge, 1937-1947.

Abrahams, Israel. "Pico Della Mirandola." HUCA, Jubilee Volume (1925), 317-331.

Abrahams, Lionel. "Menasseh ben Israel's Mission to Oliver Cromwell." JQR, 14 (1901-1902), 1-25.

Adler, Herman. "A Homage to Menasseh ben Israel." TJHSE, 1 (1895), 25-54.

Adler, Israel. **La Pratique musicale savante des quelques communantes juives en Europe aux XVII et XVIII siècles.** Paris-Hague: 1966.

-----. "The Rise of Art Music." **Jewish Medieval and Renaissance Studies**, edited by Alexander Altman. Cambridge, Mass.: 1967.

Advocates of Reform from Wyclif to Erasmus, edited by Matthew Spinka. The Library of Christian Classics, edited by John Baillie et al., Vol. XIV, including Erasmus, **The Enchiridion**. Translated by F. L. Battles. London: 1953.

Altman, Alexander. **Essays in Jewish Intellectual History**. Hanover, New Hampshire-London: 1981.

-----. **Moses Mendelssohn**. Philadelphia: 1973.

Augustine. **The City of God**. Edited and translated by Marcus Dods. 2 vols. Edinburgh: 1871.

Bacher, W. "The Sabbatarians of Hungary." JQR, 2 (1890), 465-493.

Bainton, Roland H. **Hunted Heretic: the Life and Death of Servetus, 1511-1553**. Boston: 1953.

-----. **The Reformation of the Sixteenth Century**. Boston: 1956.

Baron, Salo W. **History and Jewish Historians**. Edited by Arthur Hertzberg. Leon A. Feldman. Philadelphia: 1964.

-----. "An Italian Responsum by R. Abraham Graziano" **Studies in Jewish Bibliography History and Literature in Honor of I. Edward Kiev**. Edited by Charles Berlin. New York: 1971, 132-137 [Hebrew].

-----. John Calvin and the Jews." **Ancient and Medieval Jewish History**. Edited by Leon A. Feldman. New Brunswick, N.J.: 1972.

-----. **Modern Nationalism and Religion**. New York: 1947.

-----. **A Social and Religious History of the Jews**. 18 vols. New York and Philadelphia: Columbia University Press and Jewish Publical Society, 1955-83.

Baroway, I. "Toward Understanding Tudor-Jacobean Hebrew Studies." JSS, 18 (1956), 3-24.

Barzilay, Isaac E. "Finalizing An Issue: Modena's Authorship of the **Qol Sakhal.**" **Salo Wittmayer Baron Jubilee Volume**. Edited by Saul Lieberman. 3 vols. New York-London: 1974, 135-166.

-----. **Between Reason and Faith: Anti-Rationalism in Italian Jewish Thought (1250-1650)**. The Hague-Paris: 1967.

-----. **Yoseph Shlomo Delmedigo (Yashar of Candia). His Life, Works and Times**. Leiden: 1974.

Ben-Sasson, Haim Hillel. "Jews and Christian Sectarians: Existential Similarity and Dialectical Tensions in Sixteenth-Century Moravia and Poland-Lithuania." Viator, 4 (1973), 369-385.

-----. "Jewish-Christian Disputation in the Setting of Humanism and Reformation in the German Empire." HTR, 59 (1966), 369-390.

-----. "The Reformation in Contemporary Jewish Eyes." **Proceedings of the Israel Academy of Sciences and Humanities**, 4 (1970), 239-326 [English]; 62-116 [Hebrew].

Berlin, Charles. "A Sixteenth-Century Hebrew Chronicle of the Ottoman Empire. The Seder Eliyahu Auta of Elijah Capsali and its Message." **Studies in Jewish Bibliography, History and Literature in Honor of I. Edward Kiev**. Edited by Charles Berlin. New York: 1971.

Bettan, Israel. "The Sermons of Azariah Figo." HUCA, 7 (1930), 457-495.

-----. "The Sermons of Isaac Arama." HUCA, 12-13 (1937-1938), 583-634.

Blau, J. L. **The Christian Interpretation of the Cabala in the Renaissance**. Port Washington, New York: 1965.

Bonfil, Reuven. **The Rabbinate in Renaissance Italy [Harabanut Beitalyah Bitekufat Harenasans].** Jerusalem: 1979.

Bonnet, Jules. **Letters of John Calvin.** 2 vols. Edinburgh: 1855-1857.

Bouyer, Louis. **Erasmus and the Humanist Experiment.** Translated by Francis X. Murphy. London: 1959.

Burckhardt, Jacob. **Die Kultur der Renaissance in Italien.** 2 vols. Leipzig: 1913.

-----. **The Civilization of the Renaissance.** Translated by S. G. C. Middlemore. New York: 1954.

Calvin, John. **Commentaries.** Translated and edited by various scholars. 22 vols. rpt. Grand Rapids, Mich.: 1979.

-----. **Institution of the Christian Religion.** Translated by Ford Lewis Battles. Atlanta: 1975.

The Cambridge History of the Bible. The West From the Fathers to the Reformation. Edited by G. W. H. Lampe. 2 vols. Cambridge: 1969.

The Cambridge History of the Bible. The West From the Reformation to the Present Day. Edited by S. L. Greenslade. Cambridge: 1963.

Canons and Decrees of the Council of Trent. Translated by H. J. Schroeder. London: 1950.

Carmilly-Weinberger, Moshe. **Censorship and Freedom of Expression in Jewish History.** New York: 1977.

Cassuto, M. D. **Taqqanoth Candia V'Zikhronotěah.** Jerusalem: 1943.

Chemnitz, Martin. **Examination of the Council of Trent.** Translated by Fred Kramer. 2 vols. St. Louis, Mo.: 1971.

The Chief Works of Benedict De Spinoza. Translated by R. H. M. Elwes. 2 vols. New York: 1951.

Christian Humanism and the Reformation with Beatus Rhenanus, The Life of Erasmus. Edited by John C. Olin. New York: 1965.

Christianson, P. **Reformers and Babylon.** Toronto: 1978.

Church, Frederick C. **The Italian Reformers.** New York: 1932.

Clause, R. G. "The Rebirth of Millenarianism." **Puritans, the Millennium and the Future of Israel.** Edited by Peter Toon. Cambridge-London: 1970.

Cohen, Kitty. **The Throne and the Chariot.** The Hague-Paris: 1975.

Cohen, Mark R. "Leone da Modena's **Riti:** A Seventeenth Century Plea for Social Toleration of Jews." Jewish Social Studies, 34 (1972), 287-321.

Collinson, P. "The Beginnings of English Sabbatarianism." Studies in Church History, 1 (1964), 207-221.

The Correspondence of Spinoza. Translated and edited by A. Wolf. London: 1928.

The Creeds of Christendom. Edited by Philip Schaff. 3 vols. New York: 1877.

Daniel-Rops, Henri. **The Catholic Reformation.** Translated by John Warrington. London: 1963.

De Vita et Scripta Eliae Kapsali (Likutim Shonim Misefer Debe Eliyahu). Edited by Moses Lattes. Jerusalem: 1967-1968.

Dienstag, Jacob I. "Christian Translators of Maimonides' **Mishneh Torah** Into Latin." **Salo W. Baron Jubilee Volume.** Edited by Saul Lieberman. 3 vols. New York-London: 1974. Vol. I, 287-309.

Enelow, H. G. "Raphael Norzi: A Rabbi of the Renaissance." HUCA, Jubilee Volume (1925), 333-378.

Erasmus, Desiderius. **Enchiridion.** Translated by Ford Lewis Battles, in **Advocates of Reform From Wyclif to Erasmus.** Edited by Matthew Spinka. Vol. XIV. **The Library of Christian Classics.** Edited by John Baillie et al. London: 1953.

Ergang, Robert. **The Renaissance.** London-New York: 1967.

Fife, Robert Herndon. **The Revolt of Martin Luther.** New York: 1957.

Finkelstein, Louis. **Jewish Self-Government in the Middle Ages.** New York: 1964.

Fisch, Harold. **Jerusalem and Albion: The Hebraic Factor in Seventeenth Century Literature.** New York: 1964.

Friedman, Jerome. **Michael Servetus: A Case Study in Total Heresy.** Geneva: 1978.

-----. "Michael Servetus: A Case for a Jewish Christianity." Sixteenth Century Journal, 4 (1973), 87-110.

-----. **The Most Ancient Testimony.** Athens, Ohio: Ohio University Press: 1983.

-----. "Sixteenth Century Christian-Hebraica: Scripture and the Renaissance Myth of the Past." SCJ, 11 (1980), 67-85.

Van Gelder, H. A. Enno. **The Two Reformations in the 16th Century.** Translated by Jan F. Finlay. The Hague: 1961.

Gebhardt, Carl. **Uriel da Costa.** Amsterdam: 1922.

Graetz, Heinrich. **Geschichte der Juden von den altesten Zeiten bis auf die Gegenwart.** Leipzig: 1907.

-----. **History of the Jews.** 6 vols. Philadelphia: 1894.

Graupe, Heinz Moshe. **Die Entstehung des Modernen Judentums.** Hamburg: 1969.

-----. **The Rise of Modern Judaism.** Translated by John Robinson. Huntington, N.Y.: 1978.

Hailperin, Herman. **Rashi and the Christian Scholars.** Pittsburgh: 1963.

Henriques, H. J. Q. "The Jew and the English Law." JQR, 12 (1900), 662-673; 13 (1901), 275-295; 14 (1902), 250-264; 653-697; 16 (1904), 330-350; 623-649; 17 (1905), 203-237.

Herford, R. Travers. **Christianity in the Talmud and Midrash.** Clifton, N.J.: 1966.

Hermetica. Edited and translated by Walter Scott. 4 vols. Vol. 4 completed by A. J. Ferguson. Oxford: 1924.

Hirsch, S. A. "Johann Reuchlin, The Father of the Study of Hebrew Among Christians." JQR, 8 (1896), 445-470.

Holmio, Armas K. E. **The Lutheran Reformation and the Jews.** Hancock, Mich.: 1949.

Hunt, R. N. Carew. **Calvin.** London: 1933.

Hyamson, Albert M. "The Lost Tribes and the Return of the Jews to England." TJHSE, 5 (1908).

-----. **The Sephardim of England.** London: 1951.

Ignacio, Lemuel F. **The Life and Thought of Desiderius Erasmus and His Influence on the Reformation.** Indianapolis: 1960.

Jedin, Hubert, **Ecumenical Councils of the Catholic Church.** Translated by Ernest Graf. New York: 1960.

-----. **Geschichte des Konzils von Trient.** 4 vols. Freiburg: 1951-1975.

-----. **A History of the Council of Trent.** Translated by Ernest Graf. 2 vols. St. Louis, Mo.: 1957-1961.

The Jew in the Medieval World, edited by Jacob R. Marcus. New York: 1978.

The Jewish Christian Debate in the High Middle Ages. A Critical Edition of the
Niẓẓah Vetus. Translated by David Berger. Philadelphia: 1979.

Jewish Medieval and Renaissance Studies, edited by Alexander Altman. Cambridge,
Mass.: Harvard U. Press, 1967.

Kaplan, Y. "The Portugese Jews in Amsterdam. From Forced Conversion to a Return
to Judaism." SR, 15 (1980-1981).

Katz, David S. **Philo-Semitism and the Readmission of the Jews to England, 1603-**
1655. Oxford: 1982.

Katz, Jacob. **Exclusiveness and Tolerance.** Oxford: 1961.

Kisch, Guido. **The Jews in Medieval Germany. A Study of their Legal and Social**
Status. Chicago: 1949.

Klatzkin, J. **Baruch Spinoza: Life, Works, System** [Hebrew]. 2nd ed. Tel Aviv: 1954.

Kohut, George A. "Royal Hebraists." **Jewish Studies in Memory of Israel Abrahams,**
edited by George Alexander Kohut. New York: 1927; rpt. Arno Press,
1980.

Landsberger, F. **A History of Jewish Art.** Cincinnati: 1946.

Lasker, Daniel J. **Jewish Philosophical Polemics Against Christianity in the Middle**
Ages. New York: 1977.

Levy, S. "English Students of Maimonides." MJHSE, 4 (1942), 61-84.

Loewe, Raphael. "Jewish Scholarship in England." **Three Centuries of Anglo-Jewish**
History, edited by V. D. Lipman, 125-148. London: 1961.

-----. "The Medieval Christian Hebraists of England." HUCA, 28 (1957).

Louis Ginzberg Jubilee Volume, edited by Alexander Marx et al. New York: 1945.

Luther, Martin. "A Sincere Admonition by Martin Luther to All Christians to Guard
Against Insurrection and Rebellion." Translated by W. A. Lambert and
Walter I. Brandt, **The Christian in Society** II edited by Walter Brandt,
Luther's Works. Vol. 45. Edited by Helmut T. Lehmann. Philadelphia:
1963.

-----. "That Jesus Christ was Born a Jew." Translated by Walter Brandt, **The**
Christian in Society II, edited by Walter Brandt, **Luther's Works.** Vol.
45. Edited by Helmut T. Lehmann. Philadelphia: 1963.

-----. "Against the Sabbatarians: A Letter to a Good Friend." Translated by Martin
H. Bertram. **The Christian Society** IV. Edited by Franklin Sherman.
Luther's Works. Vol. 47. Edited by Helmut T. Lehmann. Philadelphia:
1963.

-----. **Lectures on Genesis.** 8 vols. Translated by George V. Schick et al. Edited
by Jaroslav Pelikan, Walter Hansen. **Luther's Works,** edited by Helmut
T. Lehmann. Vols. 1-8. St. Louis: 1958-1966.

-----. **Letters,** edited and translated by Gottfried G. Krodel, **Luther's Works,** edited
by Helmut T. Lehmann. Philadelphia: 1963.

-----. "On the Jews and Their Lies." Translated by Martin H. Bertram. **The Christian**
Society IV, edited by Franklin Sherman, **Luther's Works.** Vol. 47, edited
by Helmut T. Lehmann. Philadelphia: 1963.

Luther's Works. 55 vols. General Editor, Helmut T. Lehmann. Philadelphia: 1962.

Mackinnon, James. **Luther and the Reformation.** 4 vols. New York: 1962.

Marcus, Ralph. "A 16th Century Hebrew Critique of Philo." HUCA, 21 (1948).

Marx, Alexander. "Glimpses of the Life and an Italian Rabbi of the First Half of the Sixteenth Century (David Ibn Yaḥya." HUCA, 1 (1924).

-----. "R. Joseph D'Arli as Teacher and Head of an Academy in Siena." **Louis Ginzberg Jubilee Volume,** [Hebrew Section], edited by Alexander Marx et al. New York: 1945.

Maurer, Wilhelm. "Die Zeit der Reformation." **Kirche und Synagoge. Handbuch zur Geschichte von Christen und Juden, Darstellung mit Quellen,** edited by Karl H. Rengstorf, Siegfried von Kortzfleish. Stuttgart: 1968.

Meijer, J. "Hugo Grotius' **Remonstrantie,**" Jewish Social Studies, 17 (1955).

Mellone, W. E. "Seventh-Day Christians." JQR. 10 (1898), 404-429.

Menasseh ben Israel's Mission to Cromwell, edited by Lucien Wolf. London: 1901.

-----. **Vindiciae Judaeorum.** Rpt. edited by Lucien Wolf. London: 1901.

Meyer, Michael A. **The Origins of the Modern Jew.** Detroit: 1967.

Modena, Leone da. **Ḥayyeh Yehudah,** edited by A. Kahana. Kiev: 1911.

Moore, George Foote. "Christian Writers on Judaism." HTR, 14 (1921).

Natanyahu, B. **Don Isaac Abravanel: Statesman and Philosopher.** Philadelphia: 1953.

-----. **The Marranos of Spain From the Late Fourteenth to the Early Sixteenth Century.** New York: 1966.

The New Cambridge Modern History. Vol. III, **The Reformation,** edited by G. R. Elton. Cambridge: 1958.

Newman, Louis I. **Jewish Influence on Christian Reform Movements.** New York: 1925.

Olin, John C. **The Catholic Reformation: Savonarola to Ignatius Loyola.** New York-London: 1969.

Parker, T. H. L. **John Calvin: A Biography.** Philadelphia: 1973.

Peri, Hiram (Heinz Pflaum). "Leon Ebreo, Renaissance Philosopher," **Studies in Jewish Thought. An Anthology of German Jewish Scholarship,** edited by Alfred Jospe. Detroit: 1981.

Petuchowski, Jakob J. **The Theology of Haham David Nieto.** New York: Ktav, 1970.

The Philosophy of Spinoza, edited by Joseph Ratner. New York: 1927.

Popkin, Richard H. "Menasseh ben Israel and Isaac La Peyrère." SR, 8 No. 1 (1974).

-----. "Spinoza and La Peyrère," **Spinoza: New Perspectives,** edited by Robert Shaham, J. I. Biro. Norman, Oklahoma: 1978.

Popper, William. **The Censorship of Hebrew Books.** New York: 1899.

Porges, N. "Elie Capsali et sa Chronique de Venise." REJ, 77 (1923), 20-40; 78 (1924), 15-34; 79 (1924), 28-60.

Porter, H. C. **Reformation and Reaction in Tudor Cambridge.** Cambridge: 1958.

Previte-Orton. **The Shorter Cambridge Medieval History.** 2 vols. Cambridge: 1952.

Puritans, The Millennium and the Future of Israel, edited by Peter Toon. Cambridge-London: 1970.

Rankin, Oliver Shaw. **Jewish Religious Polemic.** Edinburgh: 1956.

Reyburn, Hugh Y. **John Calvin.** London-New York-Toronto: 1914.

Rivkin, Ellis. **Leon Da Modena and the Kol Sakhal.** Cincinnati: 1952.

-----. "The Sermons of Leon of Modena." HUCA, 23 (1950-1951), Part II, 295-317.

Rivkind, Isaac. "The Responsum of R. Judah Aryeh Modena on Bareheadedness," **Louis Ginzberg Jubilee Volume,** 2 vols. edited by Alexander Marx. New York: 1945. [Hebrew Section].

Robinson, Ira. "Isaac de la Peyrère and the Recall of the Jews." JSS, 40 (1978), 117-130.

Rosenthal, J. "The Anti-Christian Polemical Literature Until the End of the Eighteenth Century." Areshet, 2 (1960), 130-179; 3 (1961), 433-439.

Dei Rossi, Azariah. Meòr Einayim. Warsaw: 1899.

Rosenberg, A. W. "Hugo Grotius as Hebraist." SR, 12 (1978), 62-90.

Rosenthal, Erwin I. J. "Anti-Christian Polemic in Medieval Bible Commentaries." JSS, 11 (1960), 115-135.

-----. "Rashi and the English Bible." BJRL, (April, 1940), 138-167.

-----. "Sebastian Muenster's Knowledge and His Use of Jewish Exegesis." Essays Presented to J. H. Hertz, edited by J. Epstein et al. London: 1942.

-----. Studia Semitica. Cambridge: 1971.

Ross, Alexander. Pansebeia: A View of All Religions in the World. London: 1653.

Roth, Cecil. A History of the Jews in England. 2nd ed. Oxford: 1949.

-----. The History of the Jews of Italy. Philadelphia: 1946.

-----. The History of the Jews of Venice. Philadelphia: 1932.

-----. A History of the Marranos. New York: 1974.

-----. The Jews in the Renaissance. Philadelphia: 1959.

-----. The Jews of Medieval Oxford. Oxford: 1951.

-----. "Leone da Modena and the Christian Hebraists of His Age." Jewish Studies in Memory of Israel Abrahams, edited by George Alexander Kohut. New York: 1927; rpt. 1980.

-----. "Leone da Modena and His English Correspondents." TJHSE, 17 (1953).

-----. "Léon de Modène, ses Riti Ebraici et le Saint-Office à Venise." REJ, 87 (1929), 83-88.

-----. A Life of Menasseh ben Israel. Philadelphia: 1934.

-----. "New Light on the Resettlement." TJHSE, 11 (1928), 112-142.

Roth, Leon. Spinoza, Descartes and Maimonides. New York: 1963.

Ruderman, David B. The World of a Renaissance Jew. The Life and Thought of Abraham ben Mordecai Farissol. Cincinnati: 1981.

Salo Wittmayer Baron Jubilee Volume, edited by Saul Lieberman. 3 vols. New York-London: 1974.

Salomon, H. P. "The 'De Pinto' Manuscript." Studia Rosenthaliana, 9 (January, 1975), 1-62.

-----. "Haham Saul Levi Morteira en de Portugeese Nieuw-Christenen." Studia Rosenthaliana, 10 (1976).

Samuel, W. S. "Carvajal and Pepys." MJHSE, Part 2 (1935), 24-29.

-----. "The First London Synagogue of the Resettlement." TJHSE, 10 (1924), 1-147.

Saraiva, A. J. "Antonio Vieira, Manasseh ben Israel et Le Cinquième Empire." SR, 6 No. 1 (1972), 28-57.

Schechter, Solomon. Aspects of Rabbinic Theology. London: 1909.

Scholberg, Kenneth R. "Miguel De Barrios and the Amsterdam Sephardic Community." JQR, 53 (1962), 120-159.

Scholem, Gershom. Kabbalah. New York: 1974.

-----. The Messianic Idea in Judaism. New York: Schocken, 1971.

Scholem, Gershom G. Sabbatai Şevi. Princeton, N.J.: 1973.

Schroeder, H. J. Canons and Decrees of the Council of Trent. St. Louis, Mo.: 1950.

-----. Disciplinary Decrees of the General Councils. New York: 1937.

Secret, François. Les Kabbalistes Chrétiens De La Renaissance. Paris, 1964.

326

Seiferth, Wolfgang S. **Synagogue and Church.** Translated by Lee Chadeayne, Paul
    Gottwald. New York: 1970.

Shulvass, Moses A. **The Jews in the World of the Renaissance.** Translated by Elvin
    I. Kose. Leiden: 1973.

Sigal, Phillip. "An Inquiry Into Aspects of Judaism in Justin's **Dialogue With Trypho.**"
    Abr-Nahrain, XVIII (1978-1979), 74-100.

-----. "Aspects of an Inquiry into Dual Covenant Theology." Horizons in Biblical
    Theology, 3 (1981), 181-209.

-----. "Aspects of Dual Covenant Theology: Salvation." Horizons in Biblical Theol-
    ogy, 6 (1984).

-----. "Early Christian and Rabbinical Liturgical Affinities: Exploring Liturgical
    Acculturation." NTS, 30 (1984), 62-93.

-----. **The Emergence of Contemporary Judaism,** Vol. I, Pt. 1 **From Origins to
    the Rise and Separation of Christianity.** Pt. 2, **Rabbinic Judaism.** Pitts-
    burgh: 1980.

-----. **The Emergence of Contemporary Judaism.** Vol. II, **A Survey of Judaism from
    the 7th to the 17th Century.** Pittsburgh: 1977.

-----. **Judentum.** Stuttgart: 1984.

-----. "Luther and Calvin on Law and Gospel in their Galatians Commentaries."
    Proceedings. Calvin Studies Society, Annual Meeting, 1983.

-----. **New Dimensions in Judaism.** Jerico, N.Y.: 1972.

-----. "Responding to Christologies." Jewish Spectator, Vol. 46. (Winter, 1981),
    31-34.

Silver, Abba Hillel. **A History of Messianic Speculation in Israel.** Boston: 1959.

Sonne, Isaiah. "Leon Modena and the Da Costa Circle in Amsterdam." HUCA, 21
    (1948), 1-28.

Spinoza, Baruch. **The Ethics and Selected Letters.** Translated by Samuel Shirley,
    edited by Seymour Feldman. Indianapolis-Cambridge: 1982.

Stein, Siegfried. "Phillipus Ferdinandus Polonus." **Essays Presented to J. H. Hertz,**
    397-412, edited by I. Epstein et al. London: 1942.

Stern, Selma. **Josel of Rosheim.** Translated by Gertrude Hirschler. Philadelphia: 1965.

Stow, Kenneth R. **Catholic Thought and Papal Jewry Policy 1555-1593.** New York:
    1977.

Strauss, Leo. **Spinoza's Critique of Religion.** Translated by A. M. Sinclair. New York:
    1965.

Studies in Jewish Bibliography, History and Literature in Honor of I. Edward Kiev,
    edited by Charles Berlin. New York: 1971.

Studies in Jewish Thought. An Anthology of German Jewish Scholarship, edited
    by Alfred Jospe. Detroit: 1981.

Trachtenberg, J. **The Devil and the Jews.** Philadelphia: 1961.

Transactions, Jewish Historical Society of England. London, 1895-.

A Treasury of Jewish Letters, edited by Franz Kobler. 2 vols. Tonbridge, England:
    1952.

Troeltsch, Ernst. **Protestantism and Progress.** Translated by W. Montgomery. New
    York: 1912.

Troki, Isaac ben Abraham. **Ḥizuk Emunah.** Translated by Moses Mocatta. Rpt. New
    York: 1970.

Walker, Williston. **John Calvin.** New York: 1969.

Weil, Gérard E. **Elie Lévita humaniste et massorète, 1469–1549.** Leiden: 1963.

Wilken, Robert L. **John Chrysostom and the Jews.** London–Berkeley: 1983.

Williams, A. L. **Adversus Judaeos.** Cambridge: 1935.

Wolf, Lucien. "Crypto–Jews Under the Commonwealth." TJHSE, 1 (1895), 55–88.

-----. "The Jewry of the Restoration: 1660–1664." TJHSE, 5 (1908), 5–33.

-----. "Jews in Elizabethan England." TJHSE, 11 (1928), 1–91.

Wolfson, Harry Austryn. **The Philosophy of Spinoza.** 2 vols. in 1. Cambridge, Mass.:
        1948.

Zimmer, Eric. "Jewish and Christian Hebraist Collaboration in Sixteenth Century
        Germany." JQR, 71 (1980), 69–88.

INDEX

DR. PHILLIP SIGAL was born in Toronto, Canada. He has studied at the University of Toronto and Yeshiva University. He earned his M.A. at Columbia University and was ordained and received an MHL at the Jewish Theological Seminary, New York City. Dr. Sigal received his Ph.D. in New Testament Studies at the University of Pittsburgh for his dissertation entitled "The Halakhah of Jesus of Nazareth According to the Gospel of Matthew." Author of many articles and halakhic responsa, Dr. Sigal has written *New Dimensions in Judaism* and is engaged in the writing of this four-volume series, *The Emergence of Contemporary Judaism*. He is lecturer in Judaic Studies at Duquesne University, adjunct faculty at the Pittsburgh Theological Seminary and at Chatham College.

PICKWICK PUBLICATIONS
Allison Park, Pennsylvania
ISBN 0-915138-57-3

THE WRITING OF BOOKS ON JEWISH HISTORY has attracted many a scholar during the last century and a half. The multifaceted background of today's Jews and Judaism is itself an invitation to see relationships and to propound historiosophical theories and constructions. Yet it is only the rare Jewish historian who has actually mastered the intricacies of Rabbinic literature, and who can thus speak with real authority about a system of beliefs and practices, of legal decisions and theological opinions, which both regulated and reflected the actual life of the Jews in various parts of the world during a time-span of almost two thousand years. Rabbi Phillip Sigal has mastered that literature, and he therefore does speak with authority—and not only about that literature itself, but also about the challenges to which Rabbinic Judaism had been subjected ever since it had come into existence.

DR. JAKOB J. PETUCHOWSKI

Hebrew Union College—Jewish Institute of Religion
Cincinnati, Ohio